A Single Communal Faith?

Monographs in German History

Volume 1
Osthandel and Ostpolitik: German Foreign Trade Policies in Eastern Europe from Bismarck to Adenauer
Mark Spaulding

Volume 2
A Question of Priorities: Democratic Reform and Economic Recovery in Postwar Germany
Rebecca Boehling

Volume 3
From Recovery to Catastrophe: Municipal Stabilization and Political Crisis in Weimar Germany
Ben Lieberman

Volume 4
Nazism in Central Germany: The Brownshirts in 'Red' Saxony
Christian W. Szejnmann

Volume 5
Citizens and Aliens: Foreigners and the Law in Britain and the German States 1789–1870
Andreas Fahrmeir

Volume 6
Poems in Steel: National Socialism and the Politics of Inventing from Weimar to Bonn
Kees Gispen

Volume 7
"Aryanisation" in Hamburg
Frank Bajohr

Volume 8
The Politics of Education: Teachers and School Reform in Weimar Germany
Marjorie Lamberti

Volume 9
The Ambivalent Alliance: Konrad Adenauer, the CDU/CSU, and the West, 1949–1966
Ronald J. Granieri

Volume 10
The Price of Exclusion: Ethnicity, National Identity, and the Decline of German Liberalism, 1898–1933
Eric Kurtlander

Volume 11
Recasting West German Elites: Higher Civil Servants, Business Leaders, and Physicians in Hesse between Nazism and Democracy, 1945–1955
Michael R. Hayse

Volume 12
The Creation of the Modern German Army: General Walther Reinhardt and the Weimar Republic, 1914–1930
William Mulligan

Volume 13
The Crisis of the German Left: The PDS, Stalinism and the Global Economy
Peter Thompson

Volume 14
"Conservative Revolutionaries": Protestant and Catholic Churches in Germany After Radical Political Change in the 1990s
Barbara Thériault

Volume 15
Modernizing Bavaria: The Politics of Franz Josef Strauss and the CSU, 1949–1969
Mark Milosch

Volume 16
Sex, Thugs and Rock 'n' Roll: Teenage Rebels in Cold-War East Germany
Mark Fenemore

Volume 17
Cultures of Abortion in Weimar Germany
Cornelie Usborne

Volume 18
Selling the Economic Miracle: Economic Reconstruction and Politics in West Germany, 1952–1965
Mark E. Spicka

Volume 19
Between Tradition and Modernity: Aby Warburg and the Public Purpose of Art in Hamburg
Mark A. Russell

Volume 20
A Single Communal Faith? The German Right from Conservatism to National Socialism
Thomas Rohkrämer

A SINGLE COMMUNAL FAITH?

The German Right from Conservatism to National Socialism

Thomas Rohkrämer

Berghahn Books
NEW YORK • OXFORD

First published in 2007 by

Berghahn Books

www.berghahnbooks.com

Library of Congress Cataloging-in-Publication Data

A C.I.P. catalogue record for this book is available from the Library of Congress

British Library Cataloguing in Publication Data

A catalogue record for this book is available from the British Library

Printed in the United States on acid-free paper

ISBN 978-1-84545-368-8 hardback

CONTENTS

PREFACE

This book is, in many ways, the flip-side of my previous one, *Eine andere Moderne?* or 'An Alternative Modernity'. In response to the many scholars who had tried to show a close causal connection between cultural criticism and the fatal road to National Socialism, I emphasized the diversity of cultural criticism. I tried to take its intellectuals and movements seriously, do justice to their intellectual complexity and recognize at least some of them as critiques of modernity which were ground-breaking in pointing out very real problems of our age. While most are merely of historical interest to us, some, I have argued, have remained fascinating, challenging and stimulating to this day.

Time and some critiques of my book – ranging from the penetrating comments of Stig Förster raised in the spirit of friendship and shared historical interests to Anson Rabinbach's highly critical and, I think, one-sided, but useful review – have made me realize that my previous book needed a second half. I am still convinced that it was important to challenge the many historiographical simplifications in our understanding of cultural criticism and question too close a causal connection between this mode of thought and National Socialism. Cultural criticism cannot be reduced to its link with a certain period of German history, but is a more general 'mode of reflexion within modernity' (Bollenbeck 2005), which is present in the whole modern Western world. After this is recognized, however, there is no avoiding the question: Why did all forms of German cultural criticism – despite the deep differences between its strands – end up being among the supporters of National Socialism? The current book will try to show that one major reason was something which not only characterized cultural criticism, but much wider parts of society, especially on the Right: the desire for a single communal faith, which would transcend a deeply divided nation allegedly caught in the deadlock of incompatible interests and unable to control the often destructive dynamics of modern means.

The ideas for this book were slow to emerge. The preparation for a lecture course at Berne University in 1999 made me start to think more systematically about the 'Fatal Attraction of National Socialism', and the many discussions on that topic in seminars at Lancaster University provided important stimuli and allowed me to test my ideas. Papers given at a conference on *Utopia and Political Rule in Interwar Europe* at the Historisches Kolleg in Munich and on *Mobilized Culture: Weimar Mass Modernity from the Right* at UCLA gave me the original idea for this book. Many other conferences, discussions and publications on Richard Wagner and Ernst Jünger further helped to develop important aspects of my argument.

With rising work-loads at British universities, it becomes increasingly important to be granted time for uninterrupted research and writing. I would like to thank Lancaster University for two terms of sabbatical leave, the permission to leave for Berne University for one semester, and for several travel grants. An AHRC scholarship provided eight crucial months for writing up the final draft of this book.

More people than can be mentioned here have contributed knowingly or unknowingly to this book, but I would like to express special thanks to Sandy Grant for reading and correcting parts of the text and to Felix Schulz for many enjoyable and fruitful discussions about German History (and many other things!). Julian Young has read the whole manuscript, and our many discussions have deeply shaped my thinking on cultural criticism. Bogusia Puchalska and Paul Fletcher also took the time to read the manuscript and make useful comments. Above all, however, my thanks goes to Karin Asal for essential detective work at the University Library in Freiburg, and to Peter Kahrel and Corinna Peniston-Bird, who both went over the whole text with a fine-tooth comb. The three provided invaluable help.

It is not always easy to balance university commitments and private life, but it has been wonderful to have my family while working on this book. Philippa and Ruby did a great job in distracting me from my work; I did not always appreciate it at the time, could even become grumpy or hysterical on occasions, but altogether life would have been much poorer without them. Sylvia and I have spent uncountable hours on walks, in the garden or in front of the fish tanks discussing the topic and the many versions of the text. The book would have been a different and weaker one without her.

The book is thus dedicated to my 'harem of three'.

INTRODUCTION

How did the German Right adapt to modern society? How did it manage to rally ever increasing numbers to its cause, so that in 1932 the right-wing Nazis became the most popular political party, gaining well over a third of the vote in free elections? How was it possible that an ideology praising inequality and authoritarian rule, service to the community, and sacrifice for the glory of the nation, could outdo its progressive opponents in the age of mass participation? How did an oppressive totalitarian regime remain highly popular for large parts of its existence, and mobilize the population for its criminal policies? These questions point to what is arguably the most disturbing aspect of the German past. In studying Nazism we are faced not just with individuals or small minorities carrying out inhuman policies, but with the involvement of the nation at large. The Third Reich not only acted in the 'name of the German people', as the former Chancellor Helmut Kohl liked to put it, but also found cooperation, often even enthusiastic backing, from the vast majority of the population. Of course, Nazism's popularity did not depend on its ideological appeal alone. Its success in elections was possible only in a situation of deep crisis, and Nazi rule relied on the use of terror against any serious dissent. However, the popularity of the party's promises and policies was undoubtedly an essential aspect in its 'seizure of power', its largely unchallenged rule for twelve years, and its mobilization of the German people for the implementation of racism and the unleashing of war. After all, voters had a wide choice of political options in the early 1930s, ranging from pragmatic democratic crisis management to Socialism and Communism, and from a presidential dictatorship to National Socialism (see for example Turner 1997). And even after having secured control, the Nazis continued their untiring attempts to win the people's hearts, as they knew that a popular regime was much more effective than one that relied entirely on the whip.

This book wants to make a contribution to answering the questions raised above by showing the growing desire for a single communal faith in Germany reaching back to the Romantic period. In a deeply divided society, nationalists came to wish for a strong basis of shared cultural ideals and political goals to integrate the masses, unite the nation and mobilize it for grand heroic achievements.

Despite all their efforts, the nation became increasingly polarized, particularly as a result of the First World War. In 1933, however, many people were gripped by the enthusiastic feeling of a 'national awakening', because, for a time, the Nazis seemed to make the dream of a closely knit community in pursuit of a grand endeavour come true. In the history of the Right and the rise of Nazism, the utopian vision of a nation united in a single communal faith thus played, I shall argue, a crucial role.

The support which the political Right and National Socialism found in Germany has motivated a wide range of historical studies. In recent years, it is the perpetrators' motivations that has attracted most attention. Were Germans in the grip of a culture of exterminist hatred, as Daniel Goldhagen (1997) claims; or were they, as in Christopher Browning's opinion (1998), 'ordinary' but deeply misguided, lacking the courage to reject orders and group pressure? Was the evil based on the banal workings of an impersonal bureaucracy, as Hannah Arendt (1963) and Zygmunt Bauman (1992) have argued so persuasively? Or were the Nazi elites part of a generation radicalized – by war and defeat, revolution and paramilitary struggles, political turmoil and friend–foe thinking – to such an extent that they believed utterly in the need for a ruthless war against Germany's alleged internal and external enemies (Herbert 1991, 1996; Wildt 2002)?

This book focuses more on the wider appeal of the German Right and National Socialism on the population at large – but in that field there are many studies too. No general book on the Third Reich avoids the issue,[1] and works ranging from Fritz Stern's *National Socialism as Temptation* to Robert Gellately's *Backing Hitler*, Claudia Koonz's *The Nazi Conscience* and, most recently, Götz Aly's controversial *Hitlers Volksstaat* are specifically devoted to it. Moreover, in showing the importance of the Hitler myth for integrating a polycratic movement and attracting popular support, Ian Kershaw (1989) has highlighted a central aspect in the fatal attraction of National Socialism, while Michael Burleigh (2000 and 2006) has done the same by applying the important explanatory model of political religions to the history of the Third Reich.[2]

Such studies indicate a shift towards the history of political culture in trying to explain the rise of National Socialism (Gregor 2005: 16). The heated debate about an allegedly special path, and the comparative studies that this encouraged, have made it highly doubtful that Germany had been steering a clearly distinct *Sonderweg* since the middle of the nineteenth century. While every nation's history obviously has its distinctive features, the large majority of historians today reject the idea that one grand unifying theory can explain why Germany, in contrast to other Western nations, ended up with a fascist system.[3] A mix of modern and premodern elements in society, a piece-meal, often disrupted, process of democratization, a long continuation of authoritarian structures, and a traditional elite stubbornly trying to defend its privileges seem to have been the norm rather than the exception in the modernization process throughout the Western world. Also, the smooth democratization of West Germany after 1945 – which appears especially astonishing today when we witness the difficulties of democratization in post-totalitarian and non-Western countries – confirms that there must have been a strong democratic potential within German history. But, if the socio-economic and political structure of Germany was not particularly exceptional in comparison to other modernizing nations, then the issue of political will and all the many cultural factors that determined it must gain in significance, if we do not want to regard Nazism as merely an accident in German history.

The force of this historiographical reorientation becomes particularly clear in more recent attempts at restating peculiarities of German history. Heinrich August Winkler argues that the decisive difference between the history of Germany and that of other Western European nations lay in the myth of the Reich, which nurtured the belief that the Germans had some sort of special mission to save the world (Winkler 2000, 2002). Particularly astonishing is the shift in focus by Hans-Ulrich Wehler, the strongest advocate of a distinctive German development. While his original *Sonderweg* argument stressed the importance of economic and socio-political factors, in the most recent volume of his German history, individuals and ideas have become far more prominent. World-views are now seen as important factors in the way interests translate into actions. Also, Wehler now identifies the main reasons for a special path towards National Socialism as a radical nationalism combined with anti-Semitism, rampant expansionism and the role of charismatic leaders. In particular, the desperate desire for a political saviour, which allegedly became part of German culture with Bismarck and found its fulfilment in Hitler, has emerged as the core of his explanation for the rise of Nazism (Wehler 2003: 933–937).

My study, too, goes back to the nineteenth century in trying to demonstrate one central aspect of the attraction of the extreme Right (including Nazism) in German history. Although I do not suggest a revival of a German *Sonderweg* theory, I will focus on the importance of longer-term cultural trends and convictions for understanding the fatal attraction of National Socialism. Hitler and the Nazis could appeal to the German population because they played on deeply engrained anxieties, desires, prejudices and utopian dreams. And while the First World War certainly marked a crucial turning point in the right-wing radicalization of Germany, many of the ideas propagated under the Weimar Republic actually had older roots. The *Sonderweg* theory has been rightly criticized for reducing the multi-facetedness and openness of history too much, but there is the danger of making the pendulum swing too far in the opposite direction. Admittedly, the rise of National Socialism is unimaginable without the First World War and the crisis-ridden development of Weimar Germany; yet many important aspects of the Nazi appeal can be understood adequately only within the context of a longer-term national culture. In this loose sense Nazism did indeed draw on older German traditions.

The Nazis were obviously excellent technicians of mass propaganda, but their success also depended on the fact that many Germans already tended towards their ideas; to a large extent, Hitler and his followers were preaching to the semi-converted (Welch 1995). If the success of a Nazi movement is not imaginable in simply any country and any epoch, that raises the crucial question of what aspects of Germany's political culture made Nazi propaganda fall on such fruitful ground. My answer to this will take us back to the nineteenth century, to discover the roots of a forward-looking extreme Right, to the First World War and the 'ideas of 1914' as a decisive turning point, and to the Weimar Republic, where the Conservative Revolution and Nazism eventually triumphed in destroying Germany's first democracy and establishing a populist authoritarian regime.

Histories that deal with the intellectual roots of the Nazis are often greeted with deep suspicion, because early examples contained little more than a collection of quotations showing the existence of similar ideas in Germany's previous past. ' The exaltation of the heroic leader', as one such argument stated, ' goes back through Moeller van den Bruck, Spengler, Lamprecht, Chamberlain, Nietzsche, Lassalle, Rodbertus, and Hegel, back to Fichte's *Zwingherr zur Deutschheit* ... The Nazis said that might is right; Spengler said it; Bernhardi said it; Nietzsche said it; Treitschke had said as much; so had Haller before him; so had Novalis.'[4] Studies of Germany's political culture have, however, long since moved much beyond such simplistic statements, and now situate the expressions of convictions within their historical context.[5] They have also become much more careful about claiming causality and responsibility; just because one thing happened after the other does not mean there was a causal connection. Without denying the importance of other factors, however, thought processes clearly played an important role on the way to political actions. As Max Weber rightly argued, 'Interests (material and spiritual), not ideas dominate human action in the first instance. But the world-views, which are created through "ideas", have very often determined, like switch men of the tracks, the direction in which the dynamics of interests have steered the actions' (1988: 252). Humans live in a symbolic universe of meanings and representations, which shapes any experience of 'reality' and plays an important role in the motivation of actions.

This book does not argue for any deterministic causality between the ideas that it discusses and the rise of a radical Right. After all, intellectual and cultural history is better suited to discuss the meaning of events, not their causality. I am less concerned about direct political influences – this would require emphasis on political parties and right-wing politicians (see for example Schildt 1998) – than in ideas expressing desires for a right-wing turn. While they were most frequently expressed by an educated, predominantly Protestant middle class, whose mentality is thus most directly represented, its claim to express a more general mood of the age was not wholly unfounded, as is demonstrated by the role played by these ideas, often in vulgarized form, within the political visions of right-wing movements and parties (Stackelberg 1981: XI).

This book ends with the Nazi regime gaining and consolidating power. Such a fatal development – ending in war and genocide – raises difficult questions about responsibility and guilt. The answer is obvious with examples of direct political influence and temporal closeness; but with respect to other cases – especially concerning those who did not see themselves as part of a radical political Right, but whose ideas came to influence the shape of right-wing visions of the future – it is much less clear-cut. The philosopher Karl Löwith, for example, rejects the issue of guilt about the historical consequences of ideas by stressing 'the historical insight that "forerunners" have always prepared roads for others which they themselves did not travel' (1986: 200). In contrast, the intellectual historian Martin Jay rightly points out that only some texts are open to specific kinds of reading. 'The potential', he argues, 'for the specific distortions that do occur can be understood as latent in the original text' (1988: 33). After all, for an intellectual history, what is more important than the intentions of the individuals is the historical potential of their expressions, even if they are far removed from a literal interpretation.

Historians like Hans Mommsen, who advocate a strictly functionalist interpretation of National Socialism, have tended to minimize the role of ideology by stressing its lack of originality. All its ideas, they argue, have long been current in many different political formations, and so cannot be used to explain the stunning rise of Nazism, in contrast to other right-wing organizations, at one particular point in history. Such an argument confuses, however, the difference between a necessary and a sufficient cause. Emphasizing the importance of ideology does not imply a claim to mono-causality. Mental dispositions and cultural formations had to combine with other factors to make the 'seizure of power' possible. Furthermore, the historical influence of an ideology has nothing to do with its originality. What needs to be explained is exactly how Nazism could 'bring together and articulate a diverse ... ensemble of ideological appeals', enabling it to reach out to a broader base of popular support than any other previous party in Germany (Eley 1996: 30).

An emphasis on ideas and cultural formations can provide important impulses for an understanding of Germany's political development in the first half of the twentieth century, but the concepts put forward in the, in many ways, impressive general histories mentioned above do not tell the whole story. While the myth of a superior Reich was certainly important, the singular focus on it is too narrow. After all, the belief in the special mission of 'our own country' is part of all extreme nationalism, and a whole variety of myths of national superiority abound in German culture and the culture of other countries (Smith 2003, 2001: 144). The desire for a strong leader or a charismatic saviour is a very common reaction to a crisis situation, and does not answer the more far-reaching question, that of why an 'unperson' (Fest 1977: 697–741; Kershaw 1998: XXV) like Hitler (and not somebody else) became the object of such a desire. Only a more general comprehension of the political culture allows a historically specific understanding of the call for a particular leader or, for that matter, for a specific nationalist worldview or religion.

Above all, we need to understand not only the content and function of the right-wing mind set, but also its appeal. The cultural roots of National Socialism had such devastating consequences that the large majority of historians have naturally concentrated on its political consequences rather than on its popular attractiveness, especially as many aspects of its ideology seem, from today's perspective, to be simplistic, far-fetched and blatantly self-serving. In contrast to such a functionalist outside perspective, the subjectivist dimension takes centre stage in my attempt at providing an explanation of why so many Germans tended towards the Right and Nazism. While they accepted dangerous ideas and repulsive actions, I argue that they often did so for reasons which appeared to them to be right and proper. Most damage was 'done in the name of high-sounding ideals and moral values'.[6] This is not an attempt to play down or excuse the dark side of German history and its actors. Rather, it is the story of how 'normal people' were lured into following a highly dangerous political course for understandable, at times even seemingly harmless and idealistic, reasons. Such an endeavour means that we cannot keep these mentalities and ideologies at arm's length, but have to try to get into the minds of the people we study. 'What one wants to destroy', Walter Benjamin has claimed, 'one must not only know, one must, to do a thorough job, have felt it' (1966: 449).[7] Instead of trying to identify a completely distinct tradition of the enemies of enlightened Western thought, as for example Ian Buruma and Avishai Margalit have done in their book on 'Occidentalism', I want to show its deep connection with Western culture as a whole, even with ideas many share to this day. However, understanding has nothing to do with accepting, and the dangerous consequences of these mentalities must never be glossed over. This double perspective on the subjectivist attraction and on the political function[8] promises not only a more differentiated view of the past but also lessons for the present, as it contributes to an understanding, more generally, of the lures offered by intolerant and violent fundamentalist political movements.

My main argument is that the desire for a *single communal nationalist faith* played a decisive role in the fatal attraction that Germans felt for the extreme Right. This covers the early attempts at creating a new collective faith out of art since the early nineteenth century, the gradual emergence of ideological political movements promoting the idea of a single communal faith, the radicalization in the First World War, the uncompromising break with existing conditions with the Conservative Revolutionaries of the Weimar Republic and the eventual success at winning the masses with National Socialism. During the whole period covered, Germany was deeply divided. The conservatives, rejecting a pluralistic society, were particularly aware of the many antagonistic milieus of regions, classes and religions. In the age of nationalism, Jews and other minorities were increasingly seen as un-German. Conservatives contrasted a divided society with their ideal of a harmonious ethnic community or *Volk*, in which a single communal faith would integrate the people within the nation and mobilize their support for national goals. Without such a communal world-view, they believed, Germany would be torn apart by clashes of socio-economic interest, ideological conflicts, class war and revolution. Such a nationalist faith had the chance to gain wider appeal because people were searching for a sense of identity and belonging, a mental map for the modern world and metaphysical security. In a time of confusing ideological battles, the belief in the nation could appear as natural and beyond party differences.

In this book, the traditional conservatives, who attempted to maintain the status quo in a world of change, and the main conservative parties, whose policies were largely shaped by the material interests of their supporters, remain in the background; this struggle by conservative agricultural, and later also industrial, interests was largely defensive, and, as it did not help conservatism adapt to modern society, it was bound to fail in the long run. Instead, I examine those individuals, groups and movements which tried to preserve conservative values under new conditions. They realized the weaknesses of a static position. Could there be any realistic hope that the conservatism of the noble and agricultural classes would gain a wider appeal in a rapidly modernizing society, especially in competition with the different promises of progress? If traditional convictions had not been able to hinder the development towards a deeply divided society, why should they now become the cure? The ideological innovators I deal with were still conservative, because they held on to the belief of a hierarchically structured society with many social layers working together harmoniously, but they gradually came to be radical in rejecting current conditions and aiming for a different or alternative future.

My understanding of conservatism differs from the 'purist' definition of conservatism put forward most forcefully by Panajotis Kondylis.[9] For him, conservatism is the ideology of the nobility in their fight first against the modern state – which does away with traditional law (including noble privileges) to gain direct access to all its citizens – and then against all the other parties of change. While I am persuaded by Kondylis's argument that conservatism *emerged* as the ideology of the nobility, reducing this political ideology to its origins creates more problems than it solves. Not only does he break with the common understanding of the term, thereby over-estimating academics' power to redefine language, but he also ignores the point that an ideology can widen its appeal. In the early nineteenth century, non-noble political Romantics joined the nobility in their praise of traditional law and feudalism. Many Germans – in particular civil servants and members of the middle class – came to accept the primacy of the community over the individual, patriarchal relationships between employers and employees, and the need for a hierarchically structured, authoritarian society. Instead of describing all this as liberalism, just because conservatism is supposed to have disappeared with the nobility (and thus ending up with a wholly diffuse definition of liberalism covering a whole range of antagonistic parties), it makes more sense to allow for conservatism to change and adapt to new circumstances.

In my terminology, 'the Right' is an umbrella term for all forms of conservatism and National Socialism. Traditional conservatism is an ideology closely related to the nobility (though also expressed by middle class intellectuals), which tries to defend traditional political and legal privileges against the rise of capitalism, constitutionalism and democratic participation. While traditional conservatives thus fight a very specific battle, conservatism in a more general sense can take many different forms – but they all have in common the call for a hierarchically structured society. Against emancipatory demands for more equality, the term 'conservatism' covers all movements which insist on the need for authority and inequality. While traditional conservatives are predominantly backward-oriented, defensive and elitist, more adaptable conservatives can become populist and future-oriented in trying to develop an attractive vision of a hierarchical national community where all citizens would get their due. Their activities can lead to a historically successful conservative modernization, as for example in Prussia in response to the challenge of revolutionary France, but later they largely failed to provide adequate long-term answers to the problems German society faced. They were still part of a conservative Right, because they remained committed to authority and inequality, but at the same time they became revolutionary in trying to overturn existing conditions. The extreme Right is further characterized by an emphasis on populist mass politics (which also includes the promise of social change to win the masses), political violence and a glorification of heroism, war and expansionism. Nazism was thus a movement of the extreme Right.

The term 'Conservative Revolution' is a technical term for radical conservatives after the First World War who wanted to replace the Weimar Republic with some sort of authoritarian regime, but conservatives advocating revolutionary change emerged much earlier (to distinguish the specific name and the wider characterization, I shall write the latter in the lower case). Most of them did not have much of an immediate political impact, but they established a reservoir of concepts and ideas that larger movements could draw on in crisis-ridden times.

How can we characterize these conservative or right-wing revolutionaries? Above all, they tended to be extreme nationalists.[10] The nation was glorified, it became the highest value on earth, it could demand unconditional loyalty. Service to the nation became the highest imperative, feeling part of the nation the highest value. Germans or the Germanic race were allegedly superior to other people; they were frequently seen as having been selected for a historical mission such as spreading their culture or acquiring a hegemony. When nationalism emerged in Germany in response to the Napoleonic invasion, it was a revolutionary idea wanting to replace the existing states and dynasties by a Germany which existed only in the nationalist imagination. Despite mostly wanting to limit political rights to propertied German men, it aimed, in principle, at giving every citizen a stake in the new nation through the rule of an egalitarian law, ownership of property, and some form of political participation. While traditional conservatism opposed these demands and the whole nationalist movement as a threat to the existing order, some 'white revolutionaries' gradually came to appreciate the usefulness of nationalism as an ideology of integration and mobilization. As such, a central aspect of the nineteenth century's search for a single communal faith was the emergence of a conservative nationalism which tried to promote identification with the nation in order to maintain social order and provide increased power in international conflicts through the conscription of soldiers prepared to fight for their country and a home front unquestioningly backing the war effort. As national identity built on the construction of a communal ethnic past and eternal national values, conservatism could easily find topics with which to connect. Both nationalism and conservatism stressed the need for an authentic link with the past and for a sense of community beyond political disputes. Although nationalism could obviously be defined politically in many different ways, it was easier for Monarchists to draw on historical traditions than for Democrats or Socialists to do so.

While Bismarck and others regarded nationalism as a means to maintain the monarchy and the social status quo, its critical dimension could not be erased. Elites used it to control the masses, but it could also be turned into an attack on the existing order. If nationalism aimed at promoting solidarity among its citizens and towards the nation as a whole, it needed to advocate a sense of identity and community. Such ideals, however, involved the possibility that they could be used as yardsticks for passing critical judgement on existing conditions. Thus an ethnic nationalism became, as we shall see, a key ideology for conservative revolutionaries to challenge the status quo. From Romanticism onwards, nationalists drew the picture of a communal past, of eternal ethnic traits and of a common destiny for the German people or *Volk*. Such an idealized image of the *Volk*, constructed, of course, according to different ideological preferences, was then used to criticize the alleged shortcomings of existing conditions. While nationalism demanded close emotional ties of communal solidarity, the reality was marked by divisions and conflict or, at best, by a pragmatic balancing of divergent sociopolitical forces. Such a *modus vivendi* or power balance came to be seen as deficient, and gave rise to the call for a community based on a glorified common past, a present national solidarity and a communal future destiny. The social scientist Ferdinand Tönnies, who pinpointed these notions and the sentiments connected with them with formidable precision in his work *Community and Civil Society* (first published in German 1887, engl. 2001), distinguished an allegedly natural community based on common heritage, warm solidarity and shared beliefs from a society held together by impersonal structures, in which members act solely according to their personal interest. While Tönnies merely hinted at his wish for the regeneration of a community spirit, others were more outspoken: the call for the creation of a true community became a central rallying cry for a radical Right in their challenge to the existing order. From the beginning, conservative nationalism thus had the potential to become revolutionary in its attempt to realize their ideal of a nation.

As nationalism preceded nation building, Germany's national identity focused less on a political entity (although territorial structures such as the former Holy Roman Empire continued to play a role), but on a communal past, a communal culture and a communal race. Before German unification in 1871, it was hotly debated whether Germany should include Austria and other territories, and many ethnic nationalists such as the Pan-Germans regarded the newly founded

Reich as deficient because it did not include everyone they regarded as Germans. The difference between long-established political states like England and France, which gradually acquired a national identity within the existent state, and nationalist movements which mobilized a feeling of ethnic identity to form a nation-state, has motivated the distinction of types of nationalism. As early as 1907, the eminent German historian Friedrich Meinecke, in his book *Weltbürgertum und Nationalstaat*, contrasted the German *Kulturnation*, where Germanness is dependent on sharing the same cultural past and speaking the same language, with the older *Staatsnationen*, where the nation is defined by its territory and citizenship by place of birth and residence. The former stresses a shared cultural background, the latter, active participation in the same political entity. Influenced by Nazism, the historian Hans Kohn (1967) used a similar distinction to explain the difference between a more democratic development in Western and Eastern Europe, with Germany being classified as part of the East. He distinguished between a voluntaristic nationalism, where the rational calculation to belong together constitutes the basis of the nation, and an organicist nationalism based on a common origin of culture or race. While the former sees the nation as a voluntary association of individuals, the latter regards it as a seamless, organic whole where the collective is more fundamental than the individual. The former is based on the idea of a rational contract between individuals to work together; for the latter, belonging is an individual's historical fate.

These dichotomies are too crude and polarized to describe any nationalism fully, as all nationalism tends to contain both elements. Apart from states constructed as bureaucratic units by colonial rulers, nations tend to build on some ethnic core; this ethnic core, however, does not automatically lead to the emergence of a nation, but needs to be mobilized, shaped and constructed.[11] A liberal or progressive nationalism in Western Europe also tended to believe in a communal ethnic past and national traits, while the allegedly 'organicist' nationalism of Central and Eastern Europe frequently combined with calls for more liberal or democratic rights. In territorial discussions, ethnic and non-ethnic arguments were also used by the same nationalists. The dream of a future Germany, for example, was deeply connected with the call for a fundamental change to the political system of rule, ethnic arguments were largely rejected when minorities within the German lands like Poles or Danes wanted to go their own ways, and notions of a hegemonic medieval Reich were used as early as the revolution of 1848 to legitimate territorial demands: 'the Netherlands, the Flemish part of Belgium, Alsace and Lorraine, the Balkans, Bohemia, Moravia, the Polish-speaking Prussian province of Posen, Trieste and southern Tyrol – all were now declared part and parcel of the German nation, even if only a minority of their population was German-speaking. Germany was to stretch as far as possible from the North and Baltic seas in the north to the Adriatic and Black seas in the south' (Berger 2004: 57. See also Baycroft and Hewitson 2006). More generally, every nationalism, is, as John Breuilly reminds us, 'a form of politics' (1993: 1), and cultural or ethnic arguments are obviously never free of political bias and purpose.

The fact that it is impossible to draw a clear line between a civic nationalism on the one hand and an ethnic or cultural one on the other, has led historians like Stefan Berger and Mark Hewitson to reject the distinction completely. While I accept that, for example, Hans Kohn's value-charged distinction is too crude to do justice to the many variants of nationalism present in any given country, I still think that it is useful to distinguish between nationalisms emerging within an existing state and nationalisms calling for the creation of a new nation-state. While in both situations a whole variety of national convictions can emerge, it stands to reason that the latter type tends to use more ethnic and cultural arguments. Such a distinction thus remains, I believe, useful if the forms are understood as ideal types, which do not match reality, but help towards a more systematic understanding. German nationalists, who had to find reasons to justify the call for a unified Germany, which would overcome existing political boundaries, particularly stressed the importance of an ethnic heritage, eternal national characteristics, and the need for a single communal faith in order to unite all true Germans. While it was for a long time connected with a liberal agenda, this did not stop nationalist enthusiasm over a conservative unification in 1871. A tendency towards ethnic and cultural arguments was even more pronounced, when conservatives started to argue in nationalist terms, as they wanted to promote a sense of community and loyalty to the nation without altering the political and social status quo. In such an emphasis of a right-wing German nationalism on cultural, and often racial, homogeneity, it tended towards stressing the community over the individual, ethnicity over the state, communal characteristics over political will. Right-wing German nationalism therefore clearly leant towards what Anthony Smith names 'ethnic nationalism'. In much of the thinking considered here, the nation appears as a community of common descent and a common culture. The ethnic community or *Volk* is not seen to be based on free will and choice, but to determine the members of the community prior to any rational decision. Humans, it is emphasized, are born into a community. Therefore they share collective traits and a collective destiny, whether they like it or not.

In line with the 'classical' interpretation of scholars like Fritz Stern (1961), Kurt Sontheimer (1983) and George Mosse (1981),[12] Claudia Koonz takes the idea of an ethnic nationalism one step further by speaking of 'ethnic fundamentalism'. She interprets Nazism as a fundamentalism because it allegedly 'claims to defend an ancient spiritual heritage against the corrosive values of industrialized, urban society' (2003: 13). While the comparison with fundamentalism is a fruitful suggestion, such a characterization as essentially anti-modern or atavistic ignores the many modern elements within Nazism and the German Right as a whole (and indeed in other fundamentalist movements), which scholars have increasingly recognized over the last two decades.[13] Of course, many right-wing nationalists praised the Germanic past; yet, in reality, the extremist ones showed little respect for handed-down traditions and institutions.[14] Instead, not unlike the progressive forces, they wanted to realize their own visions of the future, largely using the past as a shopping centre where they could pick whatever they fancied. The politically decisive conservatives were conscious of the fact that the historical clock cannot be turned back, but they wanted to combine their socio-cultural convictions with the modern world of industry and technology. Furthermore, the sheer multitude of right-wing beliefs emerging after the middle of the nineteenth century reveals that these did not grow out of a solid tradition, but instead were subjective, wilful constructions. Conservatives claimed that it was only difficult times which forced them into adopting new views and measures, but this is simply part of the conservative ideology. In presenting themselves as purely reactive, they claimed to be apolitical and non-theoretical at heart, forced only by desperate conditions to enter the political arena. In truth, they not only competed with the left, frequently taking inspiration from the tactics of their political enemy, but they also developed their own hopes and ambitions for a revolutionary change to what they regarded as a better hierarchical and harmonious nation. Conservatism did not only win support from the losers in the modernization process, but also harnessed the aspirations of many who were comfortably placed in modern society. It participated in the glorification of modern means, in the progressive belief that human will can improve the world and in the aesthetic cult of self-realization. Against the idea of an atavistic 'ethnic fundamentalism', I therefore try to show that right-wing nationalism in Germany is not an anti-modern, but a modern political movement.

Similarly, I do not see that Jeffrey Herf's widely used concept of 'reactionary modernism' overcomes the difficulties connected with the multi-faceted nature of the German Right, including Nazism. While his insistance that parts of the Right reconciled themselves with modern technology since the First World War (1984: 1 f.) has been historiographically important, he does not recognize that this trend goes much further back in time. In addition, Herf reduces the highly diverse nature of National Socialism to one fundamental characteristic. But while the Nazis were certainly prepared to use modern means, their success depended on their wide appeal to very different groups. What was new, in comparison to other right-wing movements, was not their openness to technology but their success in presenting a vision of the future broad enough to rally together extremists and moderate conservatives, arrogant functional elites and large parts of the lower middle class, workers, agrarian romantics and engineers. Finally, Herf's conviction that the radical Right was reactionary is problematic (Rohkrämer 1999b). Of course, the Right rejected liberal and democratic ideas, but their more realistic, innovative and historically influential thinkers did not suggest a return to medieval or absolutist political systems or ideologies. Instead, they searched for innovative ways of integrating the masses into a hierarchical society by formulating a new communal faith. Their visions of the future incorporated elements of the past, but also some present ideals, and the arrangement as a whole was new, motivated by current concerns. It could contain the promise of security through advocating established and familiar conditions, but it could also appeal to the wish for change. The traditional and pragmatic elements are too important in right-wing thought to call the ideology a utopia, but it certainly contained utopian elements – which, I shall argue, were crucial for its popular appeal.

During the last decade, the term 'political religion' has experienced a renaissance. The work of Eric Voegelin (1996, 1952) in particular has proved an inspiration, but that of Raymond Aron, Jakob Talmon and others has also been significant (Maier 1996 ff.). George Mosse (1975) was a key figure in applying the term to German nationalism, a large number of German scholars, most convincingly Klaus Vondung (1971) and Sabine Behrenbeck (1996), have put this concept into the centre of their studies, and Michael Burleigh emphasizes it in his history of the Third Reich. As the term 'faith' in the title of the present book indicates, I agree that right-wing nationalism took on many characteristics of a religion: it tried to explain the whole individual and collective existence, to prescribe an allegedly right way of life, and to offer an ultimate meaning in the existence of the nation. Some values, objects and people appeared as sacred: the homeland was regarded as holy, every snippet from the Germanic past was valued, historical figures were idolized in public ceremonies, monuments were built to recall the great moments of the past. Awe-inspiring rituals of worship brought together the community of believers in nationalist services. Exemplary figures from the past, such as Hermann the Cheruscan, Luther, Frederick the Great and Bismarck, were seen as saviours, and the potentially eternal existence of the race or nation was offered as a way of overcoming death. While there was no promise of an individual life after death, many religions – ranging from that of ancient Greece to a number of modern Protestant theologies – have not done so either. And many believed in the special value of Germans as superior beings chosen for a historical mission, which, if accomplished, was supposed to lead towards a new paradise on earth. A cult of heroism promised an eternal existence in the memory of the nation for those who died for their fatherland. For the hard core of extreme nationalists, this ideology could undoubtedly gain the quality of a religion, if we define religion in the sense of Emile Durkheim as 'a unified system of beliefs and practices relative to sacred things, that is to say, things set apart and forbidden, beliefs and practices which unite into one single moral community … all those who adhere to them' (1915: 47). They desired to overcome the tension between religious and wordly authority – so fundamental for European history since the Middle Ages – by having a single communal faith with a total scope. It was supposed to fulfil metaphysical needs, inspire cultural production, provide a moral code of conduct and be the fundamental guide to all social and political activities.

However, there are also problems with classifying extreme nationalism as a political religion.[15] While nationalism could reach levels of religious intensity, it could also be much more pragmatic in trying to promote social stability and collective strength. As it could build on very powerful emotions, it was not simply, as the older historiography had it, a manipulative tool to integrate the masses, but it did also serve that function. The idealistic search for a communal faith was deeply intertwined, as we shall see, with the political will for a single communal world-view as a strategy for stabilizing and strengthening the nation.

Some zealots wanted to turn nationalism into a religion with its own rituals and symbols, but others, especially the politically more successful movements, preferred a more open and multi-faceted set of beliefs. While a minority of extremists wanted to replace Christianity with a Germanic religion, most – including Hitler – envisaged, or at least left space for, a more pragmatic 'division of labour': nationalism would determine all worldly values and actions, but Christianity could still provide a metaphysical answer to the question of personal redemption.

The term 'political religion' is too narrow, because it does not account for the variations within the drive for a single communal nationalist faith. It belittles the many pragmatic arrangements with the world, the frequent emphasis on scientific foundations in nationalist thought, and the will for political change. Right-wing nationalism proved popular, because it was an ideological field in which followers had to adhere to some key beliefs and taboos, but were also invited to make up their own ideas within the many undefined areas. Although nationalism stated a belief system for worldly matters, it left (apart from a radical fringe) transcendental questions to a vaguely defined Christian faith. Religious symbols and forms were frequently used simply to create a sacred or uplifting atmosphere, in other words for the effect only. The individual will to create and manipulate was often, as we shall see, stronger than the wish to adhere to a sacred truth.

The term 'political religion' also conceals the close cooperation between nationalism and German Protestantism, which became, in many ways, a politicized religion in support of German nationalism. Crudely put, Eric Voegelin and others have described the following process. Modernization was accompanied by secularization; such a loss of religion left a dangerous void; people felt disoriented, thus becoming susceptible to the lures of 'political religions' offering a clear-cut world-view. Historians of religion, however, have revealed a much more complex story in which religion is not simply a passive victim of modernization (Lehmann 1997; McLeod 2000). Most important for our topic is Protestantism, because Catholicism as the other dominant religion in Germany largely maintained its strength and distance from secular ideologies. Protestant theology, in contrast, was very much part of modern debates. Questions about the status of the Bible were raised less by atheists than by theologians trying to develop an up-to-date faith by squaring Christianity with modern knowledge. They discovered the historicity of the biblical text, noted contradictions between its different parts and had increasing difficulties believing in miracles. Many came to see the Bible as a collection of human contemplations about the godly, thus essentially equating its status with other mythical or historical stories. If the Bible was no longer seen as the one exclusive revelation of God, then God could also be discovered in other ways: 'in art, literature, or scholarship' (Williamson 2004: 15), in nature, history and political events. Jesus could appear as an exemplary figure, turning

Christianity into the call for an ethical life. Serious doubts about the Bible as literally the word of God thus opened the path for Protestantism to combine with many other beliefs and political convictions of the time. Church attendance dropped throughout the nineteenth century, first among the educated middle class, then in particular among urban workers, but the more worldly beliefs frequently remained deeply connected with a Protestant orientation. Protestantism was open to right-wing nationalism, as the church had long been close to the state, and many nationalists came to regard Luther and the Reformation as genuine parts of German ethnic identity. While secular ideologies gained religious attributes, we can also see a politicization of Protestantism.

'Political religion' is thus not a wholly appropriate concept for the phenomenon studied here, but it is useful to highlight one important aspect: that nationalism could become, for ardent believers, the ultimate source of truth and an unquestioned authority. Some, indeed, adhered to it with unquestioning faith. Like a religion, extreme nationalism claimed to hold the truth and to set the rules for the right way of life. It demanded sacrifice, even the ultimate sacrifice of giving one's life for the fatherland. Although it tolerated the Christian belief in personal redemption, it claimed ultimate authority in the political sphere. In earthly matters, Christianity was to fall in line with nationalism, not vice versa. The churches were still the prime consoler in questions of personal suffering and death, but politics was increasingly governed by ideologies with religious overtones. While Catholicism at least maintained an extra-national authority with the Pope and a strong political wing with the Centre Party, politically Protestantism largely moved in the wake of nationalism.

The term 'communal faith', which I have decided to use in this book, deliberately alludes to the many religious connotations of the search for a shared world-view in Germany between 1800 and 1945 without being as restrictive as terms like 'political' or 'secular' religion. It encompasses attempts to develop political religions in the strict sense of the word, but also other (for example, pseudo-scientific) beliefs in an absolute truth, the desire for a new communal mythology or the claim to absolute authority of one world-view in the public sphere, while allowing for a variety of different personal religious convictions as long as they are compatible with the public world-view. *In extremis* it thus means the totalitarian desire for a shared faith from which a single communal purpose emerges; in a more open sense it tends towards tolerating a variety of personal convictions, as long as they come together in a single communal political mission or a civic religion. From an analytical point of view it is obviously not ideal to have such a loose term, but exactly this openness makes it more adequate to encompass the historical reality, which does not fall neatly into the two categories, but is largely situated in the space in-between. Even the expressions of individual historical actors rarely take a wholly consistent position; it is much more characteristic for the search for a single communal faith to shift and fluctuate in the middle ground. The general term is thus used to show that we deal with a single historical phenomenon, while the text will draw a more nuanced picture by paying attention to communalities *and* differences within this historical tradition.

Conservatives had their own clear political agenda, but came to claim (and believe) that they spoke in the name of the nation. Personal convictions shaped the content of nationalism, but the belief in acting in accordance with the values of the past or with eternal Germanic traits could give it an apolitical aura, which, for the believers, protected it from critical scrutiny. Nationalism claimed to rediscover an eternal German truth, while formulating a contemporary political agenda. Of course, every faith is reinterpreted according to current conditions, but a sacred text like the Bible and a long institutional tradition put obstacles to or limits on self-serving reinterpretations. In contrast, nationalism is highly flexible and can adapt to a wide range of purposes. The combination of political ideology and a semi-religious claim to truth made such a world-view particularly dangerous. While different religious beliefs about transcendental questions can coexist without conflict, right-wing nationalism was much more intolerant in fighting for a homogeneous society according to its own conservative ideals of hierarchy and order.

Traditionally, studies of conservatism have accepted its own self-understanding that it tries to preserve old, stable and secure structures. The Austrian writer Hugo von Hofmannsthal captured this sense when characterizing Conservative Revolutionaries in the Weimar Republic: 'They do not search for freedom, but bonds [*Bindung*] … Never was a German battle for freedom more fervent and persistent than this battle for real compulsion in a thousand souls of this nation' (1927: 27). But can a freely chosen compulsion be a true compulsion? This brings us back to the question of whether conservatism grew out of the past or, like progressive political forces, was a new political movement shaped by current concerns and oriented towards the future. The same point has been debated with respect to nationalism. Like conservatism, nationalism frequently draws on the past. It stresses the importance of one communal language, old sagas and myths, folk traditions like songs and dances, costumes and festivities. All this can play an important role in shaping a national identity. In contrast to the current view of German conservatism, however, the idea that nationalism naturally emerges from an ethnic identity has been largely discredited since the 1980s. Traditions have often (to follow Eric Hobsbawm and Terence Ranger) been 'invented', or at least, according to Koshar (2000), been framed for a particular contemporary purpose through a specific 'historical gaze'. In the case of Germany, at least, the spoken language used to consist of so many dialects that Germans from different regions could hardly communicate; the fairy tales allegedly revealing a folk culture were selected by Romantics and substantially changed for publication; and seemingly old customs can frequently be shown to have a surprisingly brief history. While it would go too far to deny an older sense of ethnic belonging articulated since the early modern period and more intensely in the eighteenth century, early nationalists played a key role in mobilizing this for current purposes: a general sense of Patriotism came to be mobilized for political purposes. 'Small circles of educator-intellectuals ... were intent on purifying and mobilizing "the people" through an appeal to the community's alleged ethnic past. To do this, they had to provide cognitive maps and historical moralities for present generations ... In this way, they hoped to transform a backward traditional ethnic community into a dynamic, but vernacular, political nation' (Smith 2001a: 68 f.).

What Anthony Smith describes for nationalism in general also applies to German right-wing nationalists: they used history for present purposes. They did not accept the past as a restriction to their actions, but picked from history whatever served their current concerns and their future goals. This makes the movement modern and potentially revolutionary (Schmitt 1982).

Nations are based on the conscious belief in communalities. 'Nationalism is not the awakening of nations to self-consciousness: it invents nations where they do not exist' (Gellner 1964: 169). Nationalism emphasizes a communal past and a shared political will in trying to create a sense of collective political identity. This is clearly the case in Germany, where nationalism did not emerge within an existing state, but set out to create it. When there is no state, there can be no national past. A history of the German state had to be constructed as much as a political identity.

Nationalism did not emerge and evolve spontaneously, but was developed, shaped and promoted by a comparatively small elite of writers and artists, scholars like philologists, historians and philosophers, public intellectuals and politicians. These individuals were not, however, cool political strategists, but for the most part true believers. The later right-wing nationalism has frequently been analysed as a tool in the hand of the ruling elites, serving, it has been argued, to integrate the population, thus avoiding political upheaval and furthering a strong Germany (see above all Wehler 1985; Breuilly 1993, 2001). But even then nationalism was not simply a political tool, but first of all an answer to the elites' own anxieties and desires. And even if nationalism did come to be used as a political tool, it could only fulfil this function because it drew on a communal culture and resonated with the emotion of society at large. The political function of the ideology cannot be separated from its cultural content and popular appeal.

If previous interpretations have considered the political attraction of Conservative nationalism, it has largely been explained as a response to a crisis situation: disoriented and fearful, people looked for a clear-cut world-view; lonely in the anonymity of modernity, they sought a sense of belonging. An obvious historical example for this would be the view that the world economic crisis was a necessary prerequisite for the meteoric rise of Nazi votes – but many other situations were more ambivalent. Public intellectuals and a cultural avant-garde diagnosed a crisis of meaning before the First World War, but both the war and the rise of a new populist nationalism actually occurred, as we shall see, during an economic boom, and were maintained, in large part, by a middle class optimistic about its future role in society (Eley 1986: 266). Nationalism expressed itself in anxiety and fear, but more often it was marked by a jubilant and optimistic tone. More generally, any diagnosis of a spiritual crisis is, to a large part, dependent on the disappointment of a positive vision which is regarded as achievable (otherwise the sense of crisis turns into a mood of doom and despair). The frequent diagnosis of dangerous social divisions corresponds with the hope for a harmonious national community; using Jews or Marxists as scapegoats, for example, corresponds with the hope that a community of like-minded people would be harmonious. Even negative expressions of fear and lament tend to imply the optimistic belief in a positive alternative.

Nationalism could serve as an anchor in seemingly timeless ethnic traits for people feeling the threatening force of change. However, the reliance on a traditional faith like Christianity could have served the same function. Why did a growing number of people feel that something was lacking in traditional church doctrine, finding more life-relevant orientation in a new worldly ideology instead? Was the faith in personal redemption alone experienced as not wholly sufficient because even conservatives were infected by the desire to improve the world? To some extent, old answers lost in plausibility in the age of science, historicism and exposure to a growing multitude of different convictions, but nationalism did not mark a step towards an intellectually superior or more adequate world-view. Instead, I try to show that right-wing nationalism thrived, because it seemed to provide answers more relevant to the concerns and desires of the time than Christianity did. Nationalists spoke more about their enthusiasm and vision for the future than about their anxiety. They drew horror pictures of danger and decline, but largely in order to justify their own political remedies; and they frequently enjoyed the battles to realize their aims. Thus, while it is always possible to see signs of crisis, right-wing extremism did not decline during prosperous and optimistic periods like the turn of the twentieth century (Blackbourn 2003: 204–214; Rohkrämer 1999: 38–55).

All this is not to deny the importance of a sense of crisis for the story told here; but I shall argue that previous studies have significantly neglected the positive impulses. Many of the intellectual pioneers enjoyed the act of creating a new nationalist faith, and they frequently presented their ideas in catching imagery. From Richard Wagner's operas – which even succeed in beautifying the murderous 'twilight of the gods' by giving it heroic grandeur – to Nazism, it is easy to discern what Albert Speer rightly described as 'a striking need for beauty', a stress on the 'idyllic, the pure, the unscathed' (2002: 585). Although Nazism was certainly full of murderous hatred, its propaganda and rituals largely stressed the vision of a happily united *Volk* in a mighty Reich. While anti-Semitism and anti-Marxism were always present, propaganda emphasized heroism and grandeur, harmony and wealth.[16] It was not a desperate struggle for survival that was mainly stressed, though it undoubtedly played a key role in Hitler's world-view; instead, the emphasis was on the beauty of ideals and the joy of realizing them. How else can we explain the widespread enthusiastic sense of a national reawakening in 1933?

Aesthetics played a key role in the attempts of revolutionary conservatives to construct a nationalist vision. It was only natural that nationalists, intent on celebrating the nation, were drawn to all forms of creative expression. Artists seemed to be best suited to envisaging and disseminating nationalist ideals. While right-wing ideas about the future were often vague and inconsistent, aesthetic images could give expression to the underlying coherent sentiment. Political doctrines were often not worked out in detail, or details threatened the popular appeal. Thus it was wise to stick to a more general aesthetic expression.

Conservative revolutionaries wanted to create a world-view, a new political faith for all Germans. How could that be achieved in the modern age of rationalization and specialization? The obvious starting point is the expressive-aesthetic sphere (Klinger 1995). For most parts of its existence, art had served the glorification of God and communal ideals as the metaphoric expression of the sacred; should it now be nothing but a series of trends or a self-centred *l'art pour l'art*? The arts have never fitted into the modern trend towards differentiation and specialization, but continue to address all issues of life: dreams and desires, anxieties and hopes, political critique and utopian visions, social norms and the religious meaning of life. Their holistic orientation can appear anachronistic, but they are clearly modern and have become the prime vehicle for individuals to express their personal ideals and ambitions for shaping the world. At least since Romanticism, the rationalization, specialization and disenchantment of the world has been accompanied by artistic expressions of the desire for intimate communities, an emotional relationship to the world around us and a sense of belonging in the stream of time. More specifically, many artists and their audiences have felt that modernity has gained more and more means, but has lost any sense of an overarching purpose. Hence the call for a 'new mythology' or faith emerged, in a search for deeper meaning in the modern world (Frank 1982). A future-oriented right-wing nationalism could build on this in formulating its own dreams and goals. Personal creations in the aesthetic sphere wanted to establish themselves as a new faith. The artist's individual creation was aimed at rising to become a collective national myth, in particular when he saw himself as a medium through which a national soul found its most appropriate contemporary expression.

Aesthetic entertainment could serve as compensation or distraction, thus promoting acceptance of the hardship of life. This could be a convenient strategy in trying to stabilize existing conditions, but attempts to construct a communal faith served quite a different function. They constructed aesthetic counter-worlds which claimed to be the true world waiting for its realization. As the neo-Marxist philosopher Ernst Bloch pointed out, these two functions of aesthetic artefacts – providing a consoling surface or compensation for a harsh reality and challenging existing conditions through contrasting them with a utopian counter-world – tend to be closely intertwined. Utopias can turn into mere day-dreams if the belief in their realizability is lacking, and ideologies intended to stabilize the status quo draw their popular appeal from positive visions, which can gain an unintended dynamic if people come to demand their realization. While Marxism's self-understanding as a science inhibited German Socialists from indulging in utopian anticipations of a classless society, conservative revolutionaries worked on giving their dreams collective aesthetic expression to provide popular visions for the future. Thus Ernst Bloch rightly stressed that the popular appeal of the radical right becomes comprehensible only when we accept that their visions were more than 'mere ideology', but also opened a *Glaubensraum*, that is, a space for beliefs in a better future. Right-wing nationalism could provide the hope for a harmonious ethnic community united under a single faith to those who were sick of the 'dreariness and inhumanity' of modern society. As modernists preached the inevitability or even desirability of adapting to the 'iron cage' (Max Weber) of the bureaucratic, scientific and technological world, conservatives criticised the 'contradiction between the mechanical world' and a 'living, complete human being' (Bloch 1991: 196 f., 1985: 58), contrasting it with their hope for a strong and heroic national community where everybody would be filled by a sense of purpose and worth.

A future-oriented right-wing nationalism was predominantly carried by an educated Protestant middle class (Catholic conservatism is an important, but separate, story beyond the scope of this book[17]). The conservative artists and thinkers largely emerged from this milieu, and they found the most immediate resonance there. From Luther onwards, mainstream Protestantism had stressed that Christians owed obedience to a state which served a godly function in providing law and order. In Prussia and other states, Protestantism was basically *the* state religion, operating in close connection with the political authorities. The king was the highest church authority, and ministers had to read out official political announcements in church. Professors and grammar school teachers, church ministers and higher civil servants, who all played a central role in formulating and spreading nationalism, needed a conservative orientation if they were to pursue their careers successfully. A cultural elite largely growing out of this social milieu saw it as its mission to provide spiritual leadership for the mass of the population. Their distance from traditional Christianity grew, but simultaneously they rejected a purely secular popular culture, trying instead to maintain a sense of the sacred and a higher purpose in life.[18] The growing importance of the propertied middle class and of practical vocations like engineering, which meant a certain loss of status and influence for the humanistically educated, made them even more determined to stress the importance of spiritual values like individual civilization through a general education (*Bildung*), idealism and a deeper meaning to life.[19]

The predominance of one social milieu does not diminish the importance of this tradition. Educated Protestants (or lapsed Protestants) expressed and shaped the world-view of a functional elite which played a crucial role in promoting Conservatism and Nazism. Even if some of the individuals or small groups studied here were not immediately successful in spreading their message during their own lifetimes, they established a reservoir of ideas and images which could show its mass appeal later, when it was adopted (at a more suitable time) in a watered-down version by populist right-wing movements.[20]

The members of the educated middle class not only played an important role in right-wing activities themselves, but they also exerted an influence far beyond their number. Naturally this influence is not quantifiable, but it is clear that the high social prestige of a general education or *Bildung* gave their voices extra weight (Bollenbeck 1996). They were the most important communicative multipliers in society, strongly influencing public opinion through their role in church, education and published opinion. Of course, a wide variety of opinions existed in the German Empire and the Weimar Republic. Thus the educated middle class did not speak with one voice; nor could it 'sell' just any idea. But, as we shall see, within their circles many of the ideas emerged, which then came to be adopted by mass movements including National Socialism (Sontheimer 1983: 283 f.).

Ideas not only played their role in the historical process, but they can also enable us to comprehend the mentality which succumbed to the lure of right-wing extremism (Stackelberg 1981: XI). Engaging with the individuals who developed right-wing ideals in the most consistent, elaborate and comprehensible ways opens up an avenue towards understanding a political epoch whose thinking has become strange to us. In addition, it is hoped that close examination of an aspect of European history, in which political faith played a crucial historical role, can contribute towards gaining a better understanding, as will be shown in the conclusion, of the highly dynamic relationship between religion and politics in today's world outside of Europe.

For some decades no monograph has been published dealing with this topic as a whole. In the present book, a wealth of more specific studies, many of which are available only in German, is made more easily accessible.[21] Its main purpose, however, is to suggest a new interpretation. In contrast to the older, in many ways ground-breaking and still valuable works, it argues that right-wing extremism was not anti-modern, but developed its own visions of an alternative modernity in attempting to construct a new communal German faith. Aesthetic images played a key role, initially in the realm of high culture, but increasingly moving away from it to formulate political visions of integration and mobilization in populist ways, including political slogans and promises with wide appeal, eye-catching posters and films, spectacular rallies and rituals. Even in political actions such as the celebration of labour or the presentation of war as a short *Blitzkrieg*, the creation of appealing aesthetic images was a central concern.[22]

These nationalist representations could have an anti-modern appearance, because they used motives from an ethnic past and upheld holistic ambitions, but they were not essentially different to other modern forms of aesthetic productions. Right-wing conservatism did not want to turn back the historical clock; it did not even want to combine modern technical means with a political return to the past. Nor was it simply a panic reaction to the stress caused by a time of rapid change. Instead, it used historical opportunities for realizing its own ideals. It promoted an alternative modernity, trying to combine industrial society with social harmony and a strictly hierarchical and authoritarian political order. In addition, the label 'irrational', which has frequently been thrown about in trying to distinguish the ideology of the German Right from more moderate and humane political opinions, usually does not mean more than the interpreter's strong rejection of a particular political position and any possible reason for supporting it. After all, most human activities are to a large extent non-rational, and all political movements appeal to the emotions as well as to the mind. Like other political ideologies, the Right tried to serve the interest of their followers – for example, by promising to maintain social privileges in a hierarchical structure, to increase material security through the control of an unlimited capitalism or to make all Germans profit from a more powerful fatherland – but they also realized that they had to present more general emotional visions to be politically successful. Irrationality is thus not a distinguishing feature for the German Right. The question is rather: to what emotions did they appeal, and to what effect?

The danger was not the irrational character of the Right's ideology and propaganda, but its desire for a harmonious society united in a single communal faith and political purpose. This ambition stood for the attempt to overcome the irreducible plurality of modern society. As a consequence, citizens and political movements who did not seem to fit into this image of a tightly knit national community became targets of violent aggression – even more so when they came to be blamed for the failure in achieving that unrealistic goal. The danger was also that Germany's alleged superiority was stressed to such an extent that ruthless expansionism and an egotistical rule over others would appear justified for the improvement of humanity as a whole. Lastly, there was the further danger that this nationalist faith would immunize against critiques and doubts, partly because democracy and freedom of speech were rejected, and partly because a specific political opinion was given the religious aura of transcendental truth. Such a righteous belief in a polarized world-view of right and wrong turned the political opponent into an existential enemy and demon.

While some of the points I want to make with this book could have been demonstrated more powerfully in a more detailed study of either the nineteenth or the twentieth century, I have decided against that, because the challenge of combining two quite distinct periods raises revealing issues. A study trying to show that the search for a single communal faith was consistently at the heart of German right-wing ambitions must deal with the period before and after the First World War to show crucial continuities despite dramatic changes. Within the continued search for a communal faith, the actors became increasingly political, leaving the realm of high culture and formulating visions of integration and mobilization in increasingly populist ways. Trying to mark their distance from naive, allegedly 'romantic' notions, the Right disguised its desires behind a new matter-of-factness or 'cool conduct' (Gründel 1933; Herbert 1991; Lethen 2002). But this book will try to show that despite all these developments the dream of a nation united in a single faith did not lose its fatal attraction.

The book follows a chronological structure with the aim of showing the elements of continuity within change. It begins with the emergence of the desire for a single conservative faith in the nineteenth century, deals with the First World War as a deep dividing line producing a much more extremist political Right in the Weimar Republic, and ends with National Socialism as the right-wing movement which was able to reach out to the mass of the population on a wholly unprecedented scale. One can thus distinguish three distinct periods. The development from one to the other was by no means inevitable, but the vision of a community united in a single faith played a central role throughout the whole historical development.

A study emphasizing the political influence of an ideology needs to demonstrate the appearance of the same core idea in a wide variety of sources, particularly ones with a high circulation (see, for example, the publications of Jost Hermand and George Mosse). In contrast to this, the subjective appeal of an ideology can best be revealed through a close reading of a limited number of complex sources. I have therefore been selective in the discussion of individuals, but have used the study of social movements to show that those selected were not unrepresentative. Of course, it is possible to argue about any selection, but I hope that my choice will become plausible throughout the text. While the limitation of sources will allow for some detailed interpretation, the purpose is not to discuss works in all their complexity, but to show their place in the long search for a single communal faith.

Notes

1. Particularly useful, also in connection with right-wing traditions leading up to National Socialism, are Bracher 1984; Kershaw 1998 and 2000, Evans 2003, and Wehler 2003.
2. Burleigh 2006 was published after the manuscript for this book was completed. It is thus not systematically integrated into this study, but I do not see that it challenges my main arguments.
3. For an important recent account trying to historicize the *Sonderweg*, see Geyer and Jarausch 2002: Introduction and Ch. 1.
4. Rohan D. Butler, *The Roots of National Socialism, 1783–1933* (New York, 1968), 276–277. Similarly William M. McGovern, *From Luther to Hitler: The History of Fascist-Nazi Political Philosophy* (Boston, 1941), whose title expresses its programme.
5. The focus on culture and ideas does not imply a disregard of other aspects of history. On the contrary; social, economic and political histories offer important information to help situate ideas and understand their function. Since the early 1960s, historians like George Mosse, Fritz Stern, Kurt Sontheimer and Karl Dietrich Bracher have done so. Thomas Nipperdey's

work, in particular, offers a good example of integrating careful attention to culture and ideas into a general history.

6. Stackelberg 1981: XI. I thus reject Goldhagen's argument that Germans were drawn to Nazism by an extreme anti-Semitism. His opinion cannot account for the toning down of anti-Semitism in Nazi propaganda in the early 1930s, when the party achieved its greatest electoral successes. Even after 1933, open anti-Semitic propaganda was the exception (Koonz 2003). Robert Gellately makes a much stronger point when he stresses that the Germans who backed Hitler were fully aware of, and appreciated, the regime's terror, because it seemed to guarantee law and order. Gellately shows convincingly how much Germans knew about the terror and slave labour system, but does this mean they regarded it as a positive feature? From the beginnings, National Socialism showed its racist and militarist character, and its supporters at least tolerated these policies. However, this does not mean that those ideas and activities we rightly identify with Nazism were also the points which Germans at the time found most attractive. The Nazi elite largely shared Hitler's world-view, but the wider attraction was largely due to other factors, even to Hitler's emphasis on peace in the first years of the Third Reich. If terror was welcomed in wider circles, a key motivation was that it was seen to serve the creation of a harmonious nation united in a single communal faith.
7. In the same vein, Krockow argues that Hitler is 'a possibility inherent in humans, that is in us'. Accepting this, he no longer appears as 'ridiculous' or 'monstrous', but 'shows himself in a terrible, pressing closeness; he could return, of course disguised, behind another façade. And the question what we can do to prevent this return then becomes even more urgent' (2001: 9).
8. My distinction between subjectivist perspective and objectivist function is shaped by Jürgen Habermas's distinction between system and life world (1984 and 1987).
9. Kondylis 1986. Breuer follows Kondylis in his many publications, while Schildt raises important objections (1998: 14 f.). For a more detailed account of my position, see Rohkrämer 1999: 270–275.
10. Central for my understanding of nationalism are Anderson 1991, Berger 2004, Wehler 2004, and the publications of Anthony D. Smith.
11. As Anthony D. Smith convincingly argues, nations and nationalisms cannot be understood just as objective or wholly pragmatic entities. Instead, they all rely on national identity as well, that is, a common language or cultural sentiments and symbols. Part of nationalism is the belief in a historic territory or homeland, common historical memories, a shared culture and economic links. Nationalism needs 'bonds of solidarity among members of communities united by shared memories, myths and traditions that may or may not find expression in states of their own'. This ethnic core plays a key role in the attraction of nationalism. As individuals believe to share a communal history, cultural traits and political aims, they get a sense of who they are, where they belong and what they should do (Smith 2001a: 15 and passim; see also Brubaker 1992, Kedourie 1993 and Greenfeld 1992).
12. See also the much cruder Lukács 1962 and the summary of the arguments in Turner 1975.
13. Bavaj 2003 provides an up-to-date overview, Rohkrämer 1999b a more detailed account of my position. See the Conclusion of this book for a discussion of fundamentalism.
14. Theodor Fontane rightly observed that those trying 'to re-establish the ancient' actually broke with the 'old' (quoted in Puschner et al. 1996: 487). For an opposing view see Fritzsche (2004).
15. The articles by Klaus Schreiner and Hans Günter Hockert provide interesting critiques; Williamson (2004: Introduction) sensitively explores the complex interaction between politics and religion. See also Evans 2005: 258–260 and Gregor 2005.
16. Koonz 2003 and also Mosse 1975: 229, Behrenbeck 1996: 334. A good example is Leni Riefenstahl's documentary of the 1934 Nuremberg rally, *Triumph of the Will.*
17. Catholicism continued to be a powerful influence, both in shaping the mentality of a third of the population and in political life. While Protestantism opened itself up to current political and cultural trends, Catholicism tried to maintain its identity in a changing world. While

Catholics also tended to feel increasingly nationalist, they remained distinct to the mainstream of the extreme Right discussed here.

18. Helmuth Plessner regarded this *Weltfrömmigkeit*, that is a sacred view of the worldly, as a peculiarity of Germany as a belated nation (1959: 73 and passim). Towards the end of the nineteenth century, the voices of a largely Protestant middle class became more urgent because they came under pressure from a cultural mass market and new cultural elites. The educated middle class gradually lost its exclusive status, and adverse times eroded its homogeneous orientation (Langewiesche 1989: 112).
19. Ringer 1969. See Lepsius 1992: 11 for a suitable definition of the educated middle class. Rohkrämer 1999: 46–48 provides a more detailed discussion with references to further literature.
20. As we shall see throughout the book, the educated middle class played a key role in the rise of the extreme Right, for example, in the national leagues and in propagating the 'ideas of 1914'. Large parts of the middle class continuously worked against the Weimar Republic, and groups like students were among the first Nazi strongholds. As the Nazis did not 'seize' power, but came into power in an alliance with conservative elites, the latter's political orientation was a prerequisite for this development. Furthermore, the widely held right-wing ideals made the young elites serve the Nazi goals in the Third Reich not just for career reasons, but also as devoted and dedicated believers (Herbert 1996; Wildt 2002).
21. Important literature in English includes Aschheim 1994; Baird 1990; Burleigh 2005 and 2006; Farrenkopf 2001; Field 1981; Katz 1986; Large 1997; Rabinbach 1997; Rhodes 1980; Spotts 2002; Stackelberg 1981; Stern 1999; Wachsmann 1998; Whisker 1982; Wistrich 1996. The following books give a good idea of the main scholars in Germany working in the field: Schnurbein and Ulbricht, eds. 2001; Puschner et al., eds. 1996; Puschner 2001. The literature concerned with Nazism in a narrower sense is too numerous to be listed here. Some core texts have been mentioned in the Introduction; others, which I have found particularly useful, are pointed out throughout the text.
22. According to Albert Speer, Hitler "took the impression more seriously than the reality" (1976: 311).

CHAPTER 1

PRELUDE: THE WEAKENING OF TRADITION AND THE SEARCH FOR A NEW FAITH IN THE EARLY NINETEENTH CENTURY

First attempts at creating a new communal faith emerged around the turn of the nineteenth century with Romanticism and the newly emerging nationalist movement. Neither made their appearance in a secular void, but were productive reactions not only to enlightened thought, but also to developments within German Protestantism. A new communal faith came to be seen as *desirable* as a means of uniting the nation, and it became *possible* because the traditional foundations of Christianity and the churches were gradually eroded, not least by Protestant theologians of the nineteenth century.

Long before industrialization began to have a major impact on the many German states, the reliance on customs, traditions and long-established institutions experienced severe blows with the Enlightenment and the political revolutions of the late eighteenth century. Christianity still had a strong grip on the vast majority of the population, but a small intellectual elite was increasingly gripped by an enlightened belief in reason. Traditions were scrutinized: folk beliefs were defamed as mere superstition; church doctrine was questioned. While admitting the value of a very general rational religion, the philosopher Immanuel Kant argued in his writings that no religion could be proven as true, and he clearly expressed his rejection of beliefs such as the resurrection of the body, which failed to correspond with enlightened reason (Habermas 2005: 216–235). Johann Wolfgang von Goethe was the first outspoken non-Christian in the German-speaking lands. He rejected any belief in a personalizsed God as well as in a life after death. For him, the godly became a creative force within the material world.

A good life meant the development of all facets of one's personality, a constant exploration of the real world, the active use of one's own creative powers and useful work for one's fellow humans. For this poet, scientist and politician, the erosion of a Christian faith did not constitute a loss, but opened up the opportunity to realize one's own individual potential in the study of nature, in creative work and in love. In a pantheistic vain, he believed that one could get a sense of the godly in an open-eyed engagement with the world around us, in particular by observing nature.

Both Goethe's sense of a godly force working within the natural world and his emphasis on individual self-realization proved highly influential for the educated middle class in nineteenth century Germany. Education, a life-long engagement with a cultural canon, and self-realization became core values in the attempt to realize one's own potential. Studying great works of literature, visiting museums and galleries, going to the theatre and musical performances, all this became part of a middle-class lifestyle – undertaken not simply for fun, but as a moral duty. A cult of the creative genius emerged, because the great art work supposedly opened one's eyes for the good and godly in life; thus the building of monuments for artists, the grand celebration of anniversaries like the Schiller celebrations in 1859 and Beethoven's funeral in 1827, attended by 20 to 30 thousand people. 'The beautiful is the true, the good, the holy', Thomas Nipperdey summarized this semi-religious attitude, 'and for those, who silently or decidedly left the church in the middle of the nineteenth century it is also explicitly the arts, which maintain the religious truth in this time. The arts give comfort, offer reconciliation, redeem, become a form of salvation' (1983: 540). Even at the time, the cult of artistic genius was seen in conjunction with the weakening of Christian authority. 'Around Jesus', the theologian Strauß remarked, 'who used to stand alone, the people want to put a garland of other holy persons ... This is a mark of the time, to venerate the Spirit of God in all the spirits who have affected humanity in a vital and creative way' (quoted in Williamson 2004: 175). And even a highly influential theologian like Friedrich Schleiermacher accepted that Christianity had to overcome a literal reading of the Bible with all its unacceptable elements of superstition, to achieve harmony with modern reason and its human norms.

The enlightened critique of the Christian faith continued throughout the nineteenth century. In 1835, David Friedrich Strauß published *The Life of Jesus*. He historicized the Christian faith by interpreting the Bible like any historical text, thereby pointing out inconsistencies between the four gospels, questioning the realities of miracles and showing that the formulation of a clearly defined Christian faith occurred only *after* the death of Jesus through the workings of his believers. For Strauß, the Bible was a mythical text in the negative sense of the word: the life of Jesus had been largely distorted through an adaptation of the facts to meet traditional messianic expectations. The next important step was Ludwig Feuerbach's critique of religion in the 1840s. His work and its reception are particularly interesting in our context because he moved beyond a questioning of the truth of Christianity to an ideological critique of its psychological and social function. To him, God was dressed up with all the ideals humans held. God thus appeared as a 'super-man' with all the characteristics we secretly desire for ourselves. While such a projection of personal ideals on an imagined God might have been necessary in the past, Feuerbach now called upon his readers to realize these ideals in this world. Religious ideals thus turned into secular goals for humans with a strong faith in the possibility of progress. Instead of hoping for a better life after death, Feuerbach called for action in the real world to achieve the realization of all human ideals. God thus became a hindrance in the modern attempt of humans to become god-like by realizing their own utopia through working towards a perfect world. While religion makes humans accept an inadequate reality, they should try to realize the religious ideals in their own historical epoch: work instead of prayer, politics instead of religion (Winiger 2004; Feuerbach 1983: 443–445).

Feuerbach's message was highly optimistic. He assigned a positive historical role to religion: it had presented the space to create and formulate the most beautiful human utopia. For him, however, the time had come when this utopia had come within human reach: instead of hoping to gain it as a present from God in heaven, humans had progressed to a historical stage, where they no longer needed the illusion that a God would realize the ideal for them; they could, he believed, do it themselves. It is thus not surprising that Feuerbach's philosophy was greeted with a wave of enthusiasm, especially among a radical and activist younger generation. 'We were all, momentarily, Feuerbachians', Engels recalled (1895: 11). While the critique of religion did not remain at the centre of their thinking, he and Marx incorporated Feuerbach's ideas into their own work, claiming that religion would wither away with the realization of an ideal society. Not only did the Marxist working-class movement largely accept this argument – also because the Protestant church as a whole clearly sided with the established repressive powers – but it could also be attractive in other contexts: the later prophet of right-wing nationalism, Richard Wagner, for example, dedicated his first major theoretical work *Das Kunstwerk der Zukunft* (1849) to Feuerbach. Like many others, Marx, Engels and Wagner did not experience the erosion of Christianity with a sense of loss, but of liberation. God must not exist, because humans wanted to be their own masters, wanted to be independent, wanted to realize their own potential and redeem themselves. In his *Zarathustra*, Friedrich Nietzsche found the most pointed expression for this sentiment a few decades later: 'If there were Gods, how could I bear not to be a God. Thus there are no Gods' (II, 2: On the Blissful Islands).

There were, of course, many different strands to the weakening of church doctrine in the nineteenth century, and it was by no means always experienced as liberation. New scientific theories or the intellectual consequences of historicism did not develop within the theological discourse but were perceived as difficult challenges from outside. It seems worth pointing out, however, that church people were agents of this process much more than is often assumed. It obviously became increasingly difficult to reconcile a literal belief in the Bible with the accepted knowledge of the time, when people knew about an ever wider range of different and incompatible religions, when a mechanical world-view was so successful in explaining and controlling the world and when biblical creation came to be questioned by Darwinism. However, Kant had not only shown that human reason could not prove the existence of God, but also that it could not prove God's non-existence. More recent studies in the history of religion in the nineteenth century have questioned, with good reason, too close a deterministic link between modernization and secularization: after all, to this day, religion has not been weakened in the United States. The world religions have maintained their position in the modern world; the largely secularized post-1945 Western Europe, which many academics seem to have used as their main point of reference, appears to be the exception rather than the norm (Norris and Inglehart 2004).

Christianity in nineteenth-century Germany remained important. Even among those whose distance from the church of their parents grew, a vague belief in God and the ethics of the churches tended to survive. Church attendance gradually declined throughout the eighteenth and nineteenth centuries, first among the Protestant urban middle classes, then also among workers, but this did not necessarily mean a complete loss of faith. By and large, Christianity not only remained important in the private sphere – though among Protestants often in a less dogmatic and church-oriented form – but was also quite regularly drawn upon in political argumentation: the connection between the monarchy (as well as later other state authorities) and the Protestant church remained, for example, very close. There was simply not a secular void which was then filled by political religions, but many Protestants opened their religion to intellectual and political trends of their time. They tried to find a new synthesis between traditional Protestantism and new cultural trends, also because they were no longer convinced by a literal reading of the Bible and church doctrine. If the Bible could no longer be seen as the unmediated word of God, then one could believe in other forms of Godly revelations, for example in great art, in nature or – most importantly for the merger of religion and politics – in the history of the nation.

Up to 1945 and beyond, the vast majority of the German population still regarded themselves as Christians. What one can note, however, is that in an epoch when great opportunities for changing the social and material world seemed to open up, religion increasingly lost the ability to set the tone of political debates, to provide creative answers to the secular challenges of the time and to provide spiritual leadership. Increasingly, Protestantism in particular was no longer a prime political mover; it became reactive, adapting its own faith to the political ideologies of its time, especially to an authoritarian nationalism. In contrast, Catholicism largely came to reject modernization by becoming more dogmatic. Such a change of doctrine was at least equally unattractive to those who believed that the world was there to be improved according to their own political will (Barth 1975; Lehmann 1997; McLeod 2000; Nipperdey 1990: 428–530; Nowak 1995; Swatos et al. 2000; Walkenhorst 1996; Williamson 2004:

Introduction).

Before industrialization reached Germany with full force, the political revolutions of the late eighteenth century were the strongest demonstration for the possibility for change. The American and the French revolutions deeply challenged a cyclical understanding of history, suggesting instead that there was a chance to improve the world. In particular, the revolution in France had a strong impact on Germans, at least on a politically outspoken intellectual elite.[1] A neighbouring country was completely changed within years, and knowledge of these spectacular events crossed the border through political publications and eye-witness reports ranging from travellers to refugees and later French soldiers and administrators. At first, the revolution tended to inspire hope among progressive forces that they could also improve the political and social conditions within their own German states. Kant, for example, claimed that humans, in contrast to the rest of nature, had the ability to perfect the world; shortly afterwards, Hegel even developed a philosophy which expressed the belief that human history was progressing towards an ever more enlightened future. Such a belief in progress – that is, the irreversible improvement of humanity in the course of history – gradually spread throughout the nineteenth century. With time, it became increasingly linked with the glorification of modern science, technology and industry. For many, increased control over the natural environment and an ever more efficient industrial production of goods seemed to prove beyond doubt that society was moving with irresistible force towards a better future (Koselleck 1985).

By the middle of the nineteenth century, the railway had become a key symbol for progress.[2] To see a steam engine for the first time was an overwhelming sensual experience: the enormous scale, the clouds of smoke, the powerful noise and the unprecedented speed all worked together to create an immediate sense of an overwhelming power pushing forward. With inevitable force, the railway lines seemed to spread across the country until nobody was more than a day's walk away from a station. Separations disappeared and distances diminished; commuting, travel and migration became so much simpler. The power of steam trains connected the country, opening up the experience of very different areas, customs and living conditions. People and news travelled back and forth, exposing everybody to different ways of doing things. Steam power, and later electricity, was not simply perceived as a new technological device, but seemed to push society into a whole new era. Not surprisingly, a survey published in the *Berliner Illustrierte* on 10 February 1899 revealed that most respondents characterized the previous hundred years as the 'century of steam', the 'century of electricity', and the 'century of science and light'.

The reality of technological and industrial progress, only sketched here with focus on a few particularly striking examples, shows how the reality of change became such an intensively lived experience that people at the time were drawn to the historically new belief of living in an era of constant development towards an unprecedented future. While traditionally the term 'new time' had been used only for the time after Christ's second coming, it now came to characterize the contemporary world. Literary utopias were no longer placed in a past 'golden age' or, like Thomas More's renaissance work, in a distant country, but were projected into an allegedly better future. People gained a sense of living at the edge of time, at a moment when the known past disappeared and a different new and modern future emerged. Whether people greeted or dreaded this change, they could no longer envisage the future to be like the past. Life experience lost in value, as one had to prepare for an unknown future. The 'space of experience' no longer connected closely with the 'horizon of expectation' (Koselleck 1985: 275 f. See also Koshar 1998: 18). Systematic knowledge seemed necessary to develop plans for a different future, but one could also experience history as an anonymous force pushing forward in complete disregard of human wishes and intentions. The most influential German historian of the time, Leopold von Ranke, reflected on this new sense of open change, when he wrote his famous reflection on the purpose of history writing: 'One has given the study of history the task of judging the past and teaching contemporaries about the future [*zum Nutzen zukünftiger Jahre*]. This attempt will not try to achieve such high tasks. It simply tries to show how it has really been.' Alexis de Tocqueville's more explicitly pessimistic judgement is based on the same observation: 'Since the past has stopped to throw light on the future, the human mind is lost in darkness' (quoted in Koselleck 1985: 275 f. See also Koshar 1998: 18). Past experiences could no longer prepare adequately for revolutionary ruptures, a completely different, new future and a world deeply divided by different ideological viewpoints. As the conservative politician Friedrich Gentz remarked:

> Never before … have such a large number of important and intertwined events, such a rapid sequence of extraordinary transformations and restless movement, and such piled-up revolutions taken place. Never before have changes of such astonishing variation and with such rich significance in all their social and political aspects occurred on a stage that was so open and accessible, and never have these changes … been interpreted from such contradictory points of view. (quoted in Fritzsche 2004: 27)

While the sense that the present leads into an open future became a dominant belief with industrialization and its social consequences since the middle of the nineteenth century, a cultural avant-garde in the German lands was deeply marked by the sense of a new future as early as the opening of the century. Initially, the vision of unknown horizons was frequently greeted with an enthusiastic sense of freedom and opportunity. The Enlightenment seemed to promise a path towards a full understanding of the world solely based on reason. Humanity allegedly came of age, it freed itself from old superstitions and started to build a truly human world-view solely based on its own intelligence. No longer tied by a far-from-perfect past, it could create new and better conditions according to its own ideals.

However, doubts and disillusionment soon set in. Even liberal Germans became increasingly critical of events in revolutionary France: the reign of terror, the many conflicting factions and ideologies which failed to reach a common political ground, eventually the rise of a new authoritarian regime and Napoleon's expansionist drive, which led to the French occupation of Prussia and other states, provoked a growing alienation from revolutionary enthusiasm. Humans were, many concluded, not making good use of their new freedom from the past, they were not as reasonable as one had expected or hoped. Throwing off the shackles of tradition turned out to have deeply ambivalent results, as a turn to the better was by no means guaranteed. Edmund Burke's *Reflections on the Revolution in France* (1790), published in a German translation by the conservative writer and politician Friedrich von Gentz only three years later, became a highly influential text, expressing much of what became standard anti-revolutionary arguments far beyond conservative circles. Burke gave voice to a widely felt sense about the dangers of a ruthless break with the past. While the reliance on reason and the will for change were not wholly rejected, they should be moderated by a reference to the wisdom of tradition. Instead of basing politics on abstract principles, thereby making history and traditional knowledge irrelevant, humans should try to build on the past, adapting current conditions through constant careful reform to new circumstances. In contrast to schemes purely based on the reason of one individual, one political group or one generation, politics should grow organically out of the past. Traditional customs and institutions were not seen as perfect, but as they were seen to incorporate the collective knowledge of many generations, they gained greatly in prestige.

The belief in the wisdom of traditional values and established institutions conflicted with the belief in universal reason. Instead of accepting the idea of one universal truth discovered through human reasoning, attaching value to the past implied respect for a multitude of particularities. Paying respect to the traditions existing in different political communities, there could not possibly be one correct answer for every situation. Instead, current ideas had to be negotiated within a particular ethnic tradition, which differed from nation to nation and from region to region. Paying tribute to variety was not seen as just a necessity, however, but came to be celebrated. While most enlightened thinkers in the German-speaking lands had tended towards a cosmopolitan orientation, Johann Gottfried Herder anticipated the more nationalist orientations of the nineteenth century by glorifying the plurality in human culture. For him, every nation had its own 'genius', that is, its own culture, its own way of perceiving and doing things. Such a multitude was positive: it showed the natural richness of humanity and their history. In being creative, humans were not restricted to one form, but brought forth a wide range of equally valuable cultures. Geography, history and a particular ethnic character gave each community its unique features:

> What is the main law that we can discover in all great phenomena in history? It seems to me that in our world everything comes into existence that can come into existence in it, partly due to the features and needs of a place, partly due to conditions and opportunities of the time, partly due to the innate or evolved character of a people ...

> Only the times, the places and the national character, in short, the whole assembly of living forces in their most particular individuality make all events in the human sphere, as in natural creations, happen. (Herder 1995: 325)

While Herder was fascinated by other cultures – and spent quite some time studying, for example, songs of American Indians with deep respect (Frank 1982: 136) – he stressed that a nation should not adopt the ways of others, but build on its own historical foundations: 'Let us follow our own path ... Let all men speak well or ill of our nation, our literature, our language: they are ours, they are ourselves, and let that be enough' (quoted in Smith 2001a: 75).

The praise of multitude was only one of the responses to the growing unease about a cult of reason, which wanted to kick itself free from the past. Even if one accepted the limitations of the traditional order, what would take its place? Would the different political opinions ever lead to a new communal world-view? Would the modern rational world be wholly disenchanted, that is, emotionless and devoid of a deeper, human meaning? Where would be a place for the many non-rational human needs and desires, like the wish for a sense of belonging, for a purpose in life, for personal or communal idiosyncrasies? How did the glorification of one single reason go together with the wish for a rich multitude of individualistic artistic creations? And while reason was effective in exposing the weaknesses and limitations of traditions, how could it justify itself when subjected to the same kind of scrutiny? When political controversies in the progressive camp revealed that reason would by no means result in a single, immediately persuasive way of understanding the world and generally accepted practical improvements, then the questions emerged: What is the foundation of reason? To what extent is a full reliance on reason reasonable?

Romanticism is rightly associated with this first critical reaction to an enthusiastic enlightened cult of reason. While the usefulness of the term has been questioned – because the construction of a polar opposition between Enlightenment and its critics or between classical and non-classical art tends to conceal the far-reaching personal and substantive ground shared between the two – one can still maintain that a new generation after Kant and Goethe developed a distinct outlook on life, based on a heightened awareness of modernity's dark or problematic side.[3] The break with the past appeared no longer simply as an act of liberation, but also as a violation or destruction of irreplaceable traditions. An enlightened critique had provided ample proof that it could weaken and destroy the beliefs of the past, but scepticism emerged about its ability to put new, widely accepted beliefs into their place. At first, these doubts were at most peripheral, because an optimistic belief in the perfectability of the world held scepticism at bay. But when a German intellectual avant-garde became increasingly critical of the revolutionary terror in France and of Napoleon's ruthless restructuring of the German states, the tide began to turn. Precisely the success of the forces of change produced doubts and opposition: with the weakening of past traditions, the latter started to appear more precious; with the triumph of instrumental reason, its serious limitations became more obvious; with a liberal contract theory stressing the priority of the individual over the collective, the importance of a tightly knit community came into view; and with dramatic political changes, the wish for political stability became stronger. Old beliefs, including Christianity, were undoubtedly weakened; but did the new epoch produce more than a confusing array of incompatible political opinions?

A Romantic scepticism was particularly insightful regarding the dangers of an individualistic society, largely held together by the anonymous forces of a bureaucratic state and a capitalist market economy. In a speech about Europe in 1799, Novalis compared the Enlightenment with a 'tremendous mill', 'a mill as such, without a builder and without a miller, a real *perpetuum mobile*, a mill which grinds itself' (Novalis 1960 ff.: Vol. 3, 515). Friedrich Schelling described modern society as 'a machine which is designed to react to certain situations by itself, that is, blindly and inevitably. Although this machine is built and arranged by humans, it must act … according to its own laws, as if it existed by itself' (1856 ff.: I, 3, 584). In an anonymous text of the time, the author (probably Hegel or Schelling) even called for the abolition of a state, which was nothing but a 'mechanical clockwork' (Schelling 1975: 110). And the early conservative political Romantic Adam Müller protested in his major publications that the state should not be a machine, but an organic unit. An integration solely due to material interests was not sufficient, he argued, to function properly; a true community also needed a sense of solidarity based on a shared cultural heritage and shared political values.

The opposition organic–mechanical was fashionable not only among Romantics, but also became a staple argument in all right-wing critiques of modern society right through to National Socialism. While the theme gradually turned into a mere cliché, it held at first a precise meaning far beyond a vague nostalgia for nature. While a machine was a tool, whose sole purpose was to serve a higher function, nature was seen to have a purpose and a teleology in itself – and thus an intrinsic value. In the same way, the Romantics believed that a nation should not function without a communal purpose, solely as, say, a tool for the material well-being of its individual citizens. It should not function automatically independent of human ideals, but should incorporate *and* transcend all of its parts. Humans should not live in alienation from a purely pragmatic state, but find fulfilment and self-realization within the community. The ideal was a solidary nation united in the conscious pursuit of communal goals. As Jürgen Habermas (1987) called for the system of capitalism and power to be embedded in, and legitimated by, the life world of a communal culture, so the Romantics desired a state which would serve as the expression of a communal purpose or, in Rousseau's terminology, a *volonté générale* (Frank 1982: 161 ff.).

Romanticism has always divided opinions. Progressives have tended towards regarding it as an irrational flight from modernity. While the Romantic critique of capitalism strongly resembles Marxist ideas of alienation, many historians have stressed the far-fetched nature of their political goals, which tended to be based on a vague nostalgia for the Middle Ages, an ethnic folk culture or very personal artistic speculations. Instead of accepting the individualistic and pluralistic nature of modern society, they preached the value of the community, often in the form of an outdated corporative monarchy and a society united within a shared religion in premodern times (Schanze 1994: 509 ff., 541 ff.; Williamson 2004: 77 ff.). Instead of showing a serious commitment to firmly held convictions, Romantics allegedly followed, as Carl Schmitt has argued first in his *Political Romanticism* (1919), any path that happened to take their personal aesthetic fancy.

Growing scepticism about the idea of progress has, however, led to an important re-assessment of Romanticism, initiated above all by the works of Hartmut Böhme and Manfred Frank in the 1980s. Romantics did not fall back behind the Enlightenment, but reacted to its deficiencies when stressing the importance of emotions and personal creativity, the variety in human cultures and the importance of history in giving shape to the present. They convincingly pointed out the difficulties in trying to find a solid grounding for human reason, and they arguably had a point in highlighting the erosion of collectively held ideals. While one can question (with good reason), whether Romanticism provided more convincing answers, it certainly did not retreat into the past, but responded to very real problems raised by the revolutionary period and the Enlightenment, especially to a cult of reason, celebrated at its most naive and ruthless in the wake of the French Revolution (Burleigh 2005: 44–111; Kondylis 1979).

In general, Romantics did not argue for a simple return into the past (Schanze 1994: 509 ff.). While they undoubtedly showed a deep respect for history, they tended to acknowledge the irreversibility of temporal change, which allowed a return to the historical origins only on a higher level. Combining a high esteem for the past with a belief in progress, many tended to view history as evolving in three steps: an original natural state, a period of decline and, in their own present, a chance for the realization of a higher, conscious and self-reflected natural state. They were thus influenced by the optimism of the revolutionary period about the opportunity for bettering human conditions, but believed in achieving a future which would incorporate the ideals of the past in a more conscious and, thus, human form. In this vein, Heinrich von Kleist proclaimed: 'Paradise is bolted and barred, and the Cherub is behind us … We must make a journey round the world and see whether it may not be open at the back' (1965: 342). While they did not believe in an inevitable, determined process of improvement, at least the earlier Romantics tended to see a chance for working towards a better society.

The glorification of a distant past or a folk culture suppressed by an allegedly decadent dominant culture did not automatically lead to a conservative political orientation. On the contrary, at least the early Romantics tended to be highly critical of living traditions and current conditions. Their interest in the past was not just antiquarian and nostalgic, but aimed at finding positive elements to serve as exemplars for the present. They thus took inspiration from the past to call, not unlike their intellectual predecessors, for a revolutionary change to present conditions. Arguably, their lack of faith in a deterministic historical progression towards the better sharpened their eyes for a critique of the Enlightenment and the revolutionary epoch, but their diagnosis of a current crisis was based both on an awareness of existing deficiencies *and* a belief in the perfectability of society according to their own ideals. They did not simply show a spontaneous emotional reaction to a time of rapid and difficult change, but measured reality by the ideals they held and fought for.

An example will serve to illustrate this point. Many Romantics feared that modernization might pull society apart. The dramatic changes undermined traditional customs, integrative beliefs like Christianity were weakened, early capitalism started to create antagonistic classes, and political ideologies ranging from conservative monarchism to socialism started to emerge. Industrialization meant not only higher rates of production, but also new insecurities when people became dependent on anonymous market forces. Whole areas of production – like home weaving – became obsolete, established rights for common land or fair prices were no longer respected. The mechanization of production frequently meant monotonous manual work. Thus today's scholars tend to agree with a Romantic cultural criticism that German history of the nineteenth century faced the difficulties resulting from a rapidly changing nation divided into closed and antagonistic milieus (Lepsius 1973, 1990). On the other hand, at least the German lands of the immediate past had by no means been politically and culturally more united. The area consisted of 1,475 free lordships in the eighteenth century and was marked by deep confessional gulfs. French was the language of high society, and the strong differences between dialects meant that Germans who had not travelled widely could not understand people from other parts of the German territory. The many states meant a stupefying number of different legal, monetary and measurement systems. While market forces did not have such a wide-reaching impact, the weather could easily ruin regional parts of a highly localized food production with the consequence of regular famines. Thus it was not the immediate past which underlay the Romantics' critique of current economic and political conditions, but the ideal of a unified national culture, a caring community and the possibility of creative work. It was an ideal of the future, at least partially anticipated by the visions of the French Revolution.

Romanticism as a whole did not aim to turn back the clocks, but had, in many ways, a more complex vision of the future than enlightened thinkers did. It wanted to improve society, but without losing touch with historical tradition. It accepted reason, but wanted to combine it with an emphasis on emotions, human creativity and poetic freedom. As Romantics did not cling to old beliefs, but celebrated new trends in the arts, they clearly enjoyed the chance to create something new. They wholly shared Schiller's sentiment: 'If man is ever to solve the problem of politics in practice he will have to approach it through the problem of aesthetics' (1995: 90).

This emphasis on aesthetics and individual creativity is probably the strongest indication that Romanticism was oriented towards visions of a new and different future. This future should, however, correspond with an ideal they frequently claimed to have discovered in the past: a single communal faith, which was supposed to give humans a sense of security and communal belonging. The attempt to achieve a sense of togetherness through aesthetics led to the call for the creation of a 'new mythology' or faith for the whole community (Frank 1982).

What was meant by their frequent call for a new mythology? Romantics feared the atomization of a society purely based on self-interest; they felt alienated by a political domain, where antagonistic opinions and interests clashed without any obvious chance (or even attempt) for reconciliation. Christianity appeared as much too strict, dogmatic and in conflict with modern knowledge, while reason by itself was too cold and elitist; the ideal was an artistic creation, allegedly the true site of modern religiosity, for the whole community. 'We hear so often that the masses must have a *sensual religion.* Not only the great masses, but also the philosophers need it. Monotheism of reason and the heart, polytheism of imagination and art, that is what we need! First I will speak here of an idea that, so far as I know, has not yet occurred to anyone: we must have a new mythology. But this mythology must stand in the service of ideas: it must be a mythology of reason' (Schelling 1975: 112). Such a mythology would bring the people together in a free, enlightened and emotional community of faith: 'Then finally there would be eternal unity among us. No longer the blind shivering of the people before its wise men and priests. Only then would there be equal development of all powers, of the single person as well as of all individuals' (Schelling 1975: 112).

The call was thus for the creation of a new aesthetically shaped faith for the whole community. Romantics feared personal alienation from anonymous and cold systems – be it capitalism, the state or science – purely based on instrumental reason; thus they called for a community which would provide a feeling of solidarity and belonging. They wanted to bring the multitude of traditions within the German-speaking world together under the umbrella of one culture, but without losing the richness of pluralistic multitude. Many of them became, in time, ardent German nationalists, but they wanted to combine their dream of a powerful nation with the personal intimacy of a small community. While one can easily see the appeal of their utopia, it was rather a fanciful wish-list of all ideals imaginable than a coherent, let alone pragmatic, political programme.

The phrase *new mythology* indicates the direction of the Romantics' utopian dream of a closely integrated community. The adjective *new* signals once again that no return to, or repetition of, the past was intended, but a creation in and for the future. The noun *mythology* is rich with connotations (Fried 1985; Horstmann 1979; Jamme 1991, 1991a; Strich 1910; Williamson 2004: Introduction). It refers to a narration accepted by a whole community. It is an artistic text, but one which is given the status of sacredness. In a narrower sense, mythologies provide a whole cosmology: an explanation of the social and natural universe as well as suggestions for the proper and good way of life. It evokes associations with a pagan past which both Christianity and the Enlightenment had strongly defamed as outdated and superstitious. The choice of this term thus signalled a protest against the Christianity of the churches, against a progressive reliance on nothing but reason, and against the progressive dismissal of an allegedly irrational past. Beneath the surface the choice of this term simultaneously meant, however, a certain acceptance of an enlightened critique of religion. Historical studies of sacred texts had revealed their historical emergence through collective human agency, and the Romantic drive for a communal faith accepted this discovery which was so worrying for traditionally-minded believers. Something named 'mythology' did not claim to reveal the words of God or his actual actions; rather, it suggested the use of legends and analogies which might give the audience glimpses, suggestions and ideas about a metaphysical reality, an intuition about the infinite and the essence of existence.

Applied to a work of artistic productions, the term 'myth' makes a big claim: it rejects art as a commodity in a capitalist market or a purely pleasing *l'art pour l'art*; rather, art is to provide a collective meaning of self and world, of reality and a metaphysical essence. It reaches into the sphere of religion by wanting to be not just a purely individualistic creation, but beyond that the expression of a communal ethos and world-view. In contrast to the Bible or other sacred texts of the world religions, however, it does not claim to be the word of God or an accurate historical report of God's deeds and thus true in a literal sense, but is, like any aesthetic work, open to a wide variety of interpretations. A myth seeks to express a communal belief and communal norms, but within its frame there is a lot of freedom for personal readings. Mythologies are human-made, but the authorship is usually lost in the anonymity of time; thus they can be regarded as a collective production by a whole *Volk* or ethnic group. And, finally, the term evoked associations with classical Greece, which for the German Romantics was the prime example of a community, in which religion, customs and politics were held together by a shared celebration of communal works of art. What vision could be more attractive for poets and thinkers than a community integrated by the collective experience of art works like plays within the beautiful and sacred spaces of temples?[4]

The call for a 'new mythology' thus signalled a protest against the Enlightenment, but not its wholesale rejection. It hoped to achieve a truly communal belief, without making the absolute claims of a religion based on godly revelation. It celebrated the human act of creation,[5] but sought to be more than the product of an individual fancy. It allowed for a variety of opinions, but within the framework of a communally accepted myth, which would provide a sense of belonging and common destiny. It wanted to communicate a rational ethical and metaphysical content, but in a concrete, sensually accessible form. Put negatively, one could say that an artistic presentation of metaphysics in the shape of analogies was the only way of maintaining religion in face of an enlightened critique of allegedly godly revelations. Viewed more positively, however, one can also see it as an attempt to combine the joy of artistic freedom with the security of a communal faith. Even if a new mythology drew on a collective culture, the artist assumed the role of opening the eyes of the people to the godly, producing a contemporary expression of eternal truth and giving a community's unconscious world-view a concrete and persuasive expression. The emerging modern world of bureaucratic organization, miraculous technological means and industrial efficiency seemed acceptable or even beneficial, as long as a new mythology was able to embed it within communal meaning and purpose. In this way, one could hope to combine a new political freedom and a more comfortable standard of living with the sense of belonging and metaphysical security of a religious epoch like the Middle Ages.

Despite their stress on individual poetic creation, the Romantics preached the need for a natural harmony between individual and community. They rejected the idea that society should be based on a social contract, that is, on individual self-interest, emphasizing instead the need for a strong sense of belonging together. A community was not to be rationally constructed, but should grow organically out of the past and be united by a single communal culture or, ideally, mythology. Romantics hoped that the Enlightenment would not mark the end of religion, but only a temporary crisis: a withdrawal of the Gods (Hölderlin) and a weakening of religious sensibilities, which could be overcome by the rise of a new mythology. In this vein, Novalis argued in his speech 'Christendom in Europe' given in 1799 that the emphasis on rationality had suppressed the capacity for religious experiences, but that the Gods might return, if only humans overcame the grip of an all-encompassing rational control, thus allowing themselves to experience an unfathomable infinite.

As in many other areas, Herder was a key forerunner of the Romantics in showing an interest in mythologies. As early as 1767, he promoted the idea that mythological thinking should be revived. Instead of an antiquarian interest in old mythologies, which only petrifies them within a literary canon, Germans should aim at creating their own 'political mythology' (Herder 1877: 449) as a framework for discussing all current concerns. Such a new myth should balance enlightened reason with the 'fictional spirit' of the poet. 'The dissection of the philosopher' should go together with the 'synthesising faculty of the poet' (Herder 1877: 444), that is, with a more sensual and emotional form. In a similar vain, but with much more urgency and revolutionary fever, one of the foundational documents of Romanticism, *The Oldest Programme of German Idealism*, probably written in 1796 or 1797, recorded in Hegel's hand-writing and republished in Schelling 1975 – called, as quoted above, for a 'mythology of reason' (111f.): reason was to be accepted, but should find its metaphysical foundation within a less stringent and more poetic mythology. Instead of perceiving reality as nothing but a clockwork, it was to reveal a deeper, more human essence behind the scientific analysis of the natural world. While a purely mechanical world-view would lead to a deep alienation between humans and their environment, because we could never perceive ourselves as unfree marionettes wholly ruled by the laws of nature, an organic world-view would promote a sense of harmony between humans and their environment. This task of reconciliation between the human and the natural world was assigned to the aesthetic sphere: if it succeeded in creating such a 'new eternal gospel', poetry would become the 'teacher of humanity'. 'Then there will be eternal unity among us. No force will be suppressed any longer, then a universal spiritual freedom and equality will reign! – A higher spirit sent from heaven must found this new religion; it will be the last, greatest human achievement' (Schelling 1975: 39, 111, 112).

Such an ideal was shared by others. Friedrich Schlegel, for example, made the same point when he rejected purely personal poetry in an optimistic call for a communal mythology, In a 'Speech about Mythology' he stated: 'Our poetry, I claim, lacks a centre, as the mythology was for the Ancient, and all essential points, in which our modern poetry is inferior to the one of classical Greece, can be summarized with the words: We have no mythology. But, I add, we are close to getting one; or rather it is time that we all seriously participate in creating one' (Schlegel 1979 ff.: Vol. 1, 312).

It was much easier, however, to call for a new mythology than to create one. Individuals called for it; but a myth could not be the creation of one individual; it needed collective roots. Myth was to create a community, but it also needed a true community to bring forth a myth. Schelling saw this 'chicken-and-egg' problem, but simply delegated the answer to the future: 'Only from the spiritual unity of a people, from a truly public life, can the true and universally valid poetry emerge' (1856–1861: I/6, 573). 'But how is a new mythology itself to arise, which shall be the creation, not of some individual author, but of a new race [*Geschlecht*], personifying, as it were, one single poet – that is a problem whose solution can be looked for only … in the course of history to come' (Schelling 1856–1861: I/3, 629).

This was a core dilemma that all calls for a new myth were going to face: any single communal faith was supposed to emerge from the community as a whole, but how could one will such a spontaneous creation, especially if society was allegedly uprooted from its ethnic core and deeply divided? How could one promote an artistic creation, which was to be the expression of an anonymous, communal wisdom? Half a century later, Richard Wagner gave the following answer in his 'Work of Art in the Future' from 1849: 'Who will then be the artist of the future? The poet? The actor? The musician? The sculptor? *Let us put it briefly: the Volk. The same Volk thanks to whom we have the only true art, which is still alive today in our memory, and which we only recreate in distortion*' (Wagner n.d.: Vol. 10, 177). What Wagner meant by this, concretely, was the use of sagas and folk legends as material for the creation of a new mythology within his operas. With this viewpoint, he drew upon a long tradition. It was, after all, an obvious route to take: if Romantics had a deep admiration for the past, if they were fascinated by the wide variety of human expression, if they believed in the collective wisdom of tradition, if they wanted to move beyond personal creations to the artistic expression of a whole people, then drawing on folk art lent itself to being the most promising way forward. As early as 1773, Goethe came to propagate the gothic, in contrast to the dominant neo-classicism, as a typically German style. Herder published old folk-songs in 1874, 'not for the scholar', he claimed, 'but for the nation! People! A body called fatherland!' (quoted in Williamson 2004: 75). The shift to a celebration of supposedly authentic German art gained force in the early nineteenth century with the collection of fairy tales by the Grimm brothers, the fascination with old sagas such as the *Nibelungenlied* and the collection of folk songs by Clemens Brentano and Achim von Arnim in the three-volume *Des Knaben Wunderhorn* (published 1806–1808, reprinted 2006). We can also witness a growing interest in the German language, as it was regarded as the most comprehensive ethnic creation, even as a fundamental framework, the distinctive features of which would give rise to a typically German way of feeling and perceiving reality. As Germany did not exist as one nation, language was the supreme marker of an ethnic cultural identity. Consequently, the philologist Jacob Grimm found much support when he defined *Volk* as 'humans who speak the same language' (Grimm 1884: 557. More generally Fritzsche 2004: 142–159; Zippes 2002).

Even if the collectors of folk art might have been motivated mainly by antiquarian interest, their endeavour served contemporary goals: the creation of an ethnic identity, possibly as the basis for the formation of a future nation state. They established a culture of memory and an ethnic corpus of art, which aimed to shape a current Germanness and influence political actions. Generally, they felt quite free in adapting the old material to their own artistic taste (an extreme example is Ludwig Tieck's collection of fairy tales from 1797). These collectors were more directly concerned with identifying a German tradition rather than a new mythology, but the two goals were clearly related. Herder, for example, claimed that a nation should have 'a mythology growing out of its own language and way of thinking'. According to him, Germany lacked 'a language grown out of its own mythology, a hero epos genre developed to the present day, a poetic expression and evolvement of its originally so wide, full and beautiful ethnic ideas' (1883: 484 f., 487). When occupied by an expanding France, such convictions could turn into the call for an independent Germany, whose cultural identity was sharply contrasted with that of its dangerous neighbour in the West. In Herder's proclamation 'Germanien' (1877a), the political implications one could draw from a glorification of German culture were clearly spelled out, when he answered his own rhetorical question: 'Germany, are you still asleep?' by pleading:

> Should your name perish? And are not your fathers,
> your own heart, your language worth everything?
> Your heart, should it beat according to the Gaul's,
> the Cossack's, the Kalmuk's rhythm? Take courage!
> Whoever does not protect himself, does not deserve freedom! …
> Be one Germany
>
> (210–212)

All the many calls for a 'new mythology' remained within the realms of high culture, but they showed, nevertheless, a strong desire for a new communal belief. Artists and thinkers missed a sense of belonging, emotional warmth within the public sphere, religious security and a clear purpose in life. They reacted by promoting the dream of a tightly knit community, in which everybody would feel part of the whole, because they shared the same convictions and values. Disillusioned by lack of success, many Romantics turned to Catholicism later in their lives, but their greatest and most ambitious desire had been a *new* faith, which would take on board enlightened critiques of Christianity without losing a sense of the religious and mysterious, the emotional and the sensual. The new faith should not be hierarchically governed by one holy scripture and church dogma, but allow for poetic freedom and individual interpretations. The new myth had little to say about life after death (apart from a continued existence as part of a communal ethnic culture), but it was to promote communal values and set collective goals.

This early attempt at creating a new mythology also set an important example by its emphasis on aesthetics. Instrumental reason could serve practical purposes, many continued to believe, but it undermined any attempt to give life a deeper meaning. Rational organizations could increase society's efficiency, but integrated individuals through their interests alone. In contrast to this, the creative forces of poetry seemed to appeal to the 'Other of Reason' (Böhme and Böhme 1992): they offered a medium for the expression of anxieties and desires, provided models for defining individual existence, suggested ideas for developing a new communal identity and offered a space for society to negotiate meanings for individual and collective life.

While the call for a 'new mythology' tended to be politically progressive at first, its glorification of the past always gave it a conservative potential which was soon to become reality. From later political Romanticism with its glorification of the Middle Ages and the Catholic church onwards, the aesthetic space was also used, as we shall see, to develop right-wing ideals of a state where the citizens were to be united in a single communal faith.

While avant-garde literary discussions about a new myth remained elitist, sagas and fairy tales could reach a wider audience. But both remained peripheral in comparison to the fervent political nationalism erupting in Germany with the Napoleonic wars. In recent years, precursors of this ideology have increasingly been discovered in the eighteenth century and even earlier (Berger 2004: 13–28; Blitz 2000; Echternkamp 1998: 90–159; Hope 1995), but the movement emerging in response to the French invasion had a wholly new quality. While nationalism was still the ideology of a small minority, the belief in national differences turned into a political rallying cry for a clearly defined nation; a vague sense of identity and belonging turned into the belief that the nation should demand the highest human loyalty.

Nationalism as a political ideology of the first order emerged with the political revolutions at the end of the eighteenth century. These events indicated the enthusiasm and support a state could mobilize if citizens came to regard it as their own nation. At least a politically and culturally significant part of the population – above all from the rising middle class – desired to live in a nation they could identify with. In calling for their ideal of a nation, they fought not only for their material interest, but also for more liberty, equality and solidarity to realize a just community with participatory rights and duties. All these changes would then allow for the emergence of a nation where citizens would be filled with a sense of togetherness. They would, the nationalist utopia foresaw, feel part of the whole, and thus be prepared to make their contribution to the nation's common good. The call for more political participation was, of course, still usually limited to males with property or higher education, but these full citizens should gain the chance to identify with the nation by playing an important part in shaping and governing it. The new nationalism could evolve spontaneously among a cultural elite and gradually attract a wider following, because it promised what a growing number of people desired, namely a sense of collective belonging and emotionally charged community life at a time when a growing bureaucracy and the spread of a free-market economy made social relations increasingly anonymous and impersonal; a clear-cut political world-view through defining a strict distinction of 'us and them' in times of confusing social change; and an attractive political project for improving society and achieving a more fulfilled life.

Though patriotism for the many different states still dominated in the German-speaking world, during the Napoleonic wars an identification with the whole of Germany continuously gained force. After all, the experience with the French both as a military enemy in a war in which 5 per cent of the German population fought and many lost their lives (Fritzsche 2004: 33 f.; Hagemann 2002: 36 f.) and as invaders and occupiers promoted a sense for the common characteristics and interests of all Germans. A German nationalism could not identify with one existing state because the territory was politically so divided and the German Holy Roman Empire had ceased to be a functioning political entity long before it was formally ended in 1806, but one could try to emphasize communal cultural traits which would add up to a peculiar Germanness. While nationalism in the older states identified first and foremost with a clearly defined political entity, it was inevitable that alleged communalities of the mind and 'blood' had to be emphasized to define the communalities among all Germans, above all a common language, a communal ethnic past and a shared political destiny. The realization of shared interests and ambitions in response to the French invasion was thus backed up by a new emphasis on the importance of one language and the construction of one German history. Whether, and if so, how the different German states would form closer ties remained an open and highly controversial question, but both the idea of communal German traits and an identification of the citizens with 'their' state had entered the political stage with full force. While an earlier cultural elite had largely been cosmopolitan in their political outlook, the conflict with France made nationalism the topic of the day.

A growing willingness for political actions against the French thus led to a situation where a vague sense of national peculiarities became more clearly defined when mobilized in support of concrete goals. Furthermore, one could now justify the call for domestic reforms as a necessary step towards becoming a match for the dominating Napoleonic France. Only if serfdom was abolished, legal justice guaranteed and more participatory rights granted – so the argument went – could citizens come to identify with their state, and only this would allow for a successful mobilization of the whole population for a war against France. While a cabinet war had led to the crushing defeat of 1806, the total mobilization of the whole population in a people's war would give the strength to achieve victory and thus free the German states from foreign dominance. This was an argument one could use to convince those who were reluctant to introduce reforms which, after all, posed quite a threat to the status quo through the call for a change of both boundaries and the domestic political structure.[6]

In Prussia, a willingness for reforms thus emerged through defeat. Even many of those who would have liked to maintain the status quo came to realize that only major changes could overcome the serious weakness Prussia had shown in the short war against France and the crisis which followed. The drive for reforms in Prussia thus gained sufficient momentum only as a defensive move: if the state was to reestablish itself as one of the main military powers in Europe, then a thorough change of the social and political system was unavoidable. And the wish for political independence had to increase with the experience of occupation: the injustices of French rule, the fear that German institutions would be abolished, and German culture eroded, worked together to cause an eruption of patriotic feelings. What united quite varied opinions into one political movement was the will to break the French dominance over the German states; once Napoleon was defeated, deep political conflicts immediately sprang up again (Hagemann 2002: 42–46).

A strong nationalist movement – often still for individual states like Prussia, but increasingly also for a united future Germany – thus emerged in opposition to France; its most immediate aim was to mobilize the whole population for a nationalist people's war against France. While there is an ongoing debate on how much popular enthusiasm nationalism did actually mobilize,[7] the wars soon came to be known under the name 'wars of liberation'. Progressive interpreters argued that the nationalized population had forced reluctant rulers to take up the fight against France, while conservatives claimed that king and generals had led an enthusiastic population into the successful wars for political independence,[8] but all interpretations agreed that only a strong sense of national commitment had made the defeat of France possible. 1813–14 thus became, irrespective of the actual realities, the founding myth that a high-spirited nationalist uprising could provide a country with an irresistible military force. Furthermore, Prussia in particular was assigned a national mission, it was claimed, as the guardian and promoter of the German cause (Akaltin 1997: 87 ff.; Clark 1996; Hardtwig 1990: 58–91).

Some national extremists certainly believed that the whole population was united behind one cause. The historian and poet Ernst Moritz Arndt, for example, stated: 'To be one *Volk*, to have a strong emotion for one cause, to join together with the bloody sword of revenge, this is the religion of our times' (quoted in Nipperdey 1983: 439). As this quotation indicates, such wartime nationalism could produce extreme outbursts of hatred and destructive energy against the military enemy (Jeismann 1992). Both Fichte (1944: Conclusion) and Friedrich Schlegel (1979 ff.: Vol. 13, 166) spoke of a 'war of annihilation' (*Vernichtungskrieg* and *Ausrottungskrieg*), and Heinrich Kleist said of the French enemy: 'Kill him! History does not ask for the reason' (1923 ff.: Vol. 1, 87). Leading politicians and military officers like Freiherr vom Stein and Carl von Clausewitz shared this hatred, which was expressed in unparalleled intensity by Ernst Moritz Arndt: he called for the 'destruction' of the 'French vermin' and 'monster'. 'Damned be all humanity and cosmopolitanism ... I will work my whole life that hate and despise of that nation will take deepest roots in German hearts.' There, he wrote, 'is the German fatherland, where rage exterminates the French baubles, where every Frenchman is called enemy' (quoted in Wehler 1987: 523). Throughout the period, there were also voices expressing admiration for France, but they were undoubtedly drowned in the belligerent atmosphere.

For the hard core of the nationalist movement, however, nationalism was neither just an anti-French emotion nor a manipulative strategy to strengthen the state. On the contrary, the military conflict was seen immediately as a chance to realize long-cherished political and cultural ideals. Until the 1848 German revolution (and for the most part until 1866), nationalism was still a movement which wanted to reduce the power of the nobility, overcome feudal structures and push through liberal measures in the political and economic sphere. While the majority preferred reforms to the unpredictability of a revolution, the demand for a constitution and parliamentary representations was a step towards more participatory rights, even if most wanted a limited franchise and claimed to build on allegedly German traditions. Beyond these political goals, the conflict with France was also seen as a chance to melt the population together behind one single goal and thus establish a communal nationalist culture. As the 'father of the gymnastics movement' (*Turnvater*), Jahn exclaimed in 1815: 'Germany needs a war by itself against France ... a conflict with the French so that its own ethnic peculiarities will evolve in their full wealth' (1884: II/2, 1003).

As in other 'new nations' of the nineteenth century, there was, at first, no satisfactory institutional framework for the kind of national existence which, gradually, a growing number of people came to desire. A majority of Germans still identified with their home state, but for true nationalists the German Confederation founded in 1815 was much too loose to satisfy their dreams. Thus German nationalism did not identify with one political entity, but defined itself through the idealized construction of an ethnic past and the dream of a national future. While all perceptions of a nation are in some ways 'imaginary' (Anderson 1991), perceiving one nation where there were many independent states was even more fictitious than in long-established Western European nation states – especially as none of the German states promoted a unified Germany at the time, because it threatened the political leadership's position.

As in other countries, nationalism was first conceived and promoted within small circles of academics, higher civil servants, theologians, writers and journalists, as well as a few politicians and militaries – that is, within a newly formed educated middle class of civil servants, academics and students (Wehler 1987: 512). They were part of a new and wider communications network as they tended to study at universities away from home, move to jobs outside their home region and read national newspapers, magazines and books. With time, however, better roads, canals and the railway promoted connections for everybody, and the emerging market economy, the move towards general conscription and an increase in migration made a growing number of look beyond their region and state to identify with the wider notion of 'Germany'.

State patriotism, not German nationalism, continued to be the dominant political loyalty in the early nineteenth century, but nationalist feelings started to become a major influence in politics. The wish for a new communal mythology had been sown, a strong interest in an ethnic culture had established itself, and a belief in national stereotypes had long been present. A national history started to take shape, with heroes like the Cheruscan Armin, who allegedly defended Germanic freedom against the Roman conquerors, or powerful medieval emperors like Charlemagne and Friedrich Barbarossa, who had supposedly been early fighters for the nationalist cause. The professor of philology August Wilhelm Schlegel claimed in a letter that all his writing had only one purpose: 'to present to the Germans a picture of their old glory, their old honour and freedom in the mirror of the past' (1983 ff.: 200). Many started to emphasize a national past and present, and even a special German mission for the future. Thus the call to arms met at least with some enthusiasm when defeat in Russia showed that Napoleon was not invincible. While the later myth of a 'national awakening' in the 'wars of liberation' was obviously exaggerated, strong nationalist feelings undoubtedly had an impact on events.

There are many indications that the nationalist discourse played an important historical role (Hagemann 2002: 106–136, 395 ff.). While Prussia had censored such publications when the political elites did not feel ready for a war against France, the king of Prussia, Friedrich Wilhelm III eventually came to appeal 'to his people' (Prussians and Germans) to lead a holy war for national honour and national existence ('An Mein Volk', reprinted in Schulze 1913). The terminology was not yet truly nationalist – the king spoke of *Volk* rather than using the more political term nation, and he explicitly distinguished in the case of the Prussian *Volk* 'Brandenburgers, Prussians, Silesians, Pomeranians, [and] Lithuanians' (quoted in Breuilly 2002: 18) – but it still marked an important step towards recognizing all citizens as political actors. While it was still important for the monarch to be seen as the initiator of the war, he accepted the need to have public opinion on his side and thanked the people for their war effort after victory was achieved. The Prussian army grew between March and August 1913 from 67,000 to 245,000 soldiers without notable disquiet among the population, and 30,000 young men volunteered for war service.[9] A public role was also assigned to women: for the first time, women formed Patriotic Clubs to give support to the troops. Louise, Queen of Prussia, became a female role model, both as a caring mother and for her support for the nationalist cause.

Nationalist publications were distributed in high numbers. Leaflets by Ernst Moritz Arndt had a circulation of more than 100,000; they were discussed in clubs and reading circles. Many nationalist songs emerged (usually a new text set to a well-known melody), thus spreading the message even further. The press also reported in detail about the war, printed contributions to the nationalist debate and had lengthy articles on the many different celebrations.

Fervent nationalists like Friedrich Ludwig Jahn and Ernst Moritz Arndt also argued that Germany needed its own symbols and rituals. They initiated, for example, a lively debate about national costume. While this had no practical results, a 'national cockade' was introduced in Prussia, which many male civilians wore on their hats to show their support for the war. The army also introduced a new medal, the Iron Cross, which – a novelty – was given to soldiers of all ranks. Furthermore, Prussia also introduced a medal for patriotic women, named after Queen Louise.

Many public rituals and celebrations underlined the commitment to nation and war. The greatest event was the remembrance of the *Völkerschlacht*, a major battle near Leipzig, where the troops of all the German states had achieved an important, but costly, victory over France. Arndt and his circle initiated the idea which was taken up all over Germany. An official publication describes 780 of these events celebrated in all different parts of Germany, but this still excluded small towns and villages, where local initiatives organized simple celebrations with bonfires and thanksgiving services (Hagemann 2002: 482 ff.).

Patriotism and, increasingly, nationalism thus started to reach into everyday life, but its content was largely formulated by an avant-garde cultural elite. The scholar and political reformer Wilhelm von Humboldt, for example, stressed the importance of a *völkisch* history and culture – that is, a history and culture holding together all members of a nation. 'No German heart', he stated in 1813, could forget that Germany 'is one', because of 'common features of customs, language and literature'. He stressed the importance of a collective past in claiming a national 'memory of communally held rights and freedom, communally achieved glory and mastered dangers, a remembrance of close ties, which connected the fathers and which only lives as a desire among the grandsons'. With pathos, he stated that all this made 'Germany … always … a nation, a people, a state' for his generation. For him, the belief in one German nation found its logical conclusion in a clear political agenda: 'Germany must be free and strong' (1903 ff.: Vol. 11, 97f.).

Above all, a common language, allegedly a guarantee for a single national mentality and culture, became the defining feature of the imagined nation's identity. As Ernst Moritz Arndt wrote in his famous poem *What is the German's Fatherland?* of 1813:

> Is it Prussia? Is it Swabia?
> Is it along the Rhine where the vine resides?
> Is it along the Belt where the seagull glides?
> O no! No! No!
> His Fatherland must be greater still! ...
> As far as the German tongue rings
> And to God in Heaven Lieder sings
> That's where it should be!
> That, bold German, pertains to thee! (1894: 18–21)

The poem called for one Germany, but Arndt could refrain from a precise definition of possible borders. His sense of Germany was still not related to the idea of one state; what mattered to him was a pure ethnic identity defined by a common language and culture. The 1817 Brockhaus encyclopaedia clearly stated, however, that a national culture can be secured 'only through a united state, national virtues and religion' (quoted in Hagemann 2002: 234).

From the beginning, German nationalism was much more than a pragmatic plan for the truly faithful, but gained the status of the most fundamental and important secular mythology which was at the centre of all their political and cultural judgements. Wilhelm von Humboldt was still comparatively down to earth when he confessed that he would rather be German than any other nationality. Ernst Moritz Arndt went much further when he wanted Germans to associate 'the greatest magnificence and holiness' with the term fatherland. 'Apart from God and heaven', nationalism was supposed to be 'the highest thought' humans could hold. Within a fatherland, he wrote, the best in humans would grow towards heaven (1803: 429). In a similar vein, Friedrich Ludwig Jahn called 'a God, a fatherland, a house and a love' 'the most beautiful blessings' given to humanity (1884: I, 194). Equally, the philosopher Johann Gottlieb Fichte (1762–1814) called for a semi-religious attachment to the nation in his famous *Speeches to the German Nation*, given in the winter of 1807–08: 'Not the spirit of calm, bourgeois love of a constitution, but the consuming flame of a higher love of the fatherland, which embraces the nation as the outward cloak of eternity, for which the noble-minded sacrifices himself joyfully, and for which the not noble-minded ... has to sacrifice himself'. Fichte realized that only a minority held such sentiments, but he called on them to educate the rest: 'The majority of citizens must develop such a patriotic spirit, and to be certain of the majority, one has to try to educate everybody.' Nationalism was supposed to overcome one's narrow material interest to give a higher, more spiritual meaning to life (1944: 134, 145, 147).

Such an unreserved deification of the nation has a blasphemous ring to it, but at the time, at least in Prussia, Protestantism and nationalism were closely connected. Most nationalists also stressed, as many of the quotations above have shown, their Christian faith, and the Protestant church played a key role in promoting loyalty to the state. The vast majority of nationalists in the German lands did not see their ideology as a secular religion taking the place of a previous metaphysical faith, but as an ideology in harmony with true Christianity. As France was frequently accused of an enlightened rationalism taken to the destructive extreme of atheism, Christianity or religiosity in general even became a defining feature of German identity in alleged opposition to its Western neighbour.

State and Protestant church were deeply intertwined. The king was also the highest church authority, and he used the services to reach the population with public announcements. Patriotic war prayers were formulated for all services, and ministers were instructed in detail about how to spread war enthusiasm through their sermons. Ministers blessed soldiers before they went to war, money was collected to support the armed struggle, and the churches were used for victory celebrations. This political instrumentalization of religion was not challenged; on the contrary, the published collections of sermons strongly indicate that Protestant ministers were among the most enthusiastic supporters of their state and of a German nationalism (Altgeld 1992; Graf 1993). While Protestantism remained closely connected with nationalism throughout the period covered in this book, a later extreme nationalism became, as we shall see, increasingly critical of the allegedly un-German Christian message of love and peace.

However, there is no indication that the close ties with Protestantism had a moderating influence on the emerging nationalism. In contrast to the universalism implicit in Christianity, ardent nationalists elevated Germany to the position of a chosen nation with a special mission. Friedrich Schlegel believed, as he stated in 'To the Germans' (1800) that only 'in Germany the spring of a new time flows' (1979 ff.: Vol. 5, 300). The poet Friedrich von Schiller stated: 'The Germans' day brings the harvest of all ages', and the theologian Friedrich Daniel Schleiermacher called Germans 'a chosen tool and God's people' (quoted in Wehler 1987: 517). Wilhelm von Humboldt proclaimed: 'There is possibly no nation which deserves independence and freedom as much as Germany, as none tends to use its freedom so purely' (Humboldt and Humboldt 1968: 165). And Fichte argued that only Germany could create a perfect state, because it allegedly had the most highly educated people. Such a German state would then play a crucial role in morally improving humanity as a whole. As early as the first half of the nineteenth century, Fichte used his *Speeches to the German Nation* to turn such a claim to moral superiority into a political right and duty for Germany to govern the world (1944: 101).

A cultural chauvinism could easily translate into a legitimization of political supremacy; this reasoning continued to spread, until it became commonplace with the 'ideas of 1914'. It is true that the select role and mission many nationalists saw for their country was still moderated by the fact that they wanted Germany to act in the interest of all. Nationalism and cosmopolitanism were, as Meinecke rightly pointed out (1962: 120), deeply intertwined at the beginning of the century. It was, however, clearly a chauvinistic belief in one's own superiority, and could turn, with time, into nothing more than a convenient justification for claiming supremacy over other people.

Independent of the controversial question of how much weight nationalism had in the whole of society and in shaping the reality of war,[10] in retrospect the so-called 'wars of liberation' became a central part of the newly constructed German history (Clark 1996), for example in Friedrich Meinecke's *Das Zeitalter der deutschen Erhebung* (1906, 7th edn). In particular, the volunteers in the free corps, but also the other soldiers, were used as heroic examples of an idealism which can make a nation invincible. Prussia, in particular, was glorified as a state acting in the German interest, while the war heroes were turned into role models for all male citizens. While common soldiers had been despised outsiders for the middle class in the age of standing armies, the veterans of these wars were celebrated. All soldiers decorated with the Iron Cross were named on a plaque in their regimental church, the fallen soldiers also in the church at home. Real men, the argument now went, were prepared to fight and risk their lives. Arndt, for example, wrote a poem *Who is a man?* which included the lines: 'A man is he who can fight / for wife and dear child … A man is he who can die /for freedom, duty and justice … A man is he who can die / for God and fatherland'. In a similar vein, a teacher in a military school stated: 'Whoever cannot protect his wife, / is never suited for marriage' (quoted in Hagemann 2002: 271 and 338).

The glorification of the soldierly role, which became increasingly prominent throughout the nineteenth century, started with the wars against France and the conscript army. Serving as common soldier in the army was no longer a bloody job only desperate men chose, but the duty of every true man. War was stylized as a heroic adventure, death in battle as the ultimate sacrifice. 'Death for the fatherland', Kleist wrote, 'deserves eternal reverence. – How much I would also like to die this honourable death, when my destiny [*Verhängnis*] calls.' And Arndt did not shy away from comparing fallen soldiers with Christ: 'He is praised highly as a saviour, as a hero' (quoted in Hagemann 2002: 342, 345). Only a small minority published such poems, but their tropes were also used in many obituaries, showing that they were more widely accepted, presumably because they not only helped mobilization, but also to cope with death and loss.

The war heroes, and in particular the volunteers – for whom it was easier to claim that they had risked their lives for deeply felt convictions – continued to be praised and celebrated throughout the nineteenth century, thus presenting an important role model for male youth (Schilling 2002: 43–168). In contrast, women were supposed to focus on the home, as Ernst Moritz Arndt stated: 'And if the man does not carry weapons, / And the women does not busy herself with the kitchen, / things cannot go right in the long term, / And home and Reich must go to ruin' (quoted in Hagemann 2002: 206). Women should also be nationalistically minded, but express their conviction through infusing patriotism into their children, encourage – despite the heart-ache – the men to be heroic, and support the troops in time of war by supporting the soldiers, caring for the wounded and mourning the dead.

Perceptions matter: 'If men define situations as real, they are real in their consequences' (Thomas 1928: 114). The legend of a successful national uprising against Napoleon played a key role in teaching the following generations that nationalism was a powerful faith which was able to unite and strengthen the country. It could make individuals feel part of the whole, even to the extent of being prepared for the highest sacrifice. 'Happiness', Karl Theodor remarked categorically, lies 'only in sacrificial death' (quoted in Mosse 1990: 70). The promotion of nationalism for political aims became a model for future use. Not without reason, it appeared to be the only new myth with a chance to become *the* single communal faith of a whole nation. It seemed to have the astounding ability to anchor itself deep in the soul of many citizens and simultaneously serve the strength of the nation.

The historian Thomas Nipperdey (1983) has tried to distinguish a benign early nationalism with a later aggressive one. While it is certainly true that nationalism became, as we shall see, more extremist over time, it was by no means wholly innocent in its beginnings. Though the outbursts of hatred against the French must be seen in the context of the invasion, they still show a disturbing tendency towards demonizing the entire enemy nation and celebrating unlimited violence in the war against it (Jeismann 1992). The tendency to find one's identity in excluding others also became apparent in the anti-Semitism of ardent nationalists including Arndt, Clemens Brentano, Fichte and many less well-known figures. The Jews were called an alien people who would have to assimilate completely (which meant, as a minimum, accepting Christianity) for gaining citizenship (Hagemann 2002: 249–270). From the start, nationalism did not envisage a pluralistic state, but a community united in single communal faith.

The high-pitched nationalist fever did not last after the defeat of France, partly because such a 'war hysteria' could not be sustained, partly because many nationalists were intimidated and demoralized by the following period of restoration. But what nationalism lost in intensity after the war, it gained in overall support. With the rise of a network of communication and mobility, its sentiments gradually reached wider parts of the population. For another fifty years, nationalism continued to be largely an emancipatory ideology, aiming for more unification *and* freedom. However, non-reactionary conservatives, prepared to accept the need to adapt their ideology to changing times, gradually came to realize that nationalism was not the exclusive domain of progressive forces. After all, pride in the ethnic past, solidarity with the nation and a willingness for personal sacrifice were desirable for conservative forces too. Nationalism presented itself as a powerful ideology for the future: it could integrate citizens into the existing order and mobilize them for international conflicts, thus significantly strengthening the nation's military might. It is no surprise, then, that conservatives gradually came round to using this ideology for their own ends.

Notes

1. Dann 1996: 63–84; Echternkamp 1998; Forum für Philosophie 1989; Fritzsche 2004; Koselleck 1985; Nipperdey 1983: 1 ff.; Winkler 2000: Vol. 1, 40 ff. For a summary with reference to the more specialized literature, see Hagemann 2002: 17–45.
2. A good example for the glorification of the railway and progress in general is the article 'Eisenbahnen' in: *Meyers Conversations-Lexicon für die gebildeten Stände* (1846). More generally, on the belief in progress see Rohkrämer 1999: 48–52; on material changes, Schmoll 2004: 61–92.
3. See the contributions by Harro Segeberg and Ludwig Stockinger in Schanze 1994: 31 ff. and 79 ff. More generally Beiser 1992; Dülmen 2002.
4. See for example Frank 1982: 88 ff.; Williamson 2004. The love for the Greeks, which was particularly strong in Johann Joachim Winckelmann and Hölderlin, was so widespread as to be comparable with the Romantic fascination with the Middle Ages.
5. Friedrich Schlegel expected the new myth to be 'the most artificial of artworks, because it has to encompass all others, a new bed and container for the ancient eternal source of poetry, and itself the infinite poem, which contains the seed of all other poems' (quoted in Williamson 2004: 58).
6. For general overviews Breuilly 2001; Sheehan 1989; Wehler 1987 (with emphasis on Prussia's 'defensive modernisation'); Winkler 2000: Vol. 1, 40–78; more specifially Echternkamp 1998; Münchow-Pohl 1987; Weber 1991.
7. Following Wehler 1987, Echternkamp argues that 'a "national rising" did not take place' (1998: 216). Breuilly shares this view (2002: 17–19), while Hagemann calls the war of 1813–14 a total war (2002: 527). For a more moderate view see Sheehan 1989, Dann 2003 and 1996: 57–84.
8. The two interpretations also named the war differently: '*Freiheitskriege*', that is 'Wars of Liberty', versus '*Befreiungskriege*', that is 'Wars of Liberation' (Clark 1996: 552).
9. Such a step was not necessarily wholly voluntary, though, because it was made a prerequisite for the higher civil service. This was a strong incentive in a time of high unemployment among the university-trained, but there were also many craftsmen among the volunteers.
10. See footnote 7 for references to the literature concerning this controversy. While I tend towards assigning more historical weight to the nationalism of the time than Wehler, Echternkamp or Breuilly, the argument of the book does not depend on this. Even if it was only a later legend that a national awakening took place in the 'wars of liberation', because the nationalist sentiments were carried by 'marginal men' at the time (Elie Kedourie quoted in Berger 2004: 14), this memory would have still played an important role in the emerging desire for a single communal faith.

CHAPTER 2

FROM LEFT TO RIGHT: THE EMERGENCE OF A RIGHT-WING NATIONALIST FAITH

After German victory over France had been achieved, the nationalist movement confronted new challenges. While it had eventually met with official approval for its help in mobilizing the people for war, the attitude changed after 1815. The Congress of Vienna established a German Federation with the main intention of defending the old order. Under the 'System Metternich', promoters of a united German nation came to be regarded as threats to the restoration of stability. Practices varied across the many independent states, but on the whole nationalism faced a period of suppression. Uniting Germany threatened many principalities; for strict monarchists this amounted to an unruly policy directed against legitimate political structures. Monarchical rule was set into place, the argument went, by God and traditional custom; any challenge to this thus appeared as a dangerous revolutionary practice. The Habsburg Empire in particular had to take a strong stand against the new ideology: as it combined many different ethnic groups or nationalities under one monarchical rule, its structure was threatened by the nationalist ideal of a world where political and ethnic boundaries would correspond.

Prosecution, however, only served to prove the power of nationalism. Despite all the policies directed against it, nationalism gradually turned into a mass phenomenon. In 1817, German student fraternities (*Burschenschaften*) organized the nationalist Wartburg festival, and in 1832, 20,000 to 30,000 nationalists attended the Hambacher festival, which took place in the ruins of a medieval castle. When Prussia and other states banned student fraternities, nationalists organized in a multitude of voluntary organizations, for example, friendship circles, scholarly societies, social clubs and reading groups. They were committed to a new kind of sociability, where all members related to each other as equals (Dann 1984; Düding 1991). The most important of these nationalist associations were the gymnastic and singing clubs (*Turn-* and *Gesangsvereine*), whose membership reached approximately 150,000 by 1848, and the gun clubs (*Schützenvereine*). Nationalists developed rituals like festivals and parades with particular songs and flags, national monuments were built and a growing number of Germany-wide associations emerged. About 500 towns and cities across Germany celebrated the centenary of Friedrich Schiller's birth in 1859, praising him as *the* nationalist poet (Dann 2001), and prominent figures like Johann Gutenberg, Albrecht Dürer and Martin Luther were also turned into exemplary Germans. It is estimated that about 250,000 people were associated with the nationalist movement by the middle of the nineteenth century. Nationalist rhetoric was ever-present in Protestant sermons, in university lectures and in a growing number of newspapers, magazines and books. With time, it continued to widen its appeal, reaching out beyond a cultural elite and an educated middle class to win over large parts of the professional middle class (*Besitzbürgertum*), the petty bourgeoisie and even peasants (Düding 1985; Jarausch 1984; Mosse 1975; Wehler 1987a: 402–406; Winkler 2000: Vol. 1, 79–130).

Nationalism continued to show its usefulness for mobilizing the nation for power politics on the international scene. A national awakening had, nationalist rhetoric claimed, driven Napoleon out of Germany, and the fear of another French attack in 1840 triggered a second wave of nationalist fever. New anti-French nationalist songs like *Die Wacht am Rhein* ('Stand Guard at the Rhine') and, what was to become the national anthem *Deutschland, Deutschland über alles* ('Germany, Germany, above everything'), were composed in response to the threat. They quickly became highly popular: the Rhine-song *Sie sollen ihn nicht haben, den freien deutschen Rhein* ('They shall not have it, the free German Rhine'), for example, was apparently sung to up to 200 different melodies (Nipperdey 1983: 311). Similarly, later international conflicts, in particular about Schleswig-Holstein, always showed the nationalist movement ready to back enthusiastically the power politics of the German states. If future wars would tend towards being people's wars, as the Prussian General Carl von Clausewitz argued in his reflections *On War* at the time, then nationalism had to suggest itself as the prime means for the mass mobilization of an army devoted to the cause.

While nationalism proved its usefulness in times of international crisis, it showed its stubborn persistence in the German revolution of 1848–49 (Dowe et al. 1998). The uprising had, of course, many different causes, but the call for a united Germany constituted a core rallying cry. The revolution showed Germans acting as a political unit: the revolution reached all German states including Austria, and the national assembly in Frankfurt marked the first realization of a national institution based on elections within the whole German Confederation. Although the double goal of unifying the country and introducing liberal principles proved too much for the revolutionary forces, the old order had no reason to feel triumphant. A state cannot stabilize, prosper and develop its full strength, as people at the time fully realized, if it is ruled by the whip alone. Thus there was a strong incentive for the political elites to find a compromise with a nationalist movement which had amply demonstrated its popularity and strength.[1] The continued reliability of bureaucracy and army had given them dominance in open conflicts, but the revolution had made a growing number of conservatives see the need for a productive and innovative answer to the challenges of their time.

The revolution proved that nationalism had moved from the spiritual to the political realm. It showed the powerful role of the masses in the political sphere, and it provided the background to the emergence of political parties ranging from Conservatism to Socialism. As a consequence, political debate became more heated, more polarized and more oriented towards practical political changes. The German parliament in Frankfurt disappeared with the revolution, but not a public which wanted to have their say. No political force could ignore this trend towards popular politics; all were forced to formulate and advocate their political vision in the public sphere.

Conservatism had to travel a long way, however, before it could link with nationalism (Greiffenhagen 1986; Kraus 1995a; Mannheim 1984; Puhle 1986; Ribhegge 1992; Rohkrämer 1999: 270 ff.; Schildt 1998; Vierhaus 1972 ff.; Wehler 1987a: 440–457). As Panajotis Kondylis (1986) has shown convincingly, conservatism came into existence as an ideology of the nobility trying to justify the defence of legal privileges, first against the absolutist bureaucracy, then against all revolutionary challenges to the feudal system. Conservatism thus became the main enemy of all forces of change, trying to maintain the traditional order. In this endeavour, the nobility was soon joined by parts of the old middle class, for example, an oligarchy of craftsmen who wanted to maintain the guild system, by religious people fearing secularization and by separatists trying to maintain regional independence. While conservatism as a whole came to define itself as the political opponent of the revolutionary and progressive forces, they were not automatically opposed to all forms of change. A highly dogmatic noble conservatism – represented for example by Friedrich Ludwig von der Marwitz – rejected modernization in all its forms, but a more pragmatic and forward-looking conservatism soon emerged as well. Attempts have been made to distinguish different types of such a reformist conservatism, although there are many overlaps and shared characteristics. Fortunately, for the purpose of this book it is not necessary to enter this slippery terrain; suffice it to say that conservatives proved very successful in making pragmatic compromises with the new times. Conservative higher civil servants, most famously the Prussian politician Freiherr vom Stein, instigated dramatic reforms 'from above' to strengthen the state through abolishing serfdom and granting some political representation. Politicians like the Austrian Chancellor Prince Metternich tried to contain the forces of change through an international alliance of conservative monarchical states. The political philosophy of Friedrich Julius Stahl, who was highly influential in the middle of the century, marked another important step towards formulating an up-to-date conservatism (Berdahl 1988: 348 ff.; Kraus 1995a): he rejected any harking back to a lost past, accepting instead the possible need for a constitution, albeit only when granted voluntarily by the rightful ruler. Instead of stubbornly holding on to old privileges, he advocated a new corporative order with limited representation granted to the different professions and political classes. Above all, he tried to find a more general justification for a conservative order than respect for historical tradition. He obviously rejected the revolutionary idea that state structure should result from enlightened reason, but emphasized the importance of religion as the basis of a legitimate order. His ideal was a conservative Christian state with a close cooperation of church and secular rule: religion was to justify the monarchy, while the monarch had to rule according to Christian principles.

Stahl's vision was closely connected with politics in Prussia, where he had been teaching at the University of Berlin since 1840 and served as close adviser to the Prussian King Friedrich Wilhelm IV. As we saw in the previous chapter, Prussian Protestantism, or, more precisely, Lutheranism, had traditionally been closely linked to the worldly authorities. On a theological level, this obedience was justified with reference to the well-known passage in Paul's letter to the Romans: 'Let every soul be subject unto the higher powers. For there is no power but of God: the powers that be are ordained of God' (13.1. See also the remainder of 13). This was taken to mean that Christians had to obey the state authority in worldly matters, thus providing a perfect conservative justification for the acceptance of the existing monarchical order.[2]

Stahl's philosophy played an important part in maintaining an alliance between Protestantism and monarchy under altered circumstances.[3] His ideas further helped to prepare conservatives for the compromises deemed necessary after the revolution: the end to the relicts of feudalism, the introduction of a constitution, albeit by monarchical degree, and a more independent judicial system. At the same time, some conservatives started to discover the 'social question' as a political weapon. The liberal forces were strong advocates of a free market ideology. When a growing number of people came to suffer the price of a lack of state protection in the economic sphere – which tended to advantage the rich – social conservatives came to stress the role of the state in maintaining a fair social balance by supporting the weaker classes in society. Politically influential figures like Viktor Aimé Huber, Lorenz von Stein and Hermann Wagener emphasized the social advantages of traditional society. In contrast to a *laissez faire* doctrine, where the poor were left to fend for themselves, the conservative patriarchal system, they argued, had always offered protection for the weaker. The monarchical ruler, who was supposed to stand as impartial arbiter above all classes, would continue to offer such patriarchal protection and promote a fair compromise between different economic interests. While the nobility's economic egotism strongly hindered the realization of such ideals, Bismarck and his introduction of a social insurance system in the German Empire were also motivated by these ideas.

When Hermann Wagener, who became the editor of the leading conservative journal Kreuzzeitung, started to found 'people's clubs' (*Volksvereine*) for craftsmen and workers, he met with much ridicule, but his idea proved successful. It is estimated that at least 140 conservative clubs with a minimum of 60,000 members existed by 1849, and the movement 'For King and Fatherland' continued to play a role in the 1850s (Schwentker 1988: 87 ff., 280 ff.). By the middle of the nineteenth century, one can thus conclude, conservatism had made some careful steps towards becoming a sustainable political option for the future. Parts of the nobility still tried to hold on to all their privileges, but other conservatives accepted the change to a capitalist market economy, a constitution and reforms in the judicial system. While Catholicism went its own way with a strong orientation towards the Pope (leading to a separate brand of catholic conservatism), the alliance with the Protestant church provided a strong and lasting partnership for conservative parties. Economic liberalization and modernization soon revealed that, frequently at least, some groups in society had to pay the price for the development: they thus became targets for a conservatism reaching beyond the nobility.

The revolution had forced conservatism to become a party, competing with other political orientations for public support. With the army loyal to the king, there was, of course, always the possibility of a *coup d'état* after the constitution was granted, but this remained a desperate option: the quick initial defeat against Napoleonic France had shown, after all, that a nation needed public support to be strong, and the revolution some decades later revealed the failure of a policy of restoration to reach stable conditions. With the events of 1848, conservatism was thus forced to change: while obviously trying to hold on to its old convictions and interests, it had to adapt more thoroughly than ever before, if it did not want to become obsolete and be left behind. The founding manifest of the *Neue Preußische Zeitung* (commonly called *Kreuzzeitung*), which became the leading conservative paper in Prussia, stated quite clearly this attempt to work an up-to-date political message: 'It is not enough simply to resist and refute. Rather, there is the need, apart from the battle against the revolution and its devastating convictions and consequences, to gain simultaneously a positive attitude towards the new order of things. This is because the future belongs to those which are able to engage positively with the moving thoughts of the present' (quoted in Schildt 1998: 70). In this vein, the Conservative Party of 1861 accepted the call for a unified Germany by giving it a prominent place in their programme, albeit not through the nationalist movement, but via a legal agreement of the crowned rulers (Schildt 1998: 85 f.).

All these efforts to develop a more open-minded conservatism remained, however, rather defensive. Some conservatives accepted the need for change, but the whole smacked of concessions to new conditions only grudgingly accepted. The monarchy proved its ability to mobilize popular loyalty, but beyond that conservatism stayed in the defensive, without developing a positive vision of the future. This only gradually changed with Bismarck as chancellor since 1862, when monarchical Prussia succeeded in presenting itself as spearheading the nationalist ambitions. What the progressive nationalist movement had failed to achieve in 1848, the Prussian monarchy delivered: a unified Germany. Even those opposing Bismarck's domestic authoritarianism were often taken in by his foreign policy, which had to appear, in the age of nationalism, as a high point after centuries of German dividedness and weakness. The success of a conservative monarchical state in leading Germany to unification was the single most important event in making a merger of conservatism and nationalism possible.

Bismarck was no theoretical innovator. Following Stahl, he promoted a nation based on Christian principles, and, following social conservatism, he saw a chance for the monarchy to win over a majority of the population by pushing non-liberal social policies. On the other hand, his economic pragmatism allowed the emergence of a capitalist market economy and a constitutional legal system. The spectacular political triumph of unification together with domestic concessions to a liberal – but state-oriented – middle class forged a new compromise between conservatism and nationalism, the old political order and a rising middle class (Gall 1985).

As we shall see in more detail in the following chapter on Imperial Germany, however, this compromise always remained fragile: regional tensions continued; especially in the south a Prussian-dominated Germany was by no means automatically popular. Traditional conservatives saw Bismarck as a traitor, because he disregarded the legitimacy of long-established rulers in the interest of Prussian-German power politics. Left liberals continued to demand more freedom and parliamentary power. The exclusion of Austria from the newly founded Germany made Catholics a minority. Their sense of unease about a Germany dominated by Protestantism turned into widespread alienation with the *Kulturkampf*, that is, the conflict between state and church in Bismarckian Germany (see next chapter). Even more damaging were the severe anti-Socialist laws: the state's fierce attempt to destroy the socialist working class movement led to a deep and long-lasting alienation of the working class from the newly founded nation.

The German Empire not only remained deeply divided, it also faced difficulties in developing an official identity. After all, conservatives had not really desired a unified Germany, while the nationalist movement had envisaged it in a more liberal and parliamentary form. Many areas where German was spoken remained outside the Empire, while about 7 per cent of the population spoke French, Polish or other non-German languages (James 1991: Ch. 4). All this was a far cry from the ideal of a nation based on one communal culture. By uniting Germany, Bismarck had achieved the first goal of the nationalist movement, but the German Empire remained a pragmatic compromise between different political, economic and social forces. This might well have been, at least to a large extent, unavoidable, but there was nevertheless disappointment when the new nation fell far short of establishing a communal culture and communal political goals. It was thus only logical that the cry for inner unification, that is, the attempt to overcome the deep divisions among Germans and create a harmonious community, did not disappear.

While both traditional and more open-minded reformist conservatives were mainly concerned with politics in the narrow sense of the word, a third strand of conservatism had long voiced the desire for a single communal faith. Its origins lead us back to the previously discussed Romanticism of the early nineteenth century: while early Romantics had largely tended towards the forces of change, the glorification of a German past and the desire for a stable community united in one faith came to lead many later Romantics in a more conservative direction. Some historians suspicious of a history of ideas (most forcefully Wehler 1987a: 448) have disputed their historical relevance, because they neither entered the political sphere nor developed a political programme, but they nevertheless played a key role in formulating a critique of modern society and a utopia of a tightly knit community which extreme conservatives came to find very useful. In formulating a traditionalist unease with modern society – which was conservative only in a wide, non-political sense of the word – Romanticism provided arguments one could use to lift political conservatism from the realm of narrow material interests to the formulation of ideals with the potential for a much wider popular appeal. It thus provided thoughts, arguments, images and visions which a populist right eventually found suitable and useful. While the Romantic strand of conservatism did not consist of more than a group of individuals at first, it provided material with which a forward-looking conservatism could later build.

In criticizing the society of its time, Romanticism rejected the idea of a rational social contract between autonomous subjects as the basis of society, emphasizing instead the primacy of the community: humans are, they argued, born into a social universe and can develop their humanity only when raised and nurtured within a well-functioning community. They advocated an organic community that should be more than the sum of its parts. While largely realizing that one could not return to the past, they did not just aim for a new mythology, but also idealized an ideal original natural state, a communal folk culture or a metaphysical unity in the Christian Middle Ages (Williamson 2004: 77 and passim).

Romanticism could combine with different political orientations. Many initially sympathized with the French Revolution, and many remained nationalists who propagated a united parliamentary and constitutional Germany. It is not surprising, however, that an important number of Romantics – for example, Adam Müller, Friedrich Schlegel, Achim von Arnim and Franz von Bader – ended up as conservatives. Their idealization of the past eventually turned into the glorification of a Christianity-based monarchy; and the value they placed on tradition turned into an argument for preserving a powerful nobility. Turning against revolutionary calls for change, they idealized the Middle Ages. While they did not harbour the illusion of a complete return to the past, the vision of a hierarchically structured, stable community united by one faith became their political ideal. In their idealization of a homogeneous culture, August Wilhelm

Schlegel, for example, came to reject modern pluralism. 'The tolerance of modern Europe – what is it other than disguised indifference, self-satisfied glorification of slackness?' (quoted in Williamson 2004: 77).

As they largely remained in the realm of emotive appeals, the political Romantics never formulated a clearly defined political programme or action plan. However, both their critique of society and their suggestions about the way towards a conservative community clearly indicated their anxieties and fears as well as their dreams and desires. The main enemies were a revolutionary development, which would destroy all traditions, and the rise of anonymous political and economic systems. Drawing on Edmund Burke, they argued that historical ruptures endangered a community's relationship with its past, thus destroying a sense of belonging and direction. While revolutionaries claimed that human reason could provide the map for a better world, conservative Romantics stressed the wisdom of one's communal past. For them, the chaotic and destructive elements of the revolution served as proof that humans should not trust abstract reason, but carefully built on tradition in adapting to the future. They celebrated the family as the most important human institution, and the image of the family was then also employed as their ideal of a state: the monarch as a 'father' to all subjects, and patriarchal relationships all the way down to form a personalized and family-like hierarchy.

Such a description of traditional hierarchies between serfs and nobility as a 'heart-felt association' (Müller 1922: 313) was, of course, largely fictitious, but it served as an effective weapon in pointing out weaknesses of the newly emerging capitalist market economy. While liberal economists argued that an unrestrained rule of market forces would, at least in the long run, profit all citizens, conservatives were quick in drawing attention to the hardship the new system could produce for the poor. Anticipating socialist arguments, Adam Müller (1779–1829), in particular, stressed that the emphasis on legal equality in a free market only served to disguise the structural advantages wealth gave to the rich. He decried capitalism as nothing but a means for employers to shed their responsibility for the social welfare of their workers, which would lead to unprecedented poverty and rip society apart in revolutionary conflict between antagonistic classes (Müller 1922: 24 f., 101 f., 275 f., and passim). All these arguments became standard themes of a social conservatism, which could appeal to the many who felt threatened by modernization. The dream of a harmonious community offering more economic security was so popular that it helped decisively to establish a popular conservatism which reached far beyond the nobility to include farmers, craftsmen and small traders.

The fascination with folk culture and an ethnic past initially emerged, as we have seen, within a politically progressive nationalist ideology, but Romantic conservatives could easily employ it for their own purposes. The desire for a sense of belonging in times of rapid change came to be used to reject the revolutionary celebration of an allegedly open future. The present generation should not try to break free from the past, but value, cherish and foster the handed-down ethnic traditions: it should not decide solely according to the reason and interest of the present, but piously accept the bond with past and future generations. Respect for traditions was presented as a sacred and ennobling obligation. Against the vision of creating a new and better world, conservative Romantics developed the opposing utopia: a sense of homeland and belonging in harmony with the community's traditions. While revolutionaries were defamed as sorcerer's apprentices, who would, in naive ignorance, destroy the existing order without being able to establish a new one, a life in harmony with traditional customs was said to offer security and a clear world-view. A core root of a *völkisch* tradition intending to view and explain the whole world from an ethnic and racist perspective can thus be found in conservative Romanticism. Against an individualistic claim to autonomy and self-reliance, humans were called upon to accept and cherish themselves as determined, in essence, by the community of their birth. For political Romantics there was no necessary conflict between individual freedom and social order, because the order was supposed to provide the only ground on which the individual could flourish.

The dream of a single communal faith became the prime characteristic of the conservative Romantics' vision of an ideal community. While the more progressive strands of Romanticism searched for a new mythology, conservative Romanticism came to idealize the Middle Ages because it was regarded as an epoch united by a communal Christian belief. Long before Friedrich Julius Stahl emphasized the need for a state religion, which would serve and justify the political order, key texts of conservative Romanticism like Novalis' *Christendom in Europe* (written in 1799 and published in 1826) or Schlegel's ideas about the Middle Ages advocated the same ideal: a state religion which would serve and justify the political order. While the enlightened reliance on reason would lead to chaos, the authority of one Christian faith would provide political stability and a clear orientation for state and individual. Monarchical rule and the whole social hierarchy should thus draw their legitimacy from religion, while the state should support the church in its preaching. Political Romantics thus called upon political and religious authorities to work hand in hand in maintaining religious faith and respect for the social order.

When trying to develop concrete political goals, conservative Romantics were desperately inconsistent and impractical. Their ideal of a corporative state with a strong nobility serving the public good was proven wrong at every step by the nobility's ruthless interest politics. In their search for an authoritative order, many of them eventually turned to Catholicism, but this weakened their influence on a German history increasingly dominated by Protestant Prussia. It is not their concrete proposals, however, which are historically important, but their appealing aesthetic presentation of a desire for a harmonious community and a warm, caring world, where individuals could feel at home. They gave expression to the dream of a single communal faith, which would give a clear orientation to life. Better than in political formulas, their ideals can be seen, for example, in a core romantic *and* nationalist symbol, namely Cologne Cathedral. In the Middle

Ages, the building works were never completed, and at the beginning of the nineteenth century the cathedral in Germany's biggest medieval city was simply a long-neglected, derelict building threatened by collapse. In 1814, however, the former Jacobin, Joseph Görres, who also glorified medieval Europe as a 'festival of life' (quoted in Williamson 2004: 80), called for the restoration and completion of the building as a national task. The initiative met with surprising success: in the first third of the century restorative work started, and in 1842, two years after another military threat by France and the resulting national enthusiasm, enough money was raised to finish the cathedral. At the foundation ceremony, the Prussian king, Friedrich Wilhelm IV, said: 'The spirit which builds these portals is the same, which broke our fetters twenty-nine years ago, which brought to an end the humiliation of the Fatherland and the alien occupation of this province. It is the spirit of German unity and power' (quoted in James 1991: 48. See also Fritzsche 2004: 108–110; Nipperdey 1986).

In many ways, the cathedral was an obvious symbol for a romantic nationalism. As unfinished and as fragile as the nationalist project, Cologne Cathedral could stand for a renaissance of German culture. Since Goethe's celebration of Straßburg Cathedral, the Gothic had acquired the status of *the* quintessentially German style. The fact that both an ex-revolutionary and a Protestant king could accept a medieval Catholic church as the prime symbol of German cultural unity shows the remarkable success of the romantic idealization of the Christian Middle Ages. The imagery of a strong Reich united under one belief had grasped the imagination of a growing number of people. While most nationalists were still in favour of liberal reforms, they were at least not repelled by the imagery of a pre-modern Christian order. The hype about Cologne Cathedral anticipated that nationalism could become a conservative ideology. That such a celebration of the past was not in conflict with the modern world of technology, however, is demonstrated by another building of national significance right next to the cathedral: the new railway station. The decision to build a prime symbol of modernity next to that of the Middle Ages shows that the goal was a highly selective arrangement of old and new: the grandeur, durability and spiritual unity of the old Reich combined with the economic and technological means of the new modern world.

To the end, Romanticism as a whole remained a politically multi-faceted phenomenon. Half a century later, however, a *völkisch* conservatism emerged, which drew on many of the Romantic themes outlined above. To show such a connection is not to suggest a deterministic causal link. Even as a historical legacy, Romanticism has remained an open and fluid corpus of images and ideas that came to be used in many different ways. Thus it cannot be *reduced* to the role of an inspiration for an emerging extremist conservatism, which developed its own ideals for the future in competition to the political left, but a link nevertheless existed. A closer look at three historical figures of the middle of the century will illustrate this point.

In German history, there are no outstanding conservative thinkers in the nineteenth century with a powerful international influence comparable to, say,

Edmund Burke, Louis de Bonald or Joseph de Maistre. Within the formation of a *völkisch* or ethnic nationalism, however, Wilhelm Heinrich Riehl (1823–1897), Paul de Lagarde (1827–1891) and Richard Wagner (1813–1883) all played, in quite distinct ways, important parts. They remained intellectuals at the margins of society during their lives, but all proved influential towards the end of the nineteenth century.

The most surprising choice in this group of three might well be Riehl (Altenbockum 1994; Bergmann 1970; Ott et al. 1999: 4–14; Schmoll 2004: 111–113). He is not only the least known, but also presented himself as a traditional conservative, that is, a stout conserver of the social structure of a monarchy based on a strong nobility. As an early 'agrarian romantic', his main plea was for the preservation of agriculture and the traditional landscape. In a period of rapid historical change only a healthy farming community working in their traditional ways, he argued, could secure a sense of rootedness and social stability.

Riehl started his professional career as a journalist, who wandered through the different regions of Germany to learn about the country. At first, walking was the only means of transport he could afford, but he did not give it up even after his appointment as Professor in Cultural History and Statistics at the University of Munich. Walking became part of his image and his 'research method': for him, it was the best way to gain intimate knowledge of the countryside and its people. In academia, he made a highly successful career with his 'grass-root' studies of folk culture. In contrast to the traditional historical emphasis on high politics, he became an early pioneer of a sociological or anthropological approach in his interest for the common people and their environment. Thus, academically he was an innovator, but his political goal was the stabilization of the social status quo.

The Romantic fascination with folk culture was undoubtedly an important inspiration for Riehl. As core influences on his own work, he singled out Justus Möser, who had praised 'regional knowledge' (*Lokalvernunft*) in opposition to an enlightened claim to universalism, and his academic teacher Ernst Moritz Arndt, who had defended agriculture and the nobility in his writings (Arndt 1820; Ott et al. 1999: 4). Riehl has often been described as an early environmentalist because he called for the recognition of 'the right of the wilderness' (1854: 40), but such a characterisation misses his main intention: namely, to maintain social stability in times of rapid change. He did not deny the advantages of industry for a higher standard of living and for strengthening the state, thus accepting the inevitability of modernization, but he wanted to promote stability within such a change by maintaining as much agriculture and traditional landscape as possible.

Riehl had no interest in nature as such; any emotional meaning a viewer finds in it was to him nothing but a human projection (Riehl 1873). Like Herder, he was convinced, however, that human cultures closely correspond to their natural environments. The multitude of landscapes allegedly provided the basis for a complex social structure and the 'flexibility, richness and sensitivity of German spiritual culture and habitus [*Gesittung*]' (Riehl 1854: 37), and big forests went hand in hand with a strong aristocracy. Riehl accepted the middle and working classes as inevitable features of the modern world, but he saw them as restless forces of change, which had to be counterbalanced with a strong farming community led by the nobility, who both tended, in his opinion, naturally towards stability and conservatism.

Riehl drew on the romantic glorification of folk culture, traditional landscapes and people living in pre-modern economic circumstances, though for a political purpose. All these topoi were primarily valued because they were supposed to provide stability in times of rapid change. In his books, which he published in the wake of 1848–49, he tried to draw political lessons in order to avoid another revolution. He and his audience were aware that agriculture had not supported the revolution for long; peasants returned to be a conservative force as soon as their limited economic demands had been fulfilled. From this, Riehl drew a simple conclusion. He associated dramatic revolutionary change with the modern world of industry and workers, metropolitan cities and anonymous structures. While these new developments could not be wished away because they provided riches to the state, enough of the old structures had to be maintained to avoid an overturn of social order and secure stability. Riehl thus made use of romantic themes, but functionalized them for concrete political purposes. While the Romantics enjoyed a natural or historical order, exactly because it was not supposed to be human-made, Riehl promoted the conscious social engineering of a fine balance between the forces of conservation and those of change to allow for a gradual and conservative economic and social development.

There were obvious flaws to Riehl's thought. Nationalists had to be critical of the fact that his measures for social stability would weaken the state economically (and thus also militarily), because Riehl made only a bare minimum of concessions to industrialization. He hoped to maintain a traditional world-view among the *Volk*, but this was hardly realistic, when major historical changes had taken place and were not likely to stop, not even in agriculture. Riehl still formulated a rather defensive programme, which focused on the control of an allegedly dangerous historical development rather than opening up new and inspiring avenues. He was a defender of the old corporative order in Europe, not a conservative nationalist dreaming of a strong united Germany. Despite this, Riehl was highly influential: he became the rector of his university, a member of the Historical Commission of the Academy of Sciences (*Akademie der Wissenschaften*), the Director of Bavaria's National Museum and the Main Curator (*Generalkonservator*) for artistic and historic monuments. The seeds he had sown in his writings won a much wider audience towards the turn of the century: his claim that 'the peasant is the conserving force within the German *Volk*' (1976: 119) became a core statement of conservatism, in particular of agricultural interest; and the German *Bund Heimatschutz*, an association trying to preserve the nation's historical and natural heritage since the turn of the twentieth century, claimed him as an important forerunner. His glorification of a traditional *Volk* as well as the political use he wanted to put it to, became a standard conservative theme. It was regularly used, as Riehl had intended, to justify the political and social status quo, but soon it also came to show its potential as a critical yardstick: the existing political order was confronted with an idealized vision of the *Volk* to show the state's shortcomings and to demand reform. A stable and strong *Volk* united in a single communal faith became the prime political goal for a *völkisch* nationalism, which attacked all governments failing to achieve their ideal.

While Wilhelm Heinrich Riehl was thus a forerunner for a glorification of traditional agriculture and *Heimat* by stressing the need for a close link between a people and its land, Paul de Lagarde's main concern was the call for a new national religion (Paul 1996; Stern 1961). Never a defender of the old order, he became a conservative promoting a 'white revolution'; the creation of a hierarchically structured, homogeneous German nation united in a single faith. Despite believing in the need for a powerful authoritarian state, he distanced himself from conservative institutions and figures – the Conservative Party, the Churches as well as the majority of monarchs and conservative elites – because he came to express a new political ideology: a *völkisch* nationalism, which did not seek to preserve current conditions, but tried to realize its own ideal of a national community. Lagarde was a forerunner in formulating a radical conservatism based on the ideal of a nation united in a single faith. No conservatism was ever just about conserving, but Lagarde was unprecedented in the resoluteness of his break with the past. He believed, and this conviction was later shared by Arthur Moeller van den Bruck and the Conservative Revolutionaries of the Weimar Republic,[4] that conservatism was not about conserving everything, but about realizing the true potential of a nation. He thus wrote in 1853: 'Conservative in Prussia is ... he who tries to keep the special features of Prussian life powerful and efficient' (1920: 6).

Paul de Lagarde was an academic working in the field of Orientalism, primarily concerned with an area one would call Religious Studies today. After gaining a professorship, he started to voice his political opinion in more general articles. His prickly personality, which also slowed, it seems, his academic career, became evident in the shrill tone of a lonesome fighter against the main currents of his age. Not only did he attack liberalism, capitalism and modernization as the usual enemies of conservatism, but he also called for a new 'party, the Radical Conservatives, who are, at present, only represented by me' (1920: 16). While his different critiques did not add up to a consistent whole, the ideal on which they were all based came through quite clearly: the desire for a nation united in a single communal faith.

Like many other radical nationalists after him, Lagarde broke with Christianity, but remained a religious man in search of a religion and even a religious age. Why did he break with the faith of his childhood and youth if he clearly held a deep desire for a firm belief? Like David Friedrich Strauß in his *The Life of Jesus* (see previous chapter), Lagarde questioned that the Bible was literally the word of God. His academic work on the historical genesis of the Old and New Testament gave him a whole arsenal of reasons to conclude that the Bible was a multi-layered historical text rather than godly revelation. He stressed that we have no first-hand account of Jesus, but only many later interpretations. The Bible simply consisted, he argued, of a number of texts which were canonized by historical chance in the second century and showed strong Jewish, Greek and Roman influences. Lagarde tried to undermine the Bible's authority by pointing out contradictions within the text as well as between text and Christian dogmas. Why, for example, did Luther not question the idea of Sunday, of infant baptism or of the Trinity if none of these are mentioned in the Bible?

If Lagarde had ended up an agnostic or an atheist, one would find plausible reason for this in his historicist critique of faith. This was, however, not the case. In the last instance, his dissatisfaction with the Catholicism and Protestantism of his time was not motivated by religious doubts, but by the ideal of *one* powerful communal faith, which the *two* Christian confessions in Germany failed to provide. It was his utopian ideal of a tightly knitted religious community, which made the existing faiths look shabby. He was not satisfied with a religion for the private sphere (promising, above all, personal redemption), but wanted a single public religion to unite the nation and provide its historical destiny. Thus he could not accept a religiously neutral state, which tolerated all religions as long as they were restricted to the private sphere. Not only was the existence of two major confessions a scandal to him, but also the tension between science and religion, caused, he believed, by the insistence of the churches on the literal truth of miracles. Instead he insisted on the need for one unified religious world-view; above all harmony between metaphysics and scientific knowledge and between religion and politics so that a single world-view could wholly occupy the heart of all citizens and thus be the crucial force in motivating individual and communal action. His rejection of established forms of worship was not primarily motivated by a loss of faith, but by the desire for a much more powerful communal faith. He used a critique of the Bible to destroy the Christianity of the churches, but not to promote secularization. He was not satisfied with a religion conflicting with other forms of knowledge and national ambitions; such a crippled faith needed to be destroyed to create space for a new religious age to emerge.

What shape was this new faith supposed to take? Lagarde did not believe that a new religion could be actively created, but he formulated some criteria it had to fulfil. As the new religion should harmonize with scientific knowledge, it had to abandon any belief in miracles. As it was supposed to establish a single communal truth, it had to abandon liberal ideals of tolerance and plurality. Above all, it should be strongly nationalist. Lagarde was deeply convinced that the world consisted of categorically different ethnic cultures. He thus rejected a Christian universalism, calling instead for a German religion which would penetrate and shape all aspects of national life. For Lagarde, humans as well as nations needed 'one idea the realization of which is their sole duty' (1920: 138). The new German religion was to provide such a communal destiny. It could incorporate elements of Christianity, but should move beyond it in formulating a truly German belief.

As Lagarde distrusted the Bible and church dogmas, the new belief had to be based on personal experiences of the godly. With his critique he had destroyed the authority of any text; thus he had freed the present generation to formulate its own beliefs as religion. While this was not quite Lagarde's explicit intention, he created, in effect, the space for formulating one's own belief system. In a sense, he wanted the best of the old and the new world. Rejecting the restrictions of the Churches' teachings, he nonetheless wanted to hold on to the idea of one truth. As his kind of religion could derive only from his own experiences, thoughts and beliefs, his own personal world-view was presented with an aura of religious authority.

Lagarde called for a national religion, but the content was largely left open. He argued that one could discover God in oneself and in exemplary others; he believed that the nation was a godly creation; and serving the nation was to him a pious life. Working towards the realization of a perfect nation promised in his eyes the only real form of eternity; individual life had to perish, but the effects of one's personal life would continue to exist as part of the potentially eternal national community. Lagarde's version of religion was thus clearly focused on secular goals: it was to unite the community by giving it a great ideal. He formulated largely secular political goals, but called them religious because he did not want to miss the sense of security and the integrative force of a communal religious faith. 'I have no use for abstract truth', he stated. 'I want to bind and liberate my people' (quoted in Stern 1961: 36). At least for himself, he rejected the limitations traditional faith placed on the freedom of metaphysical thought, but he wanted to maintain religion's personal and social functions. Ideals were to have a religious authority, but this should correspond with the ideals of the time. To put it bluntly, it was a religion which allowed Lagarde (and more generally a strongly nationalist cultural elite) to have a clear conscience about all their goals. It was supposed to integrate the masses into an authoritarian national order.

As a German nation united in a single faith was Lagarde's big dream, his hate tirades were directed against all obstacles to this goal. Catholicism and Protestantism divided Germany; the Christian confessions thus had to make way for a new communal religion. Liberalism was rejected for its embrace of pluralism, and education should not provide a broad humanist knowledge, but a clear world-view. He rejected anti-nationalist conservatives, while he applauded Bismarck's unification of Germany. Even the monarch was only accepted as long as he promoted Germany's political and cultural unification.

Lagarde accepted some traditional conservative beliefs, stressing, for example, the importance of a strong nobility, agriculture and emotional ties to the homeland. His main goal, however, was not conserving a traditional hierarchy, but the unity of all Germans; not a strong state, but a state serving a strong and united German people. A *united Volk* was at the centre of his thought. Germany was for him not a political territory or a state, not even a people speaking the same language, but the totality of all those who feel, think and desire in a particularly German way (1920: 167). Germans were thus those who shared the same world-view and political will. The political unity achieved in 1871 was only one step towards realizing a nation in Lagarde's sense, as it still left the more important task of achieving 'inner unity' (1920: 94). As the German Empire lacked such unity of faith, Lagarde could write in 1875: 'Such a [communal] ideal does not exist. And thus we also have no German nationality' (1920: 136).

Lagarde promoted an ethnic nationalism which was centred on a *Volk* united in one world-view and one political will. The state and its ruler could be criticized because they were only justified as far as they served the *Volk*. In contrast to traditional conservatism, the population thus occupied the core of his thinking. This had nothing to do, however, with democracy. Lagarde stressed the importance of a religion in harmony with a German ethnic identity, but he advocated a religion *for* the people, not *of* the people. The mass of the population was not to play an active role in shaping a national culture or defining national goals. Instead he called for a cultural and political elite to express ideas in harmony with such a spurious ethnic identity. Attention should be paid to the characteristics of the German people, but the concrete form of identity could emerge only in a top-down approach. Artists and thinkers like himself were seen to play a decisive role, but also the 'heroic deed' of a great political leader. 'Only the great, firm and pure will of one man can help us, the will of a king, not parliaments, not laws, not the aspirations of a powerless individual' (Lagarde 1920: 269. See also 128 f.).

The hope for an exceptional leader which Lagarde expressed here became a core feature of the extreme Right in general. Traditional conservatives argued that the existing hierarchical chain was legitimated by historical custom and ultimately by God. A ruler did not need democratic consent, because he ruled by divine right. In contrast, new 'revolutionary' conservatives like Lagarde, who only wanted to conserve what seemed worth conserving, did not automatically accept the status quo. For them, even a monarch had to justify himself by acting for the good of Germany. Not unlike progressive forces, they thus judged leadership by its performance, but, simultaneously, they upheld the idea of authority and leadership. Their will to create an ideal hierarchical society brought them into conflict with the established forces, but their emphasis on the need for unquestioned authority made them oppose the idea of giving any real power to the people. The only way out of this contradictory position was the hope that the true leader would be immediately recognizable by his exemplary deeds and would thus establish *himself* in a position of authority. Half a century later, Adolf Hitler expressed this belief succinctly with the words: 'Sooner will a camel pass through a needle's eye than a great man be discovered by an election. In world history the man who really rises above the norm of the broad average usually announces himself personally' (1973: 81).

In the Weimar Republic, Hitler's words were no longer spectacular, because the radical Right's respect for established authorities had melted away completely. In contrast, Lagarde was still held back by a traditional respect for the monarchy based on a strong nobility. His preparedness, however, to criticize everything and everyone, his emphasis on the *Volk* as the highest authority, his wish for dramatic changes and his ideal of establishing a conservative national community made him anticipate the call for a charismatic saviour. As Lagarde could believe only in a change from 'above' – although respect for the actual rulers was largely absent – it was only logical to project one's hopes on to an ideal charismatic leader. Hope for a saviour figure fitted Lagarde's religious outlook and suggested a path for change, although he failed to provide any clear road map. He seems to have assumed that such a charismatic person would either be the monarch himself or a confidant of the monarch, because he did not reflect upon possible conflict between traditional and charismatic rule.[5]

With time, Lagarde's call for a national religion found much support among a cultural elite (Paul 1996: 74 ff.; Stern 1961: 82–94). Thomas Mann, who used Lagarde a lot in his nationalist war essays, named him *praeceptor Germaniae*, and a well-respected Protestant theologian like Ernst Troeltsch (1865–1923) could see hope in Lagarde's work for a regeneration of religion. Lagarde had contact with the sociologist Ferdinand Tönnies, and many others such as Franz Overbeck, Paul Natorp, Friedrich Naumann, Hermann Bahr, Richard Dehmel, Christian Morgenstein and Ludwig Curtius, expressed their respect. He obviously addressed issues which became standard themes of a later, more general critique of culture, namely, the weakening of religion and its growing distance from the contemporary world, the deep social divisions within society, an ethical and cultural decline, a dominance of instrumental reasons and material goals at the expense of more general philosophical and religious reflections about the meaning of life, all these arguments found much resonance among a wider reading public. As we shall see in more detail in the next chapter, Lagarde was by no means alone in his 'hope for the emergence of a religious form suitable for new and modern humans' (Lagarde 1920: 236). The call for a cultural 'regeneration' (1920: 9), first voiced by Lagarde in the early 1850s, gained its real popularity during the German Empire.

Lagarde's seemingly idealiztic call for a religious age was connected, however, with a virulent anti-Semitism and expansionism. As with many anti-Semites before and after him, Lagarde's attitude towards the Jews presented a mixture of admiration, fear and disgust. As an ethnic group united by a shared religious faith, they came, after all, close to the ideals he advocated. The Jews, Lagarde claimed, maintained their identity and achieved economic success because their faith promoted discipline and sacrifice. Such a spiritual strength in an ethnic minority he regarded, however, as a serious obstacle to the emergence of a national faith. As all Germans had to be united in one single communal religion, the Jews, he argued, had to assimilate or be forced to go.

For Lagarde, Judaism was not just different, but also dangerous and despicable. He associated Jews with everything he hated – modern democracy and capitalism, Asian traits and internationalism, and a separate alien nation within Germany. At first, he believed in the superior power of his own vision. If Germans succeeded in developing their own communal faith, the Jews would gradually fall in line and assimilate (1920: 26). With every difficulty in realizing his ideals, however, his anti-Semitism intensified until it turned into an outpouring of exterminist fantasies. Not the far-fetched nature of his ideals, but the alleged cultural dominance of Jews was blamed for the difficulties in moving towards a communal Germanic religion. Lagarde's hatred knew no bounds. He called the Jews, among other things, 'carriers of decay' and argued in 1887, 'one does not argue with trichinas and bacteria, one also does not educate trichinas and bacteria, they get destroyed as quickly and as thoroughly as possible' (1920: 396, 209).

Anti-Semitism had, of course, a long tradition in Germany. Among conservatives, a traditional Christian anti-Judaism combined with a rejection of Jewish emancipation. As Jews were seen to profit from political and economic modernization, they came to be associated with everything modern. From the beginning, nationalists could see Jews as un-German. Lagarde's exterminist fantasies, however, clearly marked a step in the radicalization of anti-Semitism. For him, the Jews were the opposite to everything German. Thus he allowed no space for them in Germany; they had to disappear either by losing their distinct identity through assimilation or by forced deportation. With this plan, he anticipated later *völkisch* thought, although he did not fully adopt a racial determinism. Germanness, he famously stated, did 'not rest in the blood, but in the mind'. As he tried to avoid a scientific determinism in favour of human freedom, he maintained that 'the spirit can also overcome race'. Jews, he grudgingly granted, could become true Germans, but they would have to overcome the alleged natural disposition of their race. While he thus allowed for exceptions, when an individual made the determined effort, he believed that Jews as a whole were a different race of 'Asiatic heathens' naturally tending towards allegedly un-German ways (1920: 255). Thus the vast majority, he came to argue, had to be removed from Germany. As early as Lagarde, such ideas of ethnic cleansing could take an implicitly genocidal turn when he mentioned a 'solution' later also temporarily considered by the Nazis, namely the deportation of all Jews to Madagascar. While Lagarde knew many enemies, ranging from the established Churches to liberal and progressive forces, he regarded the Jews alone as the incarnation of everything un-German and evil. With Lagarde's anti-Semitism it became explicit that the desire for a single communal faith could foster murderous intentions.

While Lagarde thus blamed an internal enemy for the failure of his political ambitions, he also tried to present an inspiring political goal to bring the country together. While accepting that a national religion could not be 'made', it could grow, he hoped, out of the communal pursuit of heroic nationalist goals. He thus came to promote an extreme expansionism. Calling for Germany to become a world power, he advocated nothing less than its dominance over the whole of Europe. As a first step, Lagarde envisaged unification with Austria and colonial dominance over the whole of Eastern Europe. Based on the popular belief of the imperialist age that only a few super powers would come to dominate world politics (Neitzel 2000), he regarded it as an economic and military necessity for Germany to become *the* European power. From his radicalized nationalist perspective, such a policy could even claim moral legitimacy: 'The

Germans are a peaceful nation, but they are convinced of their right to live, and to live as Germans. They are also convinced that they have a mission' in spreading German culture world-wide. 'If they are prevented from living as Germans, if they are hindered to realize their mission, they have the right to use violence' (1920: 423).

The logic of this quotation is based on Social Darwinist assumptions of relentless international competition. Nations, it was argued, either become world powers or perish: Expansion was thus seen as an inevitable survival strategy, but it was also justified in cultural terms by claiming a German mission to spread their allegedly superior culture. 'Minor' nations should lose their independence to prepare Germany for a new era dominated by a few main world powers. A glorified German culture combined with a dramatic sense that Germany would either expand or be absorbed like other weaker states was used to justify a vague, but unlimited and huge expansionist programme (Lagarde 1920: 121 ff.). Ultimately, these militaristic goals also derived from Lagarde's desire for a communal nationalist faith: only grand goals, he argued, with their demand for complete devotion to the nation could promote a sense of unity and idealizm as the ideal breeding ground for a new Germanic religion. Grand political goals, he thus hoped, could unify the nation in a single communal faith.

Fritz Stern might be right in distinguishing a 'soft' Lagarde, whose call for a Germany unified by a single communal Germanic faith came to attract a mainstream culture elite, and a 'hard' Lagarde, who became an important forerunner of extremist *völkisch* groups. He is equally right, however, in pointing out that Lagarde's two sides only increased his negative historical significance. While many of the more moderate readers criticized at least the extremity of his anti-Semitism, he was still largely accepted as a respected political essayist. His racism and expansionism did not disqualify him as a public intellectual. The fact that a prominent figure held such views further promoted an attitude that saw extreme racism and expansionism as part of the acceptable political discourse. Lagarde himself regarded the two sides of his work as inseparable. The ideal of a nationalist communal faith was so important to him that he would turn to the most brutal measures to promote it. In his fight against pluralism for a homogeneous community, the 'others' within, who would not fall into line, had to be removed without mercy. Other nations were also regarded with cynical coldness, that is, purely as a means for providing grand goals and for possible exploitation through an imperialist conquest.

While the dream of a homogeneous nation united under one nationalist faith did not necessarily lead to such brutal consequences, Lagarde provided early proof that it could. In desperate attempts to achieve this utopian vision, it could come to justify criminal policies. As a communal faith failed to emerge through preaching, brutal measures were increasingly deemed necessary to achieve it. No wonder that Lagarde was claimed to be an ideological forerunner by radical groups ranging from the Pan-German League to the Nazis around Arthur Rosenberg, who also hoped for a nationalist religion (Paul 1996: 74 f.).

Lagarde preached the need for a communal faith and tried to promote conditions in which it could grow, but he never went beyond formulating the criteria he wanted achieved; not a modest reformation of Catholicism or Protestantism, but a truly new nationalist German Religion; not liberal and tolerant, but claiming to be the only truth and winning over all true Germans (Lagarde 1920: 76). Richard Wagner went a decisive step further by trying to create an aesthetic faith which would take the place of traditional religions. He was, after all, a highly gifted artist with the ability to produce arresting images in his 'rich, sensuous, overripe' operas (Thomas Mann, quoted in Field 1981: 165). More generally, the arts never wholly followed the process of differentiation, specialization and disenchantment, which Max Weber described as core features of modernization, continuing instead to offer space for holistic ambitions. The arts have continued to address all aspects of life, including the desire for meaning within individual and collective existence. Like the Romantics discussed in the previous chapter, Richard Wagner vehemently rejected the idea of *l'art pour l'art*, that is, a self-contained aesthetic sphere, calling instead for art to provide a space in which the community could find and express their communal world-view. This utopia, he believed – like many before and after him – had been reality in classical Greece: a community where the performance of tragedies served as celebrations of a communal religious faith:

> The deeds of Gods and humans, their suffering and their joy ... here they became real and true ... Such a day of a tragedy was a religious feast, because God expressed himself distinctly and clearly here: the poet was his high priest, who was truly present in his work of art, who led the round dance, who lifted his voice in a chorus and pronounced in the song words of Godly wisdom. This was the Greek art work, Apollo personified in real art – this was the Greek people in their highest truth and beauty. (Wagner n.d.: Vol. 10, 15 f.)

This 'Greek model', which we shall encounter again in Nietzsche's and Heidegger's work, was an ideal of the past, but neither did it grow out of immediate traditions nor did it stabilize present conditions. Wagner was not only revolutionary as artist, but also called for radical political change. A new artistic myth was to infuse a longing in all Germans to work towards an ideal national community. In his later life, the Bayreuthian expressed radically conservative opinions, and the political tradition he inspired was clearly situated on the far Right. He was, however, a far more ambivalent figure than his political impact suggests. He could, I shall argue, be an exceptionally innovative force for a revolutionary conservatism, exactly because he drew on an initially left-wing or even anarchic 'political economy of love' (Williamson 2004: 181), which led to a fundamental critique of power and money.

When Richard Wagner became an established conservative figure – able to draw on the unreserved support of the Bavarian King Ludwig II to establish his own theatre – he and his disciples made tireless efforts to reinterpret his revolutionary past as the misguided prank of a politically naïve young artist. There can be no doubt, however, that Wagner was initially strongly influenced by socialist and especially anarchical ideas. Like Lagarde, his critique of existing conditions also extended to the Christian tradition. Dedicating his first major theoretical work *The Art Work of the Future* (1849) to the critic of religion, Feuerbach, Wagner rejected any belief in miracles and religious dogma. Instead of accepting the clear demarcation of the Churches between God and humans, he saw a divine potential in humanity which individuals like Buddha or Christ had developed to a godlike perfection. Wagner dreamt of a communal religion for all Germans, but this was not to be a religion in the traditional Christian sense. For him, religions were the work of man, a projection of human dreams and ideals upon an imaginary realm which can take symbolic shape with God(s) or a heaven. As he stated in a letter in 1849, God has always been for humans, 'what they communally recognized as the supreme, the strongest communal emotion, the most powerful communal belief' (Wagner 1975: 182).

Richard Wagner enthusiastically supported the 1848–49 revolution, taking part by acting as a guard for the revolutionary forces. He sharply attacked all noble privileges and called for equality among all citizens. He rejected slavery even in his beloved ancient Greece and demanded freedom for every human being. He celebrated the revolution with full pathos and expected the destruction of the old and the emergence of a new order, brought about by the people combined with the leadership of an artistic genius. Under revolutionary conditions, the genius would find the ability to produce art appropriate to the new and better time, and the population would come to recognize the art work appropriate for uniting the new community and directing it towards an ideal future. In his revolutionary writings, Wagner could remain vague about the future, because he shared the anarchic belief that an ideal community would emerge spontaneously, if only people were freed from conditions thwarting their positive potential. He celebrated the 'sublime Goddess revolution', because her destructive energies allegedly created space for an ideal community to emerge: after the revolution, he believed, 'an unimaginable paradise of happiness opens up for us … and where its [the revolution's] foot destroys, fragrant [*duftend*] flowers will sprout out of the ground, and happy songs of rejoicing of the freed humanity … will fill the air' (Wagner n.d.: Vol. 12, 29). ' One's will shall be the master of man, the own desire his only law, the own strength his whole property, because only the free human being is holy and nothing is superior to him … The equal must not rule over the equal … and as you are all equal, I shall destroy every rule of one over the other' (Wagner n.d.: Vol. 12, 33). 'Not hatred, not envy, not malevolence and enmity shall be between you in the future; you should recognize all that lives as brothers, and free, free to will, free to act, free to enjoy … Rise up, you nations of this earth! Up, you who are mournful, suppressed, poor' (Wagner n.d.: Vol. 12, 35).

All this does not sound conservative, but radically egalitarian. This strand of Wagner's thought had long been ignored, but in recent years Udo Bermbach has been highly influential in forwarding the interpretation of a progressive Richard

Wagner with strong anarchist traits. But why should the many followers before 1945 have been mistaken in taking the Bayreuth artist as a radical conservative and *völkisch nationalist*?[6] Why should Wagner never have rejected a conservative reading of his work, if it was diametrically opposed to his own intention? Bermbach's interpretation is wholly at odds with the self-understanding of Wagner and most Wagnerians; it thus served an important function in questioning all the many interpretations which simply ignored those aspects of Wagner's work which did not fit into a conservative framework. Wagner was, for example, highly critical of anonymous power relations in social institutions limiting human freedom. While conservatism celebrated the family, his operas show true love only outside of marriage (and strikingly often in incestuous relationships); while traditional conservatism cherished close links with the Christian churches, Wagner stressed personal religious experiences against all dogma. His early work *Rienzi* celebrates revolutionary fever, and his grand opera *Der Ring der Nibelungen* shows how a world becomes increasingly dehumanized through the rule of gold (i.e., capitalism) and legal contracts (i.e., formal political rule). Finally, *Parsifal* is a celebration of a community based on love and peace. Wagner diagnosed a deep alienation between individual and society, contrasting this with his ideal of a true community united by a shared collective faith. He dreamt of a communal art, which was to be freely available for all, and envisaged its production through free cooperatives of artists.

All this sounds more radical than conservative, but then we have discovered before that the two attributes are not mutually exclusive. Wagner certainly absorbed radical ideas of his time, but came to turn them into the ethnic vision of a *Volk* united by a single communal belief. What might have a radically left-wing or even anarchist ring to it today, was meant and received, largely, as the radically conservative utopia of an ideal community of the people. While his early political writings were admittedly more ambivalent, even here traces of what was to come are noticeable. In a pamphlet of 1848, he attacked the unchecked rule of money and noble privileges, but rejected an attack on the monarchy as well as the idea of communism. Instead of material changes he envisaged a society based on mutual love and solidarity; instead of constitutional controls he anticipated a king with absolutist powers acting in the interest of his subjects. Distrust of institutions played a part in such proposals, but it also has to be read as a plea for spiritual instead of structural changes. Wagner argued in favour of giving one man unlimited power, as long as he was 'destiny's man' (Wagner n.d.: Vol. 12, 15), that is, a charismatic leader in harmony with the *Volk*, and he did not spend time developing concrete plans for social change because his ultimate concern was a spiritual revolution. Wagner's vision that the population should come to feel solidary and unite in one shared faith is wholly compatible with an idealized concept of a conservative hierarchical society – a charismatic ruler allegedly representing the true will of the people in a purer form than any elected parliament. Even his revolutionary opera *Rienzi* is not about common people achieving their say in politics, but about a charismatic leader trying to open the peoples' eyes to the right course of action. It is thus not surprising that Hitler could later see a role model in the opera's hero, who tried to remove a corrupt, decadent and exploitive political elite by mobilizing a highly emotional, changeable and disoriented *Volk* to follow him in the quest for reviving a glorious national past.

In 1848, Wagner played an active part in the revolution. However, after the failure of his early political dreams and his flight from prosecution into exile, his revolutionary ambitions started to shift towards the aesthetic and ideological sphere. Instead of changes to the political structure, in his late *Regenerationsschriften* he came to encourage his followers to work for a spiritual 'regeneration' or 'redemption'. The finale of one his latest political pamphlets thus called upon his followers to act politically on the basis of Wagner's world-view: 'We recognize the reason for the historical decline of humanity and the necessity for a human regeneration. We believe in the possibility of such a regeneration, and dedicate ourselves to its implementation in every sense' (Wagner n.d.: Vol. 14, 181).

What did Wagner mean by 'regeneration'? In contrast to an optimistic faith in continuous progress, he shared an understanding of history we previously encountered in Romantic thought: a good original natural state was followed by a period of decline. The present was regarded as the lowest point of this decline, but also as offering the chance for a turn to the better; a regeneration of the original natural state, but in a more up-to-date and self-reflexive form. Wagner used the term 'redemption' interchangeably with 'regeneration'. This signalled the religious or spiritual character of such a turn as well as its radical nature; the realization of a timeless utopia in a wholly renewed world.

For Wagner, regeneration was, at least in the first instance, not a universal project, but a national or *völkisch* one. In his operas, which were intended to play the same cultural role as the tragedy had allegedly done in classical Greece, he used Germanic legends because he wanted to reveal the eternal truth of a *völkisch* mythology as well as pointing out its contemporary relevance. The grandiose and heroic dimension of all the emotions, the mythical connection between human passions and the drama of world history personified in the gods, the apocalyptic alternative between the twilight of the gods and redemption created an imaginary space for nationalist fantasies like the fear of a dangerous infiltration through alien or decadent forces and characters, the hope for an heroic age or the expectation of redemption through a purified Germanness. Polarized friend–foe thinking characterized not only the Bayreuth circle in the German Empire, but also Wagner himself. While he acknowledged that one universal human nature was more fundamental than all national and racial distinctions, he could only imagine a German-led regeneration. He was highly critical of Romanic culture and, above all, his anti-Semitism knew no bounds. In the essay 'Jewry in Music', he proclaimed that a complete Untergang of Jewish culture was a necessary prerequisite for the cultural regeneration he advocated (n.d.: Vol. 13, 29). Even if the word is intended, as the context suggests, to mean a disappearance of Jewish distinctiveness rather than extinction, it nevertheless corresponds with Lagarde's demand for a complete assimilation to a narrow nationalist ideal of German culture. His wife's diaries note that he even fantasized about physical violence and murder against Jews in private conversations (C. Wagner 1976; Vol. 2, e.g. 778, 852).

In 1879, Heinrich Treitschke wrote: 'Reaching into the circles of the highest education, among men, who distance themselves with abhorrence from every thought about religious intolerance or national chauvinism, we can hear today as if out of one mouth: "The Jews are our misfortune"' (1979: 575). The nationalist historian's notorious words met with enthusiastic support and sharp opposition, thus causing a heated controversy, but they showed that anti-Semitism was not just the opinion of a lunatic fringe. Furthermore, with Richard Wagner and the circle around him, even an apocalyptic and redemptive anti-Semitism became part of a wider public discourse (Friedländer 1997; Zelensky 2000). It diagnosed an existential historical struggle between good and evil; a triumph of evil would lead to universal destruction, a triumph of good to redemption. Despite being tempered by a Christianity-inspired belief in universal love and compassion (Wagner n.d.: Vol. 14, 198 f.), such redemptive anti-Semitism motivated outbursts of hatred and violent fantasies in Wagner. Its terrible dynamics became increasingly unchecked when Christian compassion became denounced by others as the ethics of the weak. Combined with a Social Darwinist belief of life as an eternal struggle for existence, redemptive anti-Semitism could make even the most extreme violence appear as a legitimate defence against destruction, the vilest measures as motivated by an idealiztic dream of redemption.

As Wagner's artistic oeuvre has been successful in many different historical and ideological contexts, it is obviously open to a wide variety of interpretations. It is exactly this openness, however, which made Wagner important for an extreme conservatism in Germany. The distance from middle-class gender norms, the rejection of unchecked power and a capitalist greed for wealth or the call for love and peace could have prevented a conservative glorification of the work if the audience had not been able to interpret the operas according to its convictions and selected according to its own preferences. There is at least one aspect, however, that all enthusiastic receptions share: the joy that all emotions, even base ones, gain unprecedented grandeur. Private suffering and happiness become connected with collective questions of life and death, conflicts gain heroic dimensions, battles apocalyptic significance. Even the complete destruction of good and bad at the end of the *Ring of the Nibelung* can appear as sublime, because it is such a heroic spectacle. For a receptive audience, the operas can open up a space for grand fantasies and beliefs in which their own world of petty emotions appears in a new light: full of essential drama and fateful tragedy, but clearly presented in a condensed archetypical form (Borchmeyer 2002: 277 ff.).

Wagner's operas allow for the expression of personal feelings, even the all-too-human, but lift them into the sphere of heroic grandeur. This is why they are such an easy target for caricature; a distanced view from a down-to-earth perspective can only recognise false pathos. If one identifies with the art work, however, everyday sorrows and personal interests lose their importance in the aesthetically spectacular tragedy of life. Still under the influence of Wagner, Friedrich Nietzsche expressed this sensation and attitude in the 'Birth of Tragedy': 'Only as aesthetic phenomenon does existence and the world appear justified' (1966: 24), because the tragedy of life can be transcended and thus accepted in the experience of beauty and the sublime. Works like those of Wagner encourage an aesthetic attitude towards existence; painful experiences are relativized when life is viewed as a magnificent drama to which each individual contributes. Instead of living according to metaphysical ethics or a hedonistic search for happiness, the only purpose such an aesthetic view of life can discover is to put in a good performance. In the case of Wagner, his operas served to provide a wealth of heroic role models and apocalyptic struggles which could serve to make the question of human happiness appear trivial.

Wagner himself did not go the whole way towards an aesthetization of existence. Undoubtedly, he had the ability to give many aspects of human existence an unprecedented grandeur with his aesthetic means, but he still believed in a truth humans should discover and adhere to. For many viewers, however, the aesthetics of drama and heroism could become the core message. Like Nietzsche, the lesson they drew from Wagner was the celebration of a strong and amoral life. Such a conviction could promote an attitude that not only accepted one's own personal suffering as a necessary price for living a heroic role, but also dismissed all feelings of humanity and compassion in the quest for a heroic age. A self-proclaimed heroic elite could see itself as beyond good and evil in its attempt to turn existence into a grandiose drama. As we shall see in more detail, the Nazi cult of death and Hitler's will to turn his own defeat into a universal inferno are extreme examples of a tradition which also played an important role in the 'cool conduct' (Helmut Lethen) of conservative revolutionaries like Oswald Spengler and Ernst Jünger.

Throughout his life as an artist, Wagner followed Feuerbach in regarding religion as a human projection, but this did not mean its rejection. On the contrary: the creation of a new artistic myth, which was to take the place religion used to have, was the artist's most fundamental goal. The critique of the Christian churches largely served to create space for a new communal faith for all Germans. Echoing Lagarde, he regarded the Christian confessions as incurably weak (the only point Wagner added was that Christianity had served to legitimize an unjust social system, thus permanently alienating the poor). Only a deep metaphysical art, he argued, could preserve the truth of religion in modern times: In 'dense summary of the early Romantic idea of an art religion [*Kunstreligion*]' (Frank 1982: 226), Wagner famously stated: 'One could say that at a time when religion has become artificial, art reserves itself the right to save the core of religion by interpreting the mythical symbols, which the former want to be believed as true, in an allegorical way. Through an ideal presentation of these symbols art can reveal the deep truth hidden in them' (Wagner n.d.: Vol. 14, 130). The opera *Parsifal*, which Wagner named a *Bühnenweihfestspiel* or 'holy festival for the stage', was as much part of this programme as the festivals in Bayreuth, which were to encourage a yearly pilgrimage to experience the new faith expressed in Wagner's work.

What did Wagner mean by trying to save 'the core of religion'? His conviction that religions were human-made barred the way back to traditional beliefs. For Wagner, the Divine was not an unfathomable other, but largely reduced to its worldly function. Religion turned into an ethics of love and compassion and was supposed to provide an integrative core to unite the nation. The new religion was to limit itself, as we can see in *Parsifal*, to a mythology of a few key symbols. Only by sticking to a few immediately plausible and convincing symbols, a new religion had the chance to win general acceptance and thus integrate the whole community and direct their actions. Wagner wanted to avoid religious disputes by stressing the truth allegedly present in all religions – that is, a universal human truth. He wanted to outline with clarity such a core which the audience as a whole was to share, while the highly suggestive artistic nature of the presentation should then allow individuals to make further associations, thus developing their own more concrete and highly emotive faith within the collectively shared religious framework. He did not use Germanic legends and sagas in the hope of returning into the past, but because he believed that they expressed an anonymously created eternal Germanic wisdom, which an artist could bring forth in a contemporary way. Wagner's operas were supposed to give a sensual and emotional expression to a universal truth most convincingly expressed in an ethnic German tradition. For his main work, he chose the *Niebelungen Saga*, which had been praised since Schlegel and the Grimm brothers as the quintessential national epic, but in the last respect he hoped to get at an eternal human truth.

> My studies took me through the poetry of the Middle Ages back to the foundation of the old Germanic myth. I was able to remove one garment after another, which later poetry had distortedly wrapped around it, until finally I could view it in its chaste beauty. What I now saw was no longer the historical, conventional figure … but rather the real naked human [*Mensch*] … the true man. (quoted in Williamson 2004: 196)

Richard Wagner was an intellectual artist, who read widely and reflected upon his own artistic production in theoretical works on aesthetics and the history of art. He rejected, however, the idea of conscious art production, stressing instead that the true genius is like a medium giving expression to his nation's unconscious world-view. 'You are mistaken if you look for the revolutionary power in consciousness – and if you thus want to have an effect through your intelligence: your intelligence is wrong and arbitrary … Not you, but the *Volk* – that – unconsciously – thus acting from natural instincts – will create the new' (quoted in Zelinsky 1983: 16).

Wagner was thoroughly disillusioned with enlightenment reason: it had produced, not a single communal world-view, but a multitude of personal opinions.

He thus suggested going back to an ethnic mythology (be it the *Nibelungen Saga* or the life of Jesus). In such legends he believed to discover a non-subjective, communal world-view expressed in admirable density. Drawing on such mythology would help the artist to overcome his own subjectivity to get at a more universal truth. His task was to breathe new life into legends, which had drifted out of public memory and become mere collectors' items, by re-enacting them in a new form to emphasize their current relevance.

Wagner believed in one universal truth, but he followed the Romantic praise of specificity by arguing that this one truth would reveal itself only in the trappings of different ethnic forms. While a universal truth was to shine through the specific form, his immediate goal was to create an up-to-date national mythology for all Germans. Never suffering from self-doubts, he believed to have come closer to this highest ideal in the world than anybody else. In his diary he noted:

> I am the most German human being, I am the German spirit. Search for the incomparable magic of my works, compare them with all the others: For now you cannot say anything else, but – it is German. But what is this Germanness? It must be something wonderful, because it is humanly more beautiful than everything else? Oh heaven! If only this 'Germanness' had a foundation! If I could only find my *Volk*! What a splendid *Volk* it would have to become. But I could only belong to this *Volk*. (quoted in Zelinsky 1983: 29)

The quotation clearly states Wagner's belief in the superiority of German culture as the highest expression of universal human qualities. The words also show the utopian character of Wagner's ambitions. While he believed he had created the most German art work, he had not reached his ultimate goal (yet), the connection between the art work and the people. For Wagner, art was not self-contained. It had a public function in shaping a communal world-view. Thus he believed that the German nation would become a 'splendid *Volk*' only when they were spiritually united within the mythology of his oeuvre. The Bayreuth project, a theatre far removed from the humdrum of daily life reserved for the yearly performance of his own works, was to serve his dream of regenerating the 'Greek model': the German nation gaining communal awareness and purpose in the celebration of Wagner's *Gesamtkunstwerk* (synthesis of all the arts) as the religious service of a shared nationalist faith. He was convinced that his art provided the mythology the German *Volk* needed, but it would only turn into true art once it had come to serve a communal purpose. In this vein, he could state in 1876 after the first performance of *The Ring of the Nibelung* in Bayreuth: 'If you will it, we shall have art' (quoted in Zelinsky 1983: 44).

In trying to present the Bayreuth artist as a progressive artist, Udo Bermbach calls Wagner's dream of a communal faith expressed in art a civil religion, that is, a general expression of the 'quasi-religious fundamental values' on which the community should rest 'so that all citizens, independent of their own religion, can, without force, agree on it' (1994: 219 f.). While Bermbach might be right that a society can gain stability only on the basis of shared communal values, it seems doubtful whether they should manifest themselves in the way Wagner suggested. Wagner still held on to a Christian ethos of love and compassion, but in principle such a new religion was a consciously developed, personal world-view. The creation then denied its origin in one artist's mind by presenting itself as an expression of a communal faith, which was to serve a hierarchical integration of society. The norms expressed did not emerge democratically, but were drawn from one person's reading of legends and sagas in search of allegedly eternal national traits. They were not integrative, but explicitly excluded Germans of different religious and political persuasions, above all Jews, Marxists and everybody accepting modern pluralism. In contrast to established religions like Christianity, where the range of acceptable personal views is somewhat limited by the authority of the Bible or church dogma, Wagner gave his personal inspirations a religious status. This claim removed it, at least for the faithful followers, from the realm of rational political discussion, despite the fact that the art work was intended to have far-reaching political effects. Wagner's musical dramas still allow for a wide variety of interpretations, because they are limited to a small number of rather open symbols, but more generally a consciously created national religion envisages a unity, which can easily turn, when enforced, into a cultural totalitarianism.

Richard Wagner was too multi-faceted to fit completely into the history of radical conservatism, but this is certainly where he ended up positioning himself. He also played an important role in the historical development of the extreme Right. Above all, he spelled out the dream of a single communal nationalist faith with unprecedented clarity and persuasiveness. Wagner did not join an existing political party, but wanted – as a modern subject with a strong will to create his own original world-view and alter the world accordingly – to formulate and advocate his own personal vision. Simultaneously, however, and this is his most conservative feature, he wanted the security of a true religious faith. He tried to have both the freedom for individual creation and the security of religion by developing a new faith, in other words a personal creation intended to achieve complete acceptance within the national community and thus the status of truth. In reality, this only meant that his subjective will came to be hidden behind a religious aura.

One can detect many non-conservative elements in Wagner, but his work provided a powerful imagery for the political Right, and he left powerful images: the vision of existential apocalyptic struggle with the threat of complete destruction, a glorification of heroism and charisma in an aesthetic world-view, the dream of a nationalist faith uniting the German people and, above all, the vision of a *völkisch* redemption. While such imagery used symbols of the past, it was not backward-looking, but expressed a conservative vision for the future. Wagner and his followers diagnosed a deep crisis, but this largely served as a justification for breaking with present conditions and working towards the utopia of a heroic German *Volk* united in one communal faith. In rejecting Christianity and advocating his own faith, Wagner was driven by the modern will to shape the world according to one's own subjective perspective. He worked towards a conservative modernity, in which a communal faith would guarantee cultural homogeneity and social stability. While this was an idealiztic dream, his hatred of those who did not seem to fit in signalled the potential dangers of such an endeavour. As the twentieth century showed, one could only seriously try to realize such a vision by manipulative mass propaganda and a violent exclusion of many 'others'.

In the second half of the nineteenth century, conservatism was no longer just an ideology in defence of noble privileges. Conservatism not only proved able to accept unavoidable reforms, it also widened its support base by addressing questions of social justice and by taking on board nationalism. Through German unification under Prussian leadership, the 'white revolutionary' Bismarck proved able to win much popular support far beyond the nobility. Further removed from practical politics, conservatism also succeeded in developing its own utopian ideas. From political Romanticism onwards, it competed with progressive political forces by developing its own visions of the future. Above all, conservatives contrasted an allegedly cold liberal society of individuals, where communal action is only driven by material self-interest, with their ideal of a closely knit, warm community united by a single communal faith. Like Riehl, conservatives could stress the satisfaction connected with possessing a feeling of *Heimat* – that is, a sense of belonging in a traditional countryside and in familiar social structures. Like Lagarde and Wagner, they could stress the satisfaction connected with sharing a single communal faith within the nation, which would overcome a cold enlightened disenchantment and the sense of alienation in a world where humans no longer had anything in common. While Wagner's hope of reaching the mass of the population with his sophisticated operas was obviously unrealistic, his work and that of other conservative artists produced a wide array of emotionally powerful imagery, which was ready to be used as an inspiration for conservative purposes.

Conservative visions of an ideal community could be used as a means for avoiding change: past and present conditions were praised to evoke fears of thorough reforms or a revolution with the intention of preserving the status quo. However, conservative ideals could also be so far removed from existing conditions that they triggered their own dynamics for change. Lagarde and Wagner, in particular, are early examples of conservatives who clearly recognized the deep gulf between reality and their own ideals. They became conservative revolutionaries because they advocated change through the creation of what they regarded to be a perfect hierarchical national community. With the political triumph of unification, their popular appeal was at first quite limited. When the enthusiasm of 1871 faded, however, their ideas started to fall on more fruitful grounds.

Notes

1. The fact that the old order did not use its victory to return to the status quo ante (all feudal relicts disappeared and Prussia gained a constitution) shows an awareness for the need for compromise.
2. See in particular Fischer 1977 for a sharp critique of Luther's doctrine of the two kingdoms. The journal *Evangelische Kirchenzeitung* (1827–1848), edited by the theologian Ernst Wilhelm Hengstenberg, provided an important link between Lutheranism, especially in its pietistic form, and Conservatism.
3. Such an interpretation only started to be challenged by a few theologians, such as Karl Barth, after the First World War and more generally in consequence of the conflicts with the NS state (see Conclusion).
4. According to Armin Mohler (1989: 116), Moeller van den Bruck's definition of conservatism as 'a life out of what is always valid' was the fundamental belief of the whole Conservative Revolution. He ignores, however, the older roots of such a conservatism.
5. Max Weber developed the concept of charismatic leadership systematically, Kershaw applied it convincingly to Hitler, and Wehler has made it a key component of his theory of a German *Sonderweg* (1995: 368–376; 2003: 551–563 and passim).
6. In particular Hartmut Zelinsky and Joachim Köhler read Wagner as a right-wing extremist. See Friedländer and Rüsen 2000 and Borchmeyer 2000 for good overviews.

CHAPTER 3

VISIONS OF A SPIRITUAL UNIFICATION IN THE GERMAN EMPIRE

Unification in 1871 marked, in the eyes of many, the final merger of Prussian-German policies and nationalism. This nationalist triumph had been achieved largely, it seemed, by conservative state institutions: by monarchical Prussia, by a triumphant army re-organized against liberal parliamentary will, and by the political leadership of the 'white revolutionary' Bismarck (Jefferies 2003: 44–53). Unification not only led to a truce of moderate liberals with the government which had fulfilled the greatest nationalist dream, but it also temporarily took the wind out of the sails of early *völkisch* nationalists. Enthusiasm about the new Germany pushed further-reaching dreams of a nation united in a single communal faith into the background, or at least neutralized their critical edge. Even Richard Wagner, whose insatiable ambitions always egged him towards restless dissatisfaction, offered his services to the new Empire by sending Bismarck an exalted *Kaiserlied*, hoping – in vain – that a march of his would be played on the return of the victorious troops (Zelinsky 1983: 29f.).

With time, conservatives increasingly came to accept the new modern Germany including its growing economic power, as inevitable or even useful. The German Empire possessed an unmistakably capitalist market economy with a dynamic industrial sector (Rohkrämer 1999: 37–55). Independently of ideological leanings, an open-minded look at the powerful forces of change made a growing number of people accept the reality of industrialization, of the growing regulation through law and bureaucratization. Even Wilhelm Heinrich Riehl's comparatively sophisticated romantic anti-capitalism increasingly appeared as mere nostalgia. Conservatives came to see the advantages national wealth offered for overcoming social tensions; nationalists, the importance of a strong industrial sector for Germany's international standing. Even the Agrarian League's demand for an 'agrarian *and* industrial state' (quoted in Flemming 1978: 38) implicitly accepted the continued existence of industry, and the spokesmen of the Conservation movements *Heimat- und Naturschutz* went out of their way to show the compatibility of respect for nature and the cultural heritage with economic growth (Rohkrämer 1999: 127–141).

Despite such an overall acceptance of modernization, conservatives still rejected many of its consequences, and with time their dissatisfaction re-emerged on an unprecedented scale. Modernization continued to challenge the ideal of a stable society with increased force. Massive urbanization weakened agriculture and was said to destroy a sense of belonging. The growing working class increasingly unionized and supported the Social Democratic Party with its revolutionary programme. Anti-Socialist laws promoted the emergence of a powerful workers' subculture separated from the rest of society, without curbing the movement's growth. This raised the question for the political Right: how should one deal with a fundamental Socialist opposition, which – despite repression and the introduction of social security measures – managed to win a third of the votes in 1912, thus becoming the strongest party?

The religious divide deepened with the *Kulturkampf*. While Catholicism reacted to the challenges of the nineteenth century with ultramontanism – that is, by strengthening the authority of the Pope – the newly founded state, enthusiastically supported by the liberals, tried to establish national authority over the church. Many Protestants at least implicitly tended towards seeing the new German Empire as the 'Holy Protestant Empire of the German Nation' (the minister at the Imperial Court Adolf Stoecker quoted in Wehler 2003: 438), thus failing to recognize Catholicism as a natural part of the new Reich. In the 1870s, 1,800 priests were jailed or exiled and church property worth 16 million marks was seized before the detrimental effects of such a heavy-handed approach became all too apparent. The damage was done, however, and a third of the population became deeply alienated from the new Empire. 'The *Kulturkampf* left a powerful legacy among German Catholics, a sense of being branded as pariahs that reinforced the existence of a separate Catholic subculture' (Blackbourn 2003: 198. See more generally Smith 1995).

Enthused by the moment, nationalists celebrated 1871 as the full realization of unification – though in many ways it could be only its beginning. A new state was bound to be divided and have distrustful neighbours, no seasoned institutions and a lack of integrative national symbols. The nationalist movement had wanted unity and freedom, but Bismarck's triumph allowed him to maintain the weight of conservative Prussia through an outdated election system strongly favouring agrarian regions and the rich. With heated debates about the 'right' borders of the German Empire, the remaining regional loyalties and the frequent lack of nationalist feelings outside the middle class, there was still the need to 'make Germans'. Society remained divided, and the political insistence on a single homogeneous national culture produced harsh intolerance against the national minorities within Germany: the Danes in Schleswig-Holstein, the French in

Alsace-Lorraine and, above all, the Poles, who were the largest and most despised minority in Germany. The lack of shared values of this 'great power without fundamental principles' ('*Großmacht ohne Staatsidee*', Plessner 1959: 39) becomes particularly apparent in the fact that *Sedanstag* and the song *Heil Dir im Siegerkranz* (which came closest to being a national bank holiday and a national anthem, respectively) celebrated an important battle and victory over France rather than positive features of the new state. Furthermore, the national flag in black, red and white proved divisive because it implied the rejection of the revolutionary 1848 nationalism with its black, red and gold colours. While nationalism was supposed to unite the citizens within their new state, it could also become a source of conflict between Conservative, Liberal and Socialist, Protestant and Catholic forces, when it came down to trying to determine the symbolic content of a national identity (Berger 2004: 79–96, 124–140).

Politics did not compensate for such lack of unity. The constitution favoured stability over change, and, after 1871, Bismarck was more concerned with securing the national achievements rather than with mobilizing the country for new visions. Universal male suffrage did not produce, as Bismarck had hoped, a conservative majority. The political forces were deeply divided, frequently producing uneasy stalemates. The recurring mumblings about a coup d'état reveal the growing frustration of the traditional political elites with a parliament that did not produce easy majorities for the Imperial government, while the many monarchical powers and the deep divisions between the parties thwarted attempts for furthering parliamentarization. With its many checks and balances, the constitution promoted stagnation rather than a dynamic political course.

In addition, during the first decades at least, economic development did not help the new German Empire. Although in the long run the trend showed substantial industrial growth, the economic crisis from 1873 to 1879 and the uneven growth between 1882 and 1895 revealed the dangers of the new economic order. Not until the last two decades of peace after 1895 was there any steady economic improvement, which also translated into a rise in real wages (Wehler 1995: 547–610).

The new Empire thus faced many structural difficulties, which, however, should not be over-emphasized. The state was never threatened by disintegration, nationalism gradually came to dominate over regional affiliations, and historians agree that, over the years, both Catholics and Socialists moved towards an acceptance of the Empire. By the end of the century, a Catholic initiative urged moving 'out of the ghetto', and the revisionist debate within the Social Democratic Party about the possibility of a reformist rather than a revolutionary strategy showed a growing appreciation of the Empire's positive potential. The minority parties never gained more than about 10 per cent of the vote in national elections. There was much opposition to existing conditions, but it was expressed peacefully. If there was a lot of lamentation about the divisions into deeply divided milieus, this was partly due to high expectations; reality was bound to fall far short of the dream of a nation united by a single communal faith. The German

Empire undoubtedly suffered from a lack of consensus, but the diagnosis of a deep cultural crisis was provoked by the unrealistic dream of a tightly knit national community. In comparison to other new nations, the German Empire might not have been exceptionally unstable, but it obviously did not live up to the old dream of a spiritually united nation.

Enthusiasm about unification could not last forever. With 1870–71 becoming history, the nationalist vision for the future came to be a second, inner unification of the German people. Warning cries about current conditions expressed veritable fears, but they also supported the demands for more energetic, future-oriented politics. Extreme nationalists came to accuse the political elites of complacency, demanding instead – as Lagarde had done – a policy which would unite the nation in one faith and rally its support for turning Germany into a world power. They complained that Germans did not feel German enough, but – ironically – the support they found proves that their chauvinism was increasingly shared by wider parts of society, especially among the middle classes.

Extreme nationalists came to reject what they called the materialism of the age. Historians have often interpreted this as an anti-modernist rejection of industrialization. It is true that we can detect many anti-capitalist sentiments like the attack on banks and speculative investments or the praise of agriculture and the old *Mittelstand*, that is, the traditional self-employed craftsmen and small traders. The same nationalists glorified, however, allegedly patriotic industrial magnates like Krupp and a navy equipped with the latest technology. This was not inconsistent, but based on the more fundamental belief that modern means were good so long as they served a wider, allegedly idealistic, purpose (Stackelberg 1981). Right-wing nationalists attacked a capitalist market economy aimed solely at increasing living standards for being purely materialistic, but when the same economy was embedded in a communal faith and served nationalist goals it was praised for promoting supposedly idealistic goals. Extreme nationalists accepted modern means, but only if they seemed to serve their own political ends.

The distinction between good and bad modernity became increasingly connected with anti-Semitism. As the Jewish community profited from emancipation and the opportunities available in modern society, Jews were increasingly blamed by the Right for those aspects of modernity it loathed. The targets stayed the same as with traditional anti-Judaism, but the content of the prejudices changed. Anti-Semitism – a term coined by the writer Wilhelm Marr in 1879 in reaction to the economic crash at the beginning of the Empire – no longer stood primarily for the belief that Jews were poor and unassimilable, but instead portrayed them increasingly as rich and wholly unscrupulous in using the opportunities that modern society had to offer (Blackbourn 2003: 216 ff., 231; Berding 1988: 86 ff.; Burrin 2004; Pulzer 1988, 1992, 1999; Weiss 1997; Wehler 1995: 924 ff.). The historian Heinrich Treitschke blamed the Jews for 'the vile materialism of our times' (quoted in Rosenberg 1976: 109), and the Wagnerian Hans von Wolzogen for a purely 'egoistic and utilitarian' modernization that allegedly denied 'the spirit of Christ' (quoted in Stackelberg 1981: 4). Adolf Stoecker found much agreement in conservative circles, especially among the old middle class, when he claimed that modern Jewry used 'the power of capital and the press for the ruin of the nation' (1890: 359 f.; see also ibid. 367–369). There was, of course, no sharp break, but these new anti-Semitic prejudices gained ground because they fulfilled an important function: they allowed the acceptance of modernity, despite a remaining sense of unease, because a scapegoat for its ills had been identified. Grievances were blamed on the Jews, while the vision of an efficient modern national industry serving a harmonious and strong national community came to mark the 'idealist', truly 'German' goal. Thus protests against a new economic order, by no means a reserve of the left, were increasingly channelled against the Jews; while it was claimed that a true nationalist leadership would make positive use of all the modern means. A spiritual revolution was demanded to establish a sound political and cultural framework for a better modernity – a people united in a single communal nationalist faith under the proper political leadership.

To a large extent, prejudices against the Jewish community had always been a projection which had little to do with reality. Modern anti-Semitism seems, however, even more fantastic, with the Jews being constructed as the exact polar opposite to the German identity. Increasingly, the idealization of Germanness had as its opposite the demonization of the Jew.

> The last innovation concerns the importance of the Jews for the identity of the anti-Semites, which was much bigger here than for Christianity, because the modern anti-Semitism – especially in its nationalist, and even more in its racial form – constructed an image of the Jews as absolute, negative opposite to its own defended or propagated identity. Their own physical, moral and cultural features became placed in a dualistic system, where every single feature was contrasted with alleged characteristics of the Semite. (Burrin 2004: 37 f.)

Anti-Semitism thus served to strengthen German identity in the new Reich. Germans were allegedly rooted in the soil, thus Jews had to be Nomads; Germans were supposed to be idealistic, truthful and heroic; thus Jews had to be materialistic, deceitful and cowardly. Jews could not even be seen to have a religion (although this was, after all, the defining feature of this community). As Germans were said to aim for an idealistic and metaphysical communal faith, Judaism could be regarded as nothing more than a code of conduct to promote the material well-being of all Jews and harm the rest of the world.

Traditional Conservatism, however, fell far short from the desire for a charismatic politics that would promote a communal faith and set new, inspiring political goals. For a time, Bismarck had been able to link a conservative government to a liberal nationalist agenda, but by the end of the 1870s he had returned to a more traditional defensive conservative policy (Winkler 2000: Vol. 1, 237–241). As a result, his image as the great national leader dwindled, experiencing a renaissance only after his retirement. Three victorious wars followed by unification had strengthened Bismarck and the monarchical system, but less spectacular times quickly showed that there was no way back to an unquestioning acceptance of an authoritarian system. Traditional rule continued to rely on popular support; it needed to be seen as serving the nation. The Free Conservatives were never more than a small party of notables who supported Bismarck, while the German Conservative Party became mainly concerned with a defence of noble and agricultural interest. For its survival, the Conservative Party became increasingly populist by adopting a strongly anti-Semitic critique of alleged capitalist excesses like free trade and speculation. In contrast to liberalism, it stressed the need for a protection of 'honest gainful employment', thus appealing to an old middle class frightened of free-market forces (quoted in Schildt 1998: 103. More generally, Retallack 1998: 36 ff.).

The Conservative Party's adoption of an explicit anti-Semitism at the centre of its programme signalled a growing acceptance of such prejudices within respectable circles (Stegmann 1970: 203). The main push for such a development came, however, from populist interest groups, above all the big Agrarian League (with more than 300,000 members before the First World War) and other peasant associations, but also a whole variety of organizations for craftsmen, shopkeepers and commercial employees. In contrast to the elitist notable politics of the 1870s and 1880s, these populist extra-parliamentary mass organizations used new and modern methods: aggressive political machinery with paid politicians and speakers; professional propaganda material; contacts with press and politicians; and support in election campaigns for those who committed themselves to their platform. In contrast to traditional conservatism, their style was sharp and demagogic, unashamedly hostile to government and elites. In trying to present their economic lobbying as a deep concern about wider political issues, they became virulently hostile to both Socialists and Jews, claiming that only a thriving middling class could guarantee a harmonious national community (Blackbourn 2003: 314 ff.; Chickering 1984; Eley 1980; Schildt 1998: 119–129).

The many interest groups of the *Mittelstand* – as well as the Anti-Semitic League, whose support, however, was soon largely absorbed by the increasingly anti-Semitic Conservative Party – marked an important change for the extreme Right. The ideological mix of anti-Semitism and an anti-liberal call for the protection of the traditional social order was promoted by new agitators who were carried on a wave of popular support. Despite showing little respect for authority themselves, they called for a strong state to protect professions allegedly suffering under modernization. A romantic imagery of peasants, traditional crafts and an organically structured society with many social layers was mobilized for aggressive lobbying. But, while the political style as well as the ideology proved influential for the future of right-wing extremism, its appeal had obvious weaknesses. The interest groups were successful in channelling the energies of their clientele, but because they ignored more general interests their overall success was bound to be limited. Most right-wing associations took notice of the *Mittelstand*'s concerns, if only to win support, but the Conservative Party had to pay a high price for its fully-fledged identification with the Agrarian League. Their uncompromising defence of the Prussian three-class voting system, their call for protectionism, their scepticism about social policies, and their rejection of rural settlements all clearly revealed its narrow and egotistical defence of traditional privileges.[1] As a consequence, its successes were largely limited to the agrarian east of Prussia.

Such a thinly disguised interest politics lacked appeal beyond its own clientele, but attempts to create a single communal faith could shift to more promising areas. Conservatism had accepted nationalism, but there were also many other political orientations which people chose in order to show their commitment to the new nation. Probably the most important route was 'social militarism' (Wehler 1995: 882), an ideology particularly appealing to ex-soldiers because it elevated their social status. In the age of professional armies, common soldiers had been the pariahs of society, but this changed in the nineteenth century with the shift towards conscription and people's war (see Ch. 1). For many, military service was the first move beyond the parish pump. They saw other parts of the country, experienced city life in a garrison town, met soldiers from different backgrounds. Military service was arguably the most concrete way for men to experience the nation and to present themselves as serving the nation.[2]

The army was, in Erving Goffman's terminology, a 'total institution'. Conscripts were isolated from the outside world for the first four to six weeks in order to be 'broken in'. They moved into an alien and highly disciplined world, were overwhelmed by the many rules, and experienced inadequacy and vulnerability in a strictly authoritarian setting. Unable to rebel or escape, they were forced to adapt as well as they could. In the army, soldiers experienced the power of the state and the need to obey. This setting promoted an authoritarian orientation, which accepted the value system of the superiors. Once the conscript had learned the rules, however, things became easier, which demonstrated the advantages of 'fitting in'.

Aware of the power conscription offered, the state used it to indoctrinate its citizens. The army came to be called the 'school of the nation'. The men were supposed not only to become good soldiers, but also to acquire 'transferable skills' such as discipline or cleanliness and, not least, the 'right' political attitude. Patriotic instructions preached military values, love to the monarch, and respect for the existing order. The army did everything to produce what conservatives regarded as the ideal subject: subservient, complacent, and always ready to serve the authorities.

The army could work on the bodies of the conscripts through physical exercise and drill, thus changing their whole appearance (many people noted that ex-soldiers could be recognized by their straight bearing and brisk movements). But a parallel 'schooling' of the mind could work only if ex-soldiers remembered their service positively. Many must have done so, because about 15 per cent of the adult male population in the German Empire joined veterans' and reservists' associations. This can have been only partially a reaction to their actual experience. After all, while military service offered new experiences and security, it severely limited personal freedom and was badly paid; while some regarded war as an adventure at first, they soon came to realize that it also meant hardship and mortal danger; and while many enjoyed a sense of power, they also suffered under the strict discipline and the many forms of (often physical) maltreatment. Thus the positive social image of soldiery had less to do with the experience of the role, but with the social image of the role (Parin 1978: 123). Since the so-called wars of liberation, soldiers were praised as ideal men: courageous defenders of their nation and protectors of women and children. Risking life and limb for the fatherland became the ultimate virtue, not only in official rhetoric, but also in personal war memoirs:

> Things might be rough in war ... but, nevertheless, there is no other time marked by such noble and truly grand virtues ... It produces strong enthusiasm, audacious courage, preparedness for sacrifice, a wholly altruistic sense of duty, proud nationalism and an unshakable love for king and fatherland. In short, it produces men. (Tanera 1896: 10 f.)

The military's prestige reached a climax after the victory over France, and many veterans emphasized the part they had played in the great historical event, as the following quotation from a war memoir illustrates:

> The gain I have brought home from this campaign and that I could only find there ... consists ... in the euphoric feeling that I was among those who presented the strength of the German nation in 1870–71 and who accomplished a glorious deed. I thank my God that I could participate. What self-confidence I have ... I could not have, if I had not thrown myself joyfully into the first line when the storm erupted, if I had not done my bit so that the great times did not find a petty people. (Schmitthenner 1891: 139)

Increasingly, fighting for the country – ideally voluntarily out of conviction – came to be seen as the highest service to the nation. Military service was not nearly as prestigious, but it could also serve as a rite of passage into true manhood. As conscription remained selective, only the fitter among the young men were chosen. They were put into dashing uniforms, increased their physical strengths and widened their horizons. In many areas, leaving for the army was celebrated in ritualistic ways (Frevert 2001: 228 ff.). Often, those exempt had to pay for the drinks at the goodbye celebration. Young women would give the soldiers flowers or decorate the wagons which took them away. Drums, trumpets or rifle shots gave a spectacular atmosphere to the departure, marking it as a big public occasion. Circumstantial evidence also suggests that ex-soldiers were favoured as dance- and even marriage-partners.

The army did everything to improve its prestige still further. The carefully choreographed marches and parades were pompous public performances of strength and disciplined efficiency. The army was reluctant to change to grey uniforms – even though brighter colours had long made soldiers easy targets in war – because it recognized the attraction of a spectacular military appearance. While middle-class civilians walked around in dull dark suits, soldiers emphasized their slim waists and broad shoulders, their straight bearing and – through the sabre at the side – their licence to draw blood. Hardly any memoir of the German Empire fails to mention parades and military music (Vogel 1997), and the high points of the Franco-Prussian War were marked by annual celebrations. Boys wore navy uniforms, tin soldiers were favourite toys, soldierly themes pervaded children's games, and military virtues were praised in schools. The following memory of a small-town event from a boy's perspective illustrates the cumulative effect of social militarism.

> There was one period of the year which surpassed everything else in military importance for me. It was the three days of Pentecost, when the march of the uniformed riflemen's association took place. Thirty to forty respectable burghers transformed town and surroundings. In the morning, the well-known figures of the town's musicians, today in grenadier's uniform, marched through the streets to blow the reveille. Around midday, the riflemen gathered on the market square, admiringly stared at by us, especially when the good-natured soup-boiler L. and the harmless tanner S. suddenly presented themselves in unimagined splendour and displayed a roughness and a pride we had never associated with them … The neat uniforms, the shining leather, the sparkling rifles with their long bayonets gave their bearers a completely different glamour … The main attraction was, however, when the leader Herr U., the mill owner, came galloping on a brown horse, a wide, well-fed animal which normally worked for the business, but was as garlanded for the day as its rider. To my youthful imagination he resembled Napoleon. With the dignity and pride of a commander, the 'major', as he was called today, led his troops, to the sound of trumpets and drums, to the meadow, where the target shooting took place. Late in the evening, the corps alarmed the town again on their way home. Accompanied by music, the officers were brought home in the order of their rank … My imagination as a child was intoxicated by this and similar experiences as well as from impressions taken from reading, and I made the firm decision to become a soldier. (Schubert 1909: 7 f.)

Social militarism was not purely right-wing. In its public rituals the army tried to avoid a narrow political stand, presenting itself as the force for king and country instead. Militarism could fulfil its politically crucial function as an integrative ideology only if it could appear to stand above the political squabble. Nevertheless, pride in the army implied a whole range of ideological judgements: the glorification of a purely male sphere; of power rather than peaceful action; of discipline and order rather than freedom and open discussion. More narrowly, militarism meant the glorification of an hierarchical conscript army rather than a militia, an army with the Emperor rather than parliament as supreme commander. It was an army which maintained long service, giving time for the political indoctrination of its conscripts, which mostly kept Jews out of the officer corps, and which even discriminated against the middle class, as the strikingly high percentage of nobles in the top ranks shows.

Yet, although the army was a conservative force, this did not stop its social appeal. The middle class liked to associate itself with martial rituals like the duel (Frevert 1995), and many young men wanted to become officers. While Prussian lieutenants were regarded as 'young Gods' (as the historian Friedrich Meinecke stated from his own experience), even non-commissioned officers could reach the image of 'demigods' (Meinecke 1963: 25). Such a position was proudly held by over 120,000 men, who frequently continued to make use of title and uniform to the end of their lives. Achieving the rank of officer, however, demanded more than military qualities: the soldier had 'to fit in' – that is, display social conformism, a conservative political orientation, and respect for military virtues. The army's selection was partly based on political criteria, and ensured that its members stood for politically conservative ways (Clemente 1992, John 1981).

State influence on the veterans' and reservists' associations in the German Empire was an even more far-reaching attempt at spreading a communal conservative militaristic ideology (Rohkrämer 1990: 27–82, 1999c; Zimmermann 1989). After 1871, many clubs emerged all over Germany to celebrate the memory of the wars of unification (later also of military service), to support members in need, and to provide military rituals at comrades' funerals. Many clubs remained independent, but the majority united in centralized organizations recognized by state and army. Eventually, the nation-wide *Kyffhäuserbund* became the largest association in the German Empire, with some 1.8 million members in 1900 and more than 2.8 million in 1913.

State recognition offered privileges like a semi-official flag and participation in army parades, but also exposed the clubs to continuous political pressure. From the beginning, the veterans' and reservists' associations promoted nationalism and militarism. Proud of the part they had played in German unification, they cherished the new nation and the military means used to create it. They celebrated royal birthdays and anniversaries of important battles like the Battle of Sedan. Frequently, the clubs' most important attractions were largely social, but they also enacted a communal faith. Women made flags and uniforms (as they had already done in the wars against Napoleon), while men staged rituals to celebrate days of patriotic significance or collected money for a war memorial. For many, however, such a general ritualistic practice must have been compatible with a whole variety of political decisions, because, as police reports suggest, their electoral choices did not differ significantly from the rest of the population.

With time, however, the state and some conservative activists were not satisfied with such vague militarism and nationalism, but worked towards a clear political orientation. The veterans' and reservists' associations largely consisted of petty bourgeois and workers, that is, of the class most likely to support Social Democracy. Ex-soldiers from the well-to-do classes were encouraged to join the associations to influence the political outlook of the common members. Their task was not only to communicate a monarchical and nationalist world-view, but also to combat any left-wing sympathies. Members were forbidden to vote for the Social Democrats, and even trade unions were attacked.

The justification for this course of action derived from the soldier's oath to serve emperor and nation. This oath, it was argued, continued to apply for those who chose to be part of an officially recognized soldiers' association. A vote for an anti-monarchical party stressing that workers had no fatherland was interpreted as a violation of this commitment. Beyond that, it was claimed that a whole nationalist faith followed from the identification of ex-soldiers with the Imperial army: the continuation in civil life of altruistic service to king and national community, the obedient acceptance of the hierarchical order, and the choice of camaraderie instead of class struggle. As soldierly men, the members of veterans' and reservists' associations were supposed to support Germany's foreign policy, above all the attempt in Wilhelmine Germany to become a world power with a strong navy and a colonial empire.

The strategy of manipulation did not altogether succeed, however. The few well-off who joined rarely participated actively in the regional clubs, and often left them behind because they moved to managerial positions. The attitude of the leaders was so condescending that it provoked resistance, for example when the common members, having financed a big and expensive national Wilhelm I memorial (Mai 1997) through their collections, were largely excluded from the opening ceremony to make space for state notables. Members continued to be caught voting for the Social Democrats, and the fight against the trade unions seemed lost. Nevertheless, on the whole the policy must have had a significant effect, because members without very strong political convictions would not have run the risk of being expelled from an association which offered social contacts, an insurance system, and the symbolic link with the glorified army. In any case, the policy of politicization showed the will to spread a conservative worldview more widely. It constituted a serious attempt to turn a wide-reaching but vague ideology into a more clearly defined communal political faith by spreading conservative ideals among the mass of the population. The wish to remain connected with the army was so strong that such a blatant attempt at political manipulation was accepted within a democratically structured association. The membership figures continued to grow, although there was grumbling about the attempts to increase political and ideological control. This shows that the desire for close association with state and army was stronger than any disquiet about a loss of political freedom. As the uncritical glorification of the Emperor's army did actually imply a more general conservative orientation, those – generally less well-educated – who held a more inconsistent set of beliefs might have also lacked rational counter-arguments.

The ritualistic celebration of service in the army spread not only a militaristic attitude, but also a more general conservative orientation. Its influence did not end with the members. In small towns, at least, the veterans' and reservists' nationalist celebrations were spectacular public events with music and marches, uniforms and flag-waving, drinking and dancing. They communicated the joy, pride and social prestige of the soldierly role, the authoritarian army and the conservative monarchical state. Although direct political control was only partly successful, the veterans' and reservists' associations thus played an important role in spreading a communal right-wing disposition of accepting hierarchy and glorifying military ways.

Reading about the German victory over France, Heinrich von Sybel wrote in a letter:

> My eyes continue to look at the special newspaper, and the tears flow down my cheeks. What do we deserve God's mercy for to be allowed to experience such great and powerful events? And how shall we live afterwards? That which has been the content of all wishes and actions for twenty years has now been given to us in such an absolutely beautiful way. Where shall one find a new content for future life in my age? (quoted in Hyderhoff and Wentzke: Vol. 1, 494)

For dedicated political activists, Sybel's concern about future political goals might have been an immediate problem. The vast majority were happy, however, to settle back into a more comfortable civil life, drawing pride from the new Imperial Germany and the part they believed they had played in creating it. Bismarck became the patriarch of the new nation, the unchallenged representative and custodian of nationalism (Frankel 2005). His emphasis on consolidating the nationalist achievements found widespread approval. Nationalism and militarism were largely backward-oriented, celebrating the achievements of the last decades and serving to maintain the status quo.

But with time this was bound to change. Unification became history; the German nation-state unspectacular normality. Shortcomings like the lack of political unity or the economic problems moved into the foreground of political attention; the desire grew for new nationalist goals. The problems of the Reich motivated the demand for a new and more active political orientation, but also the desire to step out of the fathers' shadow. In the long run, Sybel's comment proved prophetic: a new generation struggled to find goals which could compare with the grandeur of unification. The Wilhelmine attempt to turn Germany into a world power (Gollwitzer 1972, 1982; Neitzel 2000) was partly motivated by a Social Darwinist conviction that Germany had to become stronger if it did not want to perish, but the call for colonies and a strong navy was not based simply on fear. Recalling the experiences of his own youth, the historian Gerhard Ritter recognized a new enthusiasm gripping the circles he moved in:

> The younger generation strove beyond those borders of Germany's international power politics. Whoever remembers the Wilhelmine epoch from his own experience can clearly see how the then new catchwords of striving for 'world power' and 'sea power' were received as a salvation from the eternal backward-oriented pathos of the traditional patriotism ... (1965: 126 f.)

Other members of the cultural elite shared this view. The left-liberal politician Friedrich Naumann claimed that 'our whole youth identifies with the concept of a fleet' (1900: 182), and the sociologist Max Weber stated in his famous inaugural lecture 'that the unification of Germany was just a youthful prank which the nation committed in her old days, and which she should have avoided because of the costs involved, if it was to be the end and not the starting-point for German world politics' (1993: 571). A new militarism emerged which was not focused on maintaining the status quo, but was primarily concerned with increasing Germany's might (Förster 1985).

The veterans' and reservists' associations followed this trend by enthusiastically supporting the drive for world power in their publications, and by taking up some paramilitary activities. More importantly, there was the emergence of right-wing nationalist leagues, such as the Society for Germandom Abroad (1881), the German Language Association (1886), the Colonial Society (1887), the German Society for the Eastern Marches (1894), and the Imperial League to Combat Social Democracy (1904). The Navy League, founded in 1898 with 330,000 fee-paying members and 770,000 others affiliated to it, showed the dimensions of the phenomenon; while the Pan-German League, although it never exceeded 28,000 members, presented itself as the vanguard association. With the Army League founded shortly before the First World War in 1912, even an extremist organization succeeded in gaining 350,000 members. While the activities of the leagues were often quite limited, they could reach millions with their expert speakers, slide shows and posters whenever nationalist issues dominated the political scene (Chickering 1984; Coetzee 1990; Eley 1980, 1986; Grießmer 2000; Peters 1996).

The Navy League in particular found some support from industry, but the leagues' activists were largely notables with cultural capital. There was still a disproportionately high number of nobility – though often from its poorer and more highly educated parts (Malinowski 2004: 175–197) – but the overall appearance was dominated by higher civil servants, professors, grammar school teachers, Protestant clergymen, professionals and, to a lesser extent, entrepreneurs. When the Conservative Party became increasingly dominated by agrarian interest, the leagues offered space for a new elite to prove itself 'most German' (Roger Chickering). Turning Lagarde's ideas into their political platform, the leagues called for the creation of a harmonious national community and dramatic expansion. They enthusiastically supported the government when it pushed for colonies and an expanded navy, but the more radical activists were even quite ready to form an extra-parliamentary opposition – for example during the Moroccan crisis of 1906 – against a state leadership that shied away from conflict. The leagues were useful to the government in supporting a belligerent foreign policy, for example when trying to pass naval bills or raising colonial demands against other nations. But they proved to be a double-edged sword whenever Germany had to back down. The more German achievements fell short of the initial propaganda, the more a nationalist opposition became a destabilizing factor. After all, even Wilhelm II had argued vehemently that Germany desperately needed and deserved 'a place under the sun' second to none; how then could an Imperial policy which failed to make significant gains for more than two decades be defended? With every attempt to disguise the discrepancy between propaganda and reality, the critique of the Emperor's 'operetta politics' became more widespread, even among the top people from army and foreign office (Blackbourn 1987: 250 f.).

As pointed out in the introduction, conservatism has never been simply about conserving the status quo; hence, opposition from the right is not as surprising as often assumed. Nevertheless, Eley is right to argue that the national leagues mark an important radicalization in right-wing politics. Here right-wing extremism found a new arena, new promoters (often from the National Liberal Party), and a new political style. In contrast to the earlier individuals advocating *völkisch* ideas, the leagues were influential social movements in the political sphere. While Bismarck had stood for the merger between conservative elites and nationalism, the national leagues came to challenge this link. In claiming to be 'more German', right-wing members of the middle class staked out a radical political claim: in contrast to their fathers' generation, which had allegedly been too wishy-washy liberal, but also in contrast to a Conservative Party which compromised its nationalist claims by prioritizing egotistical interests, they demanded more political influence by presenting themselves as wholly committed servants of the fatherland. The leader and main idealogue of the Pan-Germans, Heinrich Class, thus described himself as part of a young, ultra-nationalist generation, forced by an uncompromising dedication to Germany into 'establishing a "national opposition".' 'We were purely nationalistic; we were not interested in a tolerance which spared the enemies of the *Volk* and the state' (1932: 17, 45, 61). Finally, the national leagues introduced a new style of politics on the political right: continuously sensationalist agitation, populist and disrespectful, always prepared to be hostile to government and political elites. In describing current conditions in apocalyptic terms – immediate danger of total destruction connected with the hope for redemption – they introduced a hysterical tone into German politics. The horror scenario of national doom served to justify the demand for brutal measures for uniting the nation behind one faith and taking up the battle for world power.

In his study of the Pan-Germans, Roger Chickering places particular emphasis on the fear factor in their ideological outlook (1984: 122–132): the fear of political chaos, of social disintegration, of racial decline, of a German defeat in the Social Darwinist struggle for existence. There is truth in this. Thus, despite his virulent anti-Semitism, an early *völkisch* thinker like Richard Wagner still believed that a communal national faith could emerge spontaneously from a *völkisch* culture grabbing all citizens under the guidance of an artistic genius; but, in contrast, the Pan-Germans only saw a world full of conflict and (domestic and international) mortal enemies. As their racism radicalized, their ideal of what a united *Volk* meant came to mean a (military) expansion of Germany to include all Germans and a disappearance of other races within that territory. Witnessing the rise of Social Democracy, Heinrich Class demanded legal measures against the organized working class to enforce a single political will onto the nation. Their Social Darwinism made extreme nationalists anticipate a future of murderous people's wars of existence (see above all Bernhardi's book *Germany and the next War* from 1912). In their opposition to liberalism, traditional conservatism and the government, the Pan-Germans pictured themselves as surrounded by naivety, ignorance and incompetence. To explain the failure of their policies, they employed conspiracy theories by focusing on the traditional suspects: the power of finance, reckless speculative capital, and an all-pervasive manipulative Jewish influence in politics and the press.

The diagnosis of danger and decline corresponded, however, with the strong hope for future redemption. In many ways, the national leagues' ideology was 'self-confident, optimistic and affirming', 'a vision of the future, not of the past' (Eley 1986: 266). The German Empire's extreme nationalism might have had its roots in the economic disruptions of Bismarckian Germany, but it blossomed during the prosperous decades around the turn of the century. It was precisely Germany's successes which whetted the appetite for the 'grasp for world power' (Fritz Fischer). The stress on Germany's many enemies served to turn a backward-oriented satisfaction with unification into a future-oriented desire for new goals. The sharp attack on the political establishment legitimized the demand for political influence, while self-portrayal as lonely voices gave substance to the chosen role as selfless custodian of true Germandom. Conflict and war were seen positively, as they were supposed to foster the preparedness for service and sacrifice, meld the divided nation into a community, and offer the only possible route for achieving the place Germany needed and deserved.

The leagues' extreme nationalists had a clear political vision (Chickering 1984: 74–101). Being *völkisch*, they regarded the 1871 unification as incomplete because the new state did not include the whole *Volk*. Their ideal was a Germany that would incorporate all ethnic Germans and only ethnic Germans. In domestic politics, this meant a call for measures to create a homogeneous Germany, that is, a weakening or removing of allegedly alien races, above all the Jews, but also the Poles, and forcing the others to assimilate to one dominant culture. The measures Heinrich Class advocated in his anonymously published book *If I were the Kaiser*, the core Pan-German manifesto before 1914 (Stegmann 1970: 293–304), included the following: a special law for Jews, which would ban them from work in the army, the civil service, the jurisdicature and the media, and from leading roles in banks and agriculture; the nationalization of Polish property; a dictatorship over Alsace-Lorraine; and the renewal of Bismarck's anti-Socialist legislation.

Despite their praise of the German *Volk*, the Pan-Germans – as the 'political-ideological holding company, which provided the other national leagues … with the intellectual weapons' (Kehr 1976: 144) – promoted an unashamedly self-serving oligarchical monarchy. Their leader Class demanded a constitutional reform, if necessary through a *coup d'état*, which would limit parliamentary participation to those Germans with education or property. For him, the *Volk* was by no means everybody, but a cultural elite which should act as sole advisors to the Emperor (Class 1914: 46–57, 72–85). As only a nationalist vanguard allegedly expressed the true *völkisch* culture, such a glorification of *Germanness* was largely self-glorification. The claim that Germans were superior to other nations and races was then used, however, to justify Germany's demand for world power status. Expansion at the risk of war was seen not only as an inevitable struggle for existence, but also as a way of spreading German culture for the benefit of humankind. Such allegedly idealistic motivation went hand in hand with the hope for far-reaching material advantages. Colonies appeared as a magic solution to all political conflicts: they would offer space to develop both agriculture and industry, guarantee autarky without sacrificing living standards, and allow for agrarian resettlement without infringing on established property rights. Inferior races would work for Germany's wealth, but could also, with time, be removed to make space for the growing German race. Not only the great political goal of world-power status was supposed to unite the nation into a tightly knit community, but also the material gains. Humanity as a whole was to benefit from the spread of German culture, but the main advantage would go, of course, to the German race. When such wishful thinking failed to materialize, a polarized friend–foe thinking provided a wealth of enemies (foreign nations, antagonistic races, ideological enemies) for Class and his ultra-nationalists to blame.

Yet for all their disrespectful public critique of the government, the national leagues stopped short of questioning the monarchy. They believed that only a strong leader could save Germany – but what if the *Kaiser* was weak? They saw many shortcomings in Wilhelm II, but even Heinrich Class merely expressed his hope that the Emperor would learn to listen to other advisers. Class propagated his ideals uncompromisingly in public, but had no strategy for dealing with an Emperor who would fail to listen; the idea of a charismatic leader rising from the population was still beyond his political imagination (1914: 266 f.). What is even more crucial for the topic of the present book is that the violently authoritarian and elitist plans of the leagues were in important ways at odds with the dream of a communal nationalist faith. Like the veterans' and reservists' associations, they celebrated their nationalist beliefs in ritualistically organized meetings – decorating rooms with nationalist symbols, playing music, having nationalist speeches greeted with unanimous applause, and concluding with a social event – but they never went beyond their middle-class circles to reach the lower classes. They worked towards uniting the nationalistically minded people of education and property in one belief, but not the population at large. Their violent rejection of ethnic minorities and Social Democrats made them distrust mass participation to such an extent that they could imagine only a top-down authoritarian solution. The Emperor, listening to the extreme nationalists' advice (as the new political elite), would enforce the leagues' political programme upon the nation. Of course, they hoped that grand political visions would gain popular support, but their concrete goal was an authoritarian oligarchic monarchy: the leader surrounded by an elite of clear-minded ultra-nationalists (Class 1914: 230) destroying any opposition and plurality by forcing their policy on the nation. It would be desirable to manipulate the mass of the population into supporting this policy; but failing that they envisaged a pure monarchical dictatorship. Their populism was thus focused on the nationalist mobilization of the well-off, not the population at large.

Such an openly dictatorial approach remained an important strand of right-wing extremism in the first half of the twentieth century, for example in the Hindenburg programme discussed in the next chapter. The optimistic belief that a communal German faith could emerge spontaneously under the guidance of a charismatic genius was always accompanied by more authoritarian visions which tended to view such a faith more cynically as an ideological device to integrate and mobilize the masses for the policies of a nationalist elite. For analytical purposes, it is useful to distinguish the two forms as two ideal types at either end of a polar scale, although in reality they tended to mix. The extremists in the national leagues were located towards the dictatorial end of the scale: they promoted the spread of a communal nationalist world-view among the racially correct elites of society, but, in the face of Social Democratic triumphs at the polls, had largely abandoned the idea of uniting the whole nation within one faith without force and cynical manipulation. Even Hitler, who was obviously quite ready to use terror, criticized them for alienating the working class by their elitism. By largely sacrificing the *völkisch* ideal of all Germans coming together voluntarily in a single communal faith, their vision of the future lost in its overall appeal.

In contrast to the political national leagues, 'life-reform' around the turn of the century was a very diverse, open and ambivalent cultural movement (Bucholz et al. 2001; Krebs and Reulecke 1998; Rohkrämer 1999: 117–161). Highly sensitive to the dark side of modernity, it explored a wide variety of potentially more satisfying ways of life. By and large, life-reformers realized not only the inevitability, but also the advantages, of the modernization process; but they fought against an attitude solely aimed at an increase in production and efficiency. While they accepted industrialization, they argued for the protection of places of natural beauty, of traditional features of the landscape which would maintain a sense of identity, and, more generally, of beautiful surroundings which would promote a love of *Heimat.* They advocated an allegedly healthier and more natural lifestyle, for example through healthy food, loose clothing or nudism. They promoted garden cities and aesthetically pleasing craft products. They practised new leisure activities, particularly in the youth movement: roaming in peer groups about the countryside, sleeping under the open sky or in barns and cooking on open fires. Life-reformers wanted to weaken the constraints of civilization with its authoritarian schools, stressful jobs and regimented codes of conduct.

Life-reform started with the body, but it intended to initiate a change of the whole human being. Living more naturally was supposed to promote a spiritual regeneration. Individuals were encouraged to change their lifestyles – which would lead, in the long run, to collective change. Society as a whole, the reformers argued, had become too artificial and too unnatural. Instrumental reason and egotism dominated the modern world to the extent that it destroyed any sense of community and overall purpose. Like the Romantics discussed earlier, they believed that a new faith was needed to unite the nation and give an up-to-date meaning to life. Life-reform contained a pragmatic dimension – instructions about maintaining a person's health in an increasingly artificial environment, or striking a balance between mass production and a traditional sense of quality and beauty – but ultimately it was motivated by the vision of an alternative modernity: an industrialized nation in harmony with nature, instrumental efficiency serving higher communal purposes, a great nation united by shared values and beliefs.

As usual, it was a cultural elite with a Protestant background, which was most dominant in assuming the role of guardians of Germany's spiritual life. They were suspicious that mainstream culture was not concerned enough about spiritual values, but they had no qualms in making full use of the wider circulation of books, magazines and newspapers in spreading their own ideas, thus reaching a wider audience than ever before. The reformers were convinced that life needed a higher purpose, but saw traditional convictions fading away. The semi-religious belief in a broad education (*Bildung*) as the means of achieving the individual's full potential seemed to lose its power. Learning increasingly meant a specialized vocational training, while a cultural canon of great art became, like a museum, increasingly removed from 'real life', simply serving the acquisition of a degree or the social standing. Even nationalism as the great nineteenth-century civic religion of the middle class seemed to lose strength: unification had become a historical event, and Germany's growing economic achievements lacked a non-materialistic dimension. While the national leagues wanted to find a new purpose in Germany's struggle for world power, life-reformers emphasized the need for a spiritual revival: a *Volk* coming together in the service of a non-materialist aesthetic, ethical and religious dimension of life. At the turn of the twentieth century many felt that Germany had made a great leap forward in practical matters, but had lost its alleged distinction as a *Volk* of poets and thinkers. Life-reformers therefore wanted to recover a sense of spiritual belonging from traditional communities, the aesthetic vitality of Goethe, Schiller and the Romantics and the nationalist enthusiasm of the wars of liberation. The new wealth that industrialization had produced should be used to advance a nation united in the search for a deeper, more spiritual and artistic meaning in modern times.

The publishing house Eugen Diederichs and its authors give a good sense of life-reform's intellectual landscape (Hübinger 1996, 1996a; Ulbricht 1999). Diederichs was a successful businessman with a cultural mission. He intended, as he stated in a letter to his friend, the life-reform activist Ferdinand Avenarius in 1896, to create 'a space for gathering modern spirits … against materialism for

Romanticism and a new renaissance' (quoted in Hübinger 1996a: 9). As one of the initiators of the youth movement's biggest pre-war celebration on the mountain Hoher Meissner and as participant in the life-reform *Sera*-Circle, he was at the hub of the life reform movement (Werner 1996). For him, the publishing house was not just as a commercial enterprise in the growing book market, but also as a forum for promoting a new spirituality associated with the life-reform movement. The design of his stand at the Leipzig book fair of 1914 provided a visual expression of his ambition: his books were presented in a room resembling a chapel, which was illuminated by blue light, and contained two statues from Naumburg Cathedral; above a row of his authors' portraits, the visitor could read Lagarde's call for a secret alliance of those working towards spiritual change (Hübinger 1996a: 14).

The books published by Diederichs did not push a narrow ideological line, but tried to provide a wide variety of material for a nationalist or religious revival; they included series entitled 'Fairytales in World Literature', 'Religious Voices of Ethnic Cultures', and 'Thule. Old Nordic Poetry and Prose'. Sören Kierkegaard appeared next to Wilhelm Bölsche, whose work stressed love – in contrast to a Darwinian struggle of survival – as the major force in nature. Internationally renowned writers like Tolstoy, Emerson and Ruskin were also part of Diederichs's programme, as well as more adventurous publications connected with life-reform, ranging from pedagogical reforms to garden cities, from new dance forms to the promotion of craft work and non-historicist architectural styles, from the youth movement to religious thought.[3] Diederichs published esoteric or mythical works from different cultures as material for a new spiritual turn, but there was an unmistakable emphasis on the Germanic tradition. A universal fascination with different ethnic cultures stood in tension with a glorification of an allegedly ethnic Nordic past.

Together with a group of like-minded people, Diederichs organized aesthetic feasts, for example midsummer celebrations with folk dances, medieval songs, *völkisch* theatre performances and pantheistic sermons. Such experiments hoped to provide for new community experiences, a new communal creativity and spirituality (Werner 1996). Similarly, his publishing house became 'a laboratory of religious modernity ... The search for metaphysical security or a new, binding myth stood in the centre of Diederichs' activities as publisher' (Graf 1996: 243) For him, culture gained its real importance only if it gravitated towards religion, the strongest force in life. Only a new faith could save the modern world from the danger of nihilism and bring forth true humanity. Religion could, he believed, turn egocentric individualist into social beings, materialists into idealists, a pluralistically divided society into a warm community. While humans felt alienated from their surroundings today, a new religion would make them feel at home again. We have to learn, he claimed in an advertisement, to listen to God again.

Once again we encounter the rejection of institutional church beliefs: dogmatism and pragmatic compromises had replaced religious experiences; old rituals and symbols lacked comprehensibility and contemporary relevance; and the theologians' rational approach had destroyed all sense of mystery. Instead of dogmatic systems, Diederichs desired religious fever and aesthetic fantasy. He never decided on a single faith, placing Protestant reformers and Jewish neo-Mystics next to authors who were attempting to revive Paganism or Gnosticism, the fantasies of ethical socialists about a worldly realization of a godly order next to right-wing calls for strong authority, and Buddhist-inspired theosophists next to reformers of Catholicism. The majority of his authors were German Protestants who were living in conflict with their church, but he consciously opened his programme to a wide variety of religious traditions. With Paul de Lagarde he published and popularized a core prophet of a new nationalist religion, but this did not stop him from valuing other ethnic cultures. He loved the outsiders and heretics, those living an alternative lifestyle and claiming mythical knowledge, the eclectic mergers of many traditions, the highly emotional writer addressing everyday concerns.

While Eugen Diederichs was exceptional in the range of religions he appreciated, he was typical in calling for a life-serving and life-celebrating religion. He was not concerned with life after death, but with the spiritual regeneration of individual and community. 'For me, religious ideas are ultimately helpful constructions ... Religion is a kind of perspective which allows to say yes to life; everybody has to achieve this in his own way' (quoted in Graf 1996: 250 f.). Religion was to help individuals and communities to increase their spiritual and creative powers. Heaven was to be achieved on earth. Texts, thoughts and feelings were interpreted as religious because of the effects which this claim would have on life. Diederichs allowed for individuals to choose their faith freely, but its quality was measured by the fruits it should bring forth: a harmonious community with idealistic and creative members.

Such a practical orientation was typical of the whole life-reform movement. In contrast to the national leagues, however, it was not explicitly political or manipulative towards the masses: a new faith had to emerge freely within all individuals. The reformers' vision of the future, like that of the Romantics or Wagner, was based on an optimistic view of humans and their potential for self-improvement. Life-reform included a wide variety of political directions, with some reformers even moving into socialist and anarchic directions. The widespread glorification of historically grown structures, stability and a harmonious culture tended towards conservatism, but the trust in the wisdom of nature in contrast to human customs led to a fundamental questioning of traditions. The life-reform's emphasis on spirituality and a natural harmony constituted a barrier to a Marxist class analysis, and their dream of a homogeneous national culture could result in anti-Semitism, but in contrast to the national leagues they showed little concern about Germany's international strength. At least before 1914, the life-reform movement did not really fit into a political left–right distinction.

Although life-reform did not necessarily lead to right-wing extremism, it did offer important inspirations for its development (see also Jefferies 2006). In the largely middle-class *Wandervogel*, forms and activities emerged which became characteristic for all youth organizations, including political organizations like the Hitler youth. The critique of a decadent society could connect with racism and Social Darwinism. And the dream of a spiritual community overlapped with the search for a community united in a single communal faith. There were, moreover, important personal connections. Eugen Diederichs increasingly moved to the political right, making Arthur Bonus – who called for a life-affirming and heroic Germanized Christendom – his most important theological author in the early twentieth century, promoting the anti-liberal theologian Friedrich Gogarten in the Weimar Republic, and publishing the Conservative Revolution's biggest journal *Die Tat* towards the end of the Weimar Republic. *Rembrandt als Erzieher* (1890), a core book of *völkisch* thought which went through forty-nine editions in nineteen years, was greeted with particular enthusiasm in the youth movement and other life-reform circles. In his highly associative style, the author August Julius Langbehn (1851–1907), who placed himself in the tradition of Lagarde and Nietzsche, combined ideas of the life-reform movement with a rampant anti-Semitism[4] and the call for a hierarchical society. Drawing on Wagner's theoretical work in calling for a German cultural regeneration (while rejecting the musician's art as restless and decadent, Langbehn 1922: 291 f.), he described Rembrandt as the model for the kind of artistic genius contemporary Germany needed to express and enhance the eternal spiritual traits of the *Volk*. Rejecting the scientific specialization, democratization and atomization of the modern age, he called on the supposedly unrivalled artistic and religious qualities of the German people to bring forth a new spirituality (being German means, he claimed in the book's final sentences, 'to serve God and the Godly. It means to live'). Drawing on all the ideas mentioned above without ever developing any idea thoroughly or ever commiting himself to a clear argument, he succeeded in enthusing his contemporaries with a whole string of buzz words about the need for a new spirituality: a regeneration of the arts and a communal faith as expressions of the German *völkisch* soul. Without bothering to consider differences, tensions or contradictions, Langbehn simply put forward a wish-list of an allegedly Germanic spiritualism which would combine an anti-urban love for the region and agriculture with imperialism, individuality with *völkisch* rootedness, activist will-power with a contemplative soul, creative sensibility with monumentality, a vitalistic praise of life with an artistically refined style, and a commitment to an individual view of life with a desire for metaphysical truth. Art should serve and strengthen contemporary life, while being simultaneously 'lasting, firm, necessary, inherited, eternal' (1922: 89). It should combine the alleged purity of Protestantism with a Catholic and medieval sense for artistic form in religious ceremony and a child-like devotion (1922: 374). And it should live up to the standards of high culture, but also win the heart of all Germans:

> One of the first and most fundamental laws of the German *Volk* is the right for a through and through native art, for a through and through native culture. The German heart which claims the highest rank within ourselves, also has to dominate

> public culture. Only an education (*Bildung*) and an art, which accepts *the German heart* as true authority, can provide a happy future for the Germans' inner life. (1922: 317)

Furthest to the right was the still marginal *völkisch* movement in the narrow sense of the word (Puschner 2001, 2002). A predominantly male core of about 10,000 radicals organized around journals, in loose associations, or in sect-like orders and lodges. At the centre of their thinking was an excessive glorification of Germandom, both culturally and racially, combined with a violent rejection of others, especially Jews. 'We are of holy German descent, of the blood from which will grow the salvation of the world', the ideologue Ernst Hunkel proclaimed. 'You are descended from God: set up your law in the world! The law of your blood! The law of your heart! The freedom and power of your God!'(quoted in Puschner 2002: 12). More extreme than Diederichs's authors, they called for a renewal of the German race inspired by a German Christendom or some anti-Christian pagan religion promoting the purity of the race and heroic sacrifice for the community. They drew on ideas of life-reformers about a natural lifestyle to fight the danger of racial degeneration and also promoted some re-agrarization or rural settlements for breeding a racial elite. In a controversial plan presented in the book *Mittgart* (1904), which went through five editions in a dozen years, the biologist Willibald Hentschel even suggested so-called human gardens, where 300,000 Aryans at a ratio of one man to ten women would produce the highest output of valuable racial stock. Only the racially best would be kept for further breeding, while the rest was to be used to replenish the inevitably degenerating urban population.

While such *völkisch* groups remained at the fringe of society, the glorification of the German race reached further into society. Arguably the most important promoter of such ideas for wider parts of society was the Bayreuth Circle (Châtellier 1996; Hein 1996; Schüler 1971). Richard Wagner's attempt to create a national religion through his own art had obviously not reached the nation as a whole, but it had gained a devoted circle of followers. As Riehl stated:

> The inmost, hard core of Wagner's party is more than a party, it is simultaneously a congregation which believes in its Messiah and listens to his revelations with the devotedness of believers. The veneration for his person and work grows into a cult, his books are seen as confessional writings, the outward symbols of the new, aesthetic faith. (quoted in Schüler 1971: 53)

The festivals were celebrated as services, Wagner's work as gospel. Wagner associations emerged, using the *Bayreuther Blätter* as their forum. The authors of that journal ardently followed Wagner's call to action: 'We recognize the reason for the decline of historical man as well as the necessity for a regeneration; we believe that such a regeneration is possible and devote ourselves to promoting it in every way' (Wagner n.d.: Vol. 14, 181).

Wagner's work, in particular his art, is open to a wide variety of interpretations. The Bayreuth Circle, however, drew largely on Wagner's late 'regeneration writings' and on his widow Cosima's interpretation of them, emphasizing his conservatism, his blaming of money and power – allegedly most purely incorporated by the Jews – for all ills, and his glorification of Germanness. The need for a semi-religious belief emerging from art came to be seen as the core of a future regeneration. Germany was politically unified; now an inner unification uniting the nation in a single national faith came to be seen as the next task. The Jews were regarded as the main enemies, while an undogmatic, aestheticized Christendom based on religious intuition promised salvation.

The Bayreuth Circle, as the core disseminator of Wagner's ideas, developed contacts both with *völkisch* groups and with the mainstream of society, promoting many connections between the two. Ludwig Schemann, who, encouraged by Cosima Wagner, translated the work of Gobineau and founded the Gobineau Society, was a key member,[5] and so were the academic Karl Heinrich Freiherr von Stein, Wagner's biographer Karl Friedrich Glasenapp and the Professor of Art History, Henry Thode. All these respected members of society devoted a large part of their time to promoting a Wagnerian world-view, but the most influential was Houston Stewart Chamberlain (1855–1927) (Field 1981). With time, Chamberlain became Wagner's most influential interpreter, and played a crucial role in turning his ideas into a comprehensive *völkisch* system of thought. Born in England as the son of a British admiral, brought up by English relatives in France and educated at an English boarding school, long years of travelling made Chamberlain feel desperate for roots. He got to know Germany the first time at its most martial, when it mobilized for war in 1870. Only six years later, he had become an ultra-nationalist in claiming in a letter 'that the whole future of Europe – that is, of world civilization – rests in the hands of Germany' (1919: 59). Germany became his idolized nation, Wagner its most authentic voice. 'The decisive turn in my life was the one towards Germandom … and in the centre of it stood Richard Wagner … My life's sun has been and is Richard Wagner' (1919: 160 f.). Through marriage with Richard Wagner's daughter Eva in 1908, Chamberlain also became personally connected with the family. His goal was to turn Wagner's artistic intuition into a system of thought, a forward-looking and, in contrast to a Gobineauian belief in racial decline, optimistic ideology for shaping national action.[6]

Living in Bayreuth and writing in German, Chamberlain became a highly effective propagandist for a Wagnerian nationalism. His books were easy to read but had a scientific aura. They drew on a wealth of knowledge, but were mainly concerned with popularizing a simple world-view. Chamberlain's writing was neither scientific nor intuitive, but continuously changed between the two modes. Despite the learned style, he explicitly claimed to put forward an artistic 'living truth' which was concerned with answering the key questions of his time (Chamberlain 1904: 5). He could be quite strategic, for example in toning down his anti-Semitism to reach wider circles. The enormous circulation of his work proved his strategy right: his main publication, the long two-volume *Foundations of the Nineteenth Century*, had sold more than 100,000 copies by 1915. The liberal *Frankfurter Zeitung* lamented that this core book of *völkisch* nationalism and anti-Semitism, which was discussed in scholarly circles and everyday conversations alike, 'caused more of a ferment than any other appearance on the book market in recent years' (quoted in Field 1981: 225). Even the Emperor, who read parts of the work aloud to his evening companions and frequently passed it on as a present, met the author for hours and continued to have a correspondence with him (Urbach and Buchner 2004: 127; Field 1981: 248 ff. For the following see Field 1981: 390). Chamberlain's collection of 1914 war essays, which he described as '42-centimetre bombs' (1928: Vol. 2, 244), sold 160,000 copies in half a year. With his countless newspaper and journal articles, he reached, his main biographer calculated, over a million readers. Beyond *völkisch* circles he also found resonance among more moderate conservatives and national liberals. While Catholics tended to reject his vision of a Germanic religion, it met with interest among those Protestants who saw a need for adapting to the political culture of their time.

The starting point for Chamberlain's world-view was Richard Wagner's call for regeneration. Adding a sweeping historical account, Chamberlain argued that an initial harmonious order, realized in its highest form in classical Greece (albeit based on slave exploitation), had been destroyed in the period of ethnic chaos after the fall of Rome. Since then, history has been determined by racial struggles, especially between Germanic and Jewish people. For him, these two races constituted polar opposites. They were locked in inescapable, deadly conflict. While the Jews supposedly stood for cowardly egotism, materialism and chaos, the Germanic race had the potential for realizing an ideal world of heroism and sacrifice, morality and religion, ethnic solidarity and harmonious social order.

Chamberlain was a biological racist. He allowed for individual exceptions, but believed that, as a general historical rule, racial traits determined the individuals. When the theologian Adolf von Harnack argued that racial hatred violated the second commandment of love, Chamberlain's response revealed the raw emotions involved: 'I do not view the commandment as meaning to love that which every day in all spheres defiles, poisons and drags down everything that is exalted and holy to me … With all the strength in my soul, I hate it and hate it and hate it' (quoted in Field 1981: 242). Behind everything Chamberlain hated he came to suspect Jewish influences, while he constructed wild theories to 'prove' that Jesus had probably been an Aryan (Chamberlain 1904: 211).

Chamberlain was paranoid about Jews and other alleged enemies of the Germanic people. But even stronger than this fear was his belief that an ideal Germanic future was within reach. While Wagner's critique in the *Ring* of the power of law, institutions and money made true redemption difficult to achieve, blaming 'the demon [Jew] for the decline of humanity' (Chamberlain 1925: 141) made things appear much simpler: the Germanic race would only have to overcome the Jews and realize its own positive potential to reach Chamberlain's utopia. Chamberlain's hope was 'that we Germanic people and the nations under our influence will move towards a new harmonious culture, incomparably more beautiful than any of the old ones history tells about, a culture in which humans will truly be better and happier than today' (1904: 33).

At times, Chamberlain lamented the modern age of machines and metropolitan cities, but, as with most cultural criticism, this was a critique only of a materialism that was not embedded in a wider world-view. While he approved of all material means in the service of Germany's war machine, he could never accept a material hedonism without a nationalist purpose. But with such a purpose, technology was good: while Athens still needed an immoral slave economy to support its wonderful culture, the age of technology would permit a spiritual community to include every truly German citizen (Chamberlain 1904: 481).

Developing a Germanic religion was for Chamberlain both an absolute necessity and the ultimate utopia. In the racial struggle that he diagnosed, an appropriate religion was essential to unite the people, create a strong national identity and mobilize the *Volk* for communal goals. In a twisted way, Judaism was the model, because it had kept the Jews distinct, pure and united throughout their diaspora. While the Germanic people had, in principle, the highest potential for spirituality, because they were particularly apt to experience God and lead a life devoted to ideals, history had distorted their religion: although Chamberlain regarded Jesus Christ as the most valid ideal, the Christian tradition, in particular Catholicism, allegedly suffered from Jewish distortions of the initial message (Chamberlain 1904: 543 ff.).

Chamberlain followed the general trend of nineteenth-century critiques of religion by rejecting Christian dogma. As he believed in a mechanical view of nature, the Bible did not narrate a true history for him, but was just a human story about sacred things – in other words, a mythology. He argued that the Christian belief in miracles, the Trinity and the virgin birth was mistaken because it took figurative language as literal truth. The consequences of adhering to a strict religious dogma were, Chamberlain argued, nothing short of disastrous: he perceived the papal claim for one religious truth as an imperialist project to undermine religious freedom in persons and nations. For him Catholicism was an institution which misused the term 'religion' in its drive for universal power (Chamberlain 1904: 631).

Chamberlain believed neither in one holy scripture, nor in a personal God. Instead, true religion had to be based on the personal experience of the godly and should promote the godly in humans. In contrast to a belief based on the Bible and church dogma, his was a highly subjective religion, allowing for a wide variety of religious experiences. God is, Chamberlain argued, only within the depth of the human soul. The godly was reduced to the good in human beings – most importantly, altruistic ethics and the commitment to work towards a harmonious and beautiful world.

Drawing on his reading of Kant, Chamberlain stressed the sovereignty of the human mind, but, like other calls for a new religion, his prime goal was worldly:

the realization of humans' highest potential in this world. He criticized the Catholic attempt to spread one faith, but his own vision was by no means more tolerant. The individual freedom implicit in mythical experiences disappeared due to his racism and elitism: the Nordic race allegedly experienced religion in the purest form, and within that race in particular the most valuable people. Hence a cultural elite was supposed to formulate a national religion for the mass of the population, and the best race should gain global dominance for the benefit of humanity as a whole. Chamberlain thus claimed a moral entitlement for the Nordic race to be 'the masters of the world' (1904: 503).

Chamberlain's world-view rested on a simplistic racist concept of history. He postulated a hierarchy with the Nordic people at the top and the Jews at the bottom. To realize humanity's highest potential, the Nordic people had to win the racial struggle. At present, however, not even the glorified German nation was anywhere near perfection. Its potentially mortal 'Achilles heel' (Chamberlain 1904: 750) was the lack of an appropriate racial religion, and its duty was to create such a faith. If Germany failed in this self-purification, the evil forces would triumph, but if it succeeded, the other races would stand no chance. A purified Germany could then lead all Aryan nations towards realizing the godly in this world. There was thus, we can conclude, a step-by-step plan behind the many facets of Chamberlain's work: first a spiritual regeneration within Germany; then the establishment of a 'great Nordic brotherhood' (Chamberlain 1904: 481); finally, the achievement of heaven on earth through a global culture under Aryan dominance which would realize the highest potential of humankind. For Chamberlain it was his historical mission to promote the execution of such a plan: 'Turn knowledge into action! Summarize history in such a way ... that the knowledge of the past becomes an active determining force for the present' (1904: 1003).

For conservative nationalists who had lost faith in traditional Protestantism, Chamberlain could appear as a person trying to save the best of Christianity. Shedding allegedly outdated metaphysical beliefs, he advocated a revival of a highly subjective religion through art.[7] The essence of his religion, however, turned out to be self-deification: God was not the unfathomable other, categorically distinct from all humans, but encapsulated the best of the Nordic race – Chamberlain thus advocated 'reverence for one's self' (1904: 940). In developing its positive potential and shaping the world according to its own ideals, the Germans had the opportunity to realize God's kingdom in this world. Chamberlain's call for a religion that strengthened life was a call for a Germanic cultural elite to play God. This was spelled out with unprecedented clarity in Chamberlain's war publications, which stated his old convictions in a more trenchant form. As he was convinced that Germany's triumph would benefit humanity at large, the enemies had to be wrong and evil. If a Nordic nation like England fought against Germany, then Jewish influences had to be the cause. In such a battle between good and evil, all German war efforts and war aims appeared justified. It thus comes as no surprise that this 'terrible simplificateur' (Jacob

Burckhardt) supported annexionist war aims, applauded Hindenburg's and Ludendorff's call for a total war to achieve complete victory, supported the right-wing German Fatherland's Party, and worked with Heinrich Class to found the political journal *Deutschlands Erneuerung* ('Germany's Revival'). During the war, he became increasingly disappointed with the weak Wilhelm II, but he soon found a new idol in Adolf Hitler (Bärsch 1998: 139–145; Hamann 2003). He not only gave the plans for a coup in 1923 his blessing, but also called Hitler an 'awakener of the souls' and a 'luminous figure', a 'man of the people' and 'a man of the heart' (Chamberlain 1934: 69, 65–67). In his post-war publication *Man and God*, he came to stress that the mass of the population did not need church doctrine, but instead required an exceptional human being who would serve as a mediator between them and God.

> The coming of a mediator between man and God makes the different dogmatic systems as well as the whole apparatus of church-enforced rituals appear as unnecessary ... From then on, it will be sufficient to believe in the mediator – and that means to comprehend him, everybody in the way best suited to himself, be it with a strongly beating heart or with a meditative soul. If people hold tightly onto him, then God's presence is achieved, and they enter the holy father's reign without further ado. (1921: 298 f.)

Did Hitler become such a mediator of a new religion for Chamberlain during their meeting in 1923? He did, at least, write about the Nazi leader:

> This man has worked as a blessing of God. He has strengthened hearts, he has opened eyes towards a clear goal, he has kindled the ability for love and outrage in the souls, he has inspired steel-like courage and determination. However, we still desperately need him: May God, who has given him to us as a present, still preserve him for many years for the benefit of the German fatherland! (1934: 65–67)

Chamberlain never formulated a concrete political programme, but his call for a new *völkisch* faith which should come to dominate the world offered a convenient justification for an aggressive foreign policy and a hierarchical end to cultural pluralism. The belief in a single communal faith could take many different forms and political directions, but Chamberlain's work shows it had dangerous potential even before 1914. The idealistic notion of spiritual regeneration could come to justify violence, when the whole historical development appeared as an existential struggle between a potentially good Nordic race and its adversaries, in particular the Jews. During the First World War, these views became even more extreme: allegedly, most of the major powers conspired to bring down Germany, which was the only nation still able to save humanity from decline. The interest of one nation, and all the means used to promote it, thus came to stand for 'good', and its enemies for 'evil'. Chamberlain's acknowledgement that the existing Germany was a far cry from the ideal he painted did nothing to moderate his views. On the contrary: it merely came to serve as justification for a ruthless domestic policy against all the alleged enemies within. The success of

Chamberlain as an author shows that the appeal of such a view, though still regarded as extreme, started to reach into the mainstream of society.

The last person to be discussed in this chapter, Friedrich Nietzsche (1844–1900), is obviously of a very different intellectual standing. The ideas of a figure of this calibre cannot be reduced to just one intellectual tradition, especially as Nietzsche explicitly rejected the idea of developing one system of thought, choosing instead to express the wealth of his ideas in aphoristic form. His historical influence has been even more diverse than his work: he influenced people from all political persuasions, gave support to the idea of a natural hierarchy and an anarchic joy of ecstasy, and promoted the glorification of a ruthless will to power, an epistemological scepticism and a deconstructivist critique of the metaphysical tradition. While it is impossible to give Nietzsche his full due within the framework of this study, it is equally impossible to ignore him. He became a cultural force at the turn of the century, when his ideas 'began to exert a powerful influence over all yearning and restless spirits' (Meinecke 1963: 24). The sociologist Max Weber remarked that his age 'bears largely the imprint of Marx and Nietzsche' (quoted in Baumgarten 1964: 544, n. 1). Authors of the life-reform movement frequently referred to his work, and attempts at creating a Germanic religion drew strongly on his critique of Christianity. From 1914 onwards, a right-wing reading of his philosophy, which was strongly promoted by the Nietzsche archive under his sister Elisabeth Förster-Nietzsche (wife of a well-known anti-Semitic activist), became increasingly dominant (Aschheim 1994). The sharp critic of Imperial Germany gained the stamp of official approval posthumously when 150,000 copies of his *Zarathustra* were distributed to the troops in 1914. He was used in the more intellectual war propaganda to such an extent that one book title described him as 'the philosopher of the world war' – strongly influencing, for example, Max Scheler, Werner Sombart and Thomas Mann – and Walter Flex's war novel *Wanderer Between Different Worlds*, which sold 250,000 copies in less than two years. As we shall see, he was an important source for extreme nationalists in redefining their role in the Weimar Republic after the military defeat, and he gained a central place in the Nazi pantheon of Germanic giants. While the extent of Nietzsche's true intellectual influence has always been hotly debated – the Nazi ideologue Ernst Krieck caustically remarked: 'Apart from the fact that Nietzsche was not a socialist, not a nationalist, and opposed to racial thinking, he could have been a leading National Socialist thinker' (quoted in Aschheim 1994: 253. More generally see Golomb and Wistrich 2002) – the Nazis tended to claim him as an intellectual forerunner. Hitler's visit to the Nietzsche archive in 1934 was publicized by a picture showing the thoughtful Führer next to the bust of the philosopher, Nazi language was filled with Nietzschean terms (Stern 1984: Ch. 7 f.), and the party produced anthologies of his work as well as semi-official interpretations.[8]

Nietzsche was a philosophical innovator of the first order, but politically conservative and a sharp critic of the modern age.[9] Like so many of the people and movements we have looked at already, he rejected modern economic and technological development as empty materialism and a utilitarian politics of greed, wishing instead for strong convictions and political goals. He rejected democracy and cultural pluralism because it would lead to mediocracy, and diagnosed a lack of strong beliefs, in other words, nihilism. Freedom for the masses, he believed, led to a petty age that was lacking in style and grandeur. Strongly rejecting the 'socialist rabble' (1954: 57)[10] because it would only create dissatisfaction among the common people, he argued fervently in favour of a strict hierarchical society as the only way towards grand people and a grand age.

> Every enhancement of the type 'man' has been the work of an aristocratic society – and that is how it will be, again and again, since this sort of society believes in a long ladder of rank order and value distinctions between men, and in some sense slavery. Without the *pathos of distance* as it grows out of an ingrained difference between stations, out of … the ruling caste's continuous exercise in obeying [the communal ethos] and commanding, in keeping away and below, that other, more mysterious pathos [of self-overcoming] could not have grown at all. (1966a: 257)

> The chasm between man and man, class and class, the multiplicity of types, the will to be oneself to stand out – that which I call *pathos of distance* – characterises every *strong age.* (1954b: IX, 30)

Several arguments have been employed to show a distance between Nietzsche and conservatism or nationalism. He was strongly opposed to anti-Semitism (although this led to family conflicts with his anti-Semitic brother-in-law), he mocked a self-satisfied nationalism, and his sharp critique of society had nothing to do with preservation. Not only did he criticize the idea of objective truth, thus furthering the belief in a multitude of perspectives on life, but he also rejected Christianity and the glorification of the state. His call for a caste system did not justify existing social structures, but promoted Plato's ideal of a society with spiritual leaders at the top, warriors in the middle and the producing classes at the bottom of society. Challenging established institutions, he called for 'free spirits' to live dangerously and explore new avenues.

All these points are correct, but they do not separate Nietzsche from the conservative German tradition. This tradition is, as we have seen, much more complex than most Nietzsche experts with a philosophical background assume. While extreme German nationalists were often strongly anti-Semitic, this is not a necessary ingredient of such a world-view. Nietzsche aimed, as we shall see, at a community united in a single faith, and so wanted an end to a variety of different beliefs. The anti-Semites were, however, too negative for him, too full of resentment, hatred and fear. What he called for instead was a policy of strength: the creation of strong and beautiful new values should provide an irresistible pull towards a new community of shared ideological convictions.

Nietzsche was not a conservative in the literal sense of the word, but a conservative revolutionary trying to create a new hierarchical society. Like all extreme nationalists of his time, he criticized a flag-waving glorification of the German

Empire because he saw no reason for self-satisfied contentment. He sharply criticized nationalism (for example in 1968b: 'Why I am so clever'), because he saw a strong state, but no communal culture (Bäumler 1931: 90). An ideal community which had the right to demand devotion did not exist at the time, but was a historical memory and a project for the future. This is why he defames the state as 'the coldest of cold monsters. Coldly it tells lies, too; and this lie crawls out of its mouth: "I, the state, am the people"' (1969: I, 'On the New Idol'). This quotation has been read as an expression of semi-anarchic individualism, but such interpretation shows a lack of historical knowledge. Richard Wagner held the same conviction, and so did all followers of the *völkisch* tradition down to Nazism, because they argued for the primacy of the community and, in contrast to supporters of traditional dictatorships, accepted the state only insofar as it served the realization of a *völkisch* existence. Lastly, while traditional conservatism tried to use the Christian churches to legitimise the existing social order, a critique of Christianity was, as we have seen, a central part of the more extreme *völkisch* tradition.

Nietzsche is a fascinating philosopher who proves a valuable inspiration in many different contexts, but he is also part of his time. Drawing on the life-reform movement, he stressed not only the importance of physical health, but also 'nature' or 'life' as central guiding principles for questioning the excesses of a highly artificial modern existence. He challenged the idea of a single objective truth by pointing out that the human conscience was nothing but a tool for a natural will to power. He shared Max Weber's fear that modernity would turn into an iron cage of bureaucratic rule and shallow pleasures, praising instead a martial life of conflict and struggle, of exceptional people and strongly held convictions. Like many others, he desired political drama, thus praising Napoleon or the Roman Empire as 'the most admirable of all artworks in the grand style' (1954: 58). In 'Ecce Homo', he saw himself as 'dynamite ... Only after me will there be *great politics* on earth' (96–97); and he predicted with excitement a new imperial and Social Darwinist age of unprecedented grandeur:

> *To acquire one will* by means of a new caste that would rule Europe, a long, terrible will of its own that would be able to cast its goals millennia hence – so the long-drawn-out comedy of its splinter states as well as its dynastic and democratic splinter wills would come to an end. The time for petty politics is over: the very next century will bring the fight for the dominion of the earth – the *compulsion* to large-scale politics. (1966a: 131)

Nietzsche's critical faculties might have been his main and lasting intellectual strength, but for him, deconstruction remained intrinsically linked to positive goals: 'Only as creators', he claimed, 'can we destroy' (1974: 58). Crucial to this constructive task was, as Julian Young (2006) has shown convincingly, the will for a new communal faith. A new religion was to overcome nihilism, in other words, the normative emptiness of the modern epoch. For a while he believed that

Richard Wagner would bring forth such a regeneration; but even when he lost this initial hope, the dream itself stayed with him to the end of his writing career.

In contrast to Strauß and the many other historicist critics of the Bible, Nietzsche took a different stand. Religion should remain mythology to stay flexible and proudly unscientific; once the attempt is made to adapt it to academic standards, it cannot fight off destruction:

> This is the way in which religions are wont to die off: namely, when the mythical supposition of a religion become systematized under the strict, rationalist eyes of an orthodox dogmatism into a finished sum of historical events, and one begins to fearfully defend the believability of the myth while striving against a continuation of its natural growth of life. (quoted in Williamson 2004: 246)

The desire for myth is most strongly expressed in Nietzsche's first work, *The Birth of Tragedy*, which was first published in 1872 while he was still under Richard Wagner's spell. It offered a philosophical grounding for the Bayreuth project that was far superior to anything the composer himself ever formulated. Following Wagner and many others, Nietzsche projected his own ideals on to classical Greece. That community was blessed with a joyful and life-affirming existence, while modern humans were feeling nausea about the absurdity of life. Why the difference? For Nietzsche the answer was that the modern age lacked an appropriate communal belief, while the Greeks held one, for a time, that was expressed in their tragedies. While a religious age offered a way of seeing the world as an ordered and meaningful place, as a shared faith that created a strong sense of community, and as a credible answer to the existential question of mortality, a secularized society produced a sense of absurdity and fear of death.

The Birth of Tragedy did not discuss religion in general. Secularization was taken simply as fact, and a tragic culture as the only means for overcoming it. But why tragedy? While it can be seen that plays of mythical content can communicate an explanation of the world and create a sense of community among the audience, why should it help us to understand and accept our own death? Why, in fact, does anyone leave a tragedy consoled and satisfied, if it is, by definition, about the death of admirable heroic people? The audience, Nietzsche answered, does not identify with any individual dramatic persona, but with the play as a whole. In Greek drama, the audience was the chorus that commentated on the events. It learned to understand the need for an individual's death as a necessary part of the whole drama. The absorbed viewers would experience a transcending of their own personal interests by identifying with life as a whole. Through tragedy, Nietzsche argued, we become 'the primordial being itself and we feel its unbounded greed and lust for being: the struggle, the agony, the destruction of appearances, all this now seems to us to be necessary given the uncountable excess of forms of existence thrusting and pushing themselves into life, given the exuberant fertility of the world-will' (1966: 7).

The solace Nietzsche found for the problem of death was basically, as briefly stated before, a change of perspective: humans have to learn to look at their individual existence from outside. Once they come to appreciate life aesthetically as a perfectly constructed grand drama, they learn to realize that death is a necessary part of the action. 'Only as an aesthetic phenomenon does existence and the world appear justified [or, on page 5 of the same text, 'is ... justified']; which means that tragic myth in particular must convince us that even the ugly and disharmonious is an artistic game which the Will in the fullness of its delight plays with itself' (1966: 24). An example Nietzsche used was the oil painting of a battle: as involved viewers we identify with the heroism and grandeur of the scene, accepting death and suffering as a necessary prerequisite. For Nietzsche this was the way to accept reality, even to the extent of *amor fati* or eternal recurrence, that is, the ability to say: 'Yes, I love fate and accept everything to such an extent that I want it to happen again.'

The Birth of Tragedy is based on a number of assumptions, which were addressed more or less directly in Nietzsche's later works. His decision in favour of an aesthetic religion implies acceptance that the belief in a personal afterlife should be abandoned. Such a faith seemed to him both untenable and undesirable. Like most of the other new forms of faith, Nietzsche's ideal was a religion focusing on life in this world. While Schopenhauer had regarded the Greek faith as a failed religion because it did not promise immortality, Nietzsche took the acceptance of reality 'as it is' as its main strength. A strong religion should lead, he later explicitly stated in his critique of Christianity, to a celebration of the strong life, not to its devaluation in favour of an imaginary life after death. God came to be regarded as creator, and humans could gain a god-like status, if they participated in this act of creating an impressive *Übermensch* or superman and grand drama: 'Creation – that is the great redemption from suffering and life's easement' (1969: II, 2: On the Blissful Islands).

Nietzsche's identification with existence as a whole, as well as his call, 'remain true to the earth' (1969: I, 3), also undermined Christianity's categorical distinction between God and humans. Like Feuerbach, Nietzsche insisted that the Greek gods were not other-worldly, but super-human. The proper religious respect was not for God as the other, but for an enlarged ideal self. Glorified ancestors, for example, could gain the status of gods, because gods were, in the last respect, ideal heroes.

Nietzsche's account is exceptional in showing so clearly the reason why people were drawn to the dream of a new faith. As a growing number of people found it increasingly difficult to believe in a life after death, the identification with a community, with the nation or with life as a whole could appear as the next best solution: an individual could at least hope to achieve immortality as active part of a bigger unit. To some extent this reflected a grudging acceptance that a traditional religious faith was no longer achievable, but it also had its optimistic dimension. A pantheistic deification of life also showed that not only the Left, but also the extreme Right, believed in the possibility of worldly improvements. The real world no longer appeared as a vale of tears, but seemed to offer a chance for experiencing heaven on earth. People did not want to live hoping for a salvation after death granted by an almighty God to undeserving sinners, but to take human destiny into their own hands by the creative act of realizing their own ideals.

In *The Birth of Tragedy*, Nietzsche was predominantly concerned with the question of how to accept one's own mortality, but the importance of religion was also shown in other domains. He lamented the scientific gaze which promoted a general disenchantment, calling instead for a new myth that would give a human meaning to the world. Such a myth could not be gained by a 'greedy scramble to grab at the table of others', that is, by collecting a smorgasbord of beliefs from different times and places (Eugen Diederichs springs to mind!), but by developing a consistent communal faith appropriate to the community in its time. The 'foundations of art and nation, myth and morality' were, he concluded, 'necessarily and closely entwined' (1966: 23).

This communal function of the great 'religious' art work was further developed in his *Untimely Meditations*. Here Nietzsche defined a true culture as the 'unity of feeling among a people', 'above all, unity of artistic style in all the expressions of the life of a people' (1983a; II, 4 and I, 1). He also discussed the role of history for society (1983a: II). Quite typically for the tradition under investigation, he rejected a detached historicist approach to the past. Humans should not aim for objective knowledge, but make use of the past for contemporary purposes. Only weaklings simply collect; strong people enforce their own interest on history. Some antiquarianism is necessary, simply to acquire facts to work with, but the main tasks are critical and monumental history. The former is needed to counteract a petrification of society: society has to free itself from wrong traditions, and create space for the growth of the new. The latter is, however, seen as at least equally important: society has to glorify its own ethnic tradition by stylizing exemplary men as heroes and role models, and by turning exceptional events into inspirations for the future. History should be condensed to quasi-mythical simplicity, thus exemplifying the ethos of the community and inspiring virtuous action.

In monumentalizing history into archetypical messages and monumental inspiration, in aestheticizing life into an overwhelming drama, and in avoiding ossification through cultural innovations, art always played a crucial role. The Greek tragedy was the prime historical ideal, and Richard Wagner's musical dramas were, at least for a time, the positive force of the present. The Wagnerian text based on old Germanic sagas provided the appropriate myth for the German nation, the dramatic personae provided heroic examples, and the music, a functional equivalent to the ancient chorus, served to provide an overall grandeur transcending the individual perspective. The music allegedly led the audience to identify with the 'one will' of life, accept death as 'the supreme stimulus of life', and see the 'serious and stressful' as 'an isolated fragment of' the 'total experience' (1983a: IV, 7).

It did not take long, however, before Nietzsche turned against Wagner. He came to feel that the musician sold himself to the masses with cheap effects instead of providing leadership, and he attacked his alleged romanticism as false pathos, calling instead for a classical style. Instead of providing a transvaluation of all values, Wagner had, Nietzsche believed, returned to a Christian 'herd moral' (that is, helping the weak instead of using them for heroic goals) in *Parsifal*. But this biting attack on Wagner's art should not make us overlook the fact that Nietzsche continued to agree with the Bayreuth project's intention. The concern he positively assigned to Wagner in the *Untimely Meditations*: 'How does the *Volk* come into being, and how can it be resurrected?' (1983a: IV, 8) can also be seen in the philosopher's later works.

Such a stress on Nietzsche's communitarian thinking is controversial (for the following see Young 2006): the majority of current readers emphasize Nietzsche's fascination with the strong ruthless individual, the free spirit questioning tradition and setting new values, the creative man exercising his[11] will to power by realizing his own vision of a grand life. Many passages of his writing, in particular in *Zarathustra*, show that there is truth in such a reading. Nietzsche celebrated the strong individual who breaks away from the mass in trying to live according to his own values. A self-determined, authentic existence was a core ideal that he preached in his writing. Self-reliance and vitalism are frequently praised. Is Nietzsche, then, simply inconsistent, if he simultaneously laments: 'Almost two millennia and not a single new God!' (1954: 19)?

Admittedly, there is a some tension between the call for an authentic individual existence and his admiration for cultures with a clear set of values and one style, because Nietzsche took both views to extremes. In principle, however, the two ideals were for him two sides of one coin. Firstly, being independent and developing new ideas was a lifestyle only suited, he continuously emphasized, to a spiritual elite; in contrast, the masses allegedly needed clear guidance based on a stable communal world-view. If Nietzsche did not provide such a faith for the masses, it was because he saw himself as the teacher of an elite of creative free spirits whose task was to adapt the community's faith to ever-changing conditions. Was the mass of the population then simply supposed to be slaves, providing the material means for the beautiful creativity of this elite? It is true that an aesthetic identification with the totality of life implied indifference to the suffering of individuals: after all, we do not care either how many of our bodies' cells die every day in order to maintain the whole. But in the last analysis, Nietzsche wanted both the mass of the population and the elite to serve the community. While the vast majority of the population should provide the stability needed for a grand community, a small number strong enough to be free spirits should make sure that the communal culture would not become conventional, ossified, stale and dead. Nietzsche thus envisaged a kind of spiritual Darwinism for his ideal of a community: the function of free spirits is to provide variations from the dominant communal culture. Each free spirit follows his will to power in trying to make his personal belief the new communal one. Society as a whole makes a selection, choosing the variation most suitable for communal life. While most free spirits thus perish, the successful few ensure the cultural innovations needed for a grand and lively communal life.

Despite rejecting the culture of his time, Nietzsche could thus adhere to the conservative desire for a communal culture shaped by the past as the necessary basis for a grand historical epoch. In this vein he stated:

> *Criticism of modernity.* – For institutions to exist there must exist a kind of will, instinct, imperative which is anti-liberal to the point of malice; the will to tradition, to authority, to centuries-long responsibility [*Verantwortlichkeit*], to solidarity between succeeding generations backwards and forwards *ad infinitum.* If this will is present there is established something like the *Imperium Romanum.* (1954b: IX, 39)

If a *Volk* had achieved 'hardness, uniformity, and simplicity of form' (Nietzsche 1966a: 263), it was ready to compete with other nations in trying to spread their own culture. For Nietzsche, a high communal culture did not lead to happiness, but to the will to 'rule and conquer and glitter, to the dread and envy of its neighbour' (1969: I, 15). For the future, he expected an age of war over the domination of the world (1966a: 208). Nietzsche transcended nationalism in expecting a battle over the definition of a communal European culture, akin presumably to the Roman Empire or the Christian Middle Ages, and ultimately over a global culture. Such a 'war of spirits' (Nietzsche 1968b: 327) was Nietzsche's ultimate ideal of life turned into an aesthetically overwhelming drama which would make all individual suffering and death appear justified. He, like so many, dreamed of overcoming the alleged materialism and hedonism of his time by promoting the will of an elite to realize their own utopian visions of life. While more naive 'idealists' saw only the truth of their own vision, he accepted the reality of a variety of visions growing out of different wills to power. His hope was, however, that the hard competition would promote the emergence of a healthier and stronger myth of life. After all, he once claimed, 'a dominating race can grow up only out of terrible and violent beginnings' (1968: 465).

Nietzsche's work not only provides a highly plausible explanation for the desire for a new communal faith, but also proved a strong influence on the further development of this ideal. To describe the many directions his influence took – for example, on the attempt to construct an anti-Christian Germanic religion – and the many areas his catchy images and phrases reached is well beyond the scope of this work (see for this Aschheim 1994; Wood 1996: Ch. 2). What is crucial for our topic, however, is that his utopian description of a culture united in a single faith resonated with many contemporary desires. He also succeeded in combining this vision of a harmonious community with the equally attractive call for a new cultural elite, an 'aristocracy' of 'free spirits'. The educated middle class, which provided only a tiny minority in elections and a small force in lobbying compared with the many interest groups, could find a flattering role created for itself. Readers who empathized were drawn by his pathos to see themselves as the free spirits opening up new avenues for a communal culture. Self-acclaimed guardians of (German) culture saw a heroic role cut out for themselves as spiritual leaders. If they felt isolated and ineffective in the pursuit of this goal, they could take consolation from the dramatic image Nietzsche had created for himself – that of the lonesome, heroic fighter, ridiculed by his time, but determined to keep searching for kindred spirits in the crucial battle between nihilism and the creation of a healthy community with an elite of supermen. Outsiders could, Nietzsche claimed, eventually turn into 'a new caste that will rule Europe' (1966a: 251). Such a self-definition became particularly useful when military defeat and democratization in 1918 seemed to negate all the extreme Right's political ideals in Germany. His ideal of heroic realism (Hof 1974) provided, as we shall see, a useful image for Conservative Revolutionaries and Nazis to define a politically effective attitude towards the Weimar Republic: accepting that the old forms could not be recycled from the scrapyard of history, but aiming for an up-to-date hierarchical society.

Above all, the aesthetic justification of life proved highly momentous. Seeing life from an outside perspective (as if one lived in a play or movie) is, of course, nothing peculiar to Nietzsche, but is an integral part of most heroism or of a post-modern attitude towards life. Nietzsche, however, gave a very coherent and persuasive account of it. In the first instance, such an aesthetic view of life aimed at overcoming the horror of death, but it frequently also had other, more dangerous consequences. Judging life by its dramatic effect easily led to a careless brushing aside of moral issues and human consequences. With such an attitude, human suffering and death could simply appear as inevitable parts of historical grandness.

This aspect of Nietzsche corresponds with his indulgence in martial rhetoric. He primarily had an intellectual daring in mind, but he also glorified the concept 'to live dangerously' (1974: 283) in more concrete ways, for example in his idolization of Richard Wagner's violent warrior Siegfried, or of 'some pack of blond animals of prey, a race of conquerors and rulers that is organized for war and has the drive to organize others, and that unscrupulously lays its awful paws on a population which may well be far greater in number, but is still lacking form' (quoted in Woods 1996: 36). While Nietzsche stressed the primacy of culture, his emphasis on health and strength was frequently read in a biological way. His glorification of war – 'War is the father of all good things' (1974: 145) – was useful in August 1914, and with the ideological confusion after Germany's defeat, right-wing intellectuals could draw on his decisionist glorification of fighting as such: 'You say that it is the good cause that hallows even war? I say unto you: it is the good war that hallows any cause' (1969: I, Of Wars and Warriors).

When Nietzsche talked about the will to power as the most fundamental human drive, he largely had a productive will to create and shape in mind. He advocated an honest, non-moralistic look at human nature, but wanted it to be sublimated within a higher human culture. Nietzsche's evocative images and phrases could, however, gain a momentum of their own, partly because his aphoristic and metaphorical style invited readers to take catchy parts for the whole, partly because the cruder work 'Will To Power' – assembled posthumously by his sister from notes not necessarily intended for publication – was long regarded as Nietzsche's core legacy, and partly because readers found in the texts what they wanted to find. The combination of a belief in a will to power in the sense of violent 'over-powering' (Jünger 1925: 191) as the basic human drive, combined with a rejection of liberal tolerance and a morals of compassion, could, as we shall see in the following chapters, justify as natural a ruthless fight against domestic enemies, an extreme militarism and a ruthless drive towards Imperialist expansion.

Notes

1. Hagenlücke 1997: 46 f. While many Agrarian Romantics and racial theorists promoted rural settlements, traditional Conservatives rejected breaking up big estates, even if they were no longer economically viable. The Agrarian League also provoked Protestant nationalists because it was prepared to work with the Catholic Centre Party.
2. In the German Empire, 64 per cent of the common soldiers came from villages, 22 per cent from small towns. For the following see Frevert 2001, Rohkrämer 1990 and Vogel 1997.
3. Authors included Paul Schultze-Naumburg, Hermann Muthesius, Peter Behrens, Jeannie Watt, Isadora Duncan, Mary Wigman, Rudolf Bode, Rudolf von Laban, Gustav Wyneken, Ernst Joel, Eduard Heimann, Wilhelm Flitner, Marie Luise Gothein, Bruno Taut and Leberecht Migge.
4. In the revised editions, the anti-Semitism became more pronounced. See in general Stern 1961: 97–180 and the chapter by B. Behrendt in Puschner 1996.
5. He also had contacts with Lagarde, Heinrich Class, racists like Otto Ammon, Ludwig Wilser and Wilhelm Schallmayer and the conservative revolutionary Arthur Moeller van den Bruck (see Ch. 5).
6. Chamberlain's belief in historical progression also shaped his unusual understanding of race. He does not look for an original pure race in the past, but argues that they have evolved in history through breeding and selection.
7. Chamberlain 1904: 645 and 954. After myth had lost its power, Chamberlain argued, only art was able to communicate the religious experience only available directly to a select few. In his opinion, only art was able to express the religious without turning it into a petrified dogma. His main witnesses for the role of aesthetics were Wagner and Schiller's *Letters on the Aesthetic Education of Man.*
8. Alfred Bäumler became the authorized Nietzsche expert in the Third Reich. He rejected the ideal of an eternal recurrence as overly passive, but stressed concepts such as the will to power, heroic realism and Nietzsche's critique of universal values.
9. Löwith 1986. More recent literature like Golomb and Wistrich 2002 rightly tends towards showing more understanding for the philosopher, but has difficulty accepting that Nietzsche can be philosophically important and politically dubious.
10. I shall follow the convention in Nietzsche scholarship in not quoting pages, but sections within the books.
11. The innovative philosopher was traditional in his ideas on gender, believing that women needed the authority and guidance of wilful men.

CHAPTER 4

A SINGLE COMMUNAL FAITH THROUGH WAR? THE FIRST WORLD WAR AS A WATERSHED

In 1912, the prominent pacifist Bertha von Suttner wrote: 'War does not continue to exist because there is evil, but because it is considered good.'[1] There was certainly much truth in this statement, at least as far as extreme nationalists in Germany were concerned. As mentioned in Ch. 1, the 'father of the gymnastics movement' Jahn greeted the war against France as a means for raising an awareness of Germanness; Lagarde believed that far-reaching expansionist ambitions would promote the emergence of a national religion; and the Pan-German leader Heinrich Class echoed many militarists when he exclaimed shortly before the war: 'Let us regard war as holy, like the purifying force of fate, for it will awaken in our people all that is great and ready for selfless sacrifice, while it cleanses our soul of the mire of petty egotistical concerns' (1914: 182 f.). Not only did the belief in the inevitability of war spread in the second half of the German Empire (Mommsen 1981), but also the desire for it as a means of unifying the German *Volk* and enabling the nation to achieve the status of a major world power. The young and educated, in particular students and a cultural avant-garde, expected war to intensify human existence by breaking with an allegedly sterile peace-time culture and allowing humans to live according to a 'primordial' will to power. Furthermore, published opinion overwhelmingly expected a positive influence on the morale of the nation as a whole. War was supposed to promote the altruistic willingness for service and sacrifice. While a long peace had allegedly turned the population into a philistine 'herd' satisfied with 'grassing peacefully on a rich meadow', the social scientist Werner Sombart proclaimed, in Nietzschean terminology, that war would open the chance for a great awakening (1977: 424). Even men who were not blind to the horrors of a military conflict between the major powers of Europe could come to feel that it was necessary for a revival of a true German culture. The publisher Eugen Diederichs was quite typical of the majority of public intellectuals in his expectation that the war would overcome the 'materialistic and mechanistic worldview' through a 'renewal of our *völkisch* life' (quoted in Hübinger 1996b: 262 f.). The vision of a spiritually and politically united nation was at the heart of most war-praising publications (Bruendel 2003; Flasch 2000: especially 259–267; Mommsen 1996).

In the early months of the war, many saw their dream of a united *Volk* come true. The vast majority of public intellectuals, writers and artists described August 1914 as a magical moment. With the outbreak of war, they claimed, a divided society had suddenly transformed itself into a tightly knit community. With enthusiasm, they realized what they had in common. They were not naïve about the severity of the situation, but they nevertheless experienced the euphoric sensation of being part of a *Volk* united in taking up weapons and fighting for their fatherland without hesitation.

The only message one heard from the pulpits was the call to support communally the war effort. As always, the Protestant church, in particular, was part of the nationalist fever, claiming that Germany was leading a just war in the name of God. The main minister at the Imperial Court [*Oberhofprediger*], Ernst von Dryander, was quite representative when he preached on the highly popular 'If God be for us, who can be against us?' (Romans 8.31) and commented:

> In looking up to the state, which has brought us up, to the fatherland, in which the roots of our power lie, we know that we go into a battle *for our culture against un-culture [Unkultur], for German ethics against barbarity, for the free German personality bound to God against the instincts of the disorderly mass* ... And God will be with our weapons. (quoted in Scholder 1977: 7. See also Hammer 1971; Missalla 1968)

How did such a strong and widespread belief in a nationwide 'August enthusiasm' emerge? People saw and experienced the many gatherings at news-stands and public houses, where strangers from different social spheres freely communicated. They witnessed spontaneous processions through the city centres, the waving of flags, the singing of patriotic songs, and the applause greeting political and military leaders. They noted with surprise and joy that even the Social Democrats as the feared enemy of the existing order voted in favour of war credits; that the Emperor appreciated everybody's support of the war effort by famously stating: 'I no longer recognize any parties, I know only Germans'; and that the army was overrun by young volunteers wishing to participate in the war.

Published opinion of all persuasions recognized an overwhelming communal 'spirit of 1914' (Mommsen 1994: 114). The historian Meinecke claimed that the German *Volk* had suddenly turned into 'a single, powerful, deeply breathing community' (1914: 29). Alois Riehl, a professor of philosophy at Berlin University, stated: 'Never before was our people so united as in the unforgettable early days of August … The war was preceded by a moral rise of the nation' (*Deutsche Reden* 1914 f.: Vol. I, 207). The theologian Ernst Troeltsch claimed that the call to arms had the magical ring of a 'manly-heroic ethos' (quoted in Flasch 2000: 38). His wife recalled that the sociologist Max Weber characterized the war as 'great and wonderful' (Weber 1950: 571), before he regained his critical faculties later in the war. The writer Carl Zuckmayer, who became a pacifist in the First World War, remembered: 'I have experienced such a physical and moral condition of luminosity and euphoria two or three times since, but never with that sharpness and intensity' (quoted in Leed 1979: 39). Later into the war, a cult (with an appeal even reaching into the working class) would emerge around the successful military leader Hindenburg. 'Its rituals played out in town squares in Berlin and elsewhere, where huge wooden statues of the commander were erected, then plated with metal nails purchased by townspeople with contributions to the Red Cross. "Our Hindenburg" was soon an omnipresent image, a symbol of charismatic authority' (Chickering 1998: 74).

For a long time, historians unquestioningly believed in the so-called 'August-enthusiasm', but a closer look reveals a much more complex picture (Verhey 1997). At the end of July, when the war still seemed avoidable, an estimated half a million had demonstrated for peace. People gathered in the streets because they wanted to catch the latest news, and displays of nationalism emerging in these crowds might have helped to overcome tension and anxiety. The vast majority of people did not have a choice; they thus tried to find a positive meaning in an unavoidable situation. The vision of public intellectuals and later historians alike was largely based on the visually impressive events in big cities and university towns, while a much more subdued atmosphere seems to have reigned – as regional studies have shown – in smaller towns and the countryside. Working-class newspapers expressed grave concern; there was a run on banks; food was stockpiled; and rumours spread about alleged spies. As so often, it was the middle class, especially the young educated male middle class, which was most strongly gripped by nationalist fever. People with access to public media like professors, teachers, ministers, writers and students were also those most positive about the war, generalizing from their experience to talk about the nation as a whole.

Publicly expressed opinion must be distinguished from public opinion, because political and military news were heavily censored during the war and discussion about war aims forbidden. The extreme nationalists cherished the idea of war as such, but more widespread support, including that of the Social Democrats, was gained only because the political leadership succeeded in presenting their offensive goals in defensive disguise. The Russian mobilization in particular helped to present the decision to go to war as forced upon the German people by a reactionary autocratic regime. The 'spirit of 1914' temporarily disguised political divisions, but they re-emerged in even sharper form when the war dragged on.

There is, however, another side to this argument. It is, after all, quite surprising to what extent the government's justification for war found acceptance. The Social Democrats not only pushed aside their long suspicion of German militarism and the monarchic state, but also failed to question seriously the declaration of war in the West and the violation of international law in the attack on neutral Belgium. They supported the Great War without asking for an official statement of a defensive intent, and other nations' (often true) claims of German war atrocities were rejected out of hand (Horne and Kramer 2001). The government found an unprecedented level of trust, showing a surprisingly widespread preparedness for supporting a war which was from the beginning under the control of a political and military leadership unchecked by parliament. In a moment of serious crisis, the primacy of nationalist loyalties became all too clear.

Fearing war and experiencing a sense of enthusiasm about a nation uniting in danger were not mutually exclusive feelings. Many who would have preferred peace to war were not immune to feeling enthusiastic that a nation pulled together in its preparedness to fight. Many young men certainly had far-fetched romantic ideas about war after a good forty years of peace, hoping to experience a manly adventure and a more elemental 'real life',[2] but they also wanted simply to do 'their bit', just as they had learnt from the monumental histories of the wars of liberation and unification. A few younger professors volunteered for war service, but the majority saw their students go and felt that they should at least contribute to the war effort by doing 'war service with the pen'. As Fichte had delivered the 'Speeches to the German Nation' during the Napoleonic wars, many wanted their work to be an idealistic inspiration to the nation at war. They wanted to turn feelings, which the whole nation allegedly held intuitively, into a conscious 'communal experience' and a new communal belief (*Deutsche Reden* 1914 f.: VIII f.).

Attacks from abroad brought the cultural world in Germany together in declarations of solidarity to their government. Responding to the claims of foreign colleagues that German anti-democratic militarism was responsible for a war of aggression and war crimes, the stars of German academia rose to refute the claim in a public declaration 'To the Cultural World', stating a repeated 'it is not true' to all the allegations in an act of faith without ever considering the evidence. In a similar vein, a 'Declaration of the German University Lecturers of the German Empire', which was signed by 4,000 professors, claimed: 'In the German army no other spirit reigns than in the German people, because both are one, and we are also part of it … Our belief is that the whole of European culture is dependent on the victory which German 'militarism' will gain, on the free German people's discipline, loyalty and willingness for sacrifice' (reprinted in Böhme 1975: 49). This declaration, which was signed, it is estimated, by about 80 per cent of all professors (Bruendel 2003), thus not only claimed an insoluble identity of all citizens with their army, but also a mission for Germany to save European culture by force against the will of the others. Not only for extremists like Chamberlain, but right into the mainstream of German academic culture, the claim of cultural superiority became a legitimation for military aggression.

Apart from uncritical solidarity with the German war effort, what was the content of the wave of poems and speeches delivered and published in the early weeks and months of the war? It is of course always risky to generalize from a huge corpus of texts[3] written by people of very different persuasions. An analysis of the speeches of highly respected professors of Berlin University, published in 1914 and 1915 under the title *Deutsche Reden*, reveals, however, a number of recurring themes. Above all, the speeches stressed a feeling of national solidarity in the moment of danger, in the hope that such an emphasis could promote a more lasting unity based on the recognition of a set of truly German convictions. Anonymous and alienated individuals had become, the academics believed, integral parts of a wider whole. When writers expressed a sense of euphoria, it was first and foremost about the sense that deeply divided individuals, ideological groups and social classes had at last united again in fighting for a national task: 'All of us felt', Alois Riehl claimed, 'that everybody lived for the whole, and the whole lived in each of us. Our narrow self with its personal interests disappeared into the great historical self of the nation. The fatherland calls! The parties disappear ... Thus a moral elevation of the *Volk* preceded the war' (*Deutsche Reden* 1914 f.: Vol. 1, 207). In the same vein, Riehl's colleague Gierke stated: 'Blown away from the breeze of world history were all the divisions, all party quarrels, all petty egoism, all unpatriotic behaviour. Every individual came to feel nothing but part of the whole' (*Deutsche Reden* 1914 f.: Vol 1, 88 f.).

A strengthened sense of community went, as the quotations illustrate, hand in hand with the belief in a moral or religious elevation. Cultural critics had lamented constantly about a growing materialism and egotistical hedonism. Now it was hoped, however, that the war would serve, in Rudolf Eucken's words, as a 'purification and regeneration, as an experience of the whole and the ideal' (quoted in Flasch 2000: 23). The novelist Thomas Mann was quite representative in rejoicing about the destruction of the 'dreadful world' of the pre-war years for a more authentic communal existence. 'War! It was a cleansing, a liberation that we experienced, and an incredible hope. ... It was the unprecedented, the powerful and enthusiastic unification of the nation in readiness for a fundamental trial – a readiness, a radical determination, which might not have been known before in the history of nations' (1915: 12–15). The war was supposed to evoke heroic courage and a willingness to sacrifice in the service of an ultimate ideal. In essence, the euphoric, often semi-religious glorification of the 'spirit of 1914' was based on the belief that the long-cherished ideal of a *Volk* united in a single communal purpose had at last become reality. All the modern means now allegedly gained a higher meaning in the service of the nation in arms. While Wilhelmine Germany had allegedly been lost in an egotistical materialism devoid of a higher communal meaning, the war appeared as the moment of regeneration. In the face of essential danger, Germans had mobilized, so the legend went, the best of their ethnic traits. This turned a divided society into a true community where every member felt part of the whole again and contributed selflessly to the common good.

The cry for a spiritual unity and a single faith does not have to be connected with an aggressive nationalism, but an increasingly ruthless and destructive war led to a highly polarized concept of national identities, where German culture was starkly contrasted with Western civilization. Thomas Mann was most influential in formulating and promoting this distinction. 'Culture is', he claimed, 'a closed order, style, form, attitude, taste, is any certain spiritual organization of one's world', while civilization is 'rationality, enlightenment, pacification, moralization, scepticism, decomposition' (1993: 188; more generally, Albrecht 1993). In such a view, the West came to stand for a dominance of instrumental reason combined with an enlightened scepticism with regard to metaphysics, a materialist pragmatism favouring a capitalist market economy, a primacy of individualism with an emphasis on liberal rights and a hedonistic wish for a comfortable life. In contrast, German culture was said to stand for the primacy of the community over the individual, willingness for service instead of demands for individual rights, heroism instead of materialism and the need for a deeper meaning and mission in life. The war speeches vehemently rejected the old label of Germany as a '*Volk* of poets and thinkers' (after all, this would have been a defeatist war slogan!), but they insisted that it did not fight for material goals, but for ideals. The West was seen to stand for a secular rationality, individual rights and capitalism, while Germany was said to be distinct in being metaphysical, even religious, and community-oriented. Following 1914, a greatly increased number of people came to regard the desire for a single faith uniting a national community as the essence of Germanness.

The polarized distinction between civilisation and culture marked a crucial ideological shift. The aspects of the modern epoch that were rejected were externalized by shifting the blame on to the Western nations. Allegedly, their world-view had emerged with the capitalist revolution in Britain and the political revolution in France. The nineteenth century had been their epoch, shaped by what now came to be called the 'ideas of 1789'. While these allegedly alien ideas had long infiltrated German life, the war opened the opportunity to recover the essence of Germanness. Not the West, but the 'ideas of 1914' were to shape the future, of Germany and beyond.

The 'ideas of 1914' – a term coined by the political scientist Johannes Plenge which quickly gained general currency – were born from the enmity of war. Assuming evil intentions in the military opponents served to legitimize formerly unacceptable levels of hatred, which presented itself in the morally more acceptable form of 'holy wrath' (Ziemann, forthcoming). 'May God punish England' became a common form of greeting, and all war measures including poisonous gas and unlimited submarine warfare (leading to many civilian casualties) seemed justified. Ultimately, however, the 'ideas of 1914' neither harked back to old German ways, nor were they intended to overwrite developments instigated by the 'age of revolution' (Eric Hobsbawm). Rather, the new ideas should transcend the nineteenth century by progressing towards a higher synthesis: personal freedom plus social harmony, modern means serving higher ideals, practical successes combined with a sense of community, instrumental reason integrated into a secure metaphysical world-view. Truly German values were seen as the core values needed at this historical moment where liberalism would be superseded by a more communal spirit. They were, allegedly, typically German, but also the highest universal ideas. As their fatherland had preserved, German nationalists claimed, these communal traits more than the Western European states in the age of liberalism and individualism, it was in an ideal position to lead the way in this cultural turn towards a harmonious community united in one faith – and this was supposedly confirmed by the 'August-enthusiasm', where the moment of danger was seen to have reawakened the best of Germanness: solidarity and the willingness to serve the nation, even if this meant the highest sacrifice. The new spirit of togetherness and heroism was to inspire the creation of a new Germany and ultimately a new world in which societies and states would turn into harmonious national communities united in solidarity and a communal world-view. Thus the philosopher and Nobel Prize winner for literature Rudolf Eucken could argue in his work *The World-Historic Importance of the German Spirit* that 'the future of humanity depended' on the further development of German culture (quoted in Flasch 2000: 27), and Meinecke believed that Germany fought to preserve its ideals 'for the world' (1958a: 81).

The claim *Am deutschen Wesen soll die Welt genesen* ('The German Spirit shall cure the world')[4] resounded in many war speeches, describing a German mission to spread a superior culture across the world for the benefit of humanity as a whole. In August 1914, the speakers argued, Germany had experienced a collective willingness to sacrifice life and limb for the community and its ideals. If such an emotion could gain permanency through social, cultural and, above all, spiritual reforms, then Germany would progress to an unprecedented perfection, which would then serve other nations as an exemplum. The spontaneous 'spirit of 1914' had to be turned into more clearly defined 'ideas of 1914' as the basis of a new and better community of the people. The war was thus perceived as a *Kulturkrieg* or 'war between cultures' (Beßlich 2000). With this argument, expansionist aims found a pseudo-idealistic justification. German interests were, nationalists claimed, identical with the true interests of humanity at large.

While Western propaganda portrayed the Great War as a battle against a militaristic autocratic regime to make the world safe for peace and democracy, German intellectuals glorified allegedly German communitarian values. They even took it upon themselves to defend precisely those values that opponents had singled out for criticism. Responding to the claim that the Imperial army's criminal actions violated all the values German culture had previously upheld, the war speeches tried to show the identity of German militarism and culture. The most pointed statement in support of this claim was the war publication *Händler und Helden* or 'Traders and Heroes' by the famous sociologist Werner Sombart. Many colleagues were surprised by this highly partisan contribution to war propaganda, because before 1914 Sombart had been rather dismissive of the German Empire and any nationalist praise of it. Like many, he lamented a lack of idealism. He not only believed that the mass of the population was lost in a spiritually empty hedonism, but also dismissed the political Right's emphasis on communal values by claiming that 'what is being presented as nationalism today is shallow and recycled' (quoted in Lenger 1996: 65. More generally Lenger 1994).

August 1914, however, completely changed Sombart's attitude towards the German nation. His conviction that the Germans had risen to the challenge of this historical moment made him more optimistic about a future where Germany would win the war and shape the world. Throwing aside all scholarly caution, he claimed an absolute insight into the motivations of friends and foes alike to give a sweeping account of the war as a clash between two fundamental human traits. It had taken the moment of danger, he argued, but also historic national characteristics to make the German people so prepared to fight for their country. 'The old German heroic spirit, which had only smouldered under the ashes suddenly flared up into a flame' (1915: 117). Spontaneously rising to Germany's defence, the citizens had proven, at least to Sombart's satisfaction, that they were still heroes at heart. However, such an idealistic attitude had not been present, he believed, in the most despised enemy, Great Britain. For this country, the war supposedly had no other purpose than any other business enterprise, namely profit.

Generalizing from his interpretation of the war, Sombart came to distinguish two types of human beings: traders and heroes, as 'the two poles of all human orientations' (1915: 64). While Germans were the prime example of an heroic attitude, Britain and the United States were the quintessential traders. The 'hollow English traders' culture' came to stand for everything he despised about modern times: a materialist lack of ideals, hedonism and capitalism. In contrast, a heroic attitude was associated with idealism, courage and obedient service to the nation. The war, he hoped, would be a lesson for Germany to maintain a culture in harmony with the best of their national traits. 'By no means do we want to expand, because we have more important things to do. We have to develop our own spiritual being, have to keep the German soul pure, have to take care that the enemy, the trader spirit, nowhere enters our mentality: not from the outside and not from the inside' (1915: 144f.).

Sombart remained vague about the future form a German state should take. He no longer had a problem with 'technological progress', as long as it seemed to serve higher nationalist ideas (Sombart 1915: 125), and lead towards a strong, hierarchical and self-sufficient Germany. But he claimed emphatically that the Germans would be infinitely superior to all the other nations if they succeeded in becoming true heroes. This would make them 'the chosen people of this century', who would give shape to a better future (Sombart 1915: 142. See also ibid. 143).

Sombart's ideas had a great impact on public discussion, but very few accepted them as a whole. The extreme Right rejected his dismissal of expansionist war aims, while his more moderate colleagues did not agree with such an undifferentiated attack on Anglo-Saxon culture. However, the succinctly formulated value distinction between traders and heroes hit a nerve at the time and proceeded to become a commonly used slogan. After all, the previously discussed 'Declaration of the German University Lecturers of the German Empire' showed a majority of German professors supporting the claim that the army was not only a necessary evil to defend Germany against its many enemies, but also the prime promoter of essential human traits: 'The whole of European culture is dependent on the victory which German "militarism" will gain, the discipline, loyalty and preparedness for sacrifice of the united free German *Volk*' (reprinted in Böhme 1975: 49).

I have quoted this passage a second time because it not only shows the centrality of 'militarism' as an alleged cure for the ills of the modern world, but also indicates a second core theme, the so-called 'German freedom'. Confronted with the accusation that Germany had always lacked freedom in the sense of liberal rights for its citizens, many war writers[5] responded by claiming a higher form of freedom for German culture. In France, Ernst Troeltsch argued, freedom meant a mechanistic equality; in England, space for the individual to make money (Flasch 2000: 55–58). For France, Chamberlain stated, freedom meant a complete disregard of communal values; for England, the right to walk on the grass and conquer other countries (1914: Ch. *Deutsche Freiheit*). More generally, many war writers criticized what they called a Western idea of freedom as negative and socially destructive. Western political thought, they argued, focused on freeing the individual from any communal bonds and restrictions, thus promoting anonymity and alienation, a lack of personal meaning and no sense of community. Focusing on removing all obligations, this sense of freedom not only neglected a sense of duty to the nation, but also left the individual exposed to the slavery of base instincts and arbitrary whims instead of promoting the normative idea of a right way of life. In contrast, Germany's war ideology drew on Kant in formulating a 'German idea of freedom' as a voluntary decision to fulfil one's moral obligations and duties. True freedom, the argument went, meant a state of harmony between individual and community, where everyone was happy to follow the communal norms and serve the nation. Such a freedom was not about protecting the individual from the state, but about the voluntary acceptance of social obligations to realize a higher form of existence within the larger community. It was not about social and political equality, but about accepting one's station in society. It demanded a community which deserved acceptance, but it proclaimed the primacy of a functioning community over its members, 'a communal spirit of comradeship' in the attempt to live according to worthy ideals (Plenge 1916: 142).

Ernst Troeltsch demanded in December 1914: 'Be German, remain German, become German!' (quoted in Flasch 2000: 59). Such a sense of Germanness was evoked by most war writers – in particular the primacy of the community over the individual and a heroic preparedness to serve the nation – but they largely kept a gentlemanly distance from concrete suggestions. There were some, however, who considered in more detail how the 'spirit of 1914' could gain permanency beyond the immediate military threat. After all, a new organization of the nation was called for if Germany was to lead the way towards overcoming a capitalism which allegedly destroyed a sense of idealism and communal purpose. The new visions, which gained wide currency in the early years of the war, have been variously called communal or social economy (*Gemeinwirtschaft*), war socialism, national socialism, Prussian socialism or German socialism, but they all shared the conviction that the state should become more active in trying to provide an ideal basis for the growth of a national community. Blaming an uncontrolled capitalism for class conflict and economic crisis, they wanted to replace it with a more just and efficient system. The freedom of economic actors should be limited in favour of more social harmony. Strongly rejecting Marxism – in particular the ideas of class conflict, revolution and a dictatorship of the proletariat, which all went against the ideal of a harmonious national community – they wanted the state to promote social justice as prerequisite for achieving a spiritually united nation.

One key promoter of economic change was Johann Plenge (Beßlich 2000: 261–326; Schildt 1987). Rejecting both Marxism and the 'ideas of 1789' (that is, the emphasis on individuality, democracy and an unrestricted market economy), he promoted a 'German way' with a strong state promoting efficiency and social justice. Most of his ideas were in place before the war, but they gained wider popularity when he marketed them under the new label 'ideas of 1914'. The war confirmed, he argued, that his earlier diagnosis had been correct: the inevitability of a move towards a more rational organization of industry under the direction of the state.

Following the gist of the many war proclamations, Plenge stressed the primacy of the community over the individual. Against the French Revolution's banner of 'freedom, equality and brotherhood', he propagated allegedly German communitarian values: '"Contribute!" is the freedom of action! "Fit in" is the equality of service! "Live within the whole" is the brotherhood of socialism!' (1916: 9) Taking on board the popular concept of a 'German freedom', he advocated 'a social idea of freedom, the freedom of consciously fitting into the social structure recognized as necessary'. Against the quest for individual happiness, he proclaimed a 'primacy of order, authority, discipline' (quoted in Beßlich 2000: 298, 280). His ideal was an economy directed by an efficient state bureaucracy to create a true national community.

Plenge's first principle was not the *Volk*, but the authoritarian state. The citizens were to serve, while a technocratic elite was to rule. Instead of an unstructured free market economy finding its way by trial and error, he believed in organizing material reproduction like one smooth-running machine. He called his advocacy of a strong state which would promote efficiency and social justice 'socialism', but his belief in a rational ruling elite, which would not be politically controlled by the people, obviously gave his intentions an authoritarian character. Believing in rational organization, he did not value ethnic traditions, but anticipated the emergence of an efficiently structured hierarchical and technocratic state.

Quite a diverse group of people acknowledged Plenge's importance in promoting the idea of social justice within a strong state: right-wing Social Democrats, for example Konrad Haenisch, Heinrich Cunow, Paul Lench and Kurt Schumacher, Conservative Revolutionaries like Arthur Moeller van den Bruck and Max Hildebert Boehm, as well as the Nazis Ernst Krieck, Gottfried Feder and Eduard Stadtler (Beßlich 2000: 322 f.). By far the most influential in promoting a communal economy, however, was Walther Rathenau, who not only put forward more detailed and original ideas than Plenge, but also had opportunities to implement them (Brenner 2005; Rohkrämer 1999: 71–116). This highly successful 'Jack of all trades' was director of the major electrical company AEG and also showed ambitions in the political sphere. In 1914 he was put in charge of organizing the change from a peacetime to a war economy. Although Rathenau stayed in office only until the organizational structure was in place, he unquestionably played a crucial role in preparing Germany for a longer war by directing, through political control, scarce raw materials into war-relevant sectors of production. As minister in the early Weimar Republic, he was assassinated in the summer of 1922. Right-wing extremists killed him because he was a Jew and stood for the acceptance of the Versailles treaty. Even his murderers believed, however, that he could give 'faith', 'form' and 'will' to the nation – but feared this, because it would strengthen the hated Republic (Salomon 1933: 302).

Rathenau was not only a leading figure in the practical world, but also a highly successful author. His pre-war critique of current conditions (*Zur Kritik der Zeit*) went through 18 editions in ten years, his book on the war industry (*Deutschlands Rohstoffversorgung*) through 25 editions in one year and his predictions about the future of society (*Von kommenden Dingen*) through 66 editions in five years. The philosopher Karl Jaspers called him and Oswald Spengler 'the most noted mirrors of our time' (1979: 16), and one of the main protagonists in Robert Musil's novel *Man without Qualities* (1930), Dr Paul Arnheim, is a representation of Rathenau. A decade after his death, the Conservative Revolution's leading journal *Die Tat* drew heavily on Walther Rathenau's ideas in formulating their response to the world economic crisis.[6]

For a successful man of the world, Rathenau was surprisingly critical of his time. While accepting 'mechanization' (his term for modern technology, instrumental reason and the drive for efficiency) as inevitable to feed a growing population, he attacked the concomitant social and cultural developments: the destruction of historic buildings, the decline of the arts and a loss of morality. Religious devotion, idealism and emotional attachment were allegedly fading away, making modern humans 'restless and socially distracted, changeable, in need of dabbling in fashionable thoughts' (1977: 21). Modern industry was potentially beneficial, he argued, but in order to avoid dangerous social and cultural side-effects the nation needed a non-capitalist ethos of love, respect and a sense of duty. A communal life based on 'devotion and sacrifice', on service to the nation instead of capitalist competition, would make it possible to realize a higher form of existence combining the modern material achievements with a renewed emphasis on morality, beauty and social harmony (Rathenau 1977: 69).

Before 1914, Rathenau placed his hopes mainly on a cultural change which would lead people to recognize the primacy of spiritual values: 'It is wonderful to know that the overcoming of material desires, which is no sacrifice for any truly cultured person, is enough to free humanity from the crazy cycle of mechanization and to open new ways … Material work remains serious … but it loses its prime importance, the depressing control over every hour of life … Humans will rise again and look to the stars; they will be friends with their fellow human beings, with their surroundings and with other forces in the world' (1977: 284). With the First World War, however, he came to believe that powerful historical developments were working towards realizing his own ideals. While Rathenau lamented in 1914 that the war was a human disaster and a grave danger for the future of Germany, he also saw it as a chance for achieving a higher and more satisfying level of communal existence. He was all ready to implement strict state control because he had always been critical of a free market economy. While the move towards a state-directed economy was mainly forced upon the political, military and economic leadership as an inevitable reaction to wartime shortages in raw materials and the production of essential goods, Rathenau also saw it as an opportunity for speeding up the development towards a more community-oriented future. In his eyes, the reforms were just the beginning of a fundamental change which would destroy 'the gods which the world before August 1914 had worshipped' (quoted in Schulin 1977: 558). He anticipated that capitalist competition would have to make room for a communal economy characterized by stronger state control, corporate structures and extensive social regulations. An economy in which the state would hold the ultimate power should guarantee social harmony. The emphasis on the common good would turn all citizens, rich and poor alike, into dutiful servants of the state.

The practical changes Rathenau proposed could not satisfy true socialists, but were surprisingly radical for an industrial magnate. He demanded an 'extensive, in parts nearly prohibitive, system of income duties, taxes and levies' to restrict luxury consumption, the prevention of speculation through controls and taxes, an extremely progressive property and income tax and the prohibition of every inheritance 'above a moderate property'. Equal career opportunities should both increase social justice and make more efficient use of the nation's human potential. The state was supposed to ensure that priority was given to the common good. As 'the economy is not a private, but a public measure', the state should have extensive power to prevent any inefficient, egoistic and malevolent use of entrepreneurial freedom (Rathenau 1977: 370, 373, 368, 348), for example through enforcing rationalization and closing down inefficient companies. In short, Rathenau developed a comprehensive technocratic programme for a state-directed economy. Organizing the state as a single smoothly running machine was seen not only as more efficient, but also as a necessary prerequisite for promoting social justice and encouraging an idealistic spirit of solidarity and service.

While Rathenau accused a capitalist market economy of promoting egotism and enmity, a socially just state economy would basically allow for a continuation of the 'spirit of 1914': conditions under which everybody was happy to work for the common good. Solidarity and trust between the citizens would create a community which was more than just a mechanical sum of its parts. A new spirituality or communal faith would lead to a *Reich der Seele* ('Empire of the soul'). A clear communal will would turn 'the blind play of forces into a conscious, free and truly humane cosmos' (Rathenau 1977: 322).

Rathenau's quick formulation of his economic 'ideas of 1914' as well as the public interest in them was partly due to the obvious needs of the war situation. But the ground had been prepared before the war. Many technical enthusiasts had long expressed scepticism about capitalism. It seemed to hinder the realization of important technical ideas due to a capitalist demand for immediate profits, it seemed to get in the way of an efficient economy of scale, because the same goods were produced in different companies, and it seemed to promote wasteful aberrations due to a lack of centralized planning. For technicians and engineers it was only a logical consequence of their work to develop the vision of a national economy organized as a single efficient machine. Furthermore, the German Empire was marked by a change towards corporate capitalism, with many companies merging or forming cartels. Altogether there was a widespread belief, also shared by Marxism, that the historical trend was towards concentration and planning. The majority of independent observers regarded this as a positive development, because they believed that the national economy would profit from the replacement of the chaos of competition with an over-arching economic strategy.

But there was also powerful opposition to a planned national economy. The greater majority of industrialists, whilst being open to the merging of companies, to cartels, and to agreements with the state to reduce profit-limiting competition and achieve reliable conditions for investments, were eager to maintain capitalist independence. The emergency of war made them prepared to accept an enlarged state role in economic matters, but only as a strictly temporary measure. Faced with the widespread interest in the ideas of Rathenau, Plenge and like-minded people such as the economist Wichard von Moellendorf, Gerhart von Schulze-Gaevernitz, Edgar Jaffé and Werner Sombart, employers started a big campaign attacking the measures 'against which the most radical demands of socialist revolutionaries appear comparatively harmless' (quoted in Schulin 1977: 580). Their goal was a speedy return to a peacetime economy after the end of the war (Kocka 1984: 110; Zunkel 1974: 31, 99 and passim).

A continuation of the war economy after 1918 never stood a real chance. Both employers and trade unions vehemently opposed it because it had led to gross mismanagement and social injustices. Nevertheless, the ideas maintained their importance in the future because they remained attractive especially to civil servants, the military and the educated middle class. A communal economy promised a third way between Marxism and an unregulated market economy, a way similar to that for which the imperial *Verein für Socialpolitik* ('Association for

Social Policy') had searched. With such an economic organization, a strong state would be able to overcome class divisions and the most severe social injustices; an idea particularly attractive to all those searching for a nation united in a single faith. A communal economy promised an end to the danger of social revolt and protection for a middle class which felt squeezed between powerful employers' and working class associations; it raised the hope that a competitive society based on self-interest could be replaced by a more humane cooperative and 'organic' society; and it promised nationalistically and militaristically minded people the possibility of preparing an economically strengthened Germany for a new and more successful war. The long-standing desire to reduce social tensions and unite the nation in a communal faith had become even stronger with the war, because unity came to be seen as a prerequisite for a strong Germany. Germany's defeat, revisionist enemies of the Versailles Treaty argued, only re-enforced the need for government control over the economy to prepare Germany for a future war. If self-sufficiency was seen as necessary against another future trade blockade and if industry should always be capable of changing instantaneously to war production, then an economy directed by the state appeared the most appropriate solution.

The belief in a state-directed communal economy was not limited to the political Right. After the war, Rathenau offered his services to the new Republic, and many engineers of different political persuasions supported such a trend towards a technocratic organization of society (Willeke 1995). It did, however, have a particular attraction for extreme conservatives. A communal economy appeared to be the ideal basis for a harmonious national community in which a single communal faith could emerge. Undogmatic representatives of the Right were also open to the argument that the First World War had proven the superior efficiency of such a communal economy or, as Oswald Spengler called it, 'Prussian Socialism' (1919). Despite all the problems connected with the war economy, for which one could largely blame the improvised character of the measures, members of the extreme Right were convinced that the difficult times had proven the need for more planning. Only a state-directed economy would be able to cope with the demands of a long war of attrition in the industrial age. In this line of argument, the deprivation of the population and the desolate state of the economy in 1918 were negligible in comparison with the economy's ability to maintain the war effort against the enemy's superior economic forces for four years.

Parts of the political Right thus recognized the need for more social justice to maintain national unity and a readiness for sacrifice. Others, however, remained uncompromising. Those sharing the ideas of the Pan-German leader Heinrich Class, who had promoted a *coup d'état* to establish a right-wing dictatorship before the war, never accepted the call for postponing domestic conflicts to achieve a united war front. The political truce proclaimed by the Kaiser and his Chancellor Bethmann-Hollweg had to remain fragile, because it failed to disguise fundamental political disagreements. While the stubborn forces on the Right simply expected the mass of the population to obey orders and serve their country in the war without asking questions or wanting anything in return, the Social Democrats, and to a lesser extent other reformist forces, naturally had a very different agenda. If the common people were expected to die for their country, they argued, they could not remain second-class citizens. The war was thus used to further democratization, especially to overcome the Prussian three-class voting system, which strongly privileged the rich. The war also demanded a smooth-running economy, which meant the need for a compliant workforce despite the many deprivations such as the increased burden on women with men away from home, longer working hours, a reduction in real wages and severe food shortages. The need for social harmony increased the power of the trade unions, possibly setting, some hoped and others feared, a precedent for the post-war period. The most explosive topic was, however, the war itself. While all parties had voted for the war credits in August 1914, the Social Democrats had accepted the need to defend the country, while the Right saw the conflict as an opportunity to establish Germany's hegemony in Europe. Uncompromising conservatives were thus bound to see the 'spirit of 1914' with highly ambivalent feelings.[7]

Large parts of the Right were never prepared to set back their own political goals in favour of a national truce. In particular, representatives from agriculture, heavy industry, economic middle class associations and the national leagues, which had been behind the anti-socialist 'cartel of the productive estates' in 1913, immediately formulated uncompromising policy goals. A triumphant end to the war, which, they believed, was within Germany's reach if it acted with ruthless determination, would offer the best opportunity to destroy the socialist working-class movement and establish Germany as a world power with hegemony at least over continental Europe. 'External security and a domestic rebirth of our *Volk*' was achievable, Heinrich Class argued, only if a decisive victory was achieved (quoted in Hagenlücke 1997: 50). In a memorandum he called for the annexation of Belgium as well as large French and Russian territories. France's role as a major power should end, Russia should be forced back behind the borders of Peter the Great, and Great Britain's power should be decisively weakened. Calling for ethnic cleansing, he wanted territory without people so that there would be space to resettle Germans on the land.

The government confiscated Class's petition – which he had sent to 2,000 people – because it tried to avoid any politically explosive war aim discussion. But this did not stop the Pan-Germans (supported by the Agricultural League, heavy industry and important parts of the National Liberal Party) to continue putting forth roughly identical demands. They initiated, for example, a petition of intellectuals from 8 July 1915 with the call for annexations. In response, more moderate forces published an opposing petition the next day, which expressed trust in the government and rejected the annexation of politically independent nations. The initial unity was thus soon broken, with an overwhelming majority of the intellectuals (1,347 compared to 141) supporting the annexationist camp (Hagenlücke 1997: 69).

Political conflict continued to increase throughout the war. The war ministry worked with the trade unions to organize the war economy in a form acceptable to the workers, because it believed, not unlike Plenge and Rathenau, that the best mobilization for the war effort could happen only with and not against the working class. In contrast, the military leaders Hindenburg and Ludendorff followed a much more dictatorial pro-employer line by trying to place workers under the army's jurisdiction to mobilize them, despite low wages, through military discipline and coercion. With the weakening of Chancellor Bethmann-Hollweg the demand for far-reaching expansionist war aims increasingly entered the public sphere, while, simultaneously, a growing number of people started to have doubts about a victory. The SPD fell apart, with the more radical anti-war forces forming an Independent Social Democratic Party. To the horror of the traditional right-wing hardliners, the Kaiser was persuaded to promise constitutional reform towards more democracy for the end of the war to appease the population. While the annexationists advocated the appointment of a new and tougher chancellor, parliament tried to increase its political influence. In 'a spectacular act of parliamentary defiance' the so-called 'Peace Resolution' was passed in July 1917. Over the protests of the chancellor, Hindenburg and Ludendorff, the majority of Catholic Members of Parliament joined forces with the Majority Social Democrats and Progressives in demanding a 'peace of understanding and the permanent reconciliation of the peoples' – in essence a negotiated and moderate peace (Chickering 1998: 164).

Ideas about a party uniting all right-wing annexationists first emerged in 1915, and the peace resolution was the final trigger. The later leader of a right-wing coup against the Weimar Republic, Wolfgang Kapp, was the decisive force, and Chief Admiral Alfred von Tirpitz the figure-head in the German Fatherland Party founded in September 1917. The party wanted to provide an umbrella for all individuals and associations in favour of continuing the war to a victorious end. In essence, all those previously active in formulating far-reaching war aims also provided the main drive behind the new party. It did not put forward candidates for election or formulate a precise programme, because it wanted to unite a variety of political persuasions, but the general direction was unmistakable. Dismissing parliamentary opinion, it sided with the military leadership of Hindenburg and Ludendorff in demanding a ruthless totalization of warfare to achieve a victory which would confirm Germany's hegemony in Europe and its world-power status. It thus claimed the attribute of patriotism for an aggressively anti-democratic[8] and expansionist policy, while classifying the widespread social unrest towards the end of the war as treason. Socialism remained the main enemy, and any suggestion of social compromise was rejected as a dangerous precedent for a post-war order. Its policy was still marked by the same paradox as that of the pre-war Pan-Germans. While following a populist strategy, its political ideals tended towards an authoritarian dictatorship with a complete disregard for the wishes and opinions of the citizens. It promoted neither a charismatic leader nor the ideal of a *völkisch* community to gain popularity, but tended towards the ideas Heinrich Class had formulated in 1912: a powerful monarch advised by a circle of nationalistically minded notables.

The Fatherland Party grew quickly. Internal figures claimed membership of nearly 300,000 in February 1918 and roughly 800,000 in September of the same year. While these figures are certainly somewhat inflated due to the full inclusion of the many corporate members (Hagenlücke 1997: 180), the Fatherland Party certainly constituted the most successful unification attempt of the German Empire's political Right which had started with the 'cartel of the productive estates' of 1913. This umbrella organization in favour of a ruthless war effort quickly fell apart, however, with military capitulation. Despite its initial successes, the party shared the same weakness as all the other Imperial right-wing organizations. Led by notables, it was quite elitist, thus failing to make inroads into the working class. Wolfgang Kapp's botched coup against the Weimar Republic in 1920 revealed once again that such a non-populist and anti-social dictatorial line stood no chance of success. Helped by the free corps and the army's neutrality, the rebels could seize power, but the coup faltered within days through a general strike because Kapp lacked any wider public backing.

The Fatherland Party was a major political force towards the end of the war, but it also showed the limits of such a political position. It succeeded in mobilizing the traditional nationalist circles, but had no chance to reach the workers. Adolf Hitler made a valid point when he later scorned these 'notables of the Right' (James Retallack) for their anti-social and elitist aloofness, and the old hand Junius Alter, who had been active in national leagues since pre-war times, noted self-critically in 1930:

> Gone are the days when one passed resolutions in a membership meeting or provoked a storm in a teacup in similar ways. What impact can a resolution, a petition, even a general meeting have today, when the [veterans' association] Stahlhelm or the Nazis demonstrate at the same time in the streets with the numerical size of five military corps at war! The mass has become the trump card. Political life has found new forms, the power of arms and fists often count more ... than the most substantial speech. All the old clubs and associations, in which Class matured politically, have basically lost their importance in comparison with the uniformed armies in anoraks or brown shirts ... In their political, economic and, above all, social ideas the spirit of a younger generation is starting to spread its wings towards still distant and foggy goals. (quoted in Hagenlücke 1997: 411)

The traditional conservative political style still continued to exist in the Weimar Republic, in particular in the conservative party DNVP, which many members of the Fatherland Party joined after 1918. The 'spirit of 1914' and the 'ideas of 1914' played, however, a much more important role in the formation of a more innovative extreme Right which succeeded in becoming the most popular political movement in Germany (Fritzsche 1998). While an 'August enthusiasm', which united the whole nation in a single communal national faith, never existed in 1914, it came to play a very real and powerful role as a historical legend. The writer and pacifist Stefan Zweig, for example, remembered the 'enthusiasm' of triumphant young recruits and cheering crowds, which had 'a great, entrancing and even seductive power' (1955: 206 f.). Similarly, the Nazi leader Adolf Hitler wrote:

> The struggle of the year 1914 was not forced on the masses – no, by the living God– it was desired by the whole people ... To me those hours seemed like a release from the painful feelings of my youth. Even today I am not ashamed to say that, overpowered by stormy enthusiasm, I fell down on my knees and thanked Heaven from an overflowing heart for granting me the good fortune of being permitted to live at this time. (Hitler 1992: 148)

The search for a single communal faith seemed more realistic and concrete now. As many believed that such unanimity of minds had ruled at the beginning of war, they also saw a chance for its return. 'August 1914' became a core ideal to strive for. If even the workers had been prepared to support the endangered nation, then, many nationalists believed, a true national community must be achievable, if only such a special moment would not be destroyed by re-emerging political and social conflicts. While Hindenburg, Ludendorff and the Fatherland Party still eyed the working class with suspicion, others drew the conviction from August 1914 that the whole nation could truly become a tightly knit community of fate. While one could conclude from the quick reappearance of the conflict that the political opposition had to be brutally suppressed, another lesson was to call for more social justice to create a sound basis for national solidarity. In contrast to Marxism, such ideas of a communal economy or a national socialism still proclaimed the need for hierarchy and social inequality, but they fought against stark social injustices. The well-off should not be arrogant towards manual labour, and everybody should be able to gain a "fair" income allowing for a decent and honourable life, also to make the common people feel that they had a stake in the nation. While the Right generally believed in a harder line against oppositional forces, its more open-minded representatives came to conclude that a communal economy or a national socialism was a necessary prerequisite for achieving a harmonious society. Thus right-wing nationalism was more than ever encouraged to incorporate the call for social justice into its ideal of a national community.

The belief that war would promote unity and a single national faith had a long tradition. The Napoleonic wars promoted, it was believed, the rise of a German nationalism, the wars with Denmark, Austria and France led to unification and an unprecedented acceptance of a conservative nationalism, the imperialist call for a 'place under the sun' met with enthusiasm at the turn of the century, and at least large parts of the middle class were gripped by a sense of unity in August 1914. The lesson seemed clear: expansionist goals and a war (at least, when it was short and successful), were the ideal means for uniting the nation within a single communal purpose and faith.

While the hope for a single communal faith gained a new concreteness through the legend which developed around August 1914, there was also the undeniable reality of a bitter war and defeat. War had produced social conflict on an unprecedented level, until all authority collapsed in revolution (Kocka 1984). In that sense, the Right concluded, German society had failed the test of war. Before 1914, the dream of a nation united in a single faith could still appear as a bit of a luxury, but with war and defeat it came to be regarded as a political necessity. If one wanted to avoid another revolution, if one wanted to prepare the country for another war to overcome the shackles of the Versailles treaty and re-establish Germany as a major power (a conviction held far beyond the political Right), achieving national unity had to appear as the first essential step. Consequently, post-war Germany was always expected to achieve an unprecedented level of social, cultural and political harmony, although this was obviously a goal which a Republic struggling with the consequences of a lost war could never even come close to achieving.

Not only believers in progress towards a more peaceful and humane world experienced the First World War as '*the* great seminal catastrophe' (Kennan 1979: 3) starting the twentieth century proper; the political Right in Germany did so, too. The war had obviously defied all their plans and expectations, turning all actors into helpless sorcerer's apprentices. While the Right had hoped for a short and successful war, the country had slipped into a long and bitter conflict. 'The war was a demon which demolished all pathos' (Fischer 1934: 6), because it was marked by an unprecedented destructiveness defying all strategic planning. While the Franco-Prussian war had cost about 150,000 lives, estimates put the death toll of the First World War at 20 million. In Germany alone, about 13 million men became soldiers, of which 2 million died. About 60 per cent had to leave service at least once because they were wounded or ill (Bessel 1993: 5 ff.; Eksteins 1990: 100, 144; Schulin 1994). Most Germans must have experienced a death or a serious injury in their immediate social circle. Twenty per cent of the students serving as soldiers lost their lives; according to another figure, even a shocking two-thirds of all the former members of the youth movement (Breuer 1993: 31 f.).

In the First World War all participants had soon lost control. Strategic planning and heroism long failed to overcome the defensive power of modern weapons. The German army could not defend civilians from hunger and starvation. As the war developed in unintended ways, this showed the power of material conditions over the human will. Technology seemed 'to have emancipated itself from its serving role to challenge human sovereignty' (Braun 1992: 255. See also Benjamin 1972). The heroic idealism praised before the war was faced with the stark industrial, technological, military and political demands of a war of unprecedented totality. The overpowering reality of modern industrial warfare questioned the existence of free human agency, clearly a prerequisite for creating a single communal faith. People facing up to the reality of the Great War frequently felt caught in a dilemma. Modern technology had shown its murderous side, but simultaneously the inevitability of its use. Nationalistically minded conservatives with a sense of realism had to abandon all nostalgic notions they might still have held about a return to the past; a strong nation not only needed the best weapons engineers could devise, but also a powerful industrial production to support an unprecedented war of material. Modern warfare might have destroyed all appealing notions of heroism, but those committed to a strong Germany had to accept this. Industrial and technical modernization proved to be an irresistible historical development, enforcing its logic on all political actors. Humans could try to find a productive way of incorporating this force within their ideals, but the hope to resist it turned out to be mere wishful thinking.

At least equally dramatic were the political changes. The Emperor had lost his reputation, thereby irreparably damaging the authority of the monarchy even before he was forced to flee the country. While even an extremist like Heinrich Class had stopped short of challenging the monarchy before the war, couching his critique in the form of advice to the Emperor instead, such inhibitions had disappeared by 1918. The tradition of monarchical rule was broken; an authoritarian structure was no longer handed down by history; it would have to be openly invented and implemented. The question which conservatives still aiming for an authoritarian rule faced was: how can a new ruler emerge? The return of a Hohenzollern was never a realistic political option. Thus, the only authoritarian alternative to a democratic Republic became a dictator supported by functional elites and preferably also by a majority of the population. As the monarchical tradition had collapsed, charismatic leadership became the most promising way to try to implement an authoritarian rule, especially if one still dreamt of uniting the nation in a single communal faith.

Revolutionary Conservatives had become increasingly critical of existing conditions in the nineteenth century, showing the problems of an atomized or divided society and advocating the attempt to create a more tightly knit community. As a result of the war, however, critique turned into spiteful revulsion, the call for change into a desperate apocalyptic vision of destruction and a new beginning. While nineteenth-century right-wing extremists still tended to accept large parts of reality, the lost war truly radicalized them. Germany's international might was broken, the revolution seemed to destroy all traditional authority. The civil-war conditions and the inflation of the early post-war years only confirmed the impression that the nation had fallen into chaos and misery (Geyer 1998). Seemingly desperate times went together with more extreme thinking and action. The polarization between an allegedly Western and German way, first formulated systematically during the enmity of war, continued throughout Republic and Third Reich. The widespread belief that things could not get worse seemed to justify wholly ruthless desperado strategies. Normative thinking was widely discredited; power and violence seemed to be the basis not only of international relations, but also of domestic conflicts. A Social Darwinist belief in a struggle for existence, a Nietzschean will to power and an amoral *Realpolitik* all served to justify abandoning moral inhibitions. The Left and the Jews in particular were blamed for Germany's weakness; they came to be targeted by brutal policies of exclusion and destruction. Members of the extreme Right had advocated violent measures in domestic politics before 1914; now violence became reality.

Attempts at uniting the nation in a single communal faith continued, but the years of war and revolution mark the strongest alteration in that tradition. What happened in Germany after 1918 is unimaginable without the experience of a war which was more total than anybody had anticipated. Convictions and world-views had to prove their realism by facing up to that reality, or they appeared to be naive and outdated. The sorcerer's apprentices of the Great War had to take new bearings.

Notes

1. In *Die Friedenswarte*, 14 (1912), 112.
2. Even avant-garde and progressive artists could see the war as an opportunity to gain new and more fundamental experiences as subjects for their art (Mommsen 1994).
3. An estimated 1.5 million war poems were published (Busse 1916: VI), and in 2000, Kurt Flasch's bibliography on this topic contained 13,001 titles without claiming full comprehensiveness (2000: 228).
4. This phrase derives from Geibel's poem 'Deutschlands Beruf' which ends with: 'Und es mag am deutschen Wesen / Einmal noch die Welt genesen.'
5. Particularly outspoken were Plenge, Lasson, Harnack, Jaffe, Sombart and Chamberlain (Bruendel 2003: 118–124; Mommsen 1994: 153–162).
6. This is most explicitly stated in the book of their economic expert, Ferdinand Fried (1931: 23, 46, 144 and passim). See more generally Werth 1996: 143 ff. and passim.
7. Schildt 1998: 127. Bruendel argues that the political battle was between promoters of a corporate and a democratic state, but this ignores the difference between those on the Right accepting the need for more social justice to achieve a national community and those advocating dictatorial measures. *Völkisch* thinkers also disliked that the 'ideas of 1914' largely argued in cultural, not in racist terms.
8. The party avoided an official statement against democracy to reach wider circles, but all its leading figures rejected abolishing the Prussian three-class voting system. Its extreme wing even favoured a *coup d"état* to establish a dictatorship, and Tirpitz considered a removal of the weak Emperor to bring the Crown Prince to the throne (Hagenlücke 1997: 216 ff.).

CHAPTER 5

PLAYING WITH FIRE: THE RIGHT IN THE WEIMAR REPUBLIC

Military defeat came as a shock to many Germans; especially to the extreme Right. The Fatherland Party, which demanded total war until victory would be achieved, continued to grow until autumn 1918. Official war reports and propaganda denied the increasingly bleak reality to the very end. While the situation on the Western front turned desperate after the spring offensive of 1918, leading to a 'hidden military strike' among soldiers (Deist 1992), the German army kept on fighting successfully in the East. Even after the draconic peace of Brest-Litovsk in March 1918, where Russia lost 34 per cent of its population, 54 per cent of its industry, 89 per cent of its coal fields, 33 per cent of its railway lines, 32 per cent of its agricultural land and its whole oil and cotton production, German expansion continued. A significant proportion of soldiers did not experience the disaster in the West, but a ruthless ethnic restructuring in the East, 'where even the wildest Pan-German dreams became reality' (Wehler 2003: 151–155, at 154; Liulevicius 2000).

The defeat not only destroyed, for the foreseeable future, any hope of establishing Germany as *the* great power on the continent of Europe, it even seemed to threaten Germany's existence as a major player. The continuation of the trade blockade into the summer of 1919 led to an all-time high of civilian deaths after the ceasefire (Bessel 1993: 224), seemingly confirming the suspicion that the Allies wanted to destroy Germany. The Versailles treaty, while not nearly as harsh as Germany's treaty with the Soviet Union, came as a blow to a population which had put its hopes in President Wilson's call for a lenient peace.

Military defeat shattered the right-wing dream of a national reawakening through war. While political differences had been suppressed by a widespread willingness for war in 1914, they re-emerged when the military conflict became increasingly costly and reached an unprecedented peak with military disaster. The war-weary mass of the population had gradually come to distrust the political and military elites, until popular dissatisfaction and strikes eventually culminated in the revolution. Soldiers' and workers' councils, together with a revolutionary government, took control, while the Emperor fled and the old forces capitulated without even putting up a fight. Ironically, the Right had to be grateful that the Social Democrats, long defamed as *Reichsfeinde* ('enemies of the Reich'), maintained a high degree of order and stability. After all, the Russian Revolution and the newly formed German Communist Party (KPD) proved that much more radical changes could be on the cards than the German revolutionary forces' call for a democratic national assembly.

In the new Republic, the political Right faced unprecedented challenges. They lost the privileged access traditional conservatives had maintained to the Imperial government, and they had to compete more than ever for votes. With 10.3 per cent in the first elections, the conservative DNVP gained slightly more votes than the German Conservative Party in the last pre-war election of 1912 (and only 2 per cent less than the two Imperial conservative parties taken together), but the Weimar coalition in support of the new Republic gained a clear majority, thus forming the first government.

The position of the Right was never as weak, however, as their quick retreat after the war suggested. The Weimar state remained in many ways a 'conservative Republic' because conservative functional elites and milieus largely stayed in place (Winkler 1993: 306. See also Mommsen 1989; Peukert 1991; Schildt 1998: 132–137; Wehler 2003: 284–347). The east of Germany remained a bastion of conservatism because the big agrarian estates continued mainly unchanged (Merkenich 1998); a majority of generals and 20 per cent of the officers belonged to the nobility and remained politically conservative – though often in a radicalized form typical for young conservatives and later leaning towards Nazism (Malinowski 2004: 209 ff.) – and open to adapting the army to modern conditions (Bald 1982; Carsten 1988: 164; Geyer 1988; Rusinek 1992); judges turned, as the statistician Gumbel already proved at the time, a blind eye on political crimes from the far Right; representatives of heavy industry pushed for an authoritarian political regime; the Protestant church and its ministers remained close to the conservative DNVP, while some extremist theologians like Paul Althaus, Emmanuel Hirsch and Friedrich Gogarten even tended towards *völkisch* ideas (Nowak 1995: 28 f., 35 ff., 215 ff.; Scholder 1977); and, finally, the educated middle class as a whole moved further towards a right-wing opposition to existing conditions. While this group had tended to be loyal to the monarchical state, the majority remained highly critical of the new Republic. A sharp decline in material status, the difficulties of young academics in finding jobs and the fear of a diminishing influence in the age of democracy and mass culture (although the cultural elite presumably remained the most important opinion makers) worked together to radicalize the political views of the educated middle class (Wehler 2003: 284–308). In the wake of the 'ideas of 1914', historians continued to stress that Germany's allegedly special historical development was superior to the West, universities continued to celebrate not the day of the constitution, but the memory of German unification, and students were among the most susceptible to right-wing ideologies, in particular anti-Semitism against the disproportionately high number of Jewish academics (Faulenbach 1980; Jarausch 1984).

More generally, a Republic struggling to survive for most of its existence could not win over sceptics. As the consequences of defeat were never really accepted, the new political order was blamed for its failure to regain the pre-war status. Germany's international position remained precarious, and the economy was marked by slow growth and two disastrous crises. The lack of any political consensus – much more dramatic than in the German Empire – made it extremely difficult for a democratic system to function. Large parts of the functional elites kept a distance from the Republic, which could turn into open hostility in times of crisis; the political spectrum ranged from pacifists to militarists glorifying the memory of the First World War, from advocates of the *Reichs*-legend to realists accepting the consequences of the Versailles treaty, from conservatives harking back to pre-war Germany to democrats and socialists, and from Nazis to Communists. The old industries in particular never accepted the social and political achievements of the revolution, while many workers felt disappointed by a conservative republic and a slow growth in wages. Difficult times deepened the divisions between the many milieus: Catholics, nationalistic Protestants and socialist workers all continued to have their own socio-cultural circles, leisure-time activities and political parties (Wehler 2003: 484 f.; Winkler 1985: 13–173). While a growing number of people enjoyed the products of popular culture, others defended the canon of 'high culture', defaming everything else as a dangerous 'Americanization' (Lüdtke 1996; Rohkrämer 1999: 252–260). A highly creative artistic avant-garde clashed with the search for a traditional identity in *Heimatkunst* ('folk art'), and a bubbling culture in the metropolitan cities met with deep suspicion and fear from the rest of the country (Gay 1974). Even the quite cosmopolitan author Stefan Zweig, who was later forced into exile by the Nazis, compared Berlin with Babylon, stating that 'perversity was cultivated with German thoroughness. On the Kurfürstendamm adolescents walked along with make-up and artificial waists; every grammar-school boy wanted to make some money, and in dark bars you saw ministers and senior civil servants flirt with sailors, while the police just watched benevolently' (1955: 358 f.).

Under those circumstances, it is not at all surprising that the Weimar Republic failed to win many friends. It could never profit from favourable circumstances, and it lacked the fundamental political consensus necessary to make a democracy work. If political parties see their opponent as a grave danger to the nation, they cannot really accept them governing, even if they gain a majority in elections. If radical minorities cannot see a chance for realizing their ideas democratically, they come to regard the political system as tyrannical (Schmitt 1988). As large and powerful parts of the population continued to reject the political order, it only survived until there appeared to be a viable alternative.

Could the vision of a single communal faith survive at a time when former deep political divisions frequently escalated into polarized hatred? Yes, but only in a different form. While the work of Richard Wagner, for example, remained influential, nothing of that ilk could have been produced after the First World War. The many adverse experiences made the political Right much more cautious in presenting concrete images of an ideal future. Richard Wagner appeared romantic and idealistic, while the more innovative Conservative Revolutionaries of a younger generation wanted to be realistic and down-to-earth. Their emphasis was more on the fight against political enemies; the future was frequently seen in apocalyptic terms as a complete destruction to create the necessary space for the emergence of something new; and most positive visions were left open and vague. Behind a façade of matter-of-factness, however, the dream of a community united in a single faith continued to play a crucial role.

Nietzsche had been a forerunner of an emphasis on accepting reality as it is. Again and again he stressed that humans should not lose themselves in metaphysical fantasies, but remain faithful to the earth. He preached belief in eternal recurrence, as this demanded an acceptance of all aspects of life (Hof 1974). Such an *amor fati*, then, characterized a number of influential avant-garde artists. The Expressionist painter Max Beckmann, for example, whose work has largely been seen as a critique of the First World War, wanted to serve at the front to have the chance to experience and observe life in an extreme situation. In a letter he stated: 'It is not as if I would participate in this like a historian, but that I experience this phenomenon which is essentially an aspect of life, like illness, love or voluptuousness. And exactly as I pursue, willingly or unwillingly, fear, illness and lust, love and hate to their extremes – well, so I pursue war now. Everything is life, wonderfully varied and over-rich with ideas. Everywhere I find deep lines of beauty in the suffering and the bearing of this scary fate.' His fellow-expressionist Otto Dix described his attitude towards war in similar terms: 'The war was a terrible thing, but nevertheless something powerful. I could not possibly miss this. You must have seen humans in this uninhibited state to know something about humans' (quoted in Mommsen 1994: 144).

Such an emphasis on accepting reality as it is was a defining feature of a new Right or Conservative Revolution, which did not want to provide old cures to a dramatically changed reality (Sontheimer 1983: 93). They wanted to leave all nostalgic romanticism behind to incorporate the experience of industrial warfare into their political ideology. 'The world war was a demon', a veteran and close friend of Ernst Jünger wrote, 'which broke all pathos to pieces' (Fischer 1934: 6). It not only seemed to show the reality of evil, but also that reality was much more powerful than human dreams, plans and ambitions. A belief in natural harmony lost plausibility in comparison to world-views of conflict, aggression and unforgiving hardness.[1] In a call for a 'rejection of romanticism', contemporaries denounced an openness to all facets of life in favour of strong decisions, clear attitudes and a ruthless will to power.[2] It was regarded as 'real' in that soldierly men were supposed to gird themselves with a clear, no-nonsense attitude in facing a dangerously muddled reality. Especially the younger generation who had passed through adolescence in the difficult wartimes cultivated the appearance of a new 'matter-of-factness' to 'gain control over the world of matter' through an 'instrumental, rational and economical' approach (Gründel 1933: 94. More generally Herbert 1991, 1996: 42 ff.; Merkl 1980: 110 f.; Wildt 2002).

The lies of war propaganda as well as the 'great disorder' (Gerald Feldman) after 1918 had led to both a deep distrust of big words and the wish for a clear faith which would armour the individual from being overwhelmed by a confusing and hostile world. The soldiers, initially praised as defenders of the fatherland, were disillusioned when they did not experience any particular gratitude, but instead the difficulties of getting a satisfactory job and making a career in times of high unemployment. Günther Gründel expressed a feeling common in particular among middle class youth who failed to gain the security of the previous generation: 'Where had our chance for a nice "secure bourgeois career" gone? … The generation-old firm bridges into life were broken down. We had to swim and see how and where we would end up. We ended up among [lower] classes, which had been unimaginable for our parents' (1933: 40 f.). Gründel presented a rosy picture of the past, but the feeling that his generation was exceptionally unfortunate was widespread and justified. As it was difficult for a whole generation to get into a stagnating job market, the Weimar Republic was frequently seen as an old order which tried to exclude the coming generation. Consequently, the parties of change largely attracted young members and voters (Mommsen 1985; Peukert 1991: 7–9). Disappointment with the old order could easily turn into a desire for a new faith, a positive vision for the future. It had to be more radical and hard-nosed than the pre-war ideologies, though, in order to convince in tougher times. The dream of a community united in a single faith survived the upheavals caused by the First World War, but more than ever it needed scapegoats to explain why things had gone wrong after 1914 and how this could be remedied through a ruthless battle against the alleged enemies in Germany and outside. The post-war Right did not give up the hope of uniting the nation in a single communal faith, but they tended even more than before towards a polarized distinction between friend and foe and thus towards extreme measures. The apocalyptic idea gained currency that the old had to be destroyed to create space for a better new world (Brokoff 2001; Vondung 1988).

While right-wing extremism after 1918 was dominated by veterans, the next generation immediately followed to fill the ranks. As a consequence of war, the age cohort born around 1900 had gone through a distinct socialization. They had seen their fathers and older brothers go to war and expected war service as their own future. They experienced the deprivations of the home front: hunger and need, an absent father and a mother carrying the burden of making money and looking after the children. They were the 'war-cheering' generation or 'victory watchers' (Merkl 1980: 231 ff.), which sucked in the propaganda and the celebration of victorious battles at a young age without experiencing the front line which could be a drastic cure from the rhetoric of heroism. Many lost their fathers and felt a duty to do their bit for a strong Germany. The later commandant of Auschwitz, Rudolf Höss, was typical for many nationalistically minded members of his generation when he recalled his youthful attitude towards the First World War: 'There was so much to see, and I did not want to miss anything. I pestered my mother until she gave me permission to enrol as an auxiliary with the Red Cross … I wanted to be a soldier. I was determined at all costs not to miss this war' (1995: 35 f.). A description in the NS-journal *Angriff* from 1931 expressed the same sentiments:

> We young ones, who are now around 20, greeted the soldiers when they returned from the front, walked with them through the streets. We thought to recognize in each of them our father or brother, uncle or cousin … Then came great days when we started school. [We got new] teachers, but always soldiers. They came in uniform and had medals from the Great War on their chest … When we had done our work [our teacher told us] about war and blood and great comradeship … These teachers were like older brothers, they became comrades … We went on excursions and hikes, played war games. (quoted in Reichardt 2002: 376)

A radicalization did not take place just on an ideological level, but first and foremost in a dramatic increase of political violence.[3] It has frequently been claimed that the war had reduced the inhibition to use violence, but this is too general. While the number of crimes went up, the increase was in property, not violent offences (Liepmann 1930: 37; Reichardt 2002; Schumann 2000, 2001; Weisbrod 1992, 1998, 2001). The vast majority of the 13 million veterans above all wished to return to a peaceful civilian life (Bessel 1993; Ziemann 2000). There were enough, however, who started to fight for their political convictions, thus creating a situation frequently bordering on civil war. In 1919, about 1,000 people died in such conflicts; in 1929 to 1931, about 150; in 1932, 155. With political polarization, significant numbers no longer trusted political procedures and compromises, but wanted to realize their ideals through violent means. Of course, the political violence in the wake of the war was partly due to a lack of effective political authority, but it also furthered unwillingness for compromise already present in the militaristic German Empire. Tolerance and the attempt to find a mutually acceptable consensus were defamed as weakness, while ruthlessness and determination stood for serious, manly commitment.

Both extremes of the political spectrum resorted to violence, but the Right far outdid its political opposite (Reichardt, forthcoming), also because it frequently had the backing of the army. During a Communist uprising in January 1919, the leaders of the Left, Rosa Luxemburg and Karl Liebknecht, were brutally murdered. When the council's republic in Munich was put down, 606 people lost their lives, among them 335 civilians and 38 soldiers of the government's forces (Winkler 1993: 81). Many militant right-wing organizations emerged in angry response to the revolution. The free corps with about 200,000 members constituted the most active group, continuing to fight in the name of the government on the Eastern front and against revolutionary workers or even serving as strikebreakers. While the Left loathed these forces, the Right glorified them as altruistic servants of the fatherland. With the free corps something new emerged: the openly political soldier. For these volunteers a high level of brutality became the new normality. These conflicts, like all 'little' wars and civil conflicts, [4] were very brutal, thus making the men used to a high intensity of inhumane violence. As the former member of a free corps, Ernst von Salomon, remembered in his memoirs: 'We fired into surprised crowds, and raged and shot and beat and chased ... We threw the corpses into wells and threw hand grenades after them. We slew what fell into our hands, we burnt what could be burnt. We were enraged; we no longer had human feelings in our hearts' (1933: 167 f.).

The *Einwohnerwehren* or civil guards, which were officially encouraged and were supposed to maintain law and order, had at least twice as many members as the free corps. While the latter largely consisted of ex-officers and students, the civil guards encompassed a much larger and more diverse group of citizens. Their military value was rather limited, but they 'promoted a militarized political mentality among both members and supporters that continued long after the guards' dissolution'. They claimed to be non-political, but in reality the guards provided 'a solid front against the leftist parties' (Diehl 2003: 103 f.).

The allies ordered the dissolution of German volunteer forces after 1920, but a secret *Reichswehr* as well as contacts between the army and right-wing organizations continued throughout the Weimar Republic (Carsten 1964: 276 ff.). Small circles of right-wing extremists organized political assassinations of leading Weimar politicians, but more important for the general militarization of politics was the rise of the veterans' organization *Kyffhäuserbund* with two million members, and the paramilitary *Wehrverbände* (military associations), most importantly the right-wing veterans' organization *Stahlhelm* with about 100,000 members in 1924 and four times that figure toward the end of the Republic (Berghahn 1966). Many former members of the free corps and the civil guards chose the Stahlhelm as their new ideological home. It was closely connected with the Conservative DNVP at first (later members started to drift towards the Nazis). It celebrated the cult of soldierly men and the *Frontgemeinschaft*, that is, the community of the front-line soldiers. The *Jungdeutscher Orden* was another important *Wehrverband* on the Right with about 100,000 members, and the brown shirts as the paramilitary wing of the Nazi Party even succeeded in gaining nearly 450,000 members through their image of youthful, dynamic and ruthless commitment (Reichardt 2002: 258).

The wish to be part of an ideologically committed military association was no preserve of the Right. The big and powerful *Reichsbanner* was closely connected with the Social Democrats (Rohe 1966; Ziemann 1998), while the Communist *Roter Frontkämpferbund* was the main opponent of the SA in the many street battles in the early 1930s. Despite the wide range of ideological positions, they all tried to overcome the depressing effects of military defeat by glorifying military comradeship and the heroic soldier. As it was difficult to count four years of war service as wasted, a 'soldierly nationalism' (Karl Prümm) proved fatally attractive. In stressing the quality of the soldier rather than the outcome of the war, veterans tried to find a positive meaning in the lost war. Nietzsche's claim that 'it is the good war that hallows any cause' (1969: I, Of War and Warriors) was echoed by the writer Ernst Jünger, who was also temporarily an editor of the Stahlhelm magazine *Standarte*: 'It is not essential what we fight for, but how we fight' (1922: 76). Combining all the clichés of the time, his brother Friedrich Georg Jünger glorified the soldier under the steel helmet, both the 'full, carefree, enthusiastic faces of the soldiers in August 1914' as well as the later 'rawboned, ruthlessly tense face of the fighter in the battle of material' with 'the alert hardness of the natural warrior' (1930: 65).

The Versailles treaty limited the *Reichswehr*'s size to 100,000 men. The Weimar Republic could thus no longer have a conscript army as a conservative 'school of the nation'. Militarism, however, continued to flourish, not the least through the paramilitary *Wehrverbände*, who had in total at least one million members, and through war literature, which became a mass phenomenon especially around 1930 (Wette 1979). Pacifist organizations and literature (most famously *All Quiet on the Western Front*) existed, of course, but it meant a radical break not only with the right-wing nationalism of the nineteenth century, but also with traditional ideas of manliness.[5] The cult of the soldierly man could compensate for the 'humiliation' of failing to defend nation and home in the First World War, could give meaning to dreadful years of war service, and could overcome a feeling of guilt towards the soldiers who had lost life or limb. Especially on the Right, authors felt obliged to give a positive meaning to the war, which otherwise threatened to undermine their convictions. All political ideologies found it necessary to honour the veterans by glorifying the soldierly man, but this also implied the glorification of ruthless determination and a violent answer to conflict, which was at odds with the need for tolerance and compromise in a pluralistic and democratic society. Like the social militarism of the German Empire, the 'soldierly nationalism' of the Weimar Republic could turn, as we shall see in the case of Ernst Jünger, into a political faith which aimed at establishing a homogeneous society closely resembling the total institution of an army.

In associations ranging from the free corps to the Communist Red Front and the SA, violence became a core part of their identity. Using physical force and accepting the danger of injury and death established the reputation of the members in their group. Violent conflicts created and identified a foe that could be blamed, attacked and destroyed. It also melded the group together, thus creating a sense of solidarity and camaraderie. In chaotic times, the practice of violence could help towards finding a clear orientation in life. When unemployed, it could become an activity which filled the time and gave meaning to life (Reichardt 2002; Salomon 1933). It was mainly young men who joined the actively violent groups. Many had no employment or career prospects, either never getting into a job or having experienced some kind of personal disaster. Many came from a difficult social background (Merkl 1980: 146, 154 and passim). The political effect of this, however, went far beyond these violent associations. Members of the less violent *Stahlhelm* or *Reichsbanner* identified themselves at least ideologically with such an emphasis on strength, violence and sacrifice through soldierly imagery and self-representation. Even a nationalist public could be impressed by such a display of ruthless determination as long as it seemed to serve a good cause (Weisbrod 2001). Marching in closed formation, the leader of the SA Pfeffer claimed,

> is one of the strongest forms of propaganda. The image of a great number of uniformed and disciplined men who march in step and whose will to fight is unmistakable, deeply impresses every German and speaks more strongly and persuasively to his heart than any written or spoken logic could ever do. A calm appearance and matter-of-factness underline this impression of power, the strength of the marching column and the purpose for which they march. The inner strength of conviction makes other Germans believe in its truth. When many people voluntarily risk body, soul and life for something, then it must simply be great and true. (quoted in Merkl 1980: 166)

In trying to mark their distance from 'normal' politicians, who were defamed as all talk, the Nazi Party programme played on this desire for a strong faith by ending the text with the pathos-filled words: 'The leaders of the Party promise to work ruthlessly – if need be to sacrifice their very lives – to translate this programme into action' (reprinted in Noakes and Pridham 1983: 16).

The many political displays on the Right – which were presented in films and other media long before Leni Riefenstahl – make up a 'remarkable image of a patriotic popular culture consumed by the masses' (Geyer 1998: 123). But fighting, marching and flag-waving could not be everything; the Right also had to organize in parties, find a political stand and adapt its ideology to post-war conditions. The party in which members of the old Conservative Parties, the Fatherland Party and the Pan-Germans found a new political home was the German National People's Party (*Deutschnationale Volkspartei* or DNVP). 'Conservatism' had such a bad image right after the war that the more general terms 'national' and '*Volk*' were used in the name,[6] but this shift also signalled the attempt to have just one party uniting the whole Right. This plan failed, however. The DNVP remained a Protestant Party, while Catholic conservatives largely continued to support the Catholic Centre Party, although it opted at first to support the new Republic. The DNVP found its strength mainly in the countryside and in the east of Germany, while many conservative industrialists stood closer to the more moderate DVP. By and large it remained a middle class party, strongly supported also by Protestant ministers and academics.

Conservatism was not only divided along party lines, but the struggle to find the appropriate attitude towards the new Republic also divided the DNVP. Parts of the party had been radicalizing since the summer of 1919, culminating in a coup against the government less than a year later. It was led by the former leader of the Fatherland Party, Wolfgang Kapp, who had become part of the DNVP's *völkisch* Right after 1918, and military men like Walter von Lüttwitz, who brought in the free corps as the muscle to remove the government forcefully. The right-wing forces were strong enough to make the government take flight, but the coup failed dismally within four days due to a successful general strike, amply demonstrating the complete lack of popular support for any attempt to establish a conservative dictatorship without a populist programme or an inspiring leader. The coup revealed, however, the uncertainty of conservatives about their strategy against the new Republic. The mass of the army remained neutral, and the DNVP kept its – largely tactical – distance from the rebels without clearly condemning them. Conservatives clearly found it difficult to decide between legal opposition through parliamentary means and an open fight against the Republic (Schildt 1998: 137–156).

The early DNVP also contained strong *völkisch* elements, until they left to form their own party, which gained, in a one-time high, 6.5 per cent in an election in May 1924. This party, as well as the other *völkisch* groups and sects, lost their importance with the growing weight of the Nazi Movement (see next chapter). For the DNVP, at least, this departure led to more coherence and a somewhat more constructive role in parliamentary politics, until the party moved again to the more extreme Right towards the end of the Weimar Republic. It supported the change to increasingly authoritarian presidential regimes and the attempts to win the NSDAP as a junior partner, thus hoping to gain mass support for a conservative regime. In entering a coalition government under the chancellorship of Hitler, however, they soon lost their political distinctiveness. Their independent political role ended when they were quickly drawn into the much more dynamic and powerful politics of the Third Reich (Lohalm 1970; Petzold 1980).

The DNVP clearly failed, we can conclude, to offer an inspiring vision which might have promised to unite all right-wing forces in a single communal faith. The more moderate forces harked back to the German Empire, which was, however, obviously gone for good, the more extreme members like Wolfgang Kapp were close to the dictatorial ideals which the Pan-German leader Class had already advocated in 1912, and the *völkisch* wing soon left to find more suitable associations. The party was much too backward-oriented and elitist to unite the German Right, let alone the nation as a whole in a single communal faith. Those still holding up this dream clearly had to look elsewhere.

In trying to win the masses and unite the nation, the Right was bound to hope for the emergence of a powerful charismatic leader. While the existence of the monarchy had hindered the call for a nationalist dictator, its demise set off a wave of hopeful fantasies about a new leader. Difficult and undecided times produced, as Max Weber had anticipated, the hope for a saviour. The philosopher Max Scheler diagnosed 'an unprecedented desire for leadership', the philosopher Hermann Schmalenbach described his ideal of a community which would desire 'a God, a hero, a master', and the Social Democratic politician Julius Leber criticized the widespread 'hysterical desire for a strong man'. The catholic conservative Othmar Spann called for a leader 'as saviour from the dark forces of the time' and Heinrich Class expected a new Bismarck as dictator.[7] Oswald Spengler expected, as we shall see in more detail, a new Caesarism, the conservative revolutionary Hans Zehrer waited for the decisive historical moment 'when the hour has come for the great individual – if he is available' (quoted in Woods 1996: 99), and at a celebration of the DNVP in 1924 in memory of German unification, the speaker claimed: 'The great Führer is still missing … But he will come … I call upon you to hope, you longing *Volk*, and be prepared' (quoted in Schumann 2000: 105). A popular history series called *The German Leaders* said that 'we firmly hope that they [the true leaders] will come' also for the Weimar Republic, and the nationalist journal *Deutschlands Erneuerung* wrote: 'In our misery we desire the leader. He is to show us the direction and the action … The leader does not follow the mass, but his destiny … The leader is responsible, that is, he follows the will of the God which he personifies. May God give us a leader and help us towards true leadership and obedience [*Gefolgschaft*]' (Schreiner 2003: 245, 242).

The greatest heroic model for a leader was Bismarck.[8] He was credited, after all, with saving the Prussian monarchy in the constitutional conflict in the early 1860s, with creating a powerful monarchical German Empire with a constitution favouring the conservatives, with fighting the Social Democrats and establishing Germany as a colonial power. After his retirement he had become the hero of an extreme Right, which was unhappy about the failure of his successors to establish Germany as a leading colonial and continental power. In memory of the 'Iron Chancellor', 238 Bismarck towers, financed largely by private donations, were erected all over the country. He stood as an example of an exceptional leader achieving his goals through sheer force and determination. Similarly, Hindenburg became *the* German war hero after 'his' victorious battles in the East. A cult developed around his personality during the First World War (see Ch. 4), and the greatest victory under his leadership was glorified in the Tannenberg memorial. His reputation obviously suffered through defeat, but the stab-in-the-back legend helped its revival. Those blaming 'the November criminals' for Germany's defeat regarded Hindenburg as the great leader of an army 'undefeated in battle'.

The campaign around Hindenburg's election as president in 1925 marked a turning point for the political Right in the Weimar Republic. It brought together all but the most radical right-wing forces in a large-scale populist campaign. Not only the DNVP and Stahlhelm actively supported Hindenburg, but so did conservative citizens in general. The victory celebration reminded nationalists of August 1914, when they had dominated the public scene. Imperial flags were hissed (in demonstrative rejection of the Republic's democratic colours of black, red and gold), there were proud parades and even attacks on the left. Conservative accounts of the 1918 revolution frequently describe the shock that workers dominated the streets, ripping off and destroying symbols of the old order like the officers' insignias and soldiers' medals. Now all conservatives revelled in the moment where they seemed to reconquer the public sphere. In replacing the Social Democratic president and former saddler Friedrich Ebert with the conservative war hero Hindenburg, the Right proved that they were back. In celebration of Hindenburg's eightieth birthday in 1927, such pictures of a right-wing mass politics repeated themselves with big celebrations and triumphant marches, also through working class areas, as a demonstration of strength (Fritzsche 1998: 161 ff.). While the masses had appeared as the irresistible enemy to a conservative order in 1918, the majority for Hindenburg at the polls suggested chances for the Right in a plebiscitary democracy and a populist authoritarian rule with a charismatic leader. The political fantasies of right-wing intellectuals were set in new directions (Winkler 2000: Vol. 1, 463).

Hindenburg's election marked a political landslide. A war-weary majority had overthrown the old order and had voted in favour of the parties supporting the new Republic in the winter of 1918–19. Only six years later, however, the core symbol of the Imperial army, who blamed the revolution, not the allegedly undefeated soldiers, for Germany's defeat, gained the highest political office. While Hindenburg did not ruthlessly break with the constitution, as many had certainly hoped, his sympathies clearly did not lie with the Republic. He always had an open ear for big industry, agriculture and, above all, military officers meddling in politics. Thus it was no surprise that he and his political entourage seized the opportunity of the deep economic crisis and a political stalemate in parliament at the end of the decade to destroy the republic. While Chancellor Brüning was still tolerated by a majority in parliament, the presidential regimes increasingly moved towards an authoritarian dictatorship (Winkler 2000: Vol. 1, 509 f.).

This is not the place for narrating once again the complex story of Weimar's fall (Blasius 2005; Bracher 1978; Jasper 1986; Mommsen 1989; Peukert 1991; Schildt 1981; Turner 1997; Wehler 2003; Winkler 1992, 2000). The important point for the argument of this book is that Hindenburg and the traditional conservatives around him had the power to destroy the republic, but did not dare to introduce their own ideal of an authoritarian regime. Of course, there was much common ground between Weimar conservatives and Nazis. Both were aggressively nationalist, saw Marxism as the main enemy and wanted to reestablish Germany as a world power. Many conservatives regarded the Nazis' anti-Semitism as too vulgar and extreme, but they were anti-Semitic enough not to be particularly disturbed by this aspect of Nazi ideology, which did not, in any event, play a central role in the Nazi propaganda of the early 1930s. The two political forces even drew on a similar clientele. 'Essentially', Jürgen Falter has shown in his statistical analysis of Nazi voters, 'the election of the president in 1925 can be interpreted as the first successful mobilization of conservative and *völkisch* forces, largely opposed to the constitution and even the republic, which ... later, under the catalytic influence of the world economic crisis, found their political home in the heterogeneous National Socialist movement' (1991: 125).

There was, however, also a deep distrust held by Hindenburg and his entourage against National Socialism (Kershaw 1998: 337); after all, it took nearly three years from the Nazis becoming the strongest force on the political Right and six months from them becoming the strongest party before Hitler was accepted as chancellor of a coalition government. This shows reservations which were partly due to a stubborn elitism: the President and his circle distrusted a corporal of the First World War, an unscrupulously populist mass movement and the Socialist rhetoric, especially of the SA. A conservative dictatorship would thus have been more to their liking; why, then, did Hindenburg and his surroundings not seriously try this route?

In the early 1930s, there was no chance for a popular right-wing regime without National Socialism as Hindenburg clearly lacked charisma and a positive vision of the future to keep his many right-wing voters from 1925 on board. Also, the DNVP's drop in the vote from 14.2 per cent in 1928 to 7 per cent in 1930 clearly showed the limits of their popular appeal. This conservative failure to win mass support left three possible scenarios, which were all seriously considered and attempted: firstly, an authoritarian dictatorship without popular support under Chancellor von Papen; secondly, a socially-minded, more populist authoritarian rule – somewhat reminiscent of the 'ideas of 1914' and a communal economy – under Chancellor Kurt von Schleicher; and, finally, the alliance with Hitler in 1933. Schleicher himself emphasized the problems of a dictatorship without public backing, claiming that the army could not guarantee social stability if the change to such a regime escalated into civil war (involving both Communists and Nazis) and combined with an international challenge like a Polish military attack (Blasius 2005). The argument might have been partly self-serving to remove his political rival, but it was plausible enough to carry the day against Chancellor von Papen. Why? Because even a majority of conservatives had come to accept that a stable and strong Germany needed a government popular at least with powerful parts of society. 'The tip of a bayonet is bad to sit on', von Schleicher stated, 'that is, one cannot rule long-term without being based on a broad acceptance by the people'.[9] Traditional conservatism thus accepted that there was no chance to turn back the clock. In contrast to the past, a regime had to find a sufficient degree of public acceptance under modern conditions.

The presidential regimes obviously did not aim at creating a nation united in a single communal faith, but they show the powerful influence of this vision. Despite their arrogant break with parliamentarianism, they shied away from a dictatorship by pure force. The old conservative conviction that the masses would simply go along with a wise authoritarian order had clearly vanished. A dictatorship could possibly survive for a while, but only a regime backed by a consensus within the population could, it seemed, achieve social stability and thus the military strength necessary to re-establish Germany as a world power. The presidential regimes did not wish for active popular participation or totalitarian integration, but even traditional conservatives had come round to believe in the need for a society based on shared political convictions supporting their leaders.

In accepting that the politics of the old notables, which simply expected the mass of the population to obey the elites, was no longer adequate, they accepted a core element of the vision of a single communal faith. Schleicher's attempt to base his government on the support of trade unions, the Strasser wing within the Nazi movement and the *Wehrverbände Stahlhelm, Reichsbanner* and SA was a last desperate effort to achieve this political goal without Hitler. When he failed, even Hindenburg accepted the need for an alliance with National Socialism. The conservative elites were still strong enough to destroy the Weimar Republic, but their realization that they lacked support forced them to invite the Nazis into government (Peukert 1991: 281).

Traditional conservatism suffered under the same malaise as other political parties in Weimar Germany. Right-wing liberalism, which had come to accept an authoritarian government, no longer attracted voters, and younger members of the conservative milieu increasingly turned their back on the DNVP, looking instead for new ways to unite the nation in a single communal faith. Society was deeply divided, but at the same time highly mobilized. Thomas Mann's term of the 'apolitical German', often used by older historians to describe the weakness of democracy in Germany, seems completely off the mark. Weimar was characterized by an exceptionally high degree of political mobilization. Large parts of the population were not satisfied with a government taking the political responsibility away from them, but impatiently demanded a political leadership uniting the nation and offering new avenues for the future. This is why the movements calling for a radical change – Communists, Nazis and, among the educated middle class, the Conservative Revolution – could gain ground, especially with the young generation. An increasingly desperate Republican "stumbling on" lost all its attraction, when even the Social Democrats were forced to tolerate the antisocial policies of Brüning and support Hindenburg against Hitler – making the Nazis appear the more worker-friendly force. Equally, the old guard's presidential regimes failed to suggest new avenues. With widespread economic deprivation and the government's obvious political helplessness, utopian visions of creating a different and better world could enflame the hope of more than 50 per cent of the – Communist and Nazi – voters and of most of the youthful activists. As we shall see in the following section, the vision of a nation united in a single faith played a central role in attracting people to the more forward-looking forces on the Right.

The conservative critique of existing conditions (*Kulturkritik*) of the nineteenth century dramatically increased in intensity after the First World War. While the 'ideas of 1914' had temporarily externalized such a critique by blaming the West for the ills of modernity and glorifying true Germanness, the ideological clashes in the wake of the Empire's downfall had brought the issue back home. A right-wing opposition against the new Republic became a 'powerful force of cultural formation' (Hübinger 1998: 93 f.), because increasing numbers saw nothing worth preserving after 1918. An alien democracy, it was argued, was forced upon Germany both by the victorious Western nations outside and the socialist enemy within. The Versailles treaty cut down Germany to a degree unacceptable to all nationalists, and the politics of the 1920s lacked the successes necessary to overcome initial scepticism. The right-wing rejection of the present could become a fundamental crisis of political orientation, because many also lost faith in their old political ideals. While traditional conservatives like Hindenburg and the core of the DNVP still found orientation and pride in harking back to pre-war times, an extreme Right also rejected the German Empire. It did not wholly buy the stab-in-the-back legend, but saw that monarchical Germany had failed the crucial test of war. It was disillusioned with the Emperor, who had not only been an ineffective political and military authority in war, but also 'cowardly' fled the country when facing personal danger, after having demanded so much sacrifice from others.[10] And finally, right-wing extremists not only blamed left-wing agitators and Jews for the revolution, but also recognized the importance of inequality and class conflict. Imperial Germany, they saw, had lacked the social cohesion necessary to lead total war because of elitist snobbery and a disregard for the suffering of the masses.

What could an extreme Right build on, if it no longer wanted to return to the old monarchical order? First and foremost, there was an increased emphasis on the nation and *Volk*. When the monarch could no longer be regarded as the core of the state, the *Volk* frequently became the new essence. Even if it was not defined in racial terms, as it was by the *völkisch* movement, the belief in a historically defined people could give, in times of frightening changes, a sense of eternal stability in a fundamental 'Germanness'. 'The *Volk*', the conservative Wilhelm Stapel argued, 'is a living entity of people who share a soul. It stretches back over the centuries, with the people passing on their physical and spiritual characteristics from generation to generation. They develop among themselves a shared culture and shared ideals' (1917: 17). And Arthur Moeller van den Bruck, a key figure in the emerging new Revolutionary Conservatism, clearly spelled out the consequences of such a glorification of the *Volk*: 'The conservative counter-movement … places the idea of the nation above all other ideas – even above that of the monarchy' (quoted in Klemperer 1968: 164).

The 'dishonourable' demise of the monarchy came as a shock, but it also opened new avenues. Before the war, Pan-Germans like Heinrich Class had rejected the Kaiser's policies without openly questioning the monarchy, thus remaining ambivalent and confused in their opposition to Wilhelm II. After 1918, however, the new national opposition could be more consistent: the Führer principle took the place of the monarchical ideal. A Führer did not gain his position through birth, but by his actions. He had to work his way up, prove his ability and win trust. Democratic selection was still rejected, but the law of succession made way for an ultimately indefinable and open, but still more modern merit principle. Hitler only followed widely held convictions when he declared in *Mein Kampf*: 'A philosophy of life which endeavours to reject the democratic mass idea … must … make sure that the leadership and the highest influence …fall to the best mind. Thus it builds upon the idea of personality.'

Even more pointedly, Hitler claimed: 'Sooner will a camel pass through a needle's eye than a great man be discovered by an election. In world history the man who really rises above the norm of the broad average usually announces himself personally' (Hitler 1992: 403 and 81. See also Breuer 1999: 50–57, 75–80, 132–139; Breuer 2001: 105–146, 172–180).

In these words, Hitler not only described the rise of a new leader, but also that of a new elite. A certain appreciation of the old aristocracy was left on the new radical Right (especially of their allegedly anti-bourgeois emphasis on heroism, military values and hierarchy or their pure blood), but, like the leader, a new elite had to prove its worth. The service humans could provide for the *Volk* became the ultimate measure for the social position they deserved. Being conservative, the radical Right in the Weimar Republic held on to the idea of hierarchy and an elite often still called aristocracy, but the goal was a new aristocracy of merit. The nobility could be part of it, but only to the extent that it proved its exceptional qualities (Malinowski 2004: 299–320).

The ideal of social harmony among Weimar's extreme Right made them sympathize with ideas about a communal economy. The call for a national socialism was by no means exclusive to the Nazis, but a lesson many extreme conservatives drew from war and revolution. If social injustice seriously threatened the stability of society and thus any total mobilization for war, then social harmony became the prerequisite for uniting the nation in anticipation of future military conflicts. The commitment to these ideas varied. Some largely adopted the popular term 'socialism', mainly because they did not want to leave it to the political opponents on the left, but others proposed thorough social changes or even an alliance of a nationalist Germany with Bolshevism for a joint fight against the capitalist victors of the First World War (Dupeux 1985; Schüdekopf 1960). The call for a national socialism was never connected with detailed proposals, but it distinguished a forward-looking extreme Right from the established conservative forces whose programme was still unmistakeably shaped by the interest of agriculture and social privileges in general.

Re-establishing Germany as a world power was, of course, a dream shared far beyond the political Right, thus serving as a bridge to the more moderate political forces. Paradoxically, the Republic's weakness was the ground for wild Reich-fantasies, as this loaded term recalled past glory and presented a dream for a very different future (Bosbach and Hiery 1999; Kettenacker 1983; Neurohr 1957; Winkler 2000). Without any governmental responsibility, Weimar's extreme Right could be even more uncompromising than the rest of the irresponsible revisionist enemies of the Versailles order, but another important difference was marked by attitude and style: a cult of comradeship and soldierly discipline of 'manly' commitment, of violence and determination, of apocalyptic preparedness for sacrifice in anticipation of a wholly different, utopian future was characteristic for a new Right.

The Conservative Revolution and the Ideal of a Single Communal Faith

While National Socialism eventually proved to be the decisive political movement (see Ch. 6), the so-called Conservative Revolution played an important role in formulating a future-oriented ideology of the Right, which advocated its own utopian visions of a united *Volk* in a powerful German Reich. The term refers to a wide range of very vocal individuals and circles claiming to be the intellectual avant-garde of a new conservatism. Instead of harking back to the past or accepting the present, they claimed that it 'is conservative to create things worth preserving' (Moeller van den Bruck 1932: 202). Their convictions were close to Nazism, as they shared the commitment to activism, strong leadership, hierarchy and military strength, but they were much more intellectual and elitist. Largely from middle-class backgrounds (though often struggling with starting a career in difficult times), they saw themselves as prophets and spiritual leaders of a new national faith without ever being prepared to do the donkey work necessary to establish a mass movement. They often looked with disdain upon the 'vulgarity' of the simplistic Nazi slogans and methods, but the majority jumped on the bandwagon when the Hitler movement proved its power to mobilize the masses and effect a dramatic political change to the Right. While their direct political power – despite some influence on the presidential regimes, especially on Schleicher – was limited, they clearly indicated the continued desire for a national faith in the middle class, especially among its younger and more highly educated members. The Conservative Revolution both reflected and further promoted this desire within a milieu extremely vulnerable to the fatal attraction of National Socialism. In providing a more sophisticated justification for an authoritarian change than the Nazis did, they contributed to preparing a highly trained youth to work within the Third Reich. Despite their malicious attitude towards aloof intellectuals, the Nazis liked to claim the Conservative Revolution for their own cause (Woods 1996: 127), while these right-wing thinkers frequently stressed their role in preparing the ground for the new state. As Edgar Jung claimed: 'The intellectual preconditions for the German Revolution were created outside National Socialism … Through our untold efforts, particularly among the educated, we prepared for the day when the German people voted for the National Socialist candidates. Our work was heroic, for it renounced all thought of success and public acclaim' (quoted in Sontheimer 1983: 284).

The Conservative revolutionaries promoted the ideal of a strong, hierarchically structured and united nation, but they tended to stress the cultural, not the racial dimension. While they shared the near-universal anti-Semitism of the Right, race did not constitute the core foundation of their human anthropology and their understanding of history (Winkler 2000: Vol. 1, 466). Rather, their judgement tended to be, not unlike Nietzsche's, more voluntaristic and inspired by modern aesthetic criteria. They felt no respect for either the German Empire or the Weimar Republic, because these states did not live up to their ideal of human history as a great spectacle. Instead of pragmatic compromises, they desired clear-cut decisions, utopian schemes as goals for shaping the future, full-hearted commitment, heroic struggles, grand battles and sacrifice.

As the intellectual avant-garde of the extreme Right after the war, the Conservative Revolution is marked by free-floating fantasies behind a facade of matter-of-factness. Far away from concrete political responsibilities and without emotional ties to contemporary conditions or the immediate past, the Conservative Revolutionaries were intellectually productive and artistically creative (thus the continued literary and philosophical interest in some of its key figures), but they remained committed to the right-wing agenda of destroying the Weimar Republic and establishing a new authoritarian Reich. They shared the nineteenth century dream of cultural regeneration, but their vision had a much clearer political agenda.

In what follows I shall present a wide variety of Conservative Revolutionaries to show how they built on and further developed the vision of a community united in a single faith. They never formed a coherent single party. Rather, the Conservative Revolution consisted of individuals or small groups who were all more concerned with developing their own ideals than finding a common platform for political action. They produced more interesting ideas than the rest of the Right, but they failed to transcend their own learned circles because they only half-heartedly adapted to the age of the masses. Their attitudes and actions were too elitist and highbrow, and they did not accept the political need for pragmatic compromises. They played with popular words, but were not prepared to adapt fully to the people's desires and fears. Many, like Ernst Jünger or Martin Heidegger, took ideas to such extremes that they no longer allowed for the mixed feelings of human beings, the irreversible pluralism of modern society, the compromises of down-to-earth politics. They developed interesting ideas, but remained aloof: small circles predominantly from the educated classes. When they saw the success of the Nazis, however, the majority saw the affinities and fell in line. The following thus tries to show:

(1) how the dream of a single communal faith provides a crucial key to the understanding of highly influential Weimar intellectuals;
(2) how a wide variety of motivations could lead to the desire for a single communal faith; and
(3) how the visions of the Conservative Revolutionaries, regardless of significant variations, all paved the way towards falling in line with Nazism when this movement proved to be *the* right-wing force which could promise to realize this utopian dream of a nation united behind a single right-wing vision and faith.

With the publication of the *Decline of the West*, the former grammar-school teacher and intellectual nobody Oswald Spengler (1880–1936) gained immediate fame as the most influential cultural critic of his time (Botermann 2000; Felken 1988). When writing the book, the author still expected a German victory (1971: XV); but when published right after the war, it was also read as an instruction for a 'heroic realism' in facing Germany's defeat. In situating Germany's problems within a general decline of the West, Spengler not only offered a general analysis of his time, but he also instructed his readers about the appropriate attitude for coping with this historical moment. In a later publication towards the end of the Weimar Republic, he encapsulated his ideal in the image of the obedient soldier accepting certain death:

> We are born into this age and have to go on courageously to the end destined for us. There is no other path. It is the duty to hold out in the lost position, without hope, without salvation. To hold out like the Roman soldier, whose bones were found in front of a gate in Pompeii. He died, because someone forgot to release him, when Vesuvius erupted. This is greatness, is race. This honest end is the only thing that cannot be taken away from humans. (1932: 88f.)

For Spengler, all cultures – from the Arabic to the European – were living organisms with a life cycle of youth, maturity, old age and death. In this cycle, the occident has reached old age, in his terminology 'civilization': 'The Civilization is the inevitable *destiny* ... Civilizations are the most external and artificial states of which a species of developed humanity is capable. They are a conclusion, the thing-become succeeding the thing-becoming, death following life' (1971: 31). Civilization stood for everything, cultural critics disliked about modernity: a destruction of traditions and religious faith, the decline of the arts, a mass society of isolated individuals, the dominance of instrumental reason and a materialist run for riches. In contrast to previous cultural critics, however, Spengler did not condemn these developments, but regarded them as inevitable. Instead of lamenting, humans needed to adapt. 'Henceforward it will be every man's business to inform himself ... of what with the unalterable necessity of destiny and irrespective of personal ideals, hopes or desires, *will* happen.' Humans are not free to do 'this or that, but the necessary or nothing' (1971: 39).

If the political Right criticized Spengler's work, it was mainly for promoting pessimism. A belief in decline, they feared, would lead to fatalism instead of promoting 'manly' action. Spengler, who usually tended to brush aside adverse opinions, went out of his way to refute this critique – an important indication that the Right was determined to find a forward-looking and activist outlook even in these difficult times. His claim that 'decline' could also mean the *Vollendung* (1951: 63) or completion of a culture was far-fetched, but he rightly maintained that his work did call for a politically active life.

How did Spengler square his belief in an inevitable fate with promoting action? Such a position was shared by a number of his contemporaries. Nietzsche had demanded humans to face the hard consequences of the 'death of God', and Max Weber took a similar stand, when he called on academics to accept the modern condition of general disenchantment with ascetic discipline (Treiber 1991). The cult of heroism had long dismissed human suffering in favour of grand actions, and Klaus Theweleit (1987, 1989) argues convincingly that many right-wing extremists developed a life-denying armour to protect themselves from a chaotic time. Finally, Helmuth Lethen (2002) gives many examples of a new mentality of the interwar years, which he calls 'cool conduct'. In hard times, threatening emotions were suppressed in favour of maintaining a stiff upper lip. Instead of psychological soul-searching, the decisiveness in choosing a role and sticking to it was praised.

In this vein, Spengler demanded a heroic posture. While he saw no way back to the richer culture of the past, the future still held the opportunity for heroism and grand politics. With dogmatic certainty he prophesied 'a future of hardness, Roman hardness ... There will soon be no space for anything else' (1951: 78 f.). This expectation of heroic times led him to dismiss the Weimar Republic. He rejected the November revolution for its 'indescribable ugliness ... No powerful moment, nothing exciting, no great man, no lasting word, no daring offence [*Frevel*], just the petty, disgusting, silliness' (1919: 11). Against an allegedly weak democracy, he propagated the rise of an imperialist age: 'Imperialism is Civilization unadulterated. In this phenomenal form the destiny of the West is now irrevocably set ... The expansive tendency is a doom, something daemonic and immense, which grips, forces into services, and uses up the late mankind ... willy-nilly, aware or unaware' (Spengler 1971: 36 f.). The militaristic future allegedly demanded an absolutist dictator, a Caesar who would subordinate material considerations to the imperialist endeavour.

For the future, Spengler predicted global wars. 'War is the eternal form of higher existence, and states exist for the purpose of war.' 'Even if the world will emerge tired and broken from the blood rivers of this century' (1919: 53), he maintained, the 'final battle for the domination of this planet' will be unavoidable. Full of pathos, he thundered that he, 'whose sword achieves victory here will become the master of the world. The dice of this enormous game are lying there. Who dares to throw them?' (1980: 71, 212)

Spengler claimed that his reflections were an objective historical diagnosis, but beneath a thin layer of scholarship, powerful emotions and political motives shine through. Pushing aside the horrors of the Great War, Spengler indulged in visions of grand battles, catastrophes and the heroic fulfilment of ultimately futile duties. Far outdoing his idol Nietzsche, he viewed history purely from a dramatic perspective.[11] He and, presumably, his enthusiastic readers enjoyed imagining the amoral workings of a ruthless will to power – with complete disregard for human suffering. Spengler was not unaware of his grandiose pathos; in spite of all the aura of a detached analysis, he searched for an audience sharing his fascination of tragic heroism.

> He who does not understand ... that our choice is ... between cleaving to *this* destiny or despairing of the future and of life itself; he who cannot feel that there is grandeur also in the realization of powerful intelligences, in the energy and discipline of metal-hard natures, in battles fought with the coldest and most abstract means; he who is

obsessed with the idealism of a provincial and would pursue the ways of life of past ages – must forgo all desire to comprehend history, to live through history or to make history. (Spengler 1971: 38)

The disregard for human suffering went together with a disregard for the mass of the population. Following the general trend among Conservative Revolutionaries to conquer popular terms for the Right, Oswald Spengler (1919) proclaimed a Prussian socialism, but it was devoid of any call for social justice. Socialism to him was a state-directed economy with all citizens working under a dictator for the nation's heroic goals. Like Sombart, he wanted to overcome the private profit principle of a market economy with a more heroic attitude, where people work to serve the nation. In domestic politics, he was very close to the traditional conservatives.[12] The common people, he claimed, have only one right, and that is the right 'to be governed well' (quoted in Felken 1988: 234). Failing to understand the need for popular support even for a right-wing regime, he glorified an absolutist dictatorship: 'The future Caesarism will not convince, but win with the weapon. Only when this has become obvious, when majority opinion is regarded as suspect and despicable, when someone looks down upon parties in every sense, upon programmes and ideologies, will we have overcome the revolution' (1980: 176).

The open call for violence showed parallels with fascism, but in other ways Spengler remained a traditional conservative. He had the same enemies as the Nazis and was not adverse to many of their goals, but he also showed reservations (Spengler 1980. See also Felken 1988: 195 ff.). Above all, he rejected the Hitler movement's populism. In his glorification of the strong state, there was no room for any rebellious party. He also criticized the Nazi version of racism. Although Spengler's writing was by no means free of racial prejudices (he predicted, for example, a war between the coloured and the white 'races'), a *biological* racism was too deterministic for his taste. All this did not stop him from hoping at first, however, that he could become an advisor to the new regime – a strong indication that he agreed with the general orientation of the Third Reich, but believed that they needed more sophisticated guidance. Goebbels in particular, who was keen for the Nazis to gain respectability during their securing of power by associating with big names, tried to win Spengler's support, but such a role was too passive for him (Felken 1988: 221–225). In contrast to most conservatives, Spengler was soon troubled by Nazi violence in domestic politics. The Night of Long Knives – in which not only the SA leadership but also some prominent conservatives were murdered – and a friend's death at the hands of the Nazis increased Spengler's distance from the regime (Felken 1988: 226), but he never came to oppose it or reflect upon his own role in the destruction of the Weimar Republic.

How does Spengler's thought relate to the desire for a single communal faith? At first glance, the differences might be more striking. The nineteenth-century calls for a new faith tended to emphasize the need for idealism and a thorough moral regeneration. In contrast, Spengler developed a view of history largely determined by objective forces, while human intentions and actions were largely inconsequential. Following Nietzsche, he regarded moral judgements as a childish protest against the all-pervasive human will to power. Above all, he recommended going along with the objective forces of history, fulfilling one's role with dignity and heroism. Value judgements were replaced by an aesthetics of heroism and grand politics, allegedly the true expression of the human will to power.

If we remember, however, that the seemingly objective surface was merely a cover for strong desires, the interpretation changes dramatically. Spengler believed that in the future there would be a world with few major powers. Domestically, these states would be ruled by absolute dictators, who would enforce their political will on to their nations. Each state would thus be, he believed, united in one political will. Such homogeneous national wills would then be the prerequisite for a series of wars, until the strongest dictator would gain global control. The hope for a spontaneous emergence of a single communal faith had been replaced by the vision of a brutal authoritarian integration. While the former described the evolvement of a community of communal spirits, Spengler envisaged a top-down integration, but the end result had much in common: both expected a non-pluralistic hierarchical state united in a single political will. Spengler's work reflects the growing disillusionment with 'idealistic' moral demands and the concept of human agency, but it also shows that the dream of a nation united in one political mission survived in a more ruthless and 'matter-of-fact' form.

Immediately after revolution and defeat, the bohemian **Arthur Moeller van den Bruck** (1876–1925) who turned into a political writer while working for the German war propaganda department from 1916 to 1918, played a key role in showing conservatives a forward-looking response to the revolution.[13] In contrast to Spengler, he showed no signs of fatalism, but urged an acceptance of the changes and a full use of the opportunities they provided. As he had already called for a modernization of conservatism before 1914, he was in a good position to avoid any nostalgia in sketching out new political vistas after 1918. He was the intellectual centre of an informal circle, the *Ring-Bewegung*, which was supported by the industrialists Hugo Stinnes and Alfred Hugenberg, and he wrote for newspapers, but his books became widely read only after his early death in 1925. Where Oswald Spengler preached heroic realism in facing a hard reality, Moeller van den Bruck tried to establish a new inspiring communal vision: the Third Reich.

Throughout his work, Moeller van den Bruck rejected any nostalgia about the German Empire. Like the life-reform movement at the turn of the century, he dismissed pre-war culture for its alleged materialism, spiritual emptiness and lack of artistic achievements. While he cherished August 1914 as the moment of supreme national unity, he attacked the German leadership for destroying the initial enthusiasm through rosy propaganda lies. Above all he claimed that the war had tested the Empire's spiritual strength, cruelly revealing its hollow weakness.

Moeller's dislike of the German Empire, however, did not lead to an acceptance of its destroyers. At first he showed some ambivalence towards the revolution, but he soon came to hate it. He blamed it for accepting defeat and a harsh peace settlement as well as an allegedly Western parliamentary democracy. Furthermore, the revolution did not live up to his desire for grand politics. Like Spengler and many other Conservative Revolutionaries, the author of a nationalist glorification of German history in eight volumes (1904–1910) rejected the revolution for its alleged lack of 'enthusiasm' and a catching vision (Moeller 1932: 212). More than anything, he believed, the downtrodden Germany needed a communal myth and an inspiring utopia. Such a communal faith, 'for which we have to live, if we want to survive' (1932: 243), would bring the nation together and give it strength in facing its international enemies.

Moeller van den Bruck thus welcomed the destruction of Imperial Germany, but not the direction post-war Germany took. He distanced himself sharply from reactionaries harking back to the monarchy, but was still committed to a hierarchical society rooted in a single communal identity. August 1914 had shown to him the quality of the *Volk*, which was supposedly ready to fight for nationalist goals, but he also advocated a strong and authoritarian political leadership. Rejecting both capitalism and liberalism as Western imports, he advocated an allegedly German 'communal economy' – akin to the previous war economy – to realize social justice and a hierarchy based on merit, but he also envisaged a multi-layered and 'organic' hierarchical society with an elite setting the political agenda. Instead of parliamentary procedures, his ideal was a populist leader or a syndicate of leaders winning the people over for a strong, nationalist policy (Moeller 1932: 67, 81–85 and passim).

As the November revolution had destroyed the old order without providing, in Moeller's opinion, a new one, it had left a vacuum, which had to be filled by a second, *völkisch* revolution. Full of optimism, he saw a communal desire for such an event: the '*Volk* wants to become a nation' he proclaimed (1932: 31), that is, united in a single communal faith. While Germany struggled on the verge of civil war, he proclaimed his ideal of a community founded on shared values. 'A nation is a community of norms. And nationalism is consciousness of these norms' (1932: 232). In promoting a 'Third Reich', Moeller van den Bruck aimed to provide a 'new foundation' which would serve as an integrative and inspiring myth to unite and mobilize the nation (1932: 209). Faith in a new Reich was to turn the best of the *völkisch* past into a vision for the future.

The call for a Third Reich was not original[14] but Moeller van den Bruck turned it into an effective political rallying cry. The Reich myth stressed Germany's grand history in difficult times to infuse the *Volk* with pride and hope. Like a poor aristocrat, Moeller van den Bruck emphasized Germany's old title when its real status was under threat. 'There is only one Reich', he claimed, and this one Reich was supposed to be German (1932: 245). The Reich, he emphasized, was 'an old and grand German thought', which, when realized, would complete Germany's 'destiny' (1932: 6). The term 'third' was supposed to mean not only that it would follow the first medieval and the second Empire of 1871, but also that it would be the ultimate synthesis, thus incorporating the best of the entire German tradition. 'We believe that this second Reich was only the bridge to a Third Reich, to a new and final Reich which has been promised to us' (Moeller 1932: 243). It would not reject the world of industry, but combine it with a new communal, essentially German order, anticipated already in the thoughts of Adam Müller, Lagarde and Langbehn as well as in Freiherr vom Stein's Prussian reforms and the state-directed economy of the First World War. It would use modern means of production, but avoid the atomizing social effects Moeller diagnosed in a liberal state. A *völkisch* Germany would succeed in being economically strong and maintain social harmony. The communal faith in the vision of the Reich would unite the nation, make it work together, and thus provide the basis for renewing Germany's military might.

For Moeller, the victorious allies plotted the complete destruction of Germany. Only a revolutionary conservatism could, he believed, save the state by mobilizing all nationalist forces. Such a German reawakening would have to proceed in two steps: first national unity, then the battle for world-power status. As he blamed Imperial Germany's social tensions and spiritual emptiness for its military defeat, uniting the nation in a single communal faith became essential for a military revival. The wish for a strong Germany was – as so often – a key element in the vision of a new Reich.

Despite his aversion to Communism, the Russia-loving Moeller employed the concept of 'young nations' to legitimize a revisionist Moscow–Berlin coalition. While the Western nations were allegedly long past their zenith, no longer needing the large territory they had acquired, he called Germany and Russia 'young' with a growing population and dynamic political goals. They were the 'proletarians', strangled and exploited in an unjust international system. Moeller supported the call for more social justice within Germany, but closer to his heart was the 'socialist' fight for justice between these nations. The term socialism was thus redefined to gain an aggressive meaning in the service of German revisionism. The young nations, he claimed, had a right to change the international order by force (Moeller 1919).

Moeller was not a biological racist, and anti-Semitism was peripheral to his core convictions. Like many other nationalists, however, he was convinced of Germany's cultural superiority. Germans were allegedly chosen to be 'the masters of the globe', because they could overcome liberal capitalism and Marxist collectivism through the establishment of a far superior communal order. Ultimately, the call for a Third Reich aimed at a world shaped and controlled by Germans, allegedly for the universal good. Moeller claimed for Germany a cultural mission to realize – if need be by force – the best in humankind (Moeller 1904–1910: Vol. 2, 253. See also Moeller 1932: 27, 231).

Like many people in the Weimar Republic, Moeller tended towards apocalyptic thinking. His rejection of the present and his idealization of a future Third Reich were so exaggerated, his desire for grand politics (with the usual disregard for human suffering) so strong that he rejected cautious reforms, advocating instead a heroic struggle for the Third Reich, even if it should end in disaster. 'One can imagine no grander end for a great *Volk* than its destruction in a world war, where it took a whole world to defeat a single country' (1932: 230). Ultimately, the *desire* and *will* for a nation united in the pursuit of the grand communal 'Third Reich' myth was decisive for Moeller, not the practical success.

Before the Beer Hall Putch, which established Hitler's German-wide fame, Moeller met the Nazi leader. Hitler tried to sell himself as *the* 'drummer for the nationalist cause', but the promoter of a conservative revolution was not impressed. To a friend he concluded: 'The guy will never get it!' (Pechel 1947: 279). This quotation has been used to show the distance between the thinker removed from practical politics and the populist politician. While the words certainly epitomize the widespread contempt among educated Conservative Revolutionaries for the 'vulgar' Nazis, the meeting also shows that the movement was considered as a potential coalition partner. Moeller himself stated in 1919 that the crucial challenge of the time was: 'How do we deal with our masses?' (1919: 40). The more it became clear that the Conservative Revolutionaries failed to win popular support, the more they were bound to be attracted, despite some contempt, to National Socialism as a vehicle for realizing their ideals.

At least Moeller's widow and many of his followers came to sympathize with the Nazis even before 1933. While it must remain a matter of speculation how Moeller's own views might have changed had he not taken his life in 1925, his dream of a new Reich came to play a central role in the fight against the Republic. Papen's young anti-democratic adviser Edgar Jung called for a mighty 'new Reich that has been promised and anticipated in the books of the ancestors and the history of the Germans. It will be a Reich in which God and body, spirit and power, virtue and beauty will be one again' (1930: 391). The religiously minded Conservative Revolutionary Friedrich Hielscher believed that the Germans were chosen to fulfil God's will in realizing a new Reich, which would become 'simultaneously state and church' under a powerful charismatic leader (1931: 373). And in 1932, an entire edited volume was devoted to presenting the visions of a future German Reich (Büchner 1932). The Nazis thus drew on a vibrant tradition when they called Nazi Germany the Third Reich.

Carl Schmitt was a prominent professor of constitutional and international law who has also gained recognition as a highly original political scientist. While his main intellectual influence has been as a cool analyst of power politics, Schmitt was everything but a detached Machiavellian in the Weimar Republic and Nazi Germany. Throughout his life, he was shaped by his strict Catholic background and his desire for a strong and decisive authoritarian order based on clear convictions. While the nineteenth century search for a single communal faith had largely grown out of a Protestant tradition, Schmitt was the first famous Catholic expressing similar ideas – which is an important indication that the appeal for a political communal faith began to cross Germany's deep confessional divide. Not only did he persuasively argue that all important political terms derive from theological origins, but his own ideas were also strongly motivated by the experience of religious security in his youth. In this sense, his whole work can be read in essence as a 'political theology' which promoted the destruction of democracy and an authoritarian turn towards a powerful non-pluralist state united in one faith (Blasius 2001; Bendersky 1983; Groh 1998; Kennedy 2004; Manemann 2002; Meier 1994; Meuter 1994; Wacker 1994).

Carl Schmitt's critique of modernity – which was mainly expressed in his early writings, but influenced his whole work – was strongly shaped by the religious milieu of his youth. Showing the similarities between a general cultural criticism and a Catholic rejection of modernity, he complained about 'the business as the great ... means for some shabby or meaningless end'. He pitied modern man as a 'poor devil' who

> knows everything and believes nothing ... They wanted heaven on earth, heaven as result of trade and industry ... in Berlin, Paris or New York, a heaven with washing facilities, motor cars and lounge chairs, whose holy scripture is the timetable. A universal permutation and falsification of values rules the souls. Instead of the distinction of good and evil one differentiates sublimely between usefulness and harmfulness. The confusion was terrible. (Schmitt 1991: 63–65)

While Schmitt was fascinated by some modern art, he vehemently rejected the widespread hope of creating a new religion through aesthetic means. He understood the romantic desire for 'a new religion, a new gospel, a new cult of genius, a new universal art', but argued with good reason that such endeavours could never escape their subjective origins. Instead of subordinating themselves to the will of God, they deify the creative subject who uses 'the world as occasion and opportunity for his romantic productivity'. Both the human self-deification and the 'subjective occasionalism', which playfully dismisses the demand for consistency and seriousness in any commitment to a metaphysical truth, repelled Carl Schmitt, who saw the need for a clearly defined order, which would assign humans their place and proper conduct (Schmitt 1982: 51, 23). Aesthetics can provide, he argued, an important service to religious or political convictions, but never take their place, because art was, in the last respect, nothing more than a means to an end. The romantic sin was to take the artistic more seriously than God; the naivety was to believe in being able to shape reality through playful aesthetic visions. The Romantics thus never played a decisive role: they were either ignored, Schmitt argued, or used by serious political forces committed to a clearly defined political programme.

Carl Schmitt's intellectual curiosity tempted him to engage with every stimulating viewpoint around, but the ideal world he outlined in his writings did not allow for playfulness. He could not accept the existence of a plurality of equally valuable opinions because he believed in the 'opposition of good and evil, God and devil' (quoted in Meier 1994: 25). For him, history was an ongoing battle between right and wrong. In this existential conflict there was no room for compromise or a higher synthesis, but only a stark either-or. The main enemies in the modern epoch were the revolutionary forces who stood for anarchy and disorder, ultimately an inevitable result from the modern human hubris which believed in being able to do without God. While emancipatory thought regarded humans as essentially good and perfectible, Schmitt assumed their inevitable sinfulness – and consequently the need for a strong authority controlling their evil desires. While the Left blamed bad social institutions for deforming an originally good human nature, Schmitt believed in the need for authoritarian institutions to maintain social order.

In consequence, anarchists and communists were Carl Schmitt's main political and ideological enemies. Nevertheless, he respected them as committed fighters. Such an ideologically motivated enemy, he argued, fulfils an important function in the godly order. 'It is not good that humans are without an enemy', he declared. 'The enemy is on par with me. That's why I have to struggle with him in battle to gain my own measure, my own limitations, my own identity [*Gestalt*]' (quoted in Meier 1994: 88). What he hated most was not the enemy, but liberal attempts to avoid necessary decisions. In his political theology, human existence presented itself as a battle between good and evil about the proper form of life: how, then, could anyone dare to sit on the fence? As all political decisions were for Schmitt about a metaphysical good and evil, he could scorn the liberal love for fair procedures by remarking that even if liberals were asked to decide whether Jesus or Barabbas should be crucified, they would try to call a committee or postpone the decision. They thus have, he charged, no sense that a human being has to be committed to non-negotiable principles.[15]

In consequence, Carl Schmitt was a sharp critic of parliamentary democracy. In *The Crisis of Parliamentary Democracy* originally published in 1923 he asked rhetorically: are parliamentary debates really motivated by the will to reach the best decision? Professional politicians, he argued, are not representatives of their voters, but above all mouthpieces of undemocratic parties and lobbyists who support their careers. Parliamentary procedures are nothing but a thin façade to hide an unscrupulous bargaining motivated by material interests behind allegedly objective procedures. Carl Schmitt thus provided the political Right with much-used arguments against the Republic: for him, parliamentarianism was not democratic, as parliament did not represent the voters, but interest groups. Instead of basing politics on shared metaphysical convictions, the Republic turned public life into a constant bickering over material interests. Instead of creating a strong and decisive authority to control human selfishness, the state was torn apart in endless egotistical conflicts. Instead of accepting responsibility for their actions, the decisive powers disguised their decisions behind a formalistic system of laws and procedures. The whole system was threatened, though, to be overthrown by the ideological forces from the left, because trust in the republic was fading rapidly. While the population had increasing doubts that the *Reichstag* reflected the common will, both communism and fascism made attractive promises about an identity between citizens and a new state. For Schmitt, an institution which argued formalistically that the best future will emerge from the working of a constitutional and parliamentary system had no chance in the twentieth-century battle of ideologies in which the extreme forces offered a devastating analysis of present conditions, advocated a roadmap for change and developed attractive utopian visions of a better future.

Schmitt saw modern history as a series of attempts to neutralize ideological conflicts. Thomas Hobbes had attempted to overcome the war between the two Christian confessions by stressing the highest authority of the state in all public matters, but his concession that citizens were allowed private convictions proved a deadly weakness for the *Leviathan*: ideologically motivated powers like political parties, churches and interest groups formed within society, ripping the allegedly neutral liberal state apart (Schmitt 1938). More recently, economists and technocrats claimed to provide an objective route to settle conflicts by providing the objectively best way forward, but ideologically motivated movements would always destroy this claim that there is one right way to use the forces of material reproduction beyond differences of convictions and ideals. 'Technology is no longer neutral ground', Schmitt declared in 1932, when Germany was torn apart by conflicting political forces, 'and every strong politics will make use of it. It can thus be only provisional to call the current century in a spiritual sense the technical century. The final meaning will only reveal itself when it becomes clear which kind of politics will be strong enough to gain control over the new technology, and which will be the friend–foe relations which will emerge on this new ground' (1987: 94).

Carl Schmitt described in a seemingly objective way the failure to overcome political conflict through a policy of neutralizations, but he also cherished the continuation of conflict. He vehemently rejected the technocratic belief in one instrumental truth, because he desired a state united in a single metaphysical faith. Creating an ideologically homogeneous state, he claimed in 1931, is much more demanding 'than to create other communities and social entities. In particular it is easier to realize an economic association than a political entity ... The higher and more intensive a community, the higher the consciousness and the action which realizes it. The greater also the risk of failure. The successful and perfected state is thus as great as the unsuccessful state is – morally and aesthetically – disgusting and abysmal' (Schmitt 1994: 163).

What, then, was Carl Schmitt's ideal community? In his early work, *Roman Catholicism and Political Form*, first published in 1923, he made his debut as a strong defender of the Catholic Church. Theology, he argued, was superior to the glorification of material progress because it not only provided a rationality of means, but also a rationality of ends. While the instrumental reason of economists and technocrats could increase human power over nature, only religion could provide a meaning of life which succeeds in giving material means a deeper purpose. At this stage, however, Schmitt did not advocate just any religion, but only Catholicism, because he saw it as ideal in combining decisiveness in matters of religious truth with an openness to human life and flexibility in strategic questions. This *complexio oppositorum* (combination of extremes) allows Catholicism to incorporate a wide variety of people and operate effectively in different environments without losing its distinctiveness. The authority of the Pope provides a clear dogma, which then allows for tactical flexibility without losing the ideological bearings.

Schmitt praised exactly those points about Catholicism which enlightened criticism had most condemned. What opponents saw as an opportunistic battle for the church's interest in the political sphere, Schmitt called an admirable tactical flexibility. While extreme nationalism demanded a distinct national culture and complete loyalty to the nation, Schmitt praised Catholicism's ability to be at home in different states. While the faith in the infallibility of the Pope violated the modern call for the individual to rely on his own reason, Schmitt glorified it as the most supreme example of a much-needed decisiveness.

Schmitt was not satisfied with a private religiosity, but demanded a communal religion. Against the modern stress on the importance of individual religious experiences, Carl Schmitt used Dostoevsky's famous parable from the novel *The Brothers Karamazov*, in which Jesus is scolded by a grand inquisitor that his reappearance threatens the institution of the church. While Dostoevsky criticized the distance of Catholicism from Christ's original message, Schmitt emphatically sided with institutionalized religion. Instead of personal religious feelings, which were supposed to be only an expression of subjective fantasies, he stressed Catholicism's power to establish a meaningful social form. While private religions would only destabilize the human community in glorifying the modern subject and its arbitrary will for self-realization, Christianity as an institution could provide a grand and coherent communal structure. If Catholicism succeeded in establishing universal rule, he argued, it could 'bring peace to the world' (1996b: 32).

For Schmitt, religious experiences were secondary because he valued religion for its function to stabilize and structure a community. Religion should not be limited to the private sphere, but set the essential norms for social life and provide political orientation. In sharp opposition to the liberal call for a religiously neutral state, which only allows for faith in the private sphere as long as it does not challenge the secular public order, Schmitt advocated a community whose whole existence was based on religion. Such a communal religion, he believed, should not allow for many private interpretations in key questions, but be defined clearly through dogma and one religious authority.

Carl Schmitt thus made his intellectual debut as a fervent defender of Catholicism. While his emphasis on the political and social function of the church in giving a clearly defined and meaningful form to communal life linked his arguments with the desire for a communal faith, he still strongly rejected the idea of creating an up-to-date nationalist world-view, which had largely grown out of the Protestant tradition. In the middle of the 1920s, however, his wish for a political theology became more abstract and general. The reason for his growing distance from Catholicism is not quite clear. Conflicts with the church about the separation from his wife presumably played a role, as well as his ambitions.

He could achieve, after all, a much wider intellectual and political influence if he came out of the Catholic corner to advocate more generally the need for a decisive ideological stand. Apart from such personal reasons, he gradually came to believe that Catholicism was just one interest group within the modern state, thus lacking the ability to unite the nation in a single communal faith. Catholicism or any other religion could not achieve what Carl Schmitt really wanted: to provide one ideology for the state as a whole. Such a communal faith could only be realized, Carl Schmitt came to believe, in the political sphere. 'In the meantime', he declared in the introduction to a new edition of *Political Theology* from 1933, 'we have recognized that the Political is the total', that is, not the religious (1996d: 7). He no longer wanted to revive a religious age, but promoted more pragmatic, future-oriented political attempts at establishing a powerful, hierarchically structured and ideologically firm order. Following the intellectual trend of the inter-war period, he presented his ideas in a seemingly amoral and objective analysis of power politics, but this new 'matter-of-factness' did not stop him from continuing to present, in altered fashion, many of his old ideals.

Schmitt's shift in emphasis from the religious to the political was eased by the fact that he saw the two areas as closely related. In *Political Theology* (1996d) he argued that key terms of political theory are secularized religious terms. Both religion and politics are claimed to deal with the whole of communal and individual existence; both tend towards decisiveness in determining the proper way of life. Politics based on strong principles came to be Schmitt's religion of a secular age. Like Catholicism in the past, politics was to establish an ultimate communal authority to control the evil in human beings, to distinguish between right and wrong, and to create a homogeneous community in opposition to a clearly defined political enemy.

One key element of Schmitt's political theory was his claim that no political entity could exist without a single sovereign power. While it might *seem* in untroubled times that laws and procedures rule, the state of exception proves the opposite. Laws cannot defend themselves; a power has to put them into place and ensure their authority, if need be by unlawful means. Laws and procedures thus do not establish authority, but an authority establishes and secures the rule of laws and procedures. In Schmitt's writing, the sovereign gains the features of a secular god – he has the authority and thus founds the political order. He does not have to be morally right or benign, but only decisive to give social life its form. Carl Schmitt thus emphatically agreed with Thomas Hobbes's 'famous '*Auctoritas, non veritas facit legem*' (Schmitt 1985: Ch. 1 and 2).

If a political order is based solely on a sovereign *will*, then it is, according to Schmitt's *The Concept of the Political* (1932), built on a sovereign *decision*. While religious, moral or practical reasons can be used to legitimize an order, exactly this plurality of possible reasons makes it necessary to decide. A decision is thus the essence of politics: it distinguishes who is friend or foe, what is included in the social order and what is excluded. The state, Schmitt argued, has to assume this authority; otherwise it is no longer a state, but the battleground for parties and interest groups.

While Schmitt's intellectually fascinating decisionism has frequently been taken as the amoral acceptance of a pluralistic and relativistic world, where normatively unjustified decisions are unavoidable (Krockow 1990), it is important to note that Carl Schmitt only glorified strong decisions. As all indecisive political actors would (and should) be simply brushed aside (Schmitt 1940: 80 f.), Schmitt celebrated the powerful and decisive. For him 'the high points of grand politics' were 'the moments where the enemy is seen in concrete clarity as enemy' (quoted in Meier 1994: 96). While Schmitt rejected a Republic with its emphasis on legal procedures as weak, he glorified the strong, authoritarian and militaristic state.

Friend–foe thinking not only implied a clear recognition of the political enemy, but equally a non-pluralistic definition of one's own state. In calling for 'the utmost degree of intensity of a union or separation, of an association or dissociation' (1996: 26), it advocated a nation united in a single communal faith which clearly recognized and fought its enemies. A strong state demanded, Schmitt argued as early as 1926, a homogeneous people, achieved both through promoting communal convictions and through excluding the 'other'. 'Every true democracy is based upon not only treating the equal as equal, but inevitably also the unequal as unequal. Homogeneity is thus firstly a necessary part of democracy, and secondly – if need be – the exclusion or destruction of the heterogeneous' (Schmitt 1994: 67).

As Schmitt believed that humans were evil and needed to be controlled, he emphasized the state more than the *Volk* (Voigt 2001). After the mid-1920s, however, he shared the belief in the need for a single communal faith. In trying to redefine – like Spengler and Moeller van den Bruck – a key term of the political opponent, Schmitt claimed that it was not the Weimar Republic but the radical forces which were truly democratic. While a pluralistic society with institutionalized ways of containing conflicts can never achieve a full identity between government and citizens, populist dictatorships like Bolshevism and fascism work towards overcoming domestic tensions. Agreeing with this utopian goal, Carl Schmitt advocated overcoming the Weimar Republic to establish an authoritarian rule. A decisive dictatorship should turn the nation into a homogeneous community. In deciding on one clear-cut state ideology, it would be able to define friend and foe and thus move towards a grand politics based on metaphysical principles. It would thus unite the friends into one community based on a shared communal faith and fight against the existential enemy both within and outside.

Schmitt thus transferred his initial religious dichotomy between God and devil into the political sphere. The enemy, he argued, is not necessarily morally 'evil' or 'ugly', but he is simply 'the other, the stranger; and it is sufficient for his nature that he is, in a specially intense way, existentially something different and alien, so that in the extreme case conflicts with him are possible. These can neither be decided by a previously determined general norm nor by the judgment of a disinterested and therefore neutral third party' (Schmitt 1996: 26 f.).

In foreign policy, the enemies were, for Schmitt, all competing powers. He thus tried to provide legal arguments for the fight against the Versailles treaty and in favour of German dominance within Europe (Schmitt 1940). In domestic politics he advised the presidential regimes in their destruction of the Republic. After hesitating shortly in the early months of 1933, he joined the Nazi party on May Day and worked for the new regime (even celebrating Hitler's decision to purge the SA and settle old scores in 1934). With the consolidation of the new regime, he – like many conservative supporters of Nazism – lost influence to dyed-in-the-wool Nazis, but he remained loyal to the bitter end.

While Schmitt first favoured the presidential regimes, his support for Nazism was not accidental. In 1929, he expressed his admiration for fascism and its ability to win the masses. Such a populist backing for grand goals could, he argued, justify dictatorial measures (Schmitt 1994: 123–130). He shared Nazism's rejection of universal norms and laws, because he took enmity between different communities to be part of the godly order ('Whoever says humanity wants to deceive', Schmitt 1940: 162). He celebrated the fact that nationalism could generate stronger loyalties than the Socialist utopia. Above all, he supported the Nazi turn against liberal plurality in favour of their stress on decisiveness, commitment to the community and heroic determination in fighting for its goals.

Carl Schmitt was fascinated by a decisive and populist Führer, who would succeed in uniting the country behind his political vision. While he called parliamentarianism undemocratic, he argued that Hitler truly expressed the national will. The occasional plebiscite was in his eyes sufficient to prove an identity between ruler and ruled. His emphasis on homogeneity made him accept the Nazi attacks on domestic enemies, supporting in particular their anti-Semitic propaganda with vicious denunciations of allegedly subversive Jewish thought (Blasius 2001: 153–155; Gross 2000). As early as 1933, he welcomed in a newspaper 'the purification of public life of all non-Aryan, essentially foreign elements so that ... coming generations of Germans will be pure ... No alien type can interfere with this great and profound, but also inner – I would almost say intimate – process of growth' (reprinted in Becker and Becker 1993: 301). The Nuremberg laws he praised as 'an expression of racial strength and unity' (quoted in Koonz 2003: 208), and continued – obviously less extreme – anti-Semitic comments after 1945 show that such statements had not been purely opportunistic. While Carl Schmitt was not a *völkisch* thinker, he fully shared the dream of national homogeneity.

Decisionism can appear as a resigned response to the irreducible pluralism of world-views in modern times. Questioning the possibility of rational arguments about the right way of life, decisionists stress the need for making choices to avoid paralysis. As with other Conservative Revolutionaries, the seemingly objective analysis – carried out to distance oneself from nineteenth century 'romanticism' and 'idealism' – only thinly masked Schmitt's political agenda. He advocated a powerful state to decide for all its citizens on one clear-cut worldview. He rejected freedom of thought and a plurality of opinions, calling instead for a nation united in a single communal faith. Only such an illiberal decisiveness could, he argued, give greatness to a state. Such an anti-pluralistic, authoritarian and implicitly totalitarian decisiveness was more important to him than the ideology's precise content. He could thus move away from Catholicism, when he came to doubt its ability to become an all-pervasive faith, and could later accept Nazism as the political formation most able to realize his ideals. His emphasis on the need for stable institutions and civil security marked a certain distance from the fascist movement, but the communalities were far greater: not only the vision of a nation united in a single faith, but also the goal of great power status for Germany, the rejection of communism and other progressive parties, who were seen as forces of decomposition, and a hateful distrust of Jews. Opportunism certainly played a role in Schmitt's decision to serve the Nazi state, but so did the many ideological affinities.

Ernst Jünger was a core figure of the Conservative Revolution, who advocated a nation united in militaristic determination. He initially acquired fame as the author of war books glorifying the soldiers under the steel helmet. After 1925 his political articles made him a leading 'soldierly nationalist',[16] and *The Worker* (1932), his most substantial work of the Weimar years, was arguably the most innovative and resourceful attempt to square an extreme conservatism with the modern technological age. Jünger's militant nationalism announced the demise of liberal democracy in favour of a heroic age, leading, via a 'sequence of wars and civil wars', to a new grand world order (Jünger 1932: 75).

Jünger volunteered for war service in August 1914, but his war diary (King 2003) and, more covertly, his war writings show that the initial naive enthusiasm did not survive the reality of modern industrial warfare. He had expected adventure and heroism, but the reality was dominated by murderous weapons. The war took a course nobody had intended, showing the power of modern means over all human planning. Finally, all effort seemed wasted because Germany lost the war and accepted an allegedly shameful peace. Jünger gave expression to what many nationalistically minded war veterans felt, needed and desired. In his war writings, he tried desperately to find a positive meaning for the hard war years and the shock of defeat, while his other publications of the Weimar years tried to square the power of technology with his old ideals of heroism and a conservative order.

What makes Jünger particularly interesting, however, is that he did not blend out the new realities by sticking to outdated clichés, but seriously engaged with his time. In line with Nietzsche's *amor fati* and Weimar's new-matter-of-factness, he advocated a 'heroic realism', that is, a heroism when facing even the most unpleasant aspects of reality. However, he also suggested that such an attitude would not only be stoic, but would also promote the emergence of a heroic age offering the opportunity for an adventurous existence in serving one's country in the drive for world domination. The dream Jünger had when volunteering for war service continued to drive him throughout the Weimar Republic: the desire for an adventurous existence within a grand institution. He wanted to be part of the elite within a hierarchically structured nation serving a heroic communal destiny.

Despite his 'cool conduct' (Lethen 2002), Jünger was ultimately driven by emotionally charged aesthetic visions of heroism. Like Nietzsche, he wanted to transcend individual suffering by viewing existence as a work of art. While he had sympathies for the more spectacular developments in Russia, he joined the Conservative Revolution in vehemently rejecting the German revolution and the Republic, because in his eyes the struggling democratic forces lacked courage and heroism, a grand political vision and inspiring leaders. 'There was a lack of breeding [*Rasse*]', he wrote in 1925, 'of martyrs, of dramatic developments, of inevitability' (Jünger 2001: 118). Pre-war Germany, however, also failed to find his sympathies. He valued the army and its imperialist ambitions, but rejected the Empire as a whole as weak, sterile and artificial. The Empire's defeat in war and its eventual collapse when facing the revolution revealed to him the hollow weakness of the old order. In rejecting the Weimar Republic, Jünger could thus not hark back to historical traditions, but had to look forward towards a new conservative (that is, strictly hierarchical) and heroic order. Full of self-confidence, he claimed in a letter from 1927 'that right now only I am able to give things the right direction' (quoted in Berggötz 2001: 866).

In his struggle for a new order, Jünger stylized himself as a 'Prussian anarchist' (1929: 257), that is, the ruthless destroyer of existing conditions, but only in order to create space for a new and better order. He felt justified in working towards a nihilistic or 'magic point zero' (1929: 189) because he was convinced that the allegedly heroic war generation would then be able to bring forth a better, militaristic order. His political articles written in the second half of the 1920s (Jünger 2001) thus called upon the veterans' organizations to destroy the Republic and realize their own ideal, a heroic age. The 'man under the steel helmet', which he glorified as 'a new type of human being, a harder and more courageous race', was to be 'the ideal image of the movement' in this struggle for change (Jünger 1925: 55, 73).

Jünger did not formulate a precise political programme, because the new order was to emerge spontaneously from the 'adventurous heart' of the true heroes. Taking Sombart's wartime distinction of 'merchants and heroes' (see Ch. 4) to extremes, Jünger believed that the hedonistic capitalist order did not stand a chance against the onslaught of a new warrior cast. His vision of the new order was at first largely in line with other extreme nationalists: he advocated a deep 'connection with blood, soil and emotions', praised the values of 'tradition, honour, loyalty, manliness [and] fatherland' and demanded a truly German *völkisch* future: 'Of prime importance for us is not a revolution changing the order of the state, but a revolution of the soul, which will turn the chaos into a new elemental order' (Jünger 1925: 161, 229, 114).

While Jünger stressed the need for an essentially German order, his focus was very much on the present and the future. He was conservative only in the sense of aiming for an authoritarian, rigorously organized social order. Incorporating the idea of social justice, he called for a 'nationalist, social, militant and authoritarian' future (Jünger 2001: 218). His vision was that of an army camp: a strict hierarchical order united in one purpose and completely dominated by allegedly male values of military adventure and sacrifice. This vision also included the wish for a charismatic leader who would bring forth the best of the nation by uniting it behind worthy political goals: 'There is nothing missing but a man who can bring the sum of the existing trends together' (Jünger 2001: 316. See also Jünger 1932: 12, 71).

In calling for a nation united in a single communal faith, Jünger ruled out any pluralism whatsoever. In a nationalist state, he prophesied, 'all anti-nationalist forces will have a bad day' and feel 'an iron fist on the throat' (Jünger 2001: 294). The realization of an anti-Western, essentially 'German' society would leave no space for anything un-German. While anti-Semitism was not at the centre of Jünger's convictions, the hatred of political and cultural pluralism also included the removal of Jews. 'Germans have to win their true existence – in it the alien is condemned to complete powerlessness like a fish which has been thrown onto a volcanic island' (Jünger 2001: 544). 'Do not honour this vermin too much. Only to the extent that we strengthen the German in us, is the power of all hostile forces weakened. Everything essential lies within ourselves' (Jünger 2001: 295). A truly German communal faith, Jünger thus argued, will turn Germany into a homogeneous national community or *Volksgemeinschaft*. While everything un-German was to disappear, the new order should concentrate all its energy on 'the ultimate goal', a 'great and powerful Reich of all Germans' (Jünger 1925: 83).

In the mid 1920s, Jünger entered the political arena to mobilize nationalist veterans for his political vision. Frustrated by the lack of success, he turned to a more general analysis of history and current political conditions in the early 1930s. Following the general trend to avoid normative arguments, he tried to present his thoughts as an objective analysis, but the exalted language reveals his continued fascination with heroism, grandness and sacrifice. Nevertheless, the attempt to show an objective historical logic yields original results. Drawing on a standard argument of cultural critics, Jünger blamed technology for the ills of the existing modern society. As humans allegedly lost control over their means, technology produced many unwanted effects, for example the anonymity of modern cities, the tension between traditional ideals of truth and beauty and the material reality of a dirty production process, and technology-out-of-control in the senseless destruction of trench warfare. Humans, Jünger believed, no longer lived in harmony with their means, thus failing to achieve a unified culture.

While the Great War was Jünger's prime example of technology run wild, parts of it also served as examples for an elite starting to gain control over modern means. The pilot, the tank driver and the storm trooper were his prime examples for humans who had learnt to control technology through their heroic determination. In consequence, he argued, they were also the people able to integrate technology harmoniously into society, thereby creating a homogeneous modern culture and style.

Jünger performed an intellectual somersault. Previous cultural critics tried to find a place for modern technology within culture. The overwhelming power of technology in the First World War convinced Jünger that this was impossible. He thus advocated the opposite route: if technology could not be integrated into culture, then culture had to learn the 'language' of technology (Jünger 1932: 158). Why? Obviously the dream of overcoming modern plurality by a unified cultural style was more powerful than Jünger's dislike for modern technology. He came to envisage a homogeneous culture as a so-called 'organic construction' where humans and machines would meld into a harmonious whole (Jünger 1932: 290).

According to Jünger, humans had no choice other than to use technology for military ends. While machines had served to increase the standard of living in the nineteenth century, such an utilitarian attitude would perish with increased international competition. The First World War had shown the inevitability of a 'total mobilization' of society as a whole (Jünger 1930); no nation could possibly opt out without losing the status of a great power. Competition would force the big players to become 'more cynical, Spartan, Prussian or bolshevic' (Jünger 1932: 201), all in consequence of the drive for ultimate efficiency in mobilizing maximum power. All citizens would become 'workers', either workers of production for the war or, as soldiers, workers of destruction. Jünger anticipated a series of wars of unprecedented intensity, before one nation would come to dominate the world.

This reads like a horrendous dystopia, but for Jünger and other militarists it was a vision which promised to fulfil all their desires. The nation would be turned into a fighting machine united by the single communal goal of world domination, the population would find a purpose for their existence in serving the nation, and the many conflicts would provide unprecedented heroic grandeur and sacrifice. The world of materialism would be overcome by the grandeur of war, which Jünger likened to the beauty of Homer's *Iliad*. Like Nietzsche, Jünger judged the process by aesthetic criteria of heroism, brushing aside the human suffering as unimportant. 'The goal is to find a perspective from which the locations of losses are seen as the mountain of stone chips which are lost from the block while creating a statue' (Jünger 1932: 116). Humans should willingly accept individual suffering and death as inevitable sacrifice in the process of creating a new and better 'world still hidden in the future' (Jünger 1925: 141) – that is, both in the creation of a new admirable heroic type of human and a grand world order.

Ultimately, Jünger proclaimed, the victorious nation would establish a new world order.

> For a long time the unity of one rule, which is committed to the highest [values], has not been known – and not the sword of power and justice, which alone can guarantee

> peace to the villages, grandeur to the palaces, unity among the *Völker*. And, nevertheless, everywhere this desire is still somehow present. Only in such a unity are creations and images possible, in which the sacrifice finds fulfilment and legitimation, allegories of the eternal in the harmonic rule of the space and in monuments, which will stand the passage of time. (Jünger 1932: 217 f.)

Jünger's statements about a heroic future remained vague, but the intent is clear. He dreamt of a 'unity of form', 'a consistency of institutions, habits and customs, economic security, an appreciation of the language of command and a hierarchical order, shortly a life according to a law' (Jünger 1932: 225, 233). From such an order a clear 'plan of work' or action would emerge, giving a higher purpose to all the modern economic and technological means. 'The goal, where all efforts will come together, is the planetary rule of the new type [of heroic human]. In this alone there is the benchmark of an overall stability, which incorporates all military and civil work processes' (Jünger 1932: 291). Jünger thus envisaged a world united in a single heroic faith, finding its expression in a grand, awe-inspiring world order. The empires of the past would simply pale, he claimed, in comparison with the planetary age of total mobilization.

After 1933, Jünger kept his distance from the Third Reich, but this should not disguise the affinities to Nazism and to fascism in general. Throughout the 1920s, he wished 'wholeheartedly' that National Socialism would win (2001: 517). He did not criticize Nazi principles, but criticized the movement's pragmatic compromises. While Hitler followed a legalistic strategy after the failed coup in 1923, Jünger believed that only ideological rigour could mobilize a heroic elite for a *völkisch* revolution. While Hitler accepted both agrarian romantics and technocrats in his party, Jünger praised the coming of a technological age. While Hitler promoted a high standard of living to keep the population on board, Jünger preached a cult of asceticism and sacrifice. While Hitler fought for votes, Jünger complained about 'the plebeian spirit of the movement' (Niekisch 1958: 189), putting his hope on 'the will of a new aristocracy' instead (Jünger 2001: 240). While Hitler distanced himself from the terrorism of enraged farmers in the world economic crisis to avoid a ban of the NSDAP, Jünger preached an unwavering honesty. Nazism could only be victorious, he claimed, 'if its weapons are forged from the purest metal' (2001: 517). Instead of accepting the compromises of the political battle, he came to preach the belief in the inevitable arrival of his vision of the future.

Undoubtedly, however, Jünger shared many of the Nazi ideals. Both are marked by a 'male fundamentalism' (Weisbrod 1998), celebrating the heroic soldierly man and exclusively male organizations. Both glorified violence as a value in itself. Like Nietzsche before and Goebbels after, Jünger proclaimed: 'It is not essential what we fight for, but how we fight' (1922: 76). Ideological uncertainties were overcome by a call for relentless commitment. War was to weld the community together and produce true men. Committed to an extreme militarism, both Nazism and Jünger celebrated the army, war and imperialist expansion. Both took 'the will to power and dominance' (Jünger 1925: 191) as the most fundamental human drive and promoted a cult of heroism. And while they both preached a world of international conflicts, they also propagated the vision of a mighty Reich united by a Führer and his elite in a single communal faith.

Since the publication of *Being and Time* (1927), **Martin Heidegger**[17] came to be regarded as one of the most eminent, but also controversial philosophical innovators of his time. His lectures fascinated students, colleagues and members of the wider public, and he quickly established a circle of devoted followers. His philosophy is not easily accessible, but he attracted attention because he offered fascinating reflections on a core topic of his time: the lack of meaning in the modern, secular world and the possibility of finding a new orientation. His thoughts about human existence could obviously not reach the mass of the population, but those interested in philosophy realized that this was not just another academic exercise. While engaging deeply with the historical tradition, Heidegger wanted to provide answers for his time. Philosophy, he strongly believed, should not exist within an ivory tower, but give direction to individuals, the national community and humanity at large. As his former student Karl Löwith rightly noted: 'Only half of him was an academic. The other and probably greater half was a militant and a preacher' (1986a: 28).

Heidegger was not seeking a populist arena; for that, he was much too convinced of the importance of philosophical thought. Like many of his contemporaries he felt the post-war world to be in a deep crisis, but this crisis was to him above all a spiritual one, and it could only be overcome by philosophical reflection. Heidegger followed Nietzsche in diagnosing an age of nihilism. For him, God was dead in the sense that there was no longer a communal religion powerful enough to shape history. The horrors of the First World War, in which all belligerents had claimed to fight in the name of God, was proof to him that Christianity no longer motivated or controlled human actions (Bambach 2003: 34). People still had private beliefs, but a shared communal faith, which could guide humans in their communal existence, was missing. In consequence, humanity was lost in inauthentic everyday norms and fashions instead of committing itself to a meaningful destiny; society was drifting apart because it lacked a sense of community based on shared beliefs; and academia lost its most important function of guiding humanity in the age of specialization and vocational training. He, like so many others, believed that only a new communal faith could save humanity.

In the early 1930s, Heidegger studied Jünger's *The Worker* and *Total Mobilization* with great intensity (Heidegger 2004). He valued the works as the most accurate description of nihilism: an age with no sense of an overarching purpose, which thus loses itself in an aimless technological frenzy. But while Jünger expected a heroic will to power to provide new meaning and order, Heidegger rejected such a will to power as the core symptom of nihilism. If humans know no higher purpose in life, they can only think of realizing their will – without knowing what they want to achieve with this. The modern subjects can see no meaning in the world; thus they want to control this alien environment. Knowing of no higher purpose, human life turns into an animal-like existence: the world is regarded as a hostile, inhumane and chaotic place; one has to fight and control it to secure one's survival and material well-being. Heidegger thus valued *The Worker* as the most insightful description of the modern condition, but strongly opposed Jünger's evaluation: 'The astute insight into this history [of modernity] corresponds with a delusion about the essence of this history' (Heidegger 2004: 74). Heidegger strongly opposed Jünger's hope that the heroic will to power would open up the vista towards a new and better age, arguing instead that the concept of an 'organic construction' in the world of *The Worker* was nothing but 'the last disguise of total mechanization' (2004: 201).

Martin Heidegger always stressed his humble rural background. He made a cult of his favourite workplace, a small hut deep in the Black Forest, and emphasized the importance of rootedness in contrast to modern internationalism. 'The lack of connection with the soil of current life is the root of the increasing decline ... The task is again to choose a life of simplicity and healthy orientation – a life that does not fall victim to the semblance of culture [*Scheinkultur*] in big cities, [but] that should again be an example in displaying loyalty to the soil' (2000: 53). He was clearly a romantic about rural life and the traditional lifestyles of farmers and craftsmen, but his real concern was the lack of a higher meaning in modern life: he did not reject the technological world as such, but a 'dreary technological frenzy' (Heidegger 1961: 37), that is, a fascination with technology for its own sake. Technology, he argued after the Second World War in much more detail, becomes a goal in itself if a wider purpose in life is missing. The same technology can be beneficial, however, if used strictly as a tool within a wider orientation in life. 'What is dangerous is not technology' as such (Heidegger 1978: 309), but a technology which runs wild, because it has lost any sense of a higher purpose.[18]

The purpose of Heidegger's philosophy was, then, to reflect on modern nihilism and to work towards regaining a more fundamental and satisfying meaning of existence. In *Being and Time* (1927) he already touched upon the concepts of heritage, historicity and collective destiny (1962: Ch. 5, Division 2), but the main focus was on finding an authentic existence for the individual self. Resembling other forms of a 'cool conduct' (Helmut Lethen) in trying to find orientation in the chaotic times after the First World War, the book called for *Entschlossenheit* or resoluteness in facing the realities of human existence: the fact that we are thrown into a world, that choices about what we do are of essential importance because only a limited time-span is given to us (if we waste time on trivialities we can never regain it), and that we should aim for a life in harmony with our own historical destiny. Reflecting on the essence of human existence and on the relevance of our communal heritage was shown to be an important way to question the thoughtless platitudes dominating everyday life and to work towards a more authentic existence.

One can see continuities with hindsight, but it would have been far-fetched to anticipate in 1927 the path from *Being and Time* to Heidegger's enthusiastic support for Nazism in 1933. Since 1929, however, he spoke increasingly about *das Kommende* ('the future coming'). The call for a conscious acceptance of the human condition to achieve an authentic individual existence continued, but he was also increasingly influenced by the Conservative Revolution (Habermas 1992). Sharing their contempt for constitutionalism, human rights and democracy, he favoured instead an emphasis on the well-being of the national community and the rule of an elite – which goes a long way towards explaining his support for National Socialism (Bambach 2003: XXIV f.). He agreed with the right-wing rejection of the Versailles treaty and the wish for a strong Germany; its contempt for the republic, its fear of Marxism and bolshevism; its stress on a commitment to one's nation in rejection of universalism; and the love of authoritarian structures. He could find echoes of his own thought in the Nazi blood-and-soil rhetoric (although he soon came to recognize the technocratic side of Nazism as well), and he shared their *völkisch* ideals of a harmonious nation united under a strong leadership. While he strongly opposed any biological racism, he held prejudices against Jews and everything allegedly un-German and internationalist. He regarded ideological pluralism within one community as a sign of chaos, indifference and decline. He had not fought in the First World War, but admired the front-line generation, described authentic life as a constant battle and drew strongly on a lexicon of *völkisch* militancy (fate, destiny, decision, struggle, will, self-assertion, danger, sacrifice, etc.) in formulating his philosophy.[19] He did not propagate a policy of militaristic expansion, but he wished for a strong Germany. Even after his distance from the Nazi regime had grown, he still sided with Germany in the war, also because he continued to believe to the end of his life that only Germany could overcome Western nihilism and foster a new and better beginning.

He admitted to his brother Fritz that the Nazi 'seizure of power' contained some negative aspects, but he chose to brush aside everything which could throw doubts on what he, like many, regarded as a 'German awakening'. 'You must not look at the whole movement from the bottom, but from the Führer and his great goals.' In consequence, he advised, 'not to pay any attention to what is happening around you in terms of low and non-pleasant things' (2000: 93). Why did Heidegger consciously ignore the negative, focusing instead on what he saw as the positive potential of Nazism? Partly this was motivated by an apocalyptic view of conditions in the Weimar Republic: like Ernst Jünger and so many other extremists, Heidegger was convinced that conditions could not become worse. If there was nothing left worth preserving, desperado policies appeared to be wholly justified. Despite its imperfections, the Hitler movement seemed to open up the only chance for a new age, in which the German nation would find a new communal faith. Heidegger saw only the stark alternative of continuing to participate in the general human decline or finding new strength in a German revival. The decisive question, he stated as the new Rector of his university, was whether Germans will try a truly new start, 'when the spiritual strength of the West fails and the West starts to come apart at the seams, when this moribund pseudo-civilization collapses into itself, pulling all forces into confusion and allowing them to suffocate in madness. Whether such a thing occurs or does not occur, this depends solely on whether we as a historical-spiritual *Volk* will ourselves, still and again, or whether we will ourselves no longer' (Heidegger 1991: 38).

Like Carl Schmitt, Heidegger was brought up as a Catholic, and the church financed the education of this talented son of a sexton. He initially intended to become a priest, but gradually turned into a critic of the church, because dogmatism seemed to have replaced true convictions and an unreserved inquiry into the truth of Being. His growing distance from Catholicism did not mean, however, that he lost his religiosity. Like many, he distanced himself from his childhood faith, but remained, to put it in a nutshell, a religious man in search of a religion, even of a religious age. Instead of powerless dogmatism or mere personal convictions, he desired strong collective religious feelings with the power to shape history. For a while, he believed that the Third Reich lived up to this ideal. As he stated in a lecture in the summer term of 1933:

> Now we are faced with the question ... whether we want to create a spiritual world for the development of our *Volk* and state or not. If we do not want it and if we are unable to make it happen, then some form of barbarism will sweep us away and we will have finally played out our role as a *Volk* who shapes history ... [But] if we want to succeed at this ... then we must find the will to begin to create this spiritual world and to fall in line for a second great armed conflict, a spiritual confrontation [*Auseinandersetzung*] with our whole history ... We must learn to grasp this historical moment [*Augenblick*] and to know that it is great enough and pregnant with enough forces so that we can dare to inaugurate once again the authentic beginning of our historical *Dasein*. Our sole aim here is to create a spiritual future for our *Volk* and to assure its calling among other peoples. (Heidegger 1989: 134 f.)

Heidegger's desire for an age united in a single communal faith was shaped by his background in a religiously secure Catholic environment, but his distance to the Catholic church, which was at its strongest in the 1930s, meant that he followed Nietzsche and the many other classicists to use not the Christian Middle Ages, but classical Greece as the prime example for a community united in a single communal faith.

Throughout his life, Heidegger showed a deep love for the arts. He strongly rejected the idea of *l'art pour l'art*, however, believing instead in art as a way of comprehending the world and establishing a communal way of perceiving reality. He was critical of Richard Wagner's art work (Heidegger 1977: Vol. 1, 85–88) – partly because it subordinated the word to music, partly because it was non-classical in giving expression to a wide range of personae and their individual emotions – but he fully endorsed his theoretical conviction that art should provide a communal way of perceiving and relating to the world. Following Wagner and Nietzsche he hoped that art could become, as it had in the past, 'the religion' of the people, a religion that would be a 'celebration of the national community' (Heidegger 1977: Vol. 1, 85 f.). Heidegger's ideal of great communal art shows clearly in his beautiful description of a Greek temple:

> A Greek temple ... stands there in the middle of the rock-cleft valley. The building encloses the figure of the god, and in this concealment lets it stand out into the holy precinct through the open portico. By means of the temple [figure] the god is present in the temple. This presence of the god is in itself the extension and delimitation of the precinct as a holy precinct. The temple and its precinct, however, do not fade away into the indefinite. It is the temple-work that first fits together and at the same time gathers around itself the unity of those paths and relations in which birth and death, disaster and blessing, victory and disgrace, endurance and decline acquire the shape of destiny for human being. The all-governing expanse of this open relational context is the world of this historical people. Only from this expanse does a people first return to itself for the fulfilment of its vocation.
>
> Standing there, the building rests on the rocky ground. This resting of the work draws up out of the rock the mystery of that rock's clumsy yet spontaneous support. Standing there, the building holds its ground against the storm raging above it and so first makes the storm itself manifest in its violence. The luster and gleam of the stone, though itself apparently glowing only by the grace of the sun, yet first brings to light the light of the day, the breadth of the sky, the darkness of the night. The temple's firm towering makes visible the invisible space of air. The steadfastness of the work contrasts with the raging of the surf, and its own repose brings out the surge of the sea. Tree and grass, eagle and bull, snake and cricket first enter into their distinctive shapes and thus come to appear as what they are ... The temple, in its standing there, first gives to things their look and to men their outlook on themselves. (Heidegger 1971: 41–43)

What is art understood in this way? It is not simply the art work itself, because the temple would not inspire faith in the Greek gods in a secular art historian, would not reveal a destiny to a passing tourist, and would not explain the nature of rocks to a geologist. Art is the coming together of a meaningful art work and a perceptive audience, an event in which people come to comprehend themselves and their environment. According to Heidegger, the temple gave the entire community a sense of the nature it lives in, the social world it engages with, and the gods it should obey. Art in this sense establishes a 'cultural paradigm' (Thomas Kuhn), that is, the way in which a community perceives reality. It is a 'happening of truth' (Heidegger 1971: 39, 57), because, by experiencing the art work appropriately, the community of those sharing its perspective understand a collective reality and the way to behave: they become aware of 'simple and essential decisions', 'what is holy and what is unholy', 'what is brave and what cowardly, what noble and what fugitive [*flüchtig*], what master and what slave'. They even come to recognize, Heidegger claimed, their historical 'destiny' (Heidegger 1971: 44, 48).

Heidegger's definition of art is both narrower and wider than our everyday understanding. While a 'happening of truth' hardly occurs in art galleries, it can happen in a whole variety of 'world-defining events'. Heidegger mentioned the Greek temple, Greek drama and the Olympic Games as art works (1971: 43), but one can easily think of more examples, ranging from a divine service to a spectacular rock concert like Woodstock (to use Hubert Dreyfus's example) or a Nuremberg rally.[20] Most importantly, true art can 'found a political state' (1971: 62), because it can bring people together within a single communal faith and inspire them to work towards communal goals. 'Whenever art happens ... a thrust enters history, history either begins or starts over again' (1971: 77). History in this sense was not just any sequence of events, but authentic or 'great history': a nation committing itself to communal tasks and accepting work and sacrifice to achieve them.

Heidegger wanted a communal faith in harmony with a *Volk*'s native soil and historical tradition, but he believed that it took exceptional individuals to give such a faith expression and form. He called mankind 'the violence-doer' because he tries to enforce an order on to the 'overpowering' nature around him (1961: 149 f.), and this act of giving meaning to the world he assigned to leaders. Later in his life, Heidegger came to understand the happening of truth in much more meditative and receptive terms, but he always believed that only great artists and thinkers (like himself) could formulate an appropriate world-view for the nation. Only they could awaken the *Volk* from the shallowness of everyday conventions and material concerns by bringing forth an arresting vision of the nation's higher destiny. Exceptional men were thus supposed to call the masses into the essence of their *völkisch* existence. As this essence was perceived in the singular, Heidegger rejected pluralism, calling for a *cultural totality* instead.

In 1933, Heidegger believed that he witnessed such a historic 'happening of truth'. After Nazism gained power, he shared in the widespread sense of 'the glory and greatness of this new beginning' (Heidegger 1991: 38 f.). Associating the events with the alleged 'August-enthusiasm' of 1914 (Jaspers 1977: 100 f.), he felt that Germans were at last pulling together again, experiencing a strong collective sense of purpose and starting to strive once more for communal goals. While in his early work 'authentic existence' had primarily meant that individuals should not simply follow conventions, but work towards a resolute commitment to consciously accepted convictions, the term now served to glorify Nazism. 'Authentic existence' came to mean a complete identification with the German destiny, and this destiny in turn was identified with Hitler. Ignoring the violence which played an important role in establishing the new unity, Heidegger claimed that the Führer was 'Germany's only reality and its law' (Heidegger 2000: 184). Buying into the Hitler-myth, he stated in the winter of 1933–34: 'The will of the leader [Führer] first of all recreates the others into a following out of which a *Gemeinschaft* arises. It is out of this vital solidarity of followers to leader that sacrifice [*Opfer*] and service [*Dienst*] arise, and not from sheer obedience and institutional coercion' (quoted in Bambach 2003: 158). Supporting

Hitler was for him nothing less than supporting the right destiny for Germany (Heidegger 2000: 190).

The belief that Hitler would unite the nation in a single faith was the prime reason for Heidegger to become an enthusiastic Nazi. He sympathized with the party even before 1933, he actively manoeuvred to become Rector of the university under the new regime, he publicly joined the Nazi party on May Day and the ceremony around his Rectoral Address included Nazi flags and the singing of the Nazi *Horst-Wessel* song. He not only approved in principle with the Nazi cleansing, which forced, among many others, his intimate Jewish friend Hannah Arendt to emigrate, but also used the new regime in attempts to destroy the academic careers of colleagues, for example by initiating a Gestapo investigation (Farias 1989; Ott 1994). He praised the Führer principle for the university sector, while striving to attain such a leadership position for himself.[21] If the Nazis were not all to his liking, he could accept deficiencies for the time being because he believed that Plato's vision of the philosopher as policy-making adviser to the ruler would now come true. In a combination of naivety and delusions of grandeur, he believed for a while that he himself would be *the* philosopher who would guide the Führer into uniting a *Volk* in one single faith. This pure, new faith – which was supposed to draw on the purest Greek and German traditions – would overcome the terrible crisis of modernity, that is, nihilism.

It was not the political changes that were crucial to Heidegger, but the spiritual change. Like his idealized classical Greece, Germany was to exist within one communal truth horizon or world-view and be committed to a shared understanding of Germany's historical destiny. Bound to 'the *Volksgemeinschaft*' and to 'the honour and destiny of the nation' (Heidegger 1991: 35), the university (and, above all, philosophy) was supposed to guide the German people towards establishing a national community united in a single faith. Battling 'with the opposing spirit of the communist world and not less with the dying God of Christianity' (Heidegger 2000: 72), Germany would find a faith in line with its ethnic destiny.

The philosopher from the Black Forest remained a party member to the end of the regime, kept hoping for a German victory and believed to the end of his life in the unique quality of German culture. His initial enthusiasm waned within a year, however, and he gradually came to see Nazism not as an opponent, but as an integral part of modern nihilism with its belief in the unlimited power of the human will. Later Heidegger no longer advocated an active overcoming of nihilism, but a much more meditative reflection on the absence of the gods and a preparation for their possible arrival. Despite the turn in his philosophy, however, he continued to hold on to the hope of a society united in a single communal faith. This was, I believe, Heidegger's ultimate dream.

The presentation of a variety of Conservative Revolutionaries has shown a wide range of ideas, but also crucial commonalities. These important voices within political culture could come from a Protestant or Catholic background. They could tend more towards a dictatorship or show a stronger trust in the *Volk*, could be more community-oriented or militaristic, more socially-minded or elitist, highly optimistic or believing in danger and decline. What they had in common, however, was their opposition to Marxism, liberalism and democracy, hoping instead for the rise of an authoritarian regime. They were all extreme nationalists. In contrast to traditional conservatives, they called – more or less strongly – for more social fairness to overcome the divisions in society. Above all, they all rejected a pluralistic society, advocating instead their vision of a nation united in a single faith. The Conservative Revolution shows the importance of this ideal for young and educated nationalists, and its many statements further promoted such convictions. And this dream of a nation united in a single faith was also a main reason why so many of them sympathized with Nazism and often eventually even joined them. While the movement was not always completely to their liking, its success in the polls strongly suggested that Nazism was the only force on the Right able to unite the nation.

For the Nazis, in turn, winning over this young elite was a crucial success: after all, the Third Reich needed highly trained and motivated supporters in order to maintain power and realize its political goals.

Notes

1. See above all Lethen 2002. Siegmund Freud argued in his writings about war (1915: 1933) that humans are essentially immoral. Their dangerous side emerges, he argued, as soon as they are no longer controlled by a civilized society.
2. Klugen 1938. Arthur Moeller van den Bruck, Carl Schmitt and Ernst Jünger also strongly expressed this view. See also Leed 1979: 81.
3. Political violence does not simply follow from ideological convictions, but develops its own momentum. Practicing violence integrates groups, generates friends and enemies, and leads to the acceptance of the group's convictions (Reichardt 2002; Rohkrämer 2001).
4. This is mainly due to the fact (1) that no clear line can be drawn between the enemy and neutral civilians and (2) that it is often impossible to take prisoners. Furthermore, fellow citizens must be demonized to justify the use of violence against them.
5. Hagemann 2002; Schilling 2002. For similar attitudes among the organized working class, though possibly with more of an emphasis on the strong man as worker and provider, see Fromm 1980 and Reichardt 2002: 660–695.
6. New faces also appeared in the leading positions to disguise the many conservatives who had played a major role in Imperial Germany.
7. All quotations in Wehler 2003: 555 f. See also Wehler 1995: 368–376 and 2003: 542–580; Struve 1973. Kershaw has applied this concept successfully to Hitler.
8. Gerwarth 2005. See also Wehler 1995; 368–376. While his argument that Bismarck was a charismatic leader does not seem convincing for a chancellor who always relied on the monarch, the Bismarck cult certainly *portrayed* him as charismatic.
9. Quoted in Schildt 1998: 180. The fear that a dictatorship might break down in civil war was also based on the suspicion that the army would not back the government enthusiastically. The

conviction that a right-wing regime should be based on popular support was also widespread within the army. Younger soldiers in particular thus increasingly sympathized with the Nazi movement, who could, they believed, provide a populist basis for a militarist policy.

10. The disappointment with the Kaiser reached deep into conservatism and the nobility. While the older generation especially maintained a certain nostalgia, most realized that the weakness of the monarchical family made a return to the monarchical system illusionary (Malinowski 2004: 247–258).
11. As a child he had already written chronologies and stories of great battles, in which Germany, united with Africa or Asia, was to defeat the old colonial powers (Felken 1988: 53).
12. He was closely associated with some industrialists and the elitist conservative *Herrenklub*, which supported the presidential regimes.
13. His book *Das Recht der jungen Völker* (1919) was initially written as a piece of war propaganda. On Moeller van den Bruck, see Goedel 1984; Schwierskott 1962; Silfen 1973.
14. A novel by Johannes Schlaf from 1899 was called *Das dritte Reich* or *Third Reich*, as was an analysis of different cultures by Martin Wuest from 1905 and a philosophical reflection by Gerhard von Mutius from 1916.
15. Schmitt as a person was much more ambivalent, timid and opportunistic, but he liked to see himself as a true intellectual warrior. In private notes, Schmitt stated: 'This is the secret key to my whole intellectual and scholarly existence: the battle for the essentially catholic intensification (against neutralisers, aesthetic dreamers, against abortionists, desecrators of corpses and pacifists)' (1991, 165).
16. For the term 'soldierly nationalism', see Prümm 1974. This book also covers the success of Jünger's publications (101). See also Nevin 1997; Rohkrämer 1999: 301–338; Woods 1982.
17. For my understanding of Heidegger, I am greatly indebted to Julian Young: to his books and the many discussions we have had. Particularly relevant here also are Bambach 2003; Farias 1989; Ott 1994; Pöggeler 1991; Sluga 1993; Wolin 1990.
18. For a differing view, see, above all, Bambach 2003. His argument for the centrality of rootedness in Heidegger's thought is based on using the term very loosely. Going back to the Greeks is, for example, rootedness for him (although Heidegger used this to break with existing traditions like Christianity or to distance himself from a glorification of the Germanic past), as is the critique of enlightened rationality in favour of a more situated understanding of humans.
19. See, for example, his description of university reform in 1933: 'We, who live today, participate in fighting for a new reality. We are merely a transition, merely a sacrifice. As warriors in this battle, we have to be of hard stock, one that no longer clings to anything of its own, one that commits itself to the ground of the people' (2000: 772).
20. It could well be, however, that Heidegger came to regard Nazi rallies as inauthentic and vulgar. In 1935 he called it a sign of 'the spiritual decline of the earth', 'when a boxer is regarded as a nation's great man; when mass meetings attended by millions are looked on as triumph' (1961: 38).
21. This follows from his claim that philosophy should be the foundational discipline in academia and that, as he said to Karl Jaspers, Germany needed only two or three philosophy professors (Jaspers 1977: 101).

CHAPTER 6

NAZISM AND THE CREATION OF A COMMUNAL WORLD-VIEW

The desire for a single communal faith reached its high point in the crisis of the early 1930s. The Nazis only gained such widespread support for their vision of the future because they could build on the old dream of a nation or Reich united in one shared world-view, but they also surpassed this tradition. All previous attempts at promoting a single communal faith had only resulted in an ever more divided nation. As they all failed to win over the majority of the nation, a situation emerged in which different milieus fought bitterly in trying to establish their ideals as the one and only national world-view. The angry rejection of a pluralism of world-views did not result in national unity, but in an ever greater clash of intolerant and thus incompatible convictions. In contrast, the Nazis succeeded in establishing first a mass movement and then, through terror and persuasion, a regime, which used all the propaganda means at its disposal to live up to the image of a powerful nation united in a single faith. While among historians differences of opinion continue to exist about the degree of popular support for the Third Reich (after all, public opinion is difficult to gauge with any precision in a regime aiming ruthlessly for totalitarian control), there can be no doubt that the Nazis did everything to present themselves as the force which had brought the nation together as 'one *Volk*, one Reich, [under] one Führer'.

Members of the unorthodox Left in Germany were quick to realize that fascism introduced a new political style within right-wing politics (Emmerich 1971; Reichel 1993: 21–28). Following Marx, they had expected that the logic of historical development would gradually lead the masses to join the revolutionary working-class movement; now they had to figure out why a populist mass movement could also emerge on the Right. Walter Benjamin, for example (to mention just the concepts of lasting theoretical interest), diagnosed a new fascist 'aesthetication of politics' (1963: 49), and Ernst Bloch recognized that the Nazis opened up a false but tempting utopian vision for the future. While Marxism presented itself increasingly as an objective and thus cold scientific analysis of history, fascism gained its fatal attraction by offering utopian hopes for the future. The Nazi protest against the dreary inhumanity of current conditions in favour of the vague promise of social harmony in a Nazi *Volksgemeinschaft* made them, he argued, 'false substitutes [*schiefe Statthalter*] of the revolution' (Bloch 1962: 162. See also Bloch 1976: I, 64, 178 and passim). And from a very different ideological perspective, another victim of Nazism, Thomas Mann (1942), described 'brother Hitler' as an 'artistic phenomenon'.

Since 1945, such ideas have been explored further. In 1981, for example, Susan Sontag published a stimulating article, 'Fascinating Fascism', on aspects of a fascist aesthetics, and Fritz Stern described Nazism as a 'temptation' because it provided the exciting vision of national regeneration, an Aryan national community and a strong Reich which would re-establish Germany as a world power. In his biography of Hitler, Joachim Fest stressed the aesthetic dimension of the Third Reich; Christian von Krockow speaks of 'the realization of dreams' because National Socialism took up so many desires of the time (2001: 18); and Peter Reichel emphasized in his book *The Beautiful Appearance of the Third Reich* 'the display, decoration and ritualisation of politics to overcome its dreariness and to satisfy the desire of the masses for identification, for community, entertainment and beauty' (1993: 374). As early as 1971, Klaus Vondung wrote on the *Ideological Cult and Political Religion of National Socialism.* More recently, the historians Claus Ekkehard Bärsch and Michael Ley published controversial but stimulating monographs to show that political religion is the key to understanding Nazism and the holocaust.[1] Michael Burleigh supports this view in the introduction to his general history of the Third Reich[2] and Hans-Ulrich Wehler makes frequent use of the term in his study of the Third Reich. Radical nationalism in Germany, he claims, had many characteristics of a political religion (2003: 548), 'from the fusion of extreme nationalism and faith in charisma the characteristic elements of a political religion emerge' (2003: 680), and National Socialism establishes itself as a 'monopolistic secular religion' throughout its rule (2003: 618). Richard Evans also recognizes the importance of symbolic means in the Nazi attempt to create a new fascist way of life: 'The aestheticization of politics created the illusion that social, economic and national problems were immediately being solved by acts of will.' 'Much of this was to be achieved by symbols, rituals and rhetoric. Above all, what Hitler and the Nazis wanted was a change in people's spirit, their way of thinking, and their way of behaving. They wanted a new man, and for that matter a new woman, to emerge out of the ashes of the Weimar Republic' (2005: 212, 503).

As pointed out in the introduction, I have reservations about using the term 'political religion'. It underplays, as we shall also see in this chapter, the manipulative pragmatism often involved in the attempt to establish a national faith, the frequent harmonious co-existence, respect and cross-fertilization between the new forms of political faiths and traditional religions, and the many differences of opinion within extreme nationalism and also within Nazi ideology (Kroll 1998). It also ignores the fact that many nationalists and fascists (including Hitler himself) insisted on the scientific status of their convictions, especially in the sphere of race theory and a Social Darwinist view of international relations. While the spuriousness of their arguments can be easily recognized, we should not ignore their claim to take a rational stand.

However, independent of my difference of opinion with those seeing Nazism as a political religion,[3] the studies mentioned above (as well as Behrenbeck 1996; Griffin 2005; Rißmann 2001; Tal 1975, 2002; Welch 1995) have been fruitful, because they direct attention to three crucial and interconnected points. National Socialism went far beyond pragmatic politics in trying to unite the nation in a single faith; the 'aestheticization of politics' played an important part in this endeavour; and they had unprecedented success in winning over the population for their vision of the future.

The fatal attraction of National Socialism was, of course, only one side of the coin. Even before 1933, the Nazis used violence against their political opponents, and with the 'seizure of power', force was employed ruthlessly to crush any opposition. This affected 'anyone who expressed dissent in public' (Evans 2005: 381). The SA needed little encouragement to destroy left-wing organizations and attack all allegedly un-German and unworthy members of society, especially when nobody dared to stand in their way any more. Nazi propaganda could gradually gain an increasing influence on the population because critical voices had been driven out of the country or silenced. Also, pure luck was frequently on the Nazis' side – for example, when they gained power towards the end of the economic crisis and when the Western allies were no longer determined to maintain the conditions of the Versailles treaty.

Terror and fortunate circumstances were thus important, but equally so was the fatal attraction of National Socialism. Before 1933, the Nazis used violence against political opponents, but this largely served a symbolic political function: many saw it as proof of the seriousness of the Nazi convictions, their determination to achieve change and their youthful, manly energy in fighting for their goals. Violence also found acceptance because many believed that it was only directed against 'un-German' ideologies and people, thus ultimately serving the dream of a nation united in a single communal faith. Despite such violence, however, elections were still free and people chose their favourite party before 1933. Both Nazi party members and voters fluctuated strongly, thus showing the fragility of their power basis, but they became the largest party with a good third of the votes in free elections. In sharp contrast to previous right-wing organizations, the Nazi party won support from all parts of society. While the elites and the middle class were somewhat over-represented, thus giving the NSDAP a slight middle class paunch, the Nazis were surprisingly successful in winning working class votes – numerically more indeed than either the Social Democrats or the Communists. A party with a working-class content of about 40 per cent, which also had roughly the same percentage of working-class votes in all elections between 1928 and 1933, was not a middle- or lower-middle-class party, as older scholars had it, but constituted the first people's party in German history. The Nazi claim that they were able to bring previously deeply divided social classes together under a new ideological banner was thus more than empty words (Falter 1991; Mühlberger 2003).

Such great popularity was not simply due to an all-powerful propaganda machine. While it was convenient for Germans after 1945 to stress the brainwashing power of Hitler and the Nazi aestheticization of politics to deny personal guilt, a general agreement has emerged that even the best propaganda cannot change people's minds, but only reinforce 'existing trends and beliefs, to sharpen and focus them ... Propaganda, if it is to be effective, must in a sense preach to those who are already partially converted' (Welch 1995: 5, 9. See also Welch 1983). Furthermore, Nazi propaganda before 1933 was far from perfect. As a political newcomer which largely financed itself through membership fees, Nazism operated within a tight budget. Propaganda largely had to finance itself, and neither speeches by leading Nazis nor political leaflets were free. Only those prepared to pay could experience Hitler live on stage. Goebbels dreamt of using elaborate films for propaganda purposes, even of a fascist *Panzerkreuzer Potemkin*, but the few films produced before 1933 remained cheap and amateurish. National rallies were not only much simpler than the popular image we have from Leni Riefenstahl's famous film *Triumph of the Will* about the 1934 *Reichsparteitag*; they even had to be cancelled in 1928 and between 1930 and 1932, because the Nazis could not afford both a major election campaign and a big rally in one year (Paul 1990). Thus the Nazis did not gain their electoral successes due to all-pervasive propaganda, but because they addressed the voters' fears and desires more successfully than other parties did.

After 1933, the controls on public opinion make the popularity of the regime more difficult to assess, but both the reports from the secret police and the exiled Social Democratic Party agree that the popularity of the regime increased in the first years. Until the end of the 1930s, Hitler did not stress a violent anti-Semitism or his expansionist intentions in public speeches but focused on those ideals which a majority of Germans shared: full employment, social justice within a national community, the destruction of Marxism, law and order, and a restoration of national pride. The end of the economic crisis and full employment, order in the streets at least for those not targeted by the regime, the breaking of the shackles of Versailles and the re-militarization of the Rhineland led to an ever-growing admiration for Hitler, whom a majority no longer saw as a party leader but as a true statesman realizing the nation's dreams. In 1936, Ian Kershaw concludes, 'his mastery over all other power-groups within the regime was by now well-near complete, his position unassailable, his popularity immense' (Kershaw 1998: 591). Equally, Norbert Frei describes Nazi rule after the first couple of years as 'consolidated': 'A large majority of Germans really believed in the 'national resurrection' and in their chances of a personal career, in a heroic future, and in a better life for themselves and future generations' (Frei 2001: 64. See also: Aly 2005; Frei 1993 70–108; Herbert 1996a; Peukert 1987).

The Third Reich could never stabilize; it always needed new successes to maintain popular support (see, for example, the case study Allen 1984). The enthusiasm of a 'national resurrection' was threatened by normality setting in, the new sense of community depended on full employment and an acceptable standard of living, and national pride needed international successes. The crucial point is, however, that the regime succeeded in gaining support at crucial moments (Koonz 2003: Ch. 4). It could establish its unchallenged rule because its policies were popular in the first years (even in hindsight Germans remembered the allegedly 'good years' (Niethammer 1983) of peace in the Third Reich); after the initial reluctance to go to war the Nazi regime reached the height of its popularity after the victory over France; and even the bomb plot of 1944 did not meet with majority approval. The Nazis clearly succeeded in uniting behind them a majority of the population, including a large part of the workers, for crucial periods of the Third Reich's existence and commanded obedience to the end.

The Nazis have frequently been characterized as a catch-all movement of protest, fuelled at first by the social and economic misery brought about by the World Depression, before it was kept in power by terror and short-term successes. It obviously took a deep crisis for the Nazi movement's spectacular growth, but it was not the movement of the unemployed and most deprived.[4] What influenced the attitude towards Nazism most was not social background, but previous political and religious convictions (Falter 1991). Catholics and Communists, and to a lesser extent Social Democrats, were the most unlikely to support the Nazis: they had their own associations, their own strong convictions to explain the crisis and their own social milieu to offer stability, a sense of community and group pressure against adapting to ideologically new ways. In contrast, support for the liberal parties nearly vanished in the years of the Weimar Republic; the vast majority of the political middle ground turned away from their commitment to a free society, favouring instead a more authoritarian and nationalist order. Also, many people with right-wing leanings lost their faith in traditional conservatism to save the nation, turning instead towards the new party which appeared to fight for similar goals in a more dynamic, forceful, uncompromisingly idealistic and 'modern' way. Many followed Hitler, when he contrasted the conservative Chancellor von Papen, who allegedly stood for 'everything backwards', with the National Socialist 'Young Germany, march forward!' (Domarus 1973: Vol. 1, 135). Those who had voted for the old conservative notable Hindenburg in 1925 were very likely to vote for Hitler and the Nazis in the 1930s, clearly showing a radicalization of the political Right. They stopped trusting a conservatism which was still supporting the interests of its old (often noble and agricultural) clientele, preferring instead the Nazi glorification of a powerful nation based on a socially just and efficient *Volksgemeinschaft*, where ability would determine one's social position. Conservative networks, which came to promote Nazism, were also highly important for the Nazi penetration of German society (Bösch 2002).

Only 16 per cent of Catholics voted for Hitler in July 1932, but he achieved a great majority among Protestants (Falter 1991: 176). While the former had become more dogmatic and insular when facing the challenges of modern times, the openness of the latter to new trends made it more vulnerable to the latest right-wing ideological fashions. Large sections of Protestantism had accepted the modern critique of the Bible and religious dogmatism: both were seen not as the literal words of God, but as reports of humans about their experience of God and the godly. Church attendance dropped, especially in the urban areas among the working class and the highly educated. Many non-practising Protestants continued to stick to the values of their religious milieu without sharing the belief in its traditional metaphysical foundations; they often believed that the practical consequences of a religion were decisive, not a religious truth or the promise of life after death. They often developed a more free-floating spirituality, believing in discovering a sense of the godly for themselves, for example, in nature or spectacular historical events. While many members of the Protestant tradition were thus open to new ideologies presenting themselves with a religious flair, the Protestant church as an institution was also leaning strongly towards right-wing political convictions. It had been closely linked with the monarchical system before 1918; after the shock of defeat and revolution it never adapted to the Republic, but continued to show right-wing leanings (Scholder 1977: 3 ff.; Burleigh 2006: 109 f.). While Protestantism was closest to the conservative DNVP in the 1920s, it strongly participated in the radicalization of the political Right towards the end of the Weimar Republic. While only a radical fringe would go along with ideas about a non-Christian Germanic religion, Hitler's public commitment to a 'positive [that is, trans-confessional] Christianity' was greeted in both major churches (Steigmann-Gall 2003). In elections within the church, for example, the so-called 'German Christians', who wanted to 'free' Christianity from its Semitic 'distortions' and bring it in line with allegedly German values, could gain 70 per cent of the votes and the enthusiastic support of many ministers. A majority of church representatives and common members welcomed the new Reich because they cherished 'the illusion of a new Christian authoritarian state, which would erect a bulwark against raging atheism and godless communism' (Wehler 2003: 801). While Hitler exclaimed in the early days of the regime that 'the national government regards the two confessions as the most important factors in maintaining our national characteristics [*Volkstum*]' (Domarus 1973: Vol. 1, 232 f.), a high representative of the Lutheran Church in old Prussia spoke for many when he stated:

> We share with all our Protestant fellow-believers the joy in the national awakening of the nation's deepest forces to national consciousness, to a true national community and to a religious regeneration … In the conviction that the regeneration of *Volk* and *Reich* can only be carried through and secured by these forces, the church is thankful-

> ly committed to the leadership of the new Germany. The church is eager to participate in the national and moral regeneration of our people. (quoted in Schildt 1998: 193)

Every third German voted for the NSDAP in 1932, and powerful groups came to regard the party as useful. For a majority of the traditional conservatives and functional elites, Hitler was not their first choice as chancellor, but they eventually came to regard a partnership with the Nazis as indispensable. They clearly sympathized with large parts of the NSDAP's political programme, in particular its militant nationalism and anti-Marxism, but they had serious doubts about the competence and reliability of the upstart Hitler and his populist movement. Many preferred the conservative presidential regimes, but feared the open step towards a right-wing dictatorship without popular support. The many attempts to rope the Nazis into a coalition government, eventually even with the acceptance of Hitler as chancellor, show that the desire for a communal faith had also reached the power elites. They rejected an authoritarian rule purely based on bayonets, because they saw the need for integrating the masses as much as possible into the nation and its political programme. Industry was attracted by the hope that the fascist idea of a *Volksgemeinschaft* offered an attractive alternative to socialist agitation, the military saw the need for a militaristic attitude as prerequisite for a forceful foreign policy in the age of total war, and many conservative politicians accepted the need for shared political and cultural core beliefs as the necessary basis of any truly functional community. The widespread conviction that a government needed a solid populist base led the power elites to accept the Nazis as coalition partners. Only the Hitler movement promised any chance for a right-wing regime based on popular will, and the sense of a 'national awakening' in 1933 appeared to be the fulfilment of that promise. The Nazis seemed to have what the elites lacked; namely, the ability to win the masses (Mommsen 1989: 547; Schildt 1998: 178–181; Wehler 2003: 580–588).

It was thus largely long-held political and cultural convictions that made people turn to the Nazis in a crisis situation. They could appear as a right-wing, nationalist force that had shed the conservatives' traditional elitism by committing themselves to a populist policy. The combination of strong nationalism with vague notions of a German socialism proved highly attractive to a wide range of voters. For many, it took the deep crisis of the Weimar Republic to take a gamble with a new and untested political force; but when the party seemed to fulfil its promise of a united and strong nation after January 1933, it increased its popularity even further. The Nazi stronghold was undoubtedly on the political Right, but no milieu or class proved immune to its lure. Even Catholics were taken in by the new regime when the concordat with the Pope seemed to secure the position of their church; even workers were impressed by full employment, social measures and the symbolic praise of manual labour (Lüdtke 1994). And success in winning support from different quarters produced even more success; people had hated the deep divisions within the Weimar Republic and the resulting political stalemate. The more Nazism seemed able to overcome these divisions, the more attractive it became. National unity and a strong leadership were seen as valuable in themselves, independent of the actual policy goals, and people were prepared to ignore some of the less agreeable features for the promise of a nation united in a single faith. Even the brutal attack on the political opposition, on allegedly un-German intellectuals and artists, on Jews and handicapped people – which all started in the early months of the regime – barely caught the attention of the mass of the population. They were either taken in by the spectacle of a national awakening or they accepted these measures as seemingly necessary to achieve national unity. By no means untypical was a middle-class woman who rejoiced at the time: 'The readiness to make sacrifices, their burning patriotism and this idealism! And at the same time such tight discipline and control!' (quoted in Evans 2005: 450). A general orientation and a disciplined conduct were often central in judging National Socialism; the concrete actions were then only seen within this positively tainted framework.

Profiting from the strong aversion to party politics that the deeply divided Republic had left behind, the Nazis presented themselves successfully as the only people's party or even as the only possible political orientation for all true Germans. They proved their energy, élan and determination by a militant rejection of the Weimar Republic and Communism, but became more moderate and unspecific in their propaganda in the early 1930s to integrate wider parts of society. With the emphasis on ruthless anti-Semitism and military expansionism, the Nazi movement had won unchallenged dominance on the extreme Right; now it was more opportune to use vaguer visions of national liberation through strength and unity to gain votes in the political middle ground. This change can be clearly observed in Hitler's speeches: in the election campaigns from 1930 to 1932, anti-Semitism was toned down and the brutal tirades of the early years were missing completely. 'Living space' was still important as an alternative to international economic competition, but 'the key theme now was the collapse of Germany under parliamentary democracy and party government into a divided people with separate and conflicting interests, which only the NSDAP could overcome by creating a new unity of the nation, transcending class, estate and profession. Where the Weimar parties represented only specific interest groups, Hitler asserted, the National Socialist Movement alone stood for the nation as a whole' (Kershaw 1998: 330). Of course, the Nazis' anti-Semitism was never in doubt, and Hitler never saw a need to distance himself from the SA's violence (he even backed brutal murder). But in their general propaganda, the Nazis became more mainstream; a vague anti-Semitism which many Germans shared, attacks on Versailles without explicit war-mongering, and, above all, the utopia, as Hitler stated in spring 1932, of a 'a new German Reich of greatness, power and strength, of … splendour and social justice' (Hitler 1992 ff.: Vol. 5, 31). Nazism was always a 'blend of idealism and hatred' (Koonz 2003: 19), but in the successful election campaigns the emphasis was on work and bread, national unity and a fair social order. The Nazis' programme became less distinctive in its details, but they seemed more determined and promised more than a simple change of government. 'It was a message of national redemption. In a climate of deepening economic gloom and social misery, anxiety, and division, amid perceptions of the failure and ineptitude of seemingly puny parliamentary politicians, the appeal was a powerful one' (Kershaw 1998: 331).

At the time, the NSDAP did not necessarily appear as the most extreme force on the right. Its propaganda was less radical than Ernst Jünger's praise of total war or Martin Heidegger's ideal of a nation unified within one philosophical worldview. In contrast to traditional conservative politicians like Hindenburg and von Papen, Nazism seemed to combine authoritarianism with a social conscience and an openness to the positive features of modernity. Of course, blood-and-soil propaganda was present in Nazism, but so was Hitler's enthusiasm for cars and other modern technology. Praise of military values and idealism went together with a commitment to a comfortable material standard of living, and political rituals with popular entertainment. The Nazis attacked the non-conformist aspects of German culture, but they accepted a variety of opinions and styles as long as these did not challenge their rule. Even in their rituals they were not purists; they accepted elements from high and low culture, from ancient and modern, from the Christian and the Germanic. The movement's ability to adapt and make compromises – ranging from the toning down of anti-Semitism and military expansionism to compromises with the Christian churches and the destruction of the SA leadership to maintain the alliance with functional elites like the army – was a prerequisite for their popularity among both the powerful and the masses.

The Nazis were politically successful because their visions were open to a variety of interpretations. In the 1930s, a growing number of people did not worry about the vagueness, the inconsistencies and contradictions within the movement, but saw the aspects most appealing to them as the true core. This phenomenon that people wanted to see what they liked in Nazism is most obvious in the 'Hitler myth' (Kershaw 1989). The German Right had long hoped for an exceptional leader, and they were ready to accept Hitler in this role. At first the Führer came to stand for everything positive within the Nazi movement; later this image of a charismatic leader also reached far into the population as a whole. 'No more class struggle or Marxism', a middle-class woman declared, 'no more religious antagonism – only Germany – in Hitler' (quoted in Evans 2005: 500). Hard-liners admired his uncompromising determination and ideological purity, while moderates often regarded him as a guarantee against the movement's irresponsibilities and corruptness, despite the fact that Hitler tended to side with the most extreme position when forced into a decision, and he was always loyal to his cronies. Many were taken in by what Hitler seemed to stand for; others accepted that only he could unite the extreme Right and the German nation.

Nazi successes re-enforced Hitler's charisma, which only gradually started to wane with the war turning against Germany. At the regime's height, however, Hitler even claimed an identity between himself and the *Volk*, as, for example, in September 1936 in Nuremberg:

> How deeply do we feel again in this hour the miracle which has brought us together. In time past you have heard the voice of a man, and it spoke to your heart. It aroused you, and you followed the voice ... This is the miracle of our time that you have found me ... among so many million! And that I have found you, that is Germany's fortune ... Now that we meet here we are filled by the miracle of this connection. Not everybody can see me, and I cannot see everybody. But I can sense you, and you sense me ... Now we together are Germany. (Domarus 1973: Vol. 3, 641)

Hitler thus spoke of a mystical union between Führer and *Volk*, that is, a *Volk* united in a single faith personified in the Führer. While most would not have used such an exalted expression, the statement did not meet with ridicule either. It was not only hard-core Nazis who accepted that Hitler stood for the best of his *Volk* and that he was leading the nation into a brighter future.

The brutal destruction of any opposition was one side of the coin in gaining control over the nation; the other was the so-called 'national awakening' (Fritzsche 1998). While the 1918 revolution was said to have divided and weakened the nation in a petty struggle for material gains, many shared Göring's impression that the events after 30 January 1933 'could only be compared with August 1914', when the whole nation had allegedly been united in their determination to fight for Germany (quoted in Verhey 1997: 362 f.). A huge number of civilians gathered to cheer Hitler and Hindenburg; then the nationalist demonstration started. The French ambassador, who had watched the event from his embassy, gave the following description:

> The torches [that the marchers] brandished formed a river of fire, a river with hastening, unquenchable waves, a river in spate sweeping with a sovereign rush over the very heart of the city. From these brown-shirted, booted men, as they marched in perfect discipline and alignment, their well-pitched voices bawling war-like songs, there rose an enthusiasm and dynamism that were extraordinary. The onlookers, drawn up on either side of the marching columns, burst into a vast clamour. (Francois-Poncet 1949: 48)

Gripped by the enthusiasm of the moment, a middle-class woman with obvious right-wing leanings described the demonstrations right after the 'seizure of power':

> Torchlight procession of National Socialists and *Stahlhelm*. A wonderfully elevating experience for us all. Goering says the day of Hitler's and the nationalist Cabinet's appointment was something like 1914, and this too was something like 1914 ... At 9.30 p.m. we took our positions, Gisela and us. I said she should stay till the end for the sake of the children. So far the impressions they had had of politics had been so deplorable that they should now have a really strong impression of nationhood, as we had once, and store it in their memories ... 20,000 brown-shirts followed one another like waves in the sea, their faces shone with enthusiasm in the light of the torches. "Three cheers for our Führer, our Chancellor Adolf Hitler ..." They sang "The Republic is shit" ... Now came the *Stahlhelm*, a grey stream; quieter, more spiritual

> perhaps ... Between the SA and the *Stahlhelm* marched a delegation of nationalist students ... The SS brought up the rear of the procession.
>
> We were drunk with enthusiasm, blinded by the light of the torches right in our faces, and always enveloped in their vapour as in a cloud of sweet incense. And in front of us men, men, brightly coloured, grey, brown, a torrent lasting an hour and 20 minutes ... Unity at last. (Noakes and Pridham 1983 ff.: Vol. 1, 129–131)

Especially in the first years of the regime, Hitler worked hard to promote this sense of national unity beyond party divides. His first governmental declaration (Domarus 1973: Vol. 1, 191–194) stated a right-wing consensus. He attacked the allegedly treacherous German revolution of 1918, the Weimar Republic and the Communists (without explicitly mentioning other political enemies or the Jews), which were blamed for causing Germany's domestic disunity and international weakness. His positive vision was an emotionally charged, but unspecific call for a general nationalist reawakening. 'We believe in our *Volk* and its eternal values. Peasants, workers and the middle class must together provide the building blocks for the new Reich.' Domestically, both peasants and workers, he promised, would be saved by state intervention. Internationally, the government would fight to restore the 'freedom' and equality of the German nation. 'The national government will thus regard it as its first and highest task', he then concluded, 'to restore the unity of our people in spirit and political will ... The government will again evoke the awareness in our people of the national and political unity beyond estates and classes and the duties which emerge from this. It will make reverence for our great past and pride in our old traditions the basis for the education of German youth. It will thus declare ruthless war on the spiritual, political and cultural tendency towards nihilism. Germany must not and will not perish in anarchic communism' (Domarus 1973: Vol. 1, 192 f.).

Hitler believed in a national awakening and assumed the role of a prophet in describing this vision. In strongly religious language, he declared on 10 February 1933: 'I cannot free myself from believing in my people, cannot get away from the conviction that some time the hour will come when the millions of today will stand behind us, and with us will become what has been created together, struggled for under difficulty, attained at a cost: the new German Reich of greatness and honour and strength and glory and justice. Amen' (Domarus 1973: Vol. 1, 208). Such spiritual unity of all nationalistically minded people found symbolic expression in the 'Day of Potsdam', the opening ceremony of the new parliament on 21 March 1933. It was the same day that Bismarck had opened the first parliament of the German Empire, and the garrison church together with Frederic the Great's grave offered an appropriate historical setting. Four sons of Wilhelm II were present, and one chair was left empty, thus symbolizing a space for the former Emperor. Acting the proper bourgeois, Hitler appeared in a tailcoat. Despite all his conflicts with the president and his increased power, he bowed deeply in front of Hindenburg, a gesture quickly popularized through postcards and the newsreel *Wochenschau*. In pretending to have the deepest reverence for the German tradition, he presented Nazism as a renaissance of old national values in a style suited to the present. This sentimental spectacle, which the Nazis called a 'public festival of national unification' (Reichel 1993: 150), obviously excluded Socialists, Communists and Jews, but the conservatively and nationalistically inclined were deeply impressed. In his speech, Hitler first praised 'the marriage between the symbols of old grandeur and youthful power'. He then declared: 'We want to restore the unity of the German nation's spirit and will. We want to maintain the eternal foundations of our existence: our ethnicity [*Volkstum*] and its inherent powers and values. In the organization and the leading of our state, we want to subordinate ourselves again to the principles, which have been at all times the prerequisite for the grandeur of peoples [*Völker*] and Empires' (Domarus 1973: Vol. 1, 227).

Deeply impressed by his own choreography, Goebbels described the event in his diary: 'Then the Führer speaks. He speaks with hard and forceful urgency. At the end everybody is most deeply moved. I sit close to Hindenburg and see how tears fill his eyes. All get up from their seats and jubilantly cheer the old Field Marshal, who gives the young chancellor his hand' (22 March 1933). As the following quotation shows, the ceremony could win over conservative nationalists still sceptical about Nazism:

> All cleverly done, impressive, spell-binding even, at any rate for the masses. But we too cannot and must not shut our eyes in the face of what is going on. Today and here, the marriage took place, if not for ever then at least for a time, between the masses led by Hitler and the 'Spirit of Potsdam', Prussian values, represented by Hindenburg ...
>
> Hindenburg reads his speech. Plain, strong, coming from a simple heart ... He now, soon to die, presides over the marriage of his world with the new rising one which the Austrian corporal, Hitler represents.
>
> Then Hitler speaks. It cannot be denied. He has grown in stature. Out of the demagogue and party leader, the fanatic and agitator – for his opponents surprisingly enough – a true statesman seems to be developing.

He, the commentator continued, only emphasized what every nationalist could agree with:

> the maintenance of the great traditions of our nation, firmness of government instead of eternal wavering, consideration for all the experiences of individual and human life which have proved useful for the welfare of mankind over thousands of years ...
>
> The old Field Marshal shakes hands with the World War corporal. The corporal makes a deep bow over the hand of the Field Marshal. Cannons thunder over Potsdam – over Germany.
>
> No-one can escape the emotions of the moment. (reprinted in Noakes and Pridham 1983 ff.: Vol. 1, 153 f.)

This man was not only impressed by Hitler's show of respectability, but also by Hindenburg's response. The 'day of Potsdam' signalled not only to him that all nationalists were at last uniting across previous political divides behind the new Reich. Such display of unity filled many with real enthusiasm.

Nationalists desired a community united in a single faith, and the Nazis wanted to win the population for their ideology. 'It may be a good thing to possess power that rests on arms', Goebbels stated pointedly. 'But it is better and more gratifying to win and hold the heart of the people' (1991: 138). The Nazi leadership was certainly ready to use violence to maintain control, but they much preferred a nation united behind the Führer in a single fanatical faith. But why did they get further towards realizing this goal than any group before them? The content of their propaganda was undoubtedly important. Conservatives and nationalists could hardly object, as it largely expressed the long-standing ideological obsessions of the whole right-wing and *völkisch* tradition. But precisely because Nazi propaganda of the early 1930s corresponded so much with what others had previously stated, the content by itself is insufficient to explain their success. After all, many had tried before to unite the *Volk* in a single communal faith; what distinguished the Nazis, however, was their ability to present an integrative vision of the future that was attractive to much wider and more diverse circles. As the scholar Friedrich Schreyvogel stated in 1933: ' Never before was politics filled with so many poetic speech elements, never before has it worked with so many poetic images and fantasy-inspired comparisons. The deed of the politician had to fulfil that which should have been the destiny of the poets' magic word!' (1933: 262).

From Romanticism onwards, aesthetics played a crucial role in all attempts at creating a single communal faith. These forerunners provided buildings blocks, but it took the Nazis to join them in a fatally successful way. They brought, as Walter Benjamin and Thomas Mann noted immediately, aesthetics and politics together in an unprecedented way. They took the aesthetic means out of the realm of high culture and created political symbols and rituals which gave expression to widespread fears and desires. And even among those not wholly taken in, acceptance of Nazism grew because this movement seemed to realize an old dream: the cultural integration and mobilization of the masses as a united *Volk* in a proud and self-assertive state. The Nazi imagery of a new, truly German Reich found a receptive audience – but this also included, of course, an acceptance of brutal authoritarian measures of exclusion to achieve the new unity.

Nazism and the Idea of a Single Communal Faith

While the Nazi movement was able to make compromises and adapt to changing circumstances, it was also marked by constant core convictions. Its key leaders were not just power-hungry, but also ideologically driven. The desire for a single communal faith was strong among them and played an important role in the history of the Third Reich. Within such a general orientation, however, the Third Reich was not only marked by a polycracy of differing political forces, but also by a plurality of not wholly compatible ideological convictions and utopian visions (Kroll 1998). While one strand wanted quite literally to turn Nazism into a new religion for the German people, thus doing away with an allegedly un-German Christianity, others aimed at a *political* faith to achieve national integration and mobilization, which could co-exist with religions limited to the private sphere. In the following, I shall discuss Arthur Rosenberg and Heinrich Himmler as the key representatives for the former, Adolf Hitler and Joseph Goebbels for the latter position.

Born and brought up in Estonia in Russia, the Baltic German Arthur Rosenberg (Bärsch 1998: 188–266; Bollmus 1970; Cecil 1972; Kroll 1998: 99 ff.; Mathieu 1997; Whisker 1982) came to Munich in 1918, where he moved in *völkisch* circles and joined the Nazi movement in 1919. He came to see himself as the main Nazi ideologue, but this position remained precarious. He was not as cunning as Goebbels, he lacked the power base that leading a big Nazi institution provided, and his convictions differed in important respects from those of Hitler, who never accepted another spiritual authority. He was never muted, however, but wrote an official commentary on the party programme in 1923 and served as main editor of the Nazi paper *Völkischer Beobachter*. He and the party called his main work *The Mythus of the Twentieth Century* a personal statement, after it came under fire from the churches, but his office continued to state that the work was equal in importance to *Mein Kampf* in formulating the Nazi world-view. Many leading Nazis dismissed Rosenberg as incomprehensible, but his works found their place in all official libraries and on the syllabus of Nazi instruction courses. An impressive 1.1 million copies of *The Mythus* had been published by 1944, but, not unlike *Mein Kampf* (the only Nazi work reaching an even wider circulation), often not necessarily for reading, but for symbolic purposes. Hitler himself stated in April 1942 that he had read only small parts of Rosenberg's main work and disagreed with its glorification of myth (1999: 269), but he also once praised him as 'the sharpest thinker in matters of world-view' (quoted in Bollmus 1970: 26). Rosenberg and other Nazis were asked to avoid conflict with the churches, but he was never forced to drop his ideas in favour of a party line. On the contrary: at least in private talks Hitler gradually moved, as we shall see later, closer to Rosenberg's aggressive stand against the Christian churches.

Rosenberg was strongly shaped by Houston Stewart Chamberlain (see Ch. 3), whose work he encountered while still at grammar school.[5] In the title of his book on Chamberlain (1927), he called him a 'prophet and founder of a German future'. In principle, Rosenberg accepted all Chamberlain's core beliefs: history as a struggle between the Nordic and the Jewish race, the critique of the nineteenth century as an age of division and racial impurity, and the hope that the glorified German nation would save the world. He praised Chamberlain for reconciling 'the mysterious with the rational' (1927: 23), and joined his call for a Germanic religion. In contrast to Chamberlain, Rosenberg came to reject Christianity completely, but both shared the conviction that the Germans had to find their true nature in a religion corresponding to their own racial characteristics.

For Rosenberg, the Nordic people and above all the Germans were the ideal race, but they had been weakened through losing their purity. The world was allegedly threatened by racial impurity and by the Jews – as the polar opposite to the Nordic race – while it could be saved by Germans realizing their own positive potential. Either Germany will become a true 'community of blood, ethnicity and destiny', he argued, thus realizing the highest culture imaginable, or it will perish, leaving the world to the inferior and destructive influence of the Jews (1930a: 5).

All culture was, Rosenberg believed, determined by race. What appeared as good for one was evil for another. Any universal conviction – be it the enlightened belief in one human rationality, the Christian faith in a single almighty God, or the universal Marxist utopia of communism – was dangerously wrong, because it ignored racial-*völkisch* differences. Thus Rosenberg attacked the Christian churches in Germany – especially the globally operating Catholic church, but also Protestants, including German Christians – and wanted all state support stopped. He also rejected, however, a religiously neutral, secular state, calling instead for a new national 'myth' suitable for modern times. He thus dismissed both traditional faiths and a 'mythless time' (Frank 1988: 115–17, 127 f.), calling instead for a 'religious renaissance' and a 'German national church' (Rosenberg 1930: 611). Sharing a Sorelian faith in myth as the crucial force for uniting and mobilizing the nation, he promoted a new faith expressing the eternal racial values of the Germanic race in an up-to-date fashion: 'The longing', Rosenberg emphasized, 'to give the Nordic race soul its form as a German church under the sign of the people's myth [*Volksmythos*], that is for me the greatest task of our century' (1930: 614 f.).

Rosenberg believed he lived in the era, when the Germans were discovering the godly essence of their own race. 'Today ... a new faith awakes: the mythus of blood, the faith to defend the godly essence of humankind with the blood [i.e. racial purity]. The faith based on clearest knowledge that the Nordic blood is the mystery that has replaced and overcome the old sacraments' (1930: 114). Rosenberg built on contemporary 'scientific' racism, but tried to lift this endeavour into a religious sphere. Self-servingly, he deified his own ethnic collective, thus giving godly status above all to himself and other ideal Germans, then, to a lesser degree, to allegedly true Germans and to the Nordic race as a whole.

What content should the new religion have? The myth of race basically meant giving godly status to everything allegedly truly Germanic and Nordic: a strong sense of honour, an idealistic commitment to grand goals, will-power, discipline and heroism. The stereotype that Germans were essentially (in Sombart's terminology) a nation of warriors, this time opposed to the materialistic Jews, was given religious status. Instead of praying to the allegedly weak crucified Christ, the new German Church would glorify the military hero and, in a wider sense, everybody who was fighting to understand and control the world (Ley and

Schoeps 1997: 121). It would praise the *Männerbund* or collective of men (Reulecke 2001; Rohkrämer 1995), who were said to play the crucial role in building a strong *völkisch* state (Rosenberg 1930: 485, 514). It would teach respect for social hierarchy and a Germanic socialism, that is, the altruistic service to *Volk* and race (1930: 535 f.). The new religion would teach respect for 'the eternal polarity of the sexes', 'self-sufficiency' and eugenic measures to purify the race through forced emigration, sterilization (for example, of Jews and criminals), and selective breeding (1930: 503, 545 f., 578 f.). It would, in short, give godly status to everything the Nazis stood for. Allegedly un-German opinions and influences were to be erased (1930: 545).

Using the term 'religion', Rosenberg tried to highlight the 'idealistic' nature of his thought, but he also wanted it to be practical and instrumental. Dismissing the idea of an objective truth, he favoured an 'organic truth': above all, opinions were supposed to 'improve the appearance and inner value of the race or *Volk*' and make it stronger (1930: 684). In effect, Rosenberg thus promoted a Social Darwinist understanding of truth. It simply served to make a race or collective stronger in the struggle for survival, in the struggle to realize its own form of existence, and in the struggle to gain power over the world. Different truths co-exist, but only one appropriate truth for each *Volk* and race. All cultural and political activities of a *Volk* should correspond with such an 'organic truth'. Rosenberg claimed that this 'organic truth' or new religion (the two basically stand for the same) would save the Germans from the 'desperate nihilism' of the time by the 'revival of a new sense of togetherness' and 'a renaissance of old and still eternally young values of the will' (1930: 90), but what he preached was above all intended to serve one very practical goal: a view of reality which would strengthen nation and race.

Religion was not simply supposed to serve survival, but enhance a *Volk*'s existence. Like so many others, Rosenberg promoted an aesthetics of heroism in his evaluative statements. Eugenics had to produce not only functional, but also beautiful human beings, the new politics were to intensify existence and the new Reich was supposed to be of unprecedented grandeur in giving expression to the allegedly godly essence of the Germanic race. A new nobility was to emerge, which would be a nobility both 'of blood and achievement' (1930: 596).

According to Rosenberg, the Nazis served as the vanguard in such a renaissance of a truly Germanic nation. The NSDAP, he claimed, was more than a party, because it stood for the truly German and Nordic. It had the historical function of realizing a *völkisch* revolution, but would then disappear because there was no room for parties in a nation united in a single faith. Once 'the National Socialist German Workers Party has fulfilled its mission', it 'can disappear' (1930a: 11).

Rosenberg envisaged the new Germanic Reich to be anti-Christian. The glorification of love and mercy had to be replaced, he stated, by a heroic and ruthless Germanic religion. Although periodically checked by Hitler's reluctance to enter into irreconcilable conflict with the Christian churches (see below), he never gave up his ambition of providing a superior Nazi alternative. From 1938 onwards, he developed Nazi rituals for baptism, marriages and funerals, and he promoted a yearly Nazi cycle of public holidays like the Take-over of Power Day, the Heroes Memorial Day, the Führer's Birthday, The Day of the German Nation, Mother's Day, the Summer Solstice, Thanksgiving in Autumn, Memorial Day for the Movements Martyrs, and the Winter Solstice (Bollmus 1970: 114). It was not enough, he wrote to Bormann in spring 1943, for Nazism to remain purely political; a *völkisch* ideology also had to fulfil all religious needs, above all through rituals. 'It must be accepted as a matter of principle that indoctrination and education must have the possibility of acting not simply through the spoken word in speeches and lectures, but should also appeal to the feelings of Party comrades through ceremonies. It seems to me necessary, particularly in the light of the struggle against the Church, for the Party to develop a ceremonial form which attracts Germans to the Party and allows them to dispense with what the Church has hitherto given them' (quoted in Noakes and Pridham 1983 ff.: Vol. 4, 109).

Rosenberg declared in 1938 that the power of the Christian churches would soon be broken, and there were indeed some developments in that direction. In 1939, 10 per cent of the population in Berlin registered as Deists (rather than Christians), 25 per cent of SS members called themselves Deists in 1938, and anti-Christian sentiments were also taught in the Hitler Youth. As part of Nazism's cumulative radicalization, the position of the churches became increasingly precarious (Blackburn 1985; Evans 2005: 248, 252 f. See also more generally Steigmann-Gall 2003). Only Nazi fanatics, however, used the new Nazi rituals for baptism, marriage and funeral; the large majority saw no conflict between accepting the Third Reich's policies and simultaneously using a Christian church for their religious needs. With the war, Christianity even increased in strength; for the majority, the Nazi cult of death and heroism was insufficient in the face of mass death and suffering. Rosenberg was not alone among the Nazi elite, however, in rejecting Christianity in favour of a more heroic new faith. Even outdoing Rosenberg, the leader of the SS Heinrich Himmler blamed Christianity for all ills in German history. In their political indoctrination, SS men were instructed: 'Whatever is Christian, is not German; whatever is German, is not Christian! Manly pride, heroic courage and loyalty are German – not gentleness, remorse, sin and suffering [*Sündenelende*], and an afterlife with prayers and psalms' (quoted in Ackermann 1970: 56).

Himmler grudgingly accepted Hitler's call for peace with the churches, but only half-heartedly and as a temporary measure. In public speeches, he restrained himself, but internally he continued his aggressive tirades. He was convinced he lived "in the age of final confrontation with Christianity', and the SS was to play a central role in 'giving the German people ... a non-Christian, racially suited world-view as the foundation for their conduct of life' (quoted in Ackermann 1970: 253). Himmler wanted to delve into the Germanic past to find a religion appropriate to the Nordic race. He used Heydrich's funeral to express his own faith, clearly also as guidance for the SS:

> I intentionally expressed in my oration a belief in God, a belief in fate, in the ancient one as I called him – that is the old Germanic word: *Wralda* … He [man] must once again look with deep reverence into this world. Then he will acquire the right sense of … how we are woven into the cycle. Then on a different plane, something else must happen: we must again be rooted in our ancestors and grandchildren, in this eternal chain and eternal sequence. By rooting our people in a deep ideological awareness of ancestors and grandchildren we must once more persuade them that they must have sons. We can do a very great deal. But everything we do must be justifiable vis-à-vis the clan, our ancestors. If we do not secure this moral foundation which is the deepest and the best because [it is] the most natural, we will not be able to overcome Christianity on this planet and create the Germanic Reich which will be a blessing for the earth. That is our mission as a nation on this earth. For thousands of years it has been the mission of this blond race to rule the earth and again and again to bring it happiness and culture. (quoted in Noakes and Pridham 1983 ff.: Vol. 2, 498)

For the time being, Himmler tolerated Christians within the SS as long as they did not let their religion interfere with the demand for unreserved obedience to their superiors, but a non-Christian faith obviously helped with a career. SS men should believe in a God, but it was the God of Social Darwinist conflict and racial conflict. Himmler did not believe in an individual life after death, but only a continued existence in one's offspring and race. The highest religious duty was service to a great Germanic Reich. As a SS leader stated: 'Good is that which helps our people, and bad is that which harms our people' (quoted in Ackermann 1970: 141).

Himmler's God was a highly convenient God who fully shared the SS leader's ideas and plans. In effect, he served to bless the creation of a Reich and the breeding of an ideal blond Nordic super-race. It was a religion aiming to make a difference in this world. The destruction or enslavement of 'less worthy humans' and the breeding of a Germanic 'super-race', as well as the murderous plans for the East, were all an expression of the totalitarian will to completely change the world. After all, Himmler claimed, Nordic men were men of action, defying death in trying to create the best conditions for their race. Himmler expressed this in semi-religious language, but the SS and other NS elite institutions also provided space for men who ignored Himmler's metaphysical fantasies. Obedience was demanded, as was personal initiative in 'working towards the Führer' by trying to realize his world-view, but not a particular metaphysical faith (Herbert 1995; Wildt 2002, 2003. More generally Smelser and Syring 2000; Wegner 1997). Even Himmler's second-in-command Heydrich was characterized, as his wife stated later, by a more concrete ideological fanaticism:

> Himmler was obsessed by ideas … My husband did not play with ideas. His tasks were concrete and clear … Each person interpreted National Socialism as it suited them.

> There were as many ideologies as there were members. As far as my husband was concerned, the idea of a greater Germany naturally played a decisive role – the rebirth of Germany. But that was really something obvious rather than being a matter of ideology … Naturally, he did not think about the moral aspect of his activities. He would have considered thinking about human life as a thoroughly civilian mode of thought. (Noakes and Pridham 1983 ff.: Vol. 2, 500)

In its naivety, the quotation is quite revealing. What is regarded as natural and obvious was the shared ideology of the SS – namely the commitment to a greater Germany and all the measures this allegedly took, including the ruthless 'cleansing' of society (especially of Jews, but also of other 'inferior' races and individuals) to achieve a strong *Volksgemeinschaft*, establishing cultural and political unity (also by suppressing other convictions) and a glorification of violent ruthlessness in achieving these goals. Complete commitment to the Führer served to justify the claim to be the new Nazi elite. Beyond this core, other convictions remained, at least for the time being, ultimately a matter of personal preferences. While many were more down-to-earth, Himmler was convinced that the new order needed a religious foundation to gain durability. The SS, including their carefully chosen wives and their children, was to be the new aristocracy, a semi-religious or knightly order. New SS men had to swear an oath to God, the *Volk* and the God-sent Führer, they were encouraged to use paganist NS ceremonies for baptisms, marriages and funerals, and the whole SS was supposed to develop its own faith, rituals and codes of behaviour. The high percentage of members from the nobility and the middle class and the occasional cleansing of the SS also stressed their exclusive status.

The SS was consciously set apart as a new elite. Himmler dreamt of establishing a semi-autonomous SS state, he worked towards reintroducing the duel, and the public appearance of the SS was also carefully designed: the black uniform and black boots together with the white gloves as well as the many insignia of rank and honour like the ring with a skull, the dagger and, as the highest honour, a sword. In the long run, Himmler was not satisfied with a nation united 'only' in political orientation; he also wanted a single racial religion for all Germanic people, and the SS was to lead the way.

Rosenberg and Himmler were neither silenced nor insignificant. Dietrich Eckhart, who was singled out for praise in Hitler's *Mein Kampf*, preached a Germanic religion (Bärsch 1998: 52–91), and among the prominent Nazis, Heß, Streicher, Bormann and Schirach also believed in a religious mission of the movement. Many Germans regarded the Nazis as critical of the Christian churches, and there is ample evidence, especially at the local level, of tensions between church and party (Kershaw 1987; Steigmann-Gall 2003; Süllwold 2001: 85–89). The official party line, however, was different. Taking a clear stand against all *völkisch* dreams of a Germanic religion, Adolf Hitler pushed for peace with the Christian churches (Rissmann 2001; Scholder 1980: 110–123). In *Mein Kampf* he declared that Nazism did not aim for a religious reformation, but a political reawakening of the German people, and in a conversation with the violently anti-Catholic Ludendorff he is said to have declared: 'But I need the Catholics of Bavaria and the Protestants from Prussia to build a large political movement. The rest will come later' (quoted in Scholder 1977: 115). When the Protestant churches inquired about the party's attitude towards Rosenberg's book *The Mythus*, the Nazi party claimed to be a purely political movement, which was 'carried and led by Christians' promoting a politics in harmony with Christian ethics. Despite a closer proximity to Protestantism, the party claimed to be committed to a 'positive Christianity' beyond confessional divides (quoted in Scholder 1977: 241).

In the early years of the Third Reich, Hitler continued to emphasize the important role of the Christian churches for the new Reich:

> The national government sees in the two Christian confessions the most important factors for maintaining our ethnicity [*Volkstum*]. It will respect the contracts made between the churches and the German *Länder* ... The government wants to care for the honest co-existence of church and state; the fight against the materialist world-view in favour of a true community of the people simultaneously serves the German nation and the Christian faith. (Domarus 1973: Vol. 1, 232 f.)

In contrast to *völkisch* dogmatists, Hitler thus realized that the Nazis could not succeed against the churches in a still largely Christian nation. But what were his true convictions? Despite remaining a member of the Catholic Church, he never disguised the fact that he was not much of a church-goer, and in private statements he became increasingly negative and scornful about the churches, Christianity and, to a lesser extent, religion in general. Above all, he never left any doubt that the state was the highest authority. While religions could continue to play a role in private life, they had to fall in line with the politics of the Nazi state. Hitler felt forced to make some compromises with the churches, but in principle he never accepted religious objections. In a secret wartime speech he made his totalitarian ambitions quite clear by stating that he wanted to rule Germany on the basis of the 'knowledge about the importance of blood and race ... The churches may command the German people about life after death, [but] the German nation through its leadership commands the German people in this life' (Hitler 1999: 700).

Hitler also rejected Christian ethics. In his recorded private wartime conversations and monologues, he blamed, for example, the Christian praise of love and peace for the fall of Rome and political weaknesses in German history (Hitler 1999: 131). Germany would have been better served, he argued, with a more heroic religion, promoting soldierly values and sacrifice for the race. Finally, Hitler frequently voiced a simplistic faith in science which made him reject any kind of metaphysics ranging from Christianity to *völkisch* beliefs like those of Rosenberg and Himmler. Religion became naive, he argued, in the enlightened age of knowledge; Nazism should thus base itself on science, not on faith or myth.[6]

Hitler kept wavering with regard to the political consequences the Third Reich should draw from his rejection of religion. A heroic elite like the SS and Nazi youth, he argued (1999: 111), did not need the illusion of an individual life after death: they were prepared for service and sacrifice simply to serve the community. As the mass of the population, however, needed religious fantasies to overcome their fear of death, they should still be tolerated. While he hoped for a gradual withering away of religion – as that would signal the emergence of a fanatical belief in serving nation and race – he frequently stressed the grave dangers involved in forcing such a development. With time, however, he became impatient with such a hands-off approach, partly because he believed that the churches had 'stabbed' the fighting nation 'in the back' (quoted in Bollmus 1970: 117 f.) and partly because he no longer saw the need for compromising with non-Nazi elites. As early as 1937, he claimed that 'Christianity was ripe for destruction' (quoted in Kershaw 2000: 40), and during the war his aggression against the churches came to match that of Rosenberg and Himmler. In the winter of 1941 he called it his last great task 'to solve the church problem. Only then will the German nation be truly safe', when 'the state is absolute master' (Hitler 1999: 108 f.).

Hitler thus rejected both the churches and what he called religion. This did not, however, make him non-religious. On the contrary; Hitler's thinking was crucially shaped by both his own faith and his dream of a nation united in a single communal faith. His belief in an absolute truth shows a core characteristic of religious faith. He could not see his own world-view of Social Darwinism, racism and expansionism as one opinion among others, but stressed that this basis of Nazi policy was eternally true. His opinion proved immune to counter-arguments and adverse events; even when the war turned against Germany, setbacks were interpreted as a test for hardening the Germans or, when Hitler could no longer close his eyes to the likelihood of defeat, as a sign that a weakened German race no longer deserved victory in this Social Darwinist struggle (Rissman 2001: 58–60). Hitler could not accept that he might err, but took his own world-view as gospel.

At times, Hitler tended towards a deification of nature. He once argued that a Christian 'temple of an idol' should be replaced by an astronomical observatory with the inscription 'The Sky Praises the Honour of the Eternal' (Hitler 2000: 285 f. See also Hitler 1999: 507–509). Like Himmler, the dictator claimed that the study of nature would produce a sense of consolation and humility in the confrontation with the 'all-powerful' (Hitler 1999: 701), and he frequently called the laws of nature God's will. Such pantheism, however, was largely rhetorical for Hitler. After all, there were no mysteries for him. He believed that he comprehended fully nature's laws, which, moreover, wholly corresponded with his own desire for heroism, struggle and the eventual triumph of the Aryan race (Domarus 1973: Vol. 2, 894). Talk of an awe-inspiring nature was thus little more than a cultural cliché to him.

Of crucial importance was, however, Hitler's ambition to revolutionize Germany through the Nazi 'seizure of power'. Not satisfied with pragmatic changes, he wanted to create a truly German culture based on eternal racial values, an identity of leadership and *Volk*, and a fanatical dedication to grand politics. Hitler had nothing but spiteful contempt for a relativistic intellectualism, aiming instead at a nation united in a single faith. He not only believed that the mass of the population desired a clear orientation in life, but also saw a country united in a single fascist world-view as the key to success. He not only copied from the style of working-class mass politics, but also grudgingly admired their dedication. He thus called for a right-wing equivalent. 'Marxist internationalism', he claimed in 1924, 'can only be broken through a fanatic extreme nationalism of highest social ethics and morals. One cannot take the false idol of Marxism from the people without giving it a better God' (1980: 1226). In *Mein Kampf*, he argued more generally: 'From general ideas a political programme must be stamped, from a general philosophy of life a definite political faith' (1992: 346). Such a political faith 'is intolerant' and aims at 'the complete transformation of all public life in accordance with its views' (1992: 412). This is a concise call for a nation not only sharing one faith, but also completely shaped by this faith. Strict cultural unity within a single communal faith was to overcome all plurality of opinions, thus creating cultural totalitarianism.

Despite his emphasis on science, Hitler's words were marked by many religious features (Klemperer 2000). He regularly used biblical phrases and terms, he claimed to 'go with the certainty of a sleepwalker along the path laid out for me by providence' (quoted in Kershaw 1998: 591), and he justified his fight against the Jews in religious terms. 'I believe that I am acting in accordance with the will of the Almighty Creator: *by defending myself against the Jew, I am fighting for the work of the Lord*' (1992: 60). In claiming that Aryans served as vessels for the godly in this world, they always seemed to fight for God; and the Nazi faith that the individual would live on eternally in nation or race was to provide an alternative to the Christian promise of life after death (Hitler 1999: 110 f.). Hitler thus put forward what he regarded as an enlightened version of religiosity in accordance with the racial theories of the Third Reich:

> No mysterious notion stands at the beginning of our programme, but clear knowledge and thus an open creed. By placing the maintaining and securing of a God-created being [the Aryans] at the centre of this knowledge and this creed, however, we thus serve the maintenance of a godly work and thus of a godly will, not in the mysterious twilight of a new place of worship, but in the open view of the Lord. (Domarus 1973: Vol. 2, 893 f.)

Hitler rejected the term 'cult', which he associated with an outdated irrationality (Behrenbeck 1996: 331 f.), but he advocated the development of rituals which should become a *Brauchtum* or custom for the future (Domarus 1973: Vol. 2, 893). 'We need a grand style. This style we must create for ourselves. We will thus put the celebration of our public holidays in a form which is to remain' (Hitler 2000: 99 f.). In his memoirs, Albert Speer recalled that Hitler aimed at the 'canonisation' of core rituals of Nazi Germany so that later, possibly weaker dictators could profit from the historical authority of such forms. 'It became clear to me', Speer commented, 'that Hitler aimed at something close to founding a church'. In later celebrations, he reported, Hitler no longer wanted to foreground his own person, but the architecture and the mass processions so that the rituals could work without him. Instead of enjoying the role of a 'celebrated hero of the people', he wanted to turn into the 'founder of a religion' (Speer 1976: 403).

In contrast to Christianity, however, these rituals all served an immediate political purpose. Hitler was not concerned with any individual afterlife, but with strengthening nation and race in this world. Even the cult of dead heroes was largely utilitarian, its main goal being the production of new heroes ready for sacrifice. Religious elements clearly played a role for Hitler, but they found their place within a more basic aesthetic attitude (Fest 1977; Spotts 2002). Aesthetic dream-worlds played a crucial role in Hitler's life. He lost himself in operettas and Wagner's musical dramas in Vienna and later in the feature films with which he had an obsession; he drew plans for monumental buildings when there seemed no chance of ever realizing them; he re-read Karl May's nearly seventy volumes as chancellor, claiming that they served him as a key to understanding the world; and he continued to spend much time and thought on the architectural reconstruction of Berlin and other cities. Realizing the aesthetic effect of politics came naturally to him. Working class demonstrations in Vienna inspired him to a new style of right-wing mass politics; like an actor he practised in front of the mirror; and he indulged in fantasies about the awe-inspiring effect of the new monumental political architecture. 'Whoever enters the Reich Chancellery must have the feeling that he steps in front of the master of the world. Even the way there through the triumphal arch on the wide streets past the hall of soldiers to the people's square should be breath-taking' (Hitler 2000: 101).[7] 'Even as military commander', Speer believed, 'he thought more readily about the psychological than the military effectiveness of a weapon' (1976: 278), for example, in his reluctance to introduce machine guns, which would reduce the amount of heroic face-to-face combat, or his appreciation of flame throwers. He thought of sirens on the Stuka fighter plane to demoralize the opponent, and he lost himself in fantasies of revenge and destruction when thinking about the 'miraculous' new weapons of mass destruction:

> I remember how he asked to be shown the films of burning London, of the gigantic sea of fire over Warsaw, of exploding convoys … and what greed overcame him every time. But never ever have I seen him so beside himself than towards the end of war, when he described to himself and us – as if in a delirium – the destruction of New York in storms of fire. He described how the sky-scrapers would turn into gigantic burning torches, how they would collapse into each other, how the bursting city would be reflected in the dark sky; and he commented, as if returning back from his

> ecstasy, Saur should immediately realize Messerschmidt's plans for a four-engined long-distance bomber. With its reach we could take thousand-fold revenge for the destruction of our cities. (Speer 2002: 127)

As a young man, he lost himself in fantasies about a lottery win after he had bought a ticket, only to be outraged when it came to nothing (Kershaw 1998: 22), and in 1938 he said according to Speer: 'Illusions we have to bring to the masses ... Illusions they not only need in cinema and theatre ... Precisely because life is serious, humans must be elevated out of their daily life' (1969: 155). While he knew that Nazi Germany needed to maintain a decent standard of living to keep the population happy, his ideal was – as for Nietzsche, Spengler, Jünger and many others – the heroic human wholly devoted to an aesthetics of struggle and sacrifice. 'The beautiful ought to have power over humans, and it wants to maintain its power. How else could one explain that there are always innumerable people in times of need who are ready without hesitation to risk their life for the existence of their *Volk*.' – 'Strong and beautiful I want my youth to be, masterly and fearless. The free, magnificent beast of prey must shine out of their eyes' (Hitler 1999: 108, 133).

Hitler held on to the core principles of his world-view, above all the belief in racism and expansionism in a Social Darwinist world of struggle, because 'they formed the essence of what he understood by power itself'. Otherwise, however, he could be quite pragmatic, judging political means by their effectiveness (Kershaw 1998: 253). He was taken in by grand aesthetic effects, but he also used them deliberately to gain support for his policies. Inspired by Wagner and shaped by a heroic interpretation of the First World War, he did everything for aesthetic effect. His ideal was to turn reality into a *Gesamtkunstwerk*, a grand show of national unity and strength, of heroic struggle and sacrifice, of national grandeur and victory. He accepted the egotism in his surroundings and in the nation as a whole (Aly 2005; Bajohr 2004), but he wanted to turn public life into a spectacle of devotion to the ideal of a united nation in pursuit of a grand political vision – beyond ordinary moral rights and wrongs. He had failed as a painter; but after the war he became the creator of aesthetically influenced visions of a battle between good and evil, Republican turmoil and a vague future utopia. Eclectic in his means, he combined the traditional and the modern, the religious and the banal, the romantic and the technocratic to create a vision which would unite the German people behind a single communal faith to mobilize them for grand politics.

Hitler's first political ability was his oratory skills. He criticized all conservatives from the Pan-Germans to the presidential regimes for failing to abandon their elitism and speak the language of the people. In contrast, this social upstart could claim to be 'a child of the people and will always remain so' (Domarus 1973: Vol. 1, 140). If one believed, as Hitler and an increasing number of conservatives did, 'that every government must fail and will fail which does not have a firm ideological anchorage in a supporting movement of the people' (Domarus

1973: Vol. 1, 127), then the self-acclaimed political drummer fulfilled a crucial function. The old right-wing elites had little doubt that they had the better political strategy, but they knew that they desperately needed a way to win over the population.

Hitler made sure that this point was not missed. He blamed the German Empire for having failed to win the masses, thus losing the war through a 'stab-in-the-back'. Only a country united in a single faith could be strong, and only a masterful propagandist could achieve such unity. He also mentioned the content of successful right-wing propaganda (in particular the new Nazi synthesis of nationalism and socialism), but his main emphasis was on method.

> The art of propaganda lies in understanding the emotional idea of the great masses and finding, through a psychologically correct form, the way to the attention and thence to the heart of the broad masses ... The receptivity of the great masses is very limited, their intelligence is small, but their power of forgetting is enormous. In consequence of these facts, all effective propaganda must be limited to a few points and must harp on these in slogans ...
>
> The people in their overwhelming majority are so feminine by nature and attitude that sober reasoning determines their thoughts and actions far less than emotions and feelings.
>
> And this sentiment is not complicated, but very simple and all of a piece. It does not have multiple shadings; it has a positive and a negative; love or hate, right or wrong, truth or lie, never half this way and half that way, never partially, or that kind of thing. (Hitler 1992: 165–167)

There is no need to describe once again Hitler's ideas about propaganda, which he expressed most thoroughly in Ch. 6 of *Mein Kampf*.[8] It is important to note, however, that Hitler described propaganda as a means to mobilize the people whose support can then be used for different ends. Propaganda does not need to be truthful, but effective in showing a clear world-view and inspire trust. It does not need to be beautiful, but must be catchy, vivid and full of suggestive imagery. A political movement, he believed, had to show strength and determination to convince, because the largely passive masses would go with the most courageous and dynamic force. Thus Hitler wanted to break the dominance of Socialist militancy in the public sphere by staging right-wing mass rallies with flags and uniforms, music and speeches.

It has often been ignored that Hitler's description of propaganda was not a scholarly treatise, but in itself propaganda. Hitler might have believed himself to be a perfect manipulator, but this claim was also a sales pitch, in particular to the conservative elites. They needed mass support for an authoritarian turn, and Hitler bragged that only he could get it. The leader of the Nazi party presented himself as the detached, even cynical leader, who simplified and gave emotional pathos to his differentiated political analysis, but this was largely show. Of course, Hitler was expert in deceiving people by pragmatically adapting his message to different times and audiences (this indeed was a central reason for his success).

But he was wholly convinced of the core features of his simplistic, polarized world-view, and he certainly believed in the visions of heroism, mortal sacrifice and monumental grandeur that he painted. The pathos of Wagner's operas – which plunder the whole tradition of high and low culture, the Christian and the heathen, the sophisticated and the banal to achieve powerful emotional effects – was not just a means for transmitting the message, but at the core of Hitler's attitude towards life. It was not accidental that Hitler compared the task of the successful propagandist who changes a whole nation's attitude with that of a 'really great artist' (Hitler 1999: 214 f.). His was a theatrical attitude towards reality, thinking more about aesthetic effects for the detached onlooker than the reality for the participants. Hitler's greatest ambition was that of an artist. He wanted to realize his own vision, but unfortunately he took reality as his canvas.

Hitler did not hold a political opinion which he then sold to the masses. Rather, his convictions emerged in a kind of dialogue with the population. In the first years of the Republic, when his world-view took final shape (Jäckel 1981), he constantly tested his ideas. As an orator who was sensitive to his audience, he learnt which ideas worked by a process of trial and error. In contrast to the Conservative Revolutionaries, who largely stayed within their circles, the Nazis developed their ideas in the political arena. In the ideological crisis after the First World War, the old desire on the Right for a strong leader increased even further, but an aspiring candidate had to refine his message until it found enthusiastic resonance. After all, the main test was his success at finding enthusiastic mass support.

With the writing of *Mein Kampf*, this process was largely completed. This book offers an accurate description of Hitler's belief system, though the life story describing the acquisition of this world-view is stylized and often plain invention (Kershaw 1998). Hitler's views were neither original nor insightful, but this often-noted point was politically irrelevant. Decisive was that he had succeeded

(1) in arranging the core convictions of the extreme *völkisch* Right into a coherent whole,
(2) in developing a world-view which offered an answer to everything, and
(3) in outlining a more realistic and promising political strategy than his competitors to integrate the highly divided extreme Right and further their political successes.

The characteristics of his world-view were prerequisites for his early political success within extremist circles,[9] but they were not wholly suited for the early 1930s, when the world economic crisis provided the possibility of becoming the largest party. Hitler, however, was able to make temporary ideological compromises to reach further towards the political middle ground of the Weimar Republic, for example by toning down his extreme anti-Semitism and desire for war, stressing instead the vision of a true national community as the basis of a strong Germany. His world-view proved flexible enough to adapt to unexpected political events because he valued winning a populist basis more than ideological truthfulness.

He believed in his world-view, but the primacy of the wish to win over the nation made him prepared for – at least temporary – compromises.

The importance Hitler attached to aesthetics also shows in his attitude towards art. Hitler explicitly called for 'a cultural renaissance as well as political and economic reform' (quoted in Welch 1995: 172). He accepted neither Rosenberg's emphasis on a truly Germanic art nor Goebbels's wish to provide space for parts of modern art in the new Reich. Looking for grand ancestors, he had only contempt for the Germanic tribes, claiming instead for the Aryan race whatever he regarded as most beautiful.[10] His main ideals were ancient Greece and the art of his own youth around the turn of the century, but he basically followed his aesthetic instinct in incorporating everything he fancied. Consistent with his racial world-view, though, his choice *then* had to be interpreted as a product of Aryans, allegedly the only race able to create great art.

Art was important for Hitler because it could give expression to his vision of a higher form of existence. An international art dominated by a plurality of styles was to be replaced by an art both German and eternal, expressing the essence of the German people 'in its character and life, in its feelings, its emotions and its development' (reprinted in Welch 1995: 171). Art was to express the essence of *völkisch*ness and be appealing to the general taste (Welch 1995: 174) so that it could serve as a central means to shape a communal Aryan world-view. Art was not to present the sordid or the subjective, but promote ideals as guiding utopias for the nation.

Finally, art, especially architecture, was to give eternal expression to the grandeur of Nazi Germany. It should present the best of the Third Reich to future generations by creating 'eternal values', for example, in buildings which would still look grand even when ruins. 'Our cathedrals are witnesses of past grandeur!' Hitler exclaimed, 'The grandeur of the present will one day be judged by the eternal values left behind' (Domarus 1973: Vol. 1, 529). But before this, these monumental buildings were to serve as ritualistic places for the celebration of a nationalist cult. As Speer stated with reference to the doomed hall planned for Berlin:

> This structure, the greatest assembly hall in the world ever conceived up to that time, consisted of one vast hall that could hold between one hundred and fifty and one hundred and eighty thousand persons standing. In spite of Hitler's negative attitude toward Himmler's and Rosenberg's mystical notions, the hall was essentially a place of worship. The idea was that over the course of centuries, by tradition and venerability, it would acquire an importance similar to that St. Peter's in Rome has for Catholic Christendom. Without some such essentially pseudo-religious background the expenditure for Hitler's central building would have been pointless and incomprehensible. (Speer 1976: 152 f.)

Hitler only rejected myth and religion in his own narrow understanding of the terms. He not only promoted a new world-view with many religious features (claiming, for example, to provide a full explanation of history, to establish a new individual and collective code of correct conduct or to offer a way for the individual to accept sacrifice and death), but also places of worship and sacred symbols, rituals and festivals. Hitler rejected far-fetched fantasies about a Germanic religion or myth, but he undoubtedly aimed at establishing a new communal world-view which would unite the nation in one faith and mobilize it for heroic deeds. In the early years of the movement, he declared: 'This is the greatest thing that our movement should create: [to give] the wandering and searching broad masses a new, firm faith, which does not desert them in times of chaos' (1980: 624). In 1932, Hitler claimed that Nazism was 'not only a movement, but a religion' (quoted in Behrenbeck 1996: 23), and in 1936 he stated categorically: 'Woe betide whoever does not have a belief! He sins against the meaning of all life' (Domarus 1973: Vol. 2, 647).

With power secured and consolidated, Hitler clearly identified his own world-view with the essence of Germanness, his policies with a *völkisch* destiny, thus appealing to his audience on the German Workers Day in 1935: 'Renew … your creed to your *Volk*, to our community and to our National Socialist state. My will – this must be our creed – is your faith! My faith is for me – as for you – everything in this world. The ultimate, however, that God has given me in this world, is my *Volk*! My faith is based in it' (Domarus 1973: Vol. 2, 503).

Joseph Goebbels was even more negative about Rosenberg and his followers than Hitler. Contrasting himself with this 'stubborn, headstrong dogmatic' (quoted in Reichel 1993: 92), he wanted Nazism to be open, pragmatic and result-oriented. While Rosenberg tried to stick to the true message, the propagandist Goebbels placed the emphasis on reaching his audience by being appealing. He was happy to accept entertainment as a compensation for a tough reality, limited the amount of propaganda to avoid ideological overload, and worked hard to present political messages in an aesthetically pleasing form. In his ruthless eclecticism, he used a mix of the modern and the old, the religious and the secular, the technocratic and the romantic, the witty and the solemn to package propaganda in the most effective way.

Goebbels was pragmatic in selling the Third Reich to the people, but he was by no means merely a cynic. As both his early diaries and his novel *Michael* show, he had been a man in search of a great destiny before joining Nazism. Many developments culminated to make him experience a deep crisis in the middle of the 1920s. The young and highly ambitious Doctor of German literature had serious problems starting his career in a time of high unemployment; he suffered from the loss of his Catholic faith – his parents had even wanted him to become a priest (Behrenbeck 1996: 119) – and the stumbling Weimar Republic offered little attraction to somebody looking for grandeur. Generalizing from his own university experience and drawing on a major theme of cultural criticism, he blamed relativistic intellectualism for the lack of a strong world-view in modernity.

Goebbels undoubtedly experienced personal difficulties, but his religious background strongly shaped his reaction to it. He was brought up to regard a clear orientation and purpose in life as normal. When his faith shattered, he was thus devastated and started to look for a new clear-cut world-view to guide his actions (Bärsch 1998: 100). He changed the Cartesian '*Cogito, ergo sum*' into '*Credo, ergo sum*' (1929: 25), thus postulating that faith was the ultimate basis of existence. The search for a mission, which would give meaning to a life of heroism and sacrifice, was at the centre of both his early diary entries and his novel *Michael*. There is always a looming sense that fundamental doubts marked a testing crisis, but could not last forever. Exactly at the darkest moments, he expected that an apocalyptic turn to the better would occur.

Young Goebbels was more strongly infected by modern relativism than other leading Nazis. He acknowledged that different ideological orientations were possible, but advocated a ruthless decisionism to achieve one clear orientation: 'It does not matter too much, what we believe in', he claimed, 'but only that we believe' (1929: 31). As with all decisionism, however, Goebbels was not truly neutral, but sought a decisive and heroic, grand and spectacular world-view. He continued to use the word 'God', but his God was very different to the God of the Bible. Above all, Goebbels eroded the distinction between God and humans by believing in the God-likeness of the exceptional individual. The hero of his novel (who is clearly the author's idealized self) sees it as his task to destroy the traditional faith to 'then build a new world … I fight with myself for a different God.' This new God 'is will … My God is a God of strength'. Such a warrior-like God should stand in full splendour, because 'I am God's image. The grander I make God, the grander I am.' When lost in fantasies about fighting as a soldier, Goebbels's idealized self can even claim: 'I am a hero, a God, a redeemer' (1929: 31, 32, 26, 116).

Goebbels not only rejected a categorical distinction between God and exceptional humans, thereby implicitly deifying himself and the Nazi leadership, he also came to desire a practical faith. The value of a faith showed, he argued, in worldly success: the ability to mobilize humans and achieve its goal. 'God helps the courageous and beats the weak.' 'The thought wins out that has the strongest supporters' (1929: 43, 66). Goebbels thus searched for a faith that would make a difference in this world. Rejecting the wish for material comfort, he stated that rich people make money, while idealists make history. 'We want to make history … The globe belongs to the one who takes it' (1929: 119, 148).

Goebbels found in Nazism a replacement for the lost faith of his youth. 'What is Christianity to us today? National Socialism is religion', he stated on 16 October 1928 in his diary. 'We are only lacking the religious genius which will break the old, outdated forms and build new ones. We lack the ritual, National Socialism must eventually become the state religion for the Germans. My party is my church.' His early diary entries show both a strong nationalism and the desire for a leader who would save Germany by giving it political direction and a single communal faith. Soon he found his charismatic hero in Hitler. Goebbels not only became the key promoter of the Hitler myth, he was also one of the first and most enduring believers. Despite taking the Socialist element more seriously than his Führer, he saw him as the personification of the truly German. Among the Nazi elite, Goebbels found a place to devote his life to a higher cause: 'I believe in the future! I love my people and my fatherland. Work! Sacrifice! No despair' (Diary: 9 June 1925).

Goebbels shared Hitler's polarized world-view with the Jews as a devilish counter-force to the God-like Aryans (Barth 2003). 'When Germany perishes, then the light of this world is turned off' (Goebbels 1929: 118). For him, getting rid of the Jews was thus part and parcel of establishing 'the Third Reich as a great Germany; the Third Reich as a Socialist[11] community of fate' (quoted in Bärsch 1998: 114). He believed less, however, in a science of race or Social Darwinism, but in a free power of the will to shape history (Kroll 1998: 257 ff.). Above all, he thus saw the total mobilization of the national will for the Nazi goals as decisive for success. Propaganda was key to win over the nation, but so was social justice to achieve national unity. As he stated in 1932: 'We no longer want to think in terms of class, we are not proletarians and not bourgeois, not in the first instance Catholics and not in the first instance Protestants. We do not ask whether farmer or town-dweller, whether artisan, worker or prince. May a great unity incorporate us – and then the poet's word has come true: the people rise, the storm breaks out' (1991: 47 f.). In contrast to all other parties, which allegedly fought only for their own petty interest, the Nazis were supposed to be the true voice of the people and the true Socialists who would create jobs and realize social justice. He rejected the restoration of the past with servants and class privileges, calling instead for social mobility and the universal duty to serve the nation. Social justice would win the workers for the nationalist cause and thus provide the basis for successful power politics. Then, the hero of his novel claimed, 'the globe will be in fear of us' (Goebbels 1929: 133).

Goebbels had clear convictions, but he also believed, like Hitler, that any strong conviction was better than none, because a strong communal faith was a necessary prerequisite for total mobilization. Lip-service to Nazism was not enough; only a movement which would succeed in becoming a worldly 'gospel' and a 'great faith', 'which lives so unshakably in the hearts that all of us are ready to give, if necessary, the ultimate [sacrifice]' would be an irresistible political force (Goebbels 1934: 25).

The German people, Goebbels declared, should start 'to think as one, to react as one, and to place itself in the service of the government with all of its heart' (quoted in Reuth 1995: 269). His ideal was that Nazism should grow from one political opinion to become *the* unquestioned ideology, indeed the mentality of the German people, a fundamental part of their unconscious self. 'National Socialism is not only a *political* doctrine, it is a *total* and *all-encompassing* general perspective on all public matters. So our entire life has to be based on it as a matter of natural assumption. We hope that the day will come when nobody needs to *talk* about National Socialism any more, since it has become the air that we breathe' (Goebbels 1991: Vol. 1, 227).

For Goebbels, ideological and political measures had to reinforce each other if the new German Reich was to achieve its goal. A nation united in a single faith could not be achieved without a popular and successful policy, but successes were also dependent on a united people. A good propaganda machine selling the regime's message to the people was thus essential for the national 'reawakening'. The First World War served as evidence that material mobilization was not sufficient without a corresponding 'spiritual mobilization' (quoted in Welch 1995: 148).

As integration and mobilization behind a single faith were important goals in themselves, Goebbels could be pragmatic in choosing the means that worked. 'Never mind morals', he proclaimed, 'decisive is the effectiveness' (quoted in Bollmus 1970: 105). Instead of being fixated on dogmatic purity like Rosenberg, Goebbels realized that people had to enjoy consuming Nazi culture before they could be politically influenced by it. While open political propaganda like the film *Triumph of the Will* would only speak to the already converted (Evans 2005: 127 f.), other cultural productions could have a wider effect. 'Above all do not become boring', he said to radio directors. 'Above all no dreariness. Above all, do not wear convictions on your sleeves … Convictions are a must, but convictions must not mean boredom.' During the misery of war, he could even call for culture as pure compensation. 'The darker the streets are, the brighter [should] our theatres and cinemas shine … The harder the times, the brighter art must shine over it, as the consoler of the human soul.'[12]

Goebbels had no ambition to produce art, but aimed at an aesthetics 'which still interests the sophisticated taste and which is still pleasing and understandable for the simple mind' (quoted in Reichel 1993: 168). Art was for him 'no absolute concept', but was bound to have 'political bias' and should serve the 'life of the people' (1991: Vol. 1, 131–134). Goebbels ridiculed all nostalgia, calling instead for a 'steel-like romanticism', that is, accepting modern reality, but giving it a grand and heroic meaning in showing, for example, the 'heroic attitude in SA-men, workers and farmers' or the 'almost soldierly rhythm' in Germany's economic recovery (1991: 137). Goebbels did not preach irrationalism or wishful fantasies, but he wanted all knowledge to be integrated within a powerful communal faith. Only this, he argued, would overcome the weak relativism of modern democracy.

While he dismissed the call for artistic beauty (1991: Vol. 1, 220), Goebbels also followed the classical ideal of cultural unity. What the tragedy was for classical Greece, the radio was to achieve for the Third Reich. 'The radio must drum together this one hundred percent' of the population he wanted to win; it is a crucial 'means for unifying the German people' (Goebbels 1991: 93). The propaganda minister dismissed the idea of a free and rational consensus, proclaiming instead his will 'to work on the people until they are addicted to us' (quoted in Welch 1995: 138). Allegedly, democracy had failed to achieve the necessary unity between government and people. Nazism, he admitted in the early days of the regime, was still 'terrorising' 48 per cent of the population (quoted in Welch

1995: 173), but top-down propaganda was to realize the crucial goal of ideological unity:

> This Government is, in the truest sense of the word, a People's Government. It arose from the people and will always execute the people's will ... We want to give the people their due, albeit in a different form than has been the case under parliamentary democracy. I see in the newly established Ministry for Popular Enlightenment and Propaganda a link between Government and people, the living contact between the National Government as the expression of the popular will and the people themselves ... I do not believe that we have reached our goal when, if I may use one of those old-fashioned expressions, we have a 52 percent majority in parliament. A government that faces the great and far-reaching tasks that the present Government faces could not survive for long and could not find the popular support it needs for these far-reaching measures if it were satisfied with this 52 percent majority. It must, rather, see its task as making all the necessary propaganda preparations to win the whole people over to its side in the long term. (quoted in Welch 1995: 137)

This goal was to be achieved by the greatest psychological subtlety:

> The propagandist must be the man with the greatest knowledge of souls. I cannot convince a single person of the necessity of something unless I have got to know the soul of that person, unless I understand how to pluck the string in the harp of his soul that must be made to sound ... The propagandist must understand how to speak not only to the people in their totality, but also to individual sections of the population: to the worker, the peasant, the middle class. (quoted in Welch 1995: 139)

As with Hitler we should distrust, however, Goebbels's self-representation as a cynical manipulator. Goebbels was good at popular propaganda because he himself enjoyed popular culture as well as the aesthetics of the modern age, and he believed in the message he sold. His diaries reveal a man who had all the needs he attributed to the masses: a strong leader he could trust completely; a strong faith providing a clear orientation in life; and the identification with the national community. He was a master of propaganda, but also the first victim of his own phraseology. He could hope for the death of a SA man, because propaganda needed a hero-figure, but he was the first to admire Horst Wessel's alleged heroism. Goebbels was successful because he communicated his own emotions through propaganda (Baird 1990: Ch. 4; Behrenbeck 1996: 134–148).

After university, Goebbels wanted to become a novelist, and he continued to praise the arts throughout his life. The artistic genius expressed, he believed, the best qualities of a people. He needed the connection to the *Volk*, but the *Volk* also needed him as 'the incarnation of a creative ethnicity [*Volkstum*]' (1929: 114). 'Culture is the highest expression of a *Volk*'s creative powers, the artist its blessed giver of meaning. It would be arrogant to believe that his godly mission could be realized separately from the people' (1991: 134). To those working politically towards overcoming the old by realizing their own vision of a better world he also attributed artistic qualities, because they make a *Volk* realize its highest potential. 'The statesman is also an artist', he proclaimed. 'Leader and mass, this is as little a problem as, say, painter and colour. Politics is the art of creating a state, like painting is an artistic creation with colours. Thus, politics without the people or against the people is pure nonsense. To form the masses into a *Volk* and the *Volk* into a state has always been the deepest meaning of politics' (1991: 52; similarly Goebbels 1929: 21). In an open letter to Wilhelm Furtwängler he claimed that the Nazi leadership were such creators: 'Politics, too, is an art, perhaps the most elevated art and the greatest that exists, and we – who give form to modern German politics – we feel ourselves to be artists to whom has been conferred the high responsibility of forming the solid and complete image of the people from the original brute mass. The mission of the artist is not only to unify, but goes much further. He is obliged to create, to give form, to eliminate what is sick, to open the way to what is healthy'.[13]

In comparing the statesman to the artist, Goebbels expressed his highest ambition. By serving Hitler, he wanted to play his part in creating a new artwork: a powerful German nation united in a single, truly German communal faith. He had left Catholicism behind only to find a new semi-religious political ideology in which a cultural and political elite became secular gods. 'The artist is comparable to God. Both give shape to matter. The artist is partly God. Let there be light! And there is light!' (Goebbels 1929: 22). Goebbels still wanted security through a firm world-view, but simultaneously dreamt of being a creative genius realizing his own modern subjectivity. The result is self-deification: the politician or artist as a God who creates a new world according to his own vision. And while he argued that he wanted to bring forth the best of a people, the mass of the population is in effect reduced to matter used for realizing personal fancies: 'Geniuses consume humans. That is the way it is. But, and this is consoling about it: not for themselves, but for their task' (Goebbels 1929: 41). The genius believes he knows what the true shape of the people is supposed to be; and he thus claims the right to realize it by the use of force. The vision is that, as the people come to realize that the new state is appropriate for them, those Germans regarded as worthy will eventually be united: in one national faith and a state form appropriate to it.

Towards the end of the war, when it became wholly impossible to still cling on to this illusionary vision, Goebbels came to adopt a pure aesthetics of heroism or historical grandeur to justify a continuation of the battle to the very end. 'Gentlemen', he declared in April 1945, 'in a hundred years they will show a beautiful colour film about the terrible days we live through. Do you want to play a part in this film? Hold out now so that in a hundred years the spectators will not whistle and jeer when you appear on the screen' (quoted in Leiser 1989: 120). In refusing to surrender, Goebbels (and other dyed-in-the-wool Nazis) followed the mental script of apocalyptic struggle and heroic determination to its logical conclusion. Presenting oneself to an imaginary future audience became more important for them than limiting the material damage and saving the many lives lost in the last months of war.

Rituals and Visions

Was National Socialism then a political or, in Raymond Aron's terminology, a 'secular religion', 'which takes, in the hearts of our contemporaries, the place of the lost religion and which sees human salvation in the creation of a new social order in this world in the distant future'? (quoted in Maier 2003: 155) As we have seen, a variety of opinions co-existed, sometimes even within one mind. Leading Nazis stressed that their world-view was a myth or religion, but they also stressed its scientific, political or artistic character. As these differences were never seriously debated, let alone resolved, all these opinions must have been compatible with being a true Nazi. What was non-negotiable within the movement, however, was the political primacy of the *Volk* and the Nazi movement under the Führer. The *Volk* was the Nazis' ultimately reality ('*realissimum*' in Eric Voegelin's terminology), and the movement its most truthful voice and arm. As Nazism claimed to be the ultimate authority within all realms of life, Christianity was supposed to adapt or disappear. The tension between religious and secular authority so fundamental to the whole of European history was to make place for a totalitarian unity of national culture.

National Socialism presented itself in highly ritualized form. Its public appearances were marked by military features including marches, flags and uniforms. Political speeches, especially if given by Hitler, found their place within an elaborate ritual. The room was decorated with flags and posters, and music accompanied the whole event. A march or at least a drum roll was played, while the uniformed SA marched in with flags and standards, the colour bearers placing themselves next to the speaker's stand. The time of waiting for the speaker, who deliberately came late to heighten the excitement, was passed with the singing of patriotic songs. The Badenweiler march was reserved to mark Hitler's arrival. He passed a guard of honour, the so-called *Rednerwache* (speaker's guard), reaching from the entrance to the speaker's podium, while the crowd greeted him with '*Sieg Heil*', '*Heil Hitler*' and raised arms. The same exclamations marked the end of the speech, after which the ritual was repeated in reverse order (Vondung 1971: 34).

Marches, flags, banners and uniforms, symbols like the swastika, guards and military music became the main ingredients of all Nazi rituals. They were first developed under Hitler's careful scrutiny, and then refined by Goebbels, who also added light effects, especially flames, as his own personal touch. For a while, choric speeches were frequently employed, but they proved too difficult for widespread usage. Hitler also decided on the great 'public holidays of the nation' and had an important hand in developing their ritualistic character. Protestants were more likely to fall for the dream of a nation united in a single faith, but it seems that former Catholics with their more ritualistic religious background were particularly suited to develop solemn forms for the new celebrations. The party gave directives for the different celebrations, inferior performances were censored. In 1938, Hitler declared that the main rituals should be solidified into a national custom for the future (Vondung 1971: 35–43).

Hitler banned the word 'cult' for Nazi celebrations, because he wanted to distance himself from the term's religious associations, but the regime established a cycle of national celebrations, which were intended eventually to replace the religious ones. The day of the 'seizure of power' on 30 January, the founding of the party on 24 February, Remembrance Day and the Swearing in of the Nazi Youth in March, the Führer's birthday on 20 April, the *Tag der deutschen Arbeit* ('Day of National Work') on 1 May, Mother's Day in May, the summer solstice, the national party rally in Nuremberg at the beginning of September, harvest day, the memorial day for those 'Fallen for the [Nazi] Movement' on 9 November and, finally, the winter solstice together with the Nazi people's Christmas, which stressed service to the national community and a general reawakening of life (Vondung 1971: 74–87).

Such political ceremonies could be quite popular, but the regime needed constant innovations and successes to prevent boredom and keep the public interested (Behrenbeck 1996: 436–446). For the first years, however, many indulged in the pride they felt for the surprising successes of the new Reich. These general political celebrations, which had, after all, a long tradition (Düding 1988; Mosse 1975), were fairly uncontroversial, but the Nazis' Sunday morning celebrations as alternative to church services and their rites of passage (*Lebensfeiern*) in competition with Christian baptisms, weddings and funerals (particularly promoted by the SS) caused tensions with the churches without gaining many followers in society as a whole. As an SD report concluded in 1943:

> While the Church ceremonies are gaining greatly in popularity, the national socialist marriage, christening, and funeral ceremonies, which even in peacetime were few in number, have declined still further ... The failure of the national socialist rites of passage to make a deep impression is less the result of superficial flaws and inadequacies and more the consequence of the lack of a religious element. By contrast, the priest knows how to answer all questions relating to God, fate, immortality etc. with self-assurance and thus in rural areas occupies a dominant position at all ceremonies, whereas the national socialist speaker normally takes care to avoid adopting any position on religious matters. (reprinted in Noakes and Pridham 1983 ff.: Vol. 4, 110–112. See also Vondung 1971: 107–112)

Nazi celebrations were often appreciated, it seems, in public, but not in private existence. When dealing with birth, marriage and, above all, death, people largely perceived the rhetoric of heroism, service and the eternal existence of nation and race as insufficient. Even before the hard times of war, a great majority was unwilling to give up Christianity with its ethics of love and its promise for a life after death.

Nazi rituals drew on many religious forms. The rites of passage tended to include flowers and torchbearers, symbols like bread and salt, music and a speech. They often involved a chorus, the threefold repetition known from church services and proclamations of faith and loyalty. Nazism created sacred places; above all the terrain for the national party rally in Nuremberg with buildings and spaces of unprecedented monumentality, but also the Luitpold Arena for the yearly SA and SS meetings or the *Feldherrnhalle* in Munich, where those killed in the Beer Hall Putsch were remembered. So-called *Thingplätze*, similar to the old Greek theatre, were established all over Germany, where choric plays of cultic character involving great numbers of actors and spectators (Stommer 1985), but also other activities could take place, and the Nazis also dedicated special rooms for their ritual celebrations.

The Third Reich was highly ritualized with Nazi symbols, often obligatory membership in mass organizations, elaborate rituals and rallies. Flags and uniforms – symbols of a shared ideological orientation, military heroism and a communal national identity – abounded. The rituals frequently had a clear religious ring to them. The vow of the Hitler youth, for example, is close in structure to the Lord's Prayer:

> You, Führer, are our commander!
> We stand in your name.
> The Reich is the object of our struggle,
> It is the beginning and the Amen.
>
> Your word is the heartbeat of our deeds;
> Your faith builds cathedrals for us.
> And even when death reaps the last harvest
> The crown of the Reich never falls.
>
> We are ready, your silent spell
> Welds our ranks like iron,
> Like a chain, man beside man,
> Into a wall of loyalty round you.
>
> You Führer are our commander!
> We stand in your name.
> The Reich is the object of our struggle,
> It is the beginning and the Amen.
>
> (reprinted in Noakes and Pridham 1983 ff.: Vol. 2, 422)

Choric poetry was particularly dominant in *Thing* plays, which were arguably the most obvious example of trying to establish a single communal faith. As the later president of the *Reichsschrifttumskammer* Hans Johst stated in 1933:

> The coming theatre will become a cult, or the theatre has ended its mission … The need, the despair, the misery of our people calls for help. And help comes, in the last

> respect, from the reawakening of a community of faith … Like with all primitive races [*Naturvölker*] and with all the nations we see as most cultured (for example the Greeks), the theatre again wants to lead the community of those acting and perceiving towards the mystery of a metaphysical world-view. (quoted in Behrenbeck 1996: 243)

The *Thing* plays were soon given up because, after an initial enthusiasm, the population soon tired of them, but choric texts continued to serve as liturgical texts in other Nazi rituals. One of these texts stated full of the pathos of repetition: 'Speak out, what you say, and announce, what you believe, so that we profess, what we want to believe … We believe in the blood … We believe in the land … We believe in the *Volk*' (quoted in Ley and Schoeps 1997: 37). Frequently the faith was focused on Hitler, as in the following choric dialogue for the National Day of Labour:

> Speaker: … One stands for all! Comrades! Who brought us this solution?
> Chorus: Adolf Hitler, the Führer!
> Speaker: … One stands for all! Comrades! Who has restored our honour?
> Chorus: Adolf Hitler, the Führer!
> Speaker: … One helped us, we only believe, when the One speaks.
> Chorus: Adolf Hitler, the Führer! (quoted in Vondung 1971: 142)

A dominant feature in Nazi rituals was a hero cult, which tried to reconcile individuals with death (Baird 1990; Behrenbeck 1996). While the cult quickly lost its persuasiveness when the loss of German lives shot up (many then turned back to Christianity), it initially provided an attractive ideal. The most elaborate ritual expression of the hero myth was the Memorial Day for the 'Fallen of the Movement', that is, the Nazis who had lost their lives in the Putsch of 9 November 1923 (Behrenbeck 1996: 299–312; Reichel 1993: 219–221; Vondung 1971: 160–164).

The Beer Hall Putsch was Hitler's first serious political miscalculation, from which he drew a crucial tactical lesson, namely, one could not forcefully seize power, but had to choose a legalistic route. The loss of sixteen lives (as well as the continuing death of SA men in street battles) demanded, however, a more positive interpretation. The men had not died in vain, Hitler stressed in all his speeches on 8 November to the party faithful. By giving their lives for the seemingly unachievable, these determined men had set an inspiring example. By sacrificing their lives, they had won mass support for the movement and inspired ever more sacrifice for Germany. 'All subsequent blood sacrifices', Hitler claimed, 'were inspired by the sacrifice of these first men' (reprinted in Domarus 1973: Vol. 2, 554). Similarly, a cantata exclaimed: 'The steps of the *Feldherrnhalle* [where the Nazis were shot] are now an altar, / one that secretly burns from their fervour, / and what they did not create with their fists, / erected it now stands, built on their blood' (quoted in Vondung 1971: 160).

In this interpretation, the deaths of 1923 appeared as a prerequisite for the eventual Nazi 'seizure' of power. It also served to elevate Hitler's position and that of all the old fighters. Although they survived the event, they appeared as heroes who had allegedly given a necessary signal of death-defying determination. But the Nazis were not satisfied by showing the importance of sacrifice within a general history of salvation culminating in the Third Reich; they also suggested that the heroes lived on in the Nazi movement. The evening before the ceremony of 1935, when the sixteen 'blood witnesses' were moved from their initial geographically dispersed graves to their new classicistic 'temples of honour', Hitler stated: 'They now pass into German immortality' (Domarus 1973: Vol. 2, 555), and the day after he elaborated:

> And for us they are not dead. These temples are not tombs, but an *eternal guard.* Here they stand for Germany and guard our *Volk.*[14] Here they lie as loyal witnesses of our movement. When we have celebrated this day year by year – in the times of persecution not always in the same form – and when we are determined to elevate it for all times to a public holiday for the German nation, then this does not happen just because 16 men died. Thousands die every day, and wars consume many more within hours. It happens because these 16 men suffered, with a truly faithful heart, a death which contributed to making the German people rise again. (quoted in Vondung 1971: 167)

Hitler not only stressed the historical importance of the sixteen fallen Nazis, but also denied their death. They live on, he argued, as examples and guards for the German people. This is not an explicit claim for a life after death, but at least for a personal immortality of heroes in the memory of the *Volk.*

A highly elaborate ritual in Munich – and much simpler memorials in the other parts of Germany (Behrenbeck 1996: 313 ff.) – came to symbolize the Nazi interpretation of the Beer Hall Putsch and of heroism in general. Hitler delivered a speech to old fighters on the evening of 8 November, thus reiterating the official interpretation of the event. On the day, the ceremony started with a march through town. The men were silent, only the *Horst Wessel* Song was played in a solemn tone. The procession came to a halt at the place where the shooting had started in 1923, and the music stopped. Hitler then walked by himself to the sarcophagi in the hall and stayed there in silent dialogue with the dead heroes. After that, the death march turned into a march of triumph through the *Siegestor* (arch of triumph). Flags were displayed; the national anthem played. Thus the sacrifice of 1923 became symbolically connected with the nation's alleged reawakening a decade later. Towards the end of the ceremony, just before SS men took their place again in front of the temple as 'eternal guards', a speaker called out the sixteen names. After each name, thousands of newly recruited Hitler youth responded with 'Here'.

Even more than others, this ritual commemoration of the Beer Hall Putsch clearly contained a religious message: true heroic determination and sacrifice is supposed to always reach its goal eventually. The blood of the victims was supposed to be the 'baptismal water ... for the Third Reich' (Domarus 1973: Vol. 2, 458); the dead were supposed to 'reincarnate' in the young; and new SA flags had to touch the old 'blood flag' of November 1923 to receive the original spirit. There was no mention of concrete opponents, but the ceremonies were calls to battle for a better nation. The old fighters glorified their own deeds, while the rest were to be inspired by their heroic example. Hitler always occupied an elevated position: the Führer addressing and leading a highly disciplined mass movement. The two temples were to become, the Nazis' daily newspaper noted in 1935, 'shrines of the movement' and a 'place of pilgrimage' (quoted in Behrenbeck 1996: 312). History is just, the ritual claimed, and the godly Germans will eventually triumph, if only they are dedicated and heroic enough. The ceremony thus offered the party faithful a simple, coherent and conveniently self-glorifying world-view, preparing them to face stoically difficult times. Pure sorrow and despair was banned from the Nazi vision. Even when looking at the temple for the sixteen dead, the view went through the open columned hall to the Arch of Victory behind.

Cheering crowds, often specifically selected for the occasion, symbolized the nation allegedly united in a single faith. The rituals were intended to give a feeling of solidarity and shared political goals. They also enforced conformity, as all participants were forced to play their role. Those inwardly opposed felt like lonely outsiders, isolated and weak.

The effect of a ritual is difficult to gauge. A woman remembered her burning desire 'to drown in it and be carried along with it' (Maschmann 1963: 17), but such symbolic politics could easily lose its emotional flair with time (Allen 1984: 266–273). On 3 April 1939, Goebbels noted such a development in his diary: 'We celebrate too much. I have to stop this. It cannot go on this way. The people laugh about it.' Especially when transmitted via the media of film, radio or grammophone, the appeal of rituals deteriorated, while the number of people present was necessarily limited. The rituals were undoubtedly an important instrument of integration and mobilization, but they did not work miracles (Behrenbeck 1996: 436–446).

Even more caution is demanded in interpreting the meaning of seemingly religious symbols. Throughout this book, we have noted that politics and religion were anything but separate spheres. Even Protestant preachers had no qualms about using religious language in evaluating political events, and all ceremonial language was loaded with religious metaphors. For dyed-in-the-wool Nazis their ideology could clearly become the only truth, but the majority of the population still held mixed loyalties. There is general and well-supported agreement that Nazism continued to compete with Christianity, previous political convictions, customary beliefs and pure self-interest (Aly 2005; Broszat 1977–1983; Evans 2005: 220–260; Kershaw 1987; Peukert 1987). The strongest case for truly religious sentiments was probably the 'Hitler myth' (Ian Kershaw). Again and again,

Hitler was described as the ultimate source of truth. A poem, somewhat reminiscent of the Christian Deed, may serve as example:

> Let us proclaim under the banner:
> We are Germans.
> We follow our Führer
> as the personified command
> of a higher law,
> that swings in us and above us,
> that we sense,
> and which we believe in.
> We believe in our Führer
> as a revelation of this law
> for us
> his *Volk*. (quoted in Ley and Schoeps 1997: 38)

Many letters to newspapers show that such an attitude was more than official rhetoric and opportunism. In their collection of sources, Noakes and Pridham have reprinted some revealing examples (1983ff.: Vol. 2, 572). 'Just as in my youth the dear Lord used to appear in my dreams, so now the Führer appears', one person claimed. 'These nights are times of celebration.' Another person wrote: 'As my "creator", his portrait hangs both in my work room and in the parlour at home. A look at him has often produced in me what "pious people" allegedly feel when deep in prayer.' To quote one more of the examples: 'He who serves the Führer serves Germany, and he who serves Germany serves God.'

The enthusiastic support for National Socialism, we can conclude, could take religious forms. A clear-cut ideology and a strong sense of community offered a new orientation and a sense of collective belonging; the Führer was seen as the bearer of truth, the eternal existence of race and nation was to overcome death; and a fanatical will was taken as guarantee for success. We can even note magical elements like the touching of the 'blood flag' or the miraculous qualities of blood. I would still be sceptical, however, about labelling Nazism as a whole a political religion. After all, the movement never pushed one single doctrine or one single liturgy. Hitler claimed that some rituals, like the one for 9 November, had found their definite form, but the variation always continued. Not even Hitler himself could solve the tension between his naive faith in science, his call for a fanatical will to overcome all odds, and his religious belief in a benign fate. Even within clearly defined rituals, the viewer was free to interpret religious elements literally, metaphorically or simply as aesthetic means to create some vague form of elevated, solemn and grand aura for a special occasion.

Most Nazis never expected that the population would take on Nazism as a religion. While a primacy of politics was enforced, Nazism never provided one dogmatic system, but a general framework within which a variety of individual convictions was tolerated and accepted. Some careerists tried to show that they were the true Nazis, thus reducing the influence of intellectual opponents, but there was no witch-hunt for ideological heretics within the movement. Moreover, for the mass of the population and many party members, a variety of loyalties continued to coexist. Most importantly, Christianity continued to play an important role. It was often reinterpreted in more nationalist and racist ways, but many were not prepared to let go of it as prime consolation in the private sphere. In many people's minds, Nazism and Christianity co-existed harmoniously (Schreiner 2003: 43; Steigmann-Gall 2003), and with the sorrows of war, church-going actually increased.

Leading Nazis were increasingly annoyed with the churches, but the regime continued to shy away from an open conflict. It seemed more sensible to use the many Nazi sympathies among believers to undermine the Bible's message and work towards a Nazi-compatible Christianity. In this vein, Goebbels noted in his diary on 23 February 1937: 'Christianity is the slogan to destroy the priests, as formerly socialism was to destroy the Marxist bigwigs.' And Hitler, Goebbels's diary recalled on 28 April 1939, said the same: 'The best way to finish with the churches is if one claims to be a positive Christian oneself.' Religious symbols in Nazi rituals could thus also serve as a bridge between religion and politics.

The Nazi leadership was emotionally moved by its own rituals, but also used them for manipulative purposes: as a means to integrate the population, secure Nazi rule and mobilize for political goals. Even if people enjoyed rituals as special events to experience a sense of community, grandeur and heroism, they did not necessarily accept their messages as binding norms for everyday life (after all, most people still tried to avoid sacrificing their lives). Studies about everyday life in Nazi Germany tend to agree that only a small fanatical minority accepted Nazism as the only truth and thus as a secular religion. But this was not necessarily a disadvantage for the regime. Rituals and symbols could appeal to a majority of the population, precisely because they fulfilled a wider and less specific function; these highly emotive aesthetic spectacles could be perceived and experienced in a wide variety of different ways. The ritualistic side of Nazism did not develop into a precisely defined dogma, but opened a *Glaubensraum* (Ernst Bloch), that is, a space for a wide variety of communal, nationalist, militaristic and racist fears and desires, visions and utopias. Nazism obviously drew a sharp line of exclusion against some convictions and some groups within society, but it got closer than any of its predecessors in uniting a majority within the nation in a single communal faith, because this faith was expressed in a vague and suggestive way. At least at the many political high points in the Third Reich, a majority could see Nazism as the realization of their political wishes because its suggestive aesthetics allowed the projection, within limits, of one's own visions of the future onto the new regime.

Rituals and symbols could create, temporarily, a strong sense of a community united by a single communal faith and a communal political vision. On special occasions, they could lift people out of everyday life into an aura of heroism and grand historical drama. But the Nazi aestheticization of politics did not end here. Visions of integration and mobilization had to go beyond the 'theatrical-aesthetic staging of an emotionally powerful world of appearance' (Paul 1990: 16) to include attractive political measures which promised to realize these visions of a more harmonious and grander Germany. Hitler had spoken of 'the desire for a true community of the German people, which has motivated the best of our nation for centuries' (Domarus 1973: Vol 1, 175); when in power he thus had to show how he would realize this promised 'unity between leadership and followers [*Gefolgschaft*]' (Domarus 1973: Vol. 1, 182).

As a new party, the Nazis made many, frequently incompatible, promises in many different directions. Once in power, however, no powerful disappointment spread through the country. On the contrary: all the evidence we have strongly suggests that their popularity continued to increase in the first years of the regime until Hitler was probably more popular than any German statesman before him. Strongly fluctuating attitudes show that the Nazis needed a constant flow of successes to maintain such a high level of support, but before the war turned against Germany they largely achieved this. The dependency on successes made the regime highly unstable and prone to end in disaster, but the majority of the population believed for a while that it was able to deliver the goods.

As the Nazis were able to create such a euphoria about their 'seizure of power', they faced a tricky task after gaining it. They had made far-reaching promises; now they could not afford to disappoint seriously any of their major support-groups. They had promised not only well-considered reforms, but also the beginning of a new era: a national 'awakening' in a grand Third Reich. Thus they could not simply stumble on, trying not to annoy anyone, but had to present themselves as a dynamic and visionary force. Many believed that Nazism offered goals that 'were great and essential' (Maschmann 1963: 18), but such high hopes demanded spectacular political measures beyond the many deadlocks of the Weimar Republic.

The Nazis failed to show a sustainable way forward; even the material achievements and the limited rise in the standard of living were paid for by a huge deficit (see below). Many Germans, however, experienced 1933 to 1939 as the 'good times' between a dire Weimar Republic and a destructive Second World War, because the Nazis seemed to suggest promising ways forward out of bitter battles of interest with no winner and out of old ideological conflicts paralysing all political initiative. These visions of the future were largely deceptive, because the tensions were not really solved, and the cumulative radicalization of the regime made it inherently unstable. The many factions of Nazism competed against each other in 'working towards the Führer', thus promoting a constant ideological radicalization which eventually undermined the popularity of Nazi policies and the sustainability of the Reich. For a time, however, these visions suggested to many a constructive way forward by an innovative political force towards a more harmonious national order. It will take another book to treat this topic adequately, but I want to sketch briefly three particularly suggestive examples in the remainder of the chapter.

A Reconciliation of Nature and Technology

In German history, a deep-seated unease about modernity went back a long way (Rohkrämer 1999, 2002, 2003). Most cultural critics soon came to accept the need for modern industry and technology as unavoidable parts of modern society, but they continued to lament its allegedly dangerous consequences: mechanization would make the world cold and anonymous; an over-emphasis on a purely material well-being would secularize the world and undermine all higher ideals; a ruthless technological drive would destroy nature's beauty and pollute the environment; and living in a man-made world seriously threatened the health of the population. While believers in progress argued that modern industry and technology would eventually find a solution to all problems, these cultural critics believed in the need for protecting parts of nature and society from the logic of the technological world. In the nineteenth century, associations emerged with the intention of protecting nature and the countryside, German traditions and architecture. They did not want to stop modernization, but aimed at moderating the single-minded drive for efficiency with a concern for maintaining a healthy natural environment and a traditional German identity.

The cultural critics and their associations, which always remained numerically small, never exerted a great influence, but with the economic difficulties of the Weimar Republic, non-material concerns slipped even further down the political agenda. This lack of success radicalized the movement. While it had by no means been all right-wing in the German Empire, it increasingly rejected the Republic after 1918 and over time a majority of its members came to sympathize with the Nazis and their 'blood-and-soil' rhetoric (Blackbourn 2006: 239–296; Radkau and Uekötter 2003).

While environmentalists and conservationists thus tended to be disgruntled with the political developments, engineers, whose existence and status was closely linked with modern technology, had no reason for jubilation either. Many of them saw their technological dreams – and, with high unemployment among technical occupations, even their careers – thwarted by narrow economic concerns. Their professional ideal often remained the independent inventor, while in reality they were increasingly a cog in the machine of huge companies. The social prestige of an engineering degree remained lower than that of more established academic subjects, and the higher ranks of the civil service remained largely closed to them. While cultural critics stressed the purely material character of modern technology, engineers tried to show that they were serving the nation in increasing the material means for nationalist goals, were heroic in daring to reach out for new and unpredictable technical means, and were creative in realizing the previously unthinkable. Dissatisfied with their social status and the working conditions in the economic crisis of the early 1930s, engineers were open to a new political force like Nazism with its stress on the importance of technology, of practical knowledge and of an instrumental rationality to strengthen Germany.

Since Ralf Dahrendorff and David Schoenbaum in the 1960s, historians have debated the Nazi attitude towards technology and modernity in general (Bavyj 2003), which partly reflects that both the *völkisch* movement and Nazism were simply inconsistent. One important strand, most prominently represented by Walther Darré, emphasized the importance of maintaining a strong agricultural sector as a prerequisite for a natural lifestyle and a healthy race, for a high birth rate and self-sufficiency in food production. While the concern for autarky and a growing, healthy population was widely shared, most Nazis emphasized promoting modern technology as a necessary means for strengthening Germany. No Weimar politician associated himself as closely with modern technology as Hitler, for example, the motorways, a car for the people, the radio and, later, war technology like the 'miraculous' rockets. Equally, Goebbels celebrated a modern 'steel-like romanticism'. He fully accepted that Germany existed in an age of technology, but he simultaneously claimed: 'We are all more or less romantics in a new German way ... The realm of roaring engines, of sky-conquering technical inventions, of grand industrial creations, of vast, nearly unexplored space which we have to settle for our nation – that is the realm of our romanticism' (1991: 253).

Environmentalists rejoiced both in the rhetoric of Germanness and the first national law for the protection of nature in 1935, but lamented the loss of wilderness which came under the plough in the effort to achieve self-sufficiency. With the four-year-plan and war, their complaints were largely ignored. For the individual engineer, however, the situation turned out to be much better. They had been sceptical about blood-and-soil propaganda at first, but soon found unprecedented career opportunities with mobilization for war. The engineering profession suffered from a dramatic decline in student numbers, a dropping of standards because of a shortened degree scheme and the recruitment of engineers for service in war, but those working as engineers had more opportunities than ever before.

But this material side only tells one part of the story. The Nazis also succeeded in launching a new vision of a 'German technology' which proved attractive both to cultural critics and engineers. Their slogan *Gemeinnutz geht vor Eigennutz* ('public need before private greed'), was interpreted as promising a technology no longer thwarted by the capitalist obsession with immediate profits, and Nazi ideas about an 'organic economy' were in fact both taking account of environmental concerns and quite similar to the technocratic ideal held by many engineers. The images of both 'organism' and 'machine' suggested organizing production as one coherent and thus more efficient (and less harmful) whole. Nazis wanted to overcome the capitalist emphasis on competition in the capitalist market by considering a whole range of factors like efficiency of production and contribution, the actual needs of the population, job creation and environmental impact. While the environmentalists got a law for the protection of nature, ideas about a state representation for engineers (*Reichskammer der Technik*) raised hopes about more political influence for experts; and a Führer with dictatorial power in support of large, but also beautiful technical projects made their implementation much easier than in the Weimar Republic, where Berlin and the *Länder*, the public and private owners all demanded a say.

Above all, the famous *Autobahnen* became the core symbol for a 'German technology' which could attract the enthusiasm of the whole population, including the polar poles of both engineers and cultural critics (Zeller 2002). Stylized as the 'Führer's roads', the motorways enjoyed the highest priority. As the largest job creation scheme, the building project symbolized a national community caring for the unemployed. Engineers were enthusiastic about the new technical tasks, ranging from street and bridge building to the development of new cars to fill the new roads, above all the *Volkswagen* which would open the age of mass motorization for Germany. Backed by the highest support, planners enjoyed realizing their plans without the need for compromises with local authorities or regional protests, while cultural critics praised the introduction of *Landschaftsanwälte* (literally, environmental lawyers). They were supposed to guarantee the beauty and ecological character of the project. The motorways were to merge with the landscape, allow public access to the countryside and provide easy viewing of its beauty. The planning thus tried to adapt to the unevenness of the ground and achieve a constant change of scenery, for example, between meadows and forests or from valleys to spectacular heights (although it was clear that this would cause problems for motorists, especially in winter). All this fulfilled the core wishes of cultural critics (in particular the respect for the traditional character and beauty of the German landscape), while also giving modern technology its due. 'We live, work and die for the eternal Germany', the highest-ranked planner Fritz Todt wrote with pathos, 'and in our technical interference with nature we do not just want to gain immediate profit, but also want to implement our technical means ... in a way that they correspond with nature's great laws and maintain eternal values in the eternal Germany' (Todt 1941). And Goebbels stated with a slightly different emphasis on the car exhibition of 1939:

> Today we live in the age of technology ... There is hardly any event which is not strongly influenced by modern technology. From this undoubtedly also the danger emerges that modern technology makes humans soulless. And thus it has been one of the main tasks of National Socialism to give technology – which we do not reject or fight, but consciously affirm – an inner soul, to discipline it and to place it in the service of our *Volk* and its high standard of culture and living ... We live in an age that is simultaneously romantic and steel-like, that has not lost its depth of feeling, but also discovers a new romanticism in the results of modern inventions and technology. While bourgeois reactionaries have been alienated and estranged from technology ... National Socialism has succeeded in overcoming technology's soulless character and filling it with the rhythm and the hot impulses of our time. (1939: 105 f.)

The ideal of a 'German technology' opened up the vision of a harmony between the German *Volk* and its technical means. Nazism promised to develop a technology that would not be soulless, but heroic and beautiful, not ruthless, but in harmony with nature, not internationalist, but closely linked to allegedly eternal German traits. Cultural critics saw their concerns addressed, while techno-enthusiasts appreciated both the wider social acceptance technology achieved in this way and the technocratic vision of a perfectly designed technology without negative side-effects. While the discourse about the dangers of modern technology had reached an unprecedented intensity during the world economic crisis of the early 1930s, the Nazis now promised a higher synthesis: a technology in harmony with the German *Volk*. If they had worked on implementing this ideal in all areas of life, conflicts about priorities between the different objectives would soon have re-emerged, but before the war demanded a ruthless mobilization of all resources, the prestige object of the *Autobahn* could stand for an ideal Nazi future beyond the conflicts of the past. And for the time after a victorious war, the General Plan East should guide the development in Eastern Europe in an ecologically sound way (Rohkrämer forthcoming).

The Vision of a Harmonious Community of the People (*Volksgemeinschaft*)

There seems to be general agreement that the promise to establish a fair, harmonious and efficient *Volksgemeinschaft* was probably at the centre of the fatal attraction of Nazism to the German people (Aly 2005; Evans 2003: 218; Frei 2001; Kershaw 1998: 316 f., 330 ff. and passim; Peukert 1987; Süllwold 2001: 95–97; Wehler 2003: 548). There are strong indications that even for the party faithfuls this general vision constituted a core attraction of National Socialism. Asked in 1934 by the American social scientist Abel to describe their reasons for joining the Nazi movement, one-third of the 581 respondents emphasized the idea of national solidarity and *Volksgemeinschaft* as the prime reason, 20 per cent expressed their faith in the Führer and over half their belief in a 'national resurrection' (Merkl 1980: 32 f., 147, 453, 522 f.). Of course, we cannot be sure how representative the sample is, but the figures do indicate the widespread hope for a new unity based on social harmony. While the movement's violent militancy and anti-Semitism seems to have been a prime motivation for many activists (Evans 2003: 217–230; Reichardt 2002), the vision of a *Volksgemeinschaft* could meet with an enthusiastic response also from within the mainstream of society. While conservative parties and associations had been closely linked with the interests of its privileged clientele, a new Right emphasized the primacy of national commitment and solidarity: everybody was expected to serve, first and foremost, the nation, but, at the same time, the nation should also care for all true Germans.

There was, of course, nothing original about the idea of a national socialism. In Imperial Germany, the professorial *Verein für Socialpolitic* or Association for Social Policy advocated state measures to promote social justice; the 'ideas of 1914' were all about maintaining a sense of national solidarity and service; and

Conservative Revolutionaries continued to stress the need for providing a 'German socialism' as a right-wing alternative to the Marxist utopia. The film *Metropolis*, whose director Fritz Lang emigrated from Nazism in 1933, shows that the vision of a *Volksgemeinschaft* was by no means a reserve of the Right (Elsaesser 2000). This science fiction from 1926 provides a powerful visualisation of the anti-Marxist idea of *Volksgemeinschaft*, which has not lost its aesthetic appeal over time. The action takes place in a futuristic city divided into two classes: the workers, whose life underground is all misery, and an upper class, which never meets the poor and wastes its lives in idle, playful luxury. The injustice provokes on the one hand a worker's rebellion: angry crowds destroy the machines which force an inhumane work pattern upon them. Such an aggressive Luddism is shown to be wrong, however, because the machines are needed to keep the workers' homes from flooding. While the film thus suggests that class war and revolution are ultimately self-destructive and suicidal, injustice is eventually overcome by the son of the city's dictatorial ruler and a female social worker, who both promote Christian charity and compassion, respect and a sense of communal responsibility. In the end, these representatives of a younger generation convince the ruler and an old-fashioned worker to shake hands, thus vowing to work together towards a more solidaric and humane communal future.

This was exactly the message of the Nazis, who, after all, wrote the call for a national socialism into their party's name. The Nazis were the most important political force on the Right calling for a *Volksgemeinschaft*, and they always stressed this social commitment to distinguish themselves from traditional conservatives. A police officer, for example, reported on a speech by Hitler of 26 October 1920:

> Now Hitler turned to deal with the Right and the Left. The Nationals on the Right lack a social sense, the Socialists on the Left a nationalist one. He appeals to the parties on the Right: if you want to be nationalist then come down among your people and put away all your class pride. To the Left he appeals: you who proclaim your solidarity with the whole world, first show your solidarity with your own compatriots, be Germans first and foremost. Do they look like heroes who want to smash the world and yet crawl before foreigners for fear they might not like something they see here? (*applause*) You who are real revolutionaries, come over to us and fight with us for our whole nation (*loud applause*). Your place is not over there with the procurers of international capital, but with us, with your own people!! (*stormy applause*). (reprinted in Noakes and Pridham 1983 ff.: Vol. 1, 17 f.)

Throughout his political career, Hitler always stressed his humble beginnings to show himself as a man of the people. 'I', he claimed, 'did not issue from a palace: I came from the worksite. Neither was I a general: I was a soldier like millions of others' (Domarus 1973: Vol. 2, 892) He stressed his humble beginnings to claim first-hand knowledge about the plight and needs of the common people. In the successful election campaigns of the early 1930s, the key theme 'was the collapse of Germany under parliamentary democracy and party government into a divided people with separate and conflicting interests, which only the NSDAP could overcome by creating a new unity of the nation, transcending class, estate and profession' (Kershaw 1998: 330), and in the early months of Nazi rule Hitler claimed to be the honest broker between the different classes. He called himself the representative of those Germans, 'who cannot defend themselves well', and finished his speech with the words: 'I shall have no greater pride in my life, than if I can say at the end of it: I have won over the German worker for the German Reich' (Domarus 1973: Vol. 1, 267–269).

The goal was not a Socialist society, but, as Hitler stated in an interview on 27 January 1934, a 'Germany as a corporate body, as a single organism.'

> People's community, that means a community of all productive labour, that means the oneness of all vital interests, that means over-coming bourgeois privatism and the unionised, mechanically organised masses, that means unconditionally equating the individual fate and the nation, the individual and the people ... The bourgeois must become a citizen of the state; the red comrade must become a citizen of the state. Both must, with their good intentions, ennoble the sociological concept of the worker and raise the status of an honorary title for labour. The patent of nobility alone puts the soldier and the peasant, the merchant and the academic, the worker and the capitalist under oath to take the only possible direction in which all purposeful German striving must be headed: towards the nation. (Domarus 1973: Vol. 1, 415–417).

The Nazis' call for more social justice was necessary for winning over significant numbers of workers and turning the NSDAP into a right-wing people's party, but the ideal of a *Volksgemeinschaft* also appealed to many others. It promised protection for the fearful and economically squeezed, for example, for farmers against banks and the world market, but it also promised, by challenging traditional privileges, equal opportunities for professions like the engineers and other members of the new middle class, who called for a recognition of their abilities (Wehler 2003: 686, 773), and a chance for the young generation to make a quick career. The ideal of social harmony promised social justice to the poor, but also freedom from trade unions and social unrest to the rich. Historians have often noted the indeterminate and contradictory nature of the Nazi ideal of the *Volksgemeinschaft*, but such vagueness was necessary for its propaganda success.

Like many Conservative Revolutionaries, some young Nazis, especially those from conservative middle-class family backgrounds, connected the idea of the *Volksgemeinschaft* with the dream of a harmoniously united and strong *Volk*: Melita Maschmann, for example, who tried to explain retrospectively her enthusiastic participation in the Nazi movement, stated:

> For me it was decisive: I wanted to go a different way than the conservative one which family tradition prescribed. For my parents terms like 'social' and 'socialist' had derogatory connotations. They used them when they were angry that the hunchbacked tailor dared to become politically active ... No other slogan was as fascinating to me as the 'community of the people'. I heard it first from the mouth of the crippled

> tailor, and on the evening of 30 January it got a magic air. The way I encountered it determined the content. I felt that it could only be realized in opposition to the snobbery of the class from which I came and that it should give protection and rights to the weak. What tied me to this utopia was the hope for conditions in which the human beings of all classes would live together like brothers and sisters ... I believed in the promise of the Nazis that they would overcome unemployment and thus the misery of six million humans. I believed that they would lead the German *Volk* from the fragmentation of more than 40 parties to unity, and that they would overcome the consequences of the Versailles treaty. If my faith in January 1933 was only based on hope, it soon enough seemed to be supported by facts. (Maschmann 1963: 16 f.)

In trying to show idealistic reasons for joining the Nazi movement, Melita Maschmann stressed the desire for a nation united in a single faith. There is no reason to doubt her words; such a desire was, as we have seen, widespread. But a closer look soon reveals that there continued to be many quite different visions of a truly united nation. From a militarist perspective, any kind of unity was deemed necessary as a prerequisite for a future war; industrialists hoped for an end to social unrest and the Communist threat (Blasius 2005); and the deprived hoped for improvement of their material conditions and more social acceptance.

In his book on the Nazi 'people's state' (2005), Götz Aly argues that Nazi Germany was a convenience dictatorship in that it allegedly found support to the end because the majority of Germans profited from the plunder of Nazi victims in Germany and in the occupied territories. Reviewers like Mark Spoerer and Adam Tooze were quick in pointing out serious weaknesses in his argument.[15] While the enemies of the Third Reich were certainly plundered (and the mass of the population showed little concern about their fate), it seems unlikely that the mass of Germans profited. Most experts agree that German society did not become significantly richer or more egalitarian after 1933. It is for economic historians further to discuss these questions, but if such trends did actually take place, they were clearly not strong enough to be easily noticeable. People did not talk about an unmistakable rise in the standard of living or in material equality. They did not profit from the Nazis when they started to vote for them in large numbers in 1930, and they did not profit from the plundering of others in the early years when the regime consolidated its rule. There was very little solidarity with the victims of the new regime, but the policies against them were not discussed in terms of personal profit. People clearly listened to the many Nazi promises, they very much appreciated the end of high unemployment, and they proudly celebrated a 'national reawakening': a more united country gaining respect in the world, establishing security and order, offering splendour and career opportunities.

The majority of the population probably believed that things improved under the new regime. The argument, however, that profit was the all-decisive reason for the fatal attraction of National Socialism, while ideology and propaganda were nothing but superfluous window-dressing, results from a crude materialism.

The two factors are obviously not mutually exclusive, but even tend to reinforce each other: interests are usually perceived, interpreted and justified within an ideological framework. With the Nazi ideal of *Volksgemeinschaft*, moreover, the many often inconsistent promises it contained to attract the many different interests made any straightforward realization wholly unimaginable. Only propaganda in combination with often mainly symbolic policies could avoid the alienation of important supporters: the fearful who wanted protection, the confident who demanded opportunities in a socially mobile society, the elites who wanted protection from trade unions and strikes, and the nationalists desiring a community united in a single faith. Both the general emphasis on a 'national awakening', which would benefit the whole of Germany, and a propagandistic celebration of all labour as service to the nation were needed to suggest that the regime was really working towards realizing the original ideal.

Many early measures of the regime clearly went against the interests of the working population, above all the destruction of the trade unions and a wage freeze at the low level of the world economic crisis. The new regime blocked those in the Nazi movement who wanted social reforms, stressing instead the 'Führer-principle' also for industry, that is, a strict hierarchy with power to the bosses (Noakes and Pridham 1983 ff.: Vol. 1, 134 f.). Only in agriculture did Nazism try to help small enterprises, but even in this sector over-regulation, the lack of credits and fixed prices led to understandable discontent (Corni 1990). All consumers suffered from food shortages even before the war, especially of fat and butter. Industry had to accept new state regulations, but they enjoyed freedom from Socialist organizations, strikes and rising labour costs. For the workers, however, the positive features in the decisive period of regime consolidation were basically restricted to job creation schemes and the gradual drop in unemployment. With full employment since 1936, wages started to creep up, career opportunities opened, and the regime did everything to maintain a decent standard of living for all Germans they considered worthy (even if it meant compromising the rearmament programme), but an important aspect of winning the nation was based on promises and make-believe through attractive visions of communal wealth in a harmonious *Volksgemeinschaft*. Altogether, the priority of war preparation left little room for real social changes.

Possibly the strongest symbol of solidarity within a single communal faith was the Nazi movement itself. Marches, mass rallies and the Nazi organizations for all parts of society suggested that the movement offered a space for all true Germans. Everybody could make a contribution, the rich through donations and the poor through distributing leaflets, the clever through spreading the message verbally and the strong and courageous through physical commitment in the SA, the men through public political battle and the women through promoting Nazi values within the family and private circles. All were supposed to contribute according to their ability, while the movement not only offered a social network, but also claimed to take care of all its members, for example, by providing food and a sleeping place to poor SA men or by the so-called 'socialism of the deed' of One-

Pot Sundays and Winter Relief Programmes. The comradeship of the trenches in the First World War, which had allegedly united soldiers from all kinds of social and ideological backgrounds in service to the nation, was also supposed to be similar to the active participation in the Nazi movement and the Third Reich.[16]

In contrast to Marxism, the Nazi regime respected private property, but they marked their distance from conservatism by stressing the social obligation of wealth. Goebbels stated, for example, that there must be no way back to the age of maidservants. More generally, anti-capitalist impulses were directed against allegedly non-productive wealth (generally associated with the Jews), for example war-profiteers, department stores or banks. When the realities of rule showed the need for many of these services, 'Jewish capitalism' as such became the term for 'bad capitalism'. This ideological phrase allowed, as Götz Aly has stressed, for the exploitation of a minority group, but it also fulfilled an important ideological function: all capitalist activities could continue and all non-Jewish businesses could feel safe, while the anti-capitalist aggressions present in the movement were directed against clearly specified targets.

The end to conservative arrogance against the working class was also emphasized through a celebration of all labour. 'Labour ennobles', the slogan went, and this included both manual and non-manual work. The destruction of the trade unions was closely connected with the celebration of the worker to show that Nazism ultimately followed a positive vision: a fair and harmonious *Volksgemeinschaft* as an alternative to a destructive class war (Reichel 1993: 214 ff.). May Day became a national public holiday, the day of national labour under the motto: 'Honour work and respect the worker.' The trade unions were replaced by the German Labour Front, which encompassed both workers and industrialists to show the new unity in one Nazi faith, and its leader Robert Ley called out to the workers: 'We will not let you alone until you give us your entire and genuine support … For we know that without the German worker there is no German nation' (reprinted in Noakes and Pridham 1983 ff.: Vol. 2, 331 ff.). Hitler made the ideological message even more explicit:

> We want to destroy the arrogance with which unfortunately so many intellectuals feel that they must look down upon labour … We wish to contribute to the mutual understanding of the different classes in order to reinforce the tie which binds together the community of the people … The hammer will become once more the symbol of the German worker and the sickle the sign of the German peasant, and with them the intellect [*Geist*] must conclude an alliance that nothing shall dissolve … Today, on May Day, we meet to celebrate the fame of the army of those millions who, as unknown and nameless Soldiers of Work, in the sweat of their faces, in town and country, in the fields, in the factory and the workshop, cooperate to produce those goods which rightly raise our people into the ranks of the civilised nations of the world and enable it to hold that place of honour (reprinted in Noakes and Pridham 1983 ff.: Vol. 2, 354)

German *Volk*! You are strong, if you become one, if you remove the spirit of class war and discord from your heart. You can put incredible power into your work, if you connect the work with the will to live of your whole ethnicity. (Domarus 1973: Vol. 1: 260 f.)

The Nuremberg Rally, known primarily through Leni Riefenstahl's famous documentary *Triumph of the Will* (1934), gave aesthetic expression to this vision of a people united in service to the new Reich (Reichel 1993: 128 f.). For more than two hours, members of the Reich Labour Service marched, until the 50,000 workers came to stand in precise blocks, holding their spades as if presenting a rifle. The continued call: 'Comrade, where do you come from?' was answered in dialect: 'From Frisia, from Bavaria, from the Rhine' and so on, until the list of all regions united in one service to the nation cumulated in: 'One *Volk* – one *Führer* – one *Reich*! *Heimat*!' The chorus then celebrated communal service to the nation by exclaiming: 'Nobody is too good to work for Germany. Nobody is too low to work for Germany, the fatherland.' Finally, work found its ultimate glorification by being linked to the celebrated service in war and civil war. 'We raise our gaze and remember our brothers', the speaker called out, 'who suffered in the trenches, and those who fought murder and hate in the streets. They died for Germany.' The chorus responded: 'But we may live for Germany.'

Such rituals were a convenient way of praising manual labour without significantly changing the economic structure. While the promotion of both industry and agriculture were bound to conflict in reality, they could simultaneously be glorified in aesthetic rituals: the industrial worker, for example, as a Promethean giant (Paul 1990: 242 ff.), labour day and agriculture through a huge Thanksgiving Day celebration as well as pseudo-historic rituals like folk dance, traditional costumes, and celebrations for passing on a farm to the next generation (Farquharson1976: 202–220).

The 'strength through joy' programme was another attempt to please the mass of the population (Baranowski 2004; Reichel 1993: 243–255; Semmens 2005; Welch 1995: 57–60). It offered not only evening entertainment, but also the first mass tourism in Germany. While the more expensive trips were out of the financial reach of most workers, the 10 million overnight stays per year meant that millions must have made use of these opportunities to go on their first holiday. In 1934, 400,000 went on a package tour; in 1937, it was 1.7 million plus 7 million shorter weekend excursions. While a cruise on one of the eight ships (four more were hired on a semi-permanent basis) or a trip to Madeira were still quite expensive, such offers could still instil hope that a more affluent consumer society for everybody was a realistic prospect for the future. There were complaints about better treatment for the rich and Nazi officials, but even a report collected by the exiled SPD grudgingly had to admit: 'Strength through joy is very popular. The events appeal to the yearning of the little man who wants an opportunity to get out and about himself and to take part in the pleasures of the "top people". It is a clever appeal to the petty bourgeois inclinations of the unpolitical workers. For such a man it really means something to have been on a trip to Scandinavia, or even if he only went to the Black Forest or the Harz Mountains, he imagines that he has thereby climbed up a rung on the social ladder.' The announcement of a car affordable for the mass of the population had a similar effect: 'For a large number of Germans the announcement of the People's Car came as a pleasant surprise. There developed a real KdF-Car psychosis. For a long time the KdF-Car was a big talking point among all classes of population' (reprinted in Noakes and Pridham 1983 ff.: Vol. 2, 353). One can thus see the first signs of a consumer society – albeit limited through the priority placed on rearmament.

The reality of the Third Reich could not wholly contradict the propaganda; otherwise it would have lost all credibility. Propaganda promised a better life in a harmonious national community, and the population wanted to see at least steps in that direction (although the short period of peace with many dramatic events and the demands of war could serve to justify the situation if achievements remained limited). There was an obvious reason, however, why the Nazi regime put so much energy and thought into propaganda and symbolic gestures: not only was it cheaper and less risky to change appearances and attitudes than the actual economic and social structure, it also enabled them to accommodate, at least temporarily, a wide variety of interests (Lüdtke 1994). Only the aestheticization of politics could satisfy workers both in agriculture and in industry, and all this without unsettling the elites whose support the regime desperately needed. Only the aestheticization of politics could not only promise more prestige to all workers, but also a new *völkisch* harmony to the population as a whole: a strong and successful Germany united in a single faith. Despite some Socialist rhetoric, even the elites were bound to be pleased by such an appeasement of the masses.

The 'beautiful appearance of the Third Reich' presented a vision of a harmonious national community which 'disguised class antagonisms and status differences, preached a public spirit, propagated happiness and *völkisch* solidarity' (Reichel 1993: 111). Of course, there was some dissatisfaction with the political reality or even resistance, but 'the majority of Germans really believed in the "national resurrection" and in their chance of a personal career, in a heroic future, and in a better life for themselves and future generations' (Frei 2001: 64). While the industrial working class might not have been quite as enthusiastic as the rest of the population, it was certainly not immune to the Nazis' wooing (Herbert 1996a). While all this could not last – as the dramatically growing national deficit shows – it provided the Nazi leadership with a supportive population at least well into the war.

The Rhetoric of Heroism and a Grand Reich

The dream of heroism and historic grandeur belonged to the core of Nazi ideology, but was also – as we have seen – part of a widespread mentality in modern

German history, at least since the Napoleonic wars. If anything, such an attitude intensified after 1918, above all among the nationalist Right. The call for a fight against the Versailles treaty, the glorification of the 'man under the steel helmet' and the 'comradeship of the trenches' (also as a model for a future society), the fascination with marches and uniforms, the glorification of the body and physical hardness, the later popularity of Hitler's foreign policy successes which peaked after the defeat of France, all this shows quite clearly that not only 'soldierly nationalists' desired heroism and a strong Germany which would regain a position of international might or even succeed in its second 'grasp for world power' (Fritz Fischer). Pacifism existed, of course, and it even intensified in the wake of the First World War, but it was clearly a minority opinion.

Within such widespread support for national assertiveness there existed, however, important differences. Many extremists, as we have seen, viewed reality as an apocalyptic struggle between good and evil. A compromise was deemed impossible; everything moved towards a murderous struggle in which the Germans would either perish or destroy their enemies and realize an ideal *völkisch* future, which would also benefit the world as a whole. The much-noted lack of enthusiasm at the beginning of the Second World War,[17] however, shows that even many of those enjoying militaristic rituals and cheering nationalist triumphs remembered the horrors of industrial warfare. They liked the images of heroism and grandeur, but feared a repetition of the First World War. This ambivalence showed again after victory over France: as long as military success was achieved without too much bloodshed, a majority celebrated the Führer – until the tide of war turned (Noakes and Pridham 1983 ff.: 526 ff.; Peukert 1987: 49–66).

The same ambivalence holds true for the soldierly role. Many men loved to associate themselves with the image (and the aesthetics) of the role, but much less with the reality of the role (Parin 1978: 123). It was one thing to indulge in fantasies of heroism and grandeur, service and sacrifice, but only a minority volunteered for war service and disregarded their personal plight to achieve the military goals. Many had gained a sense of pride and freedom from being in the Hitler Youth, but simultaneously grumbled about the hard military drill. As George Orwell stated more generally: 'There is one part of you that wishes to be a hero or a saint, but another part of you is a little fat man who sees very clearly the advantage of staying alive with a whole skin. He is your unofficial self, the voice of the belly protesting against the soul. His tastes lie towards safety, soft beds, no work, pots of beer and women with "voluptuous" figures' (Orwell 1968: 163).

The dream of a strong Germany found many expressions, but a core image was that of the Reich (Empire). The term indicated a claim for universal primacy which never became reality. With the gradual demise of the Holy Roman Empire of German Nation, the title was the only thing left to maintain some patriotic pride, thus serving the same function as the 'title for an impoverished noble' (Kettenacker 1983: 264;. See also Bosbach and Hiery 1999; Winkler 2000, 2002). In 1871, the old grandeur reemerged in the name of the new Germany, only to perish again soon in military defeat and revolution. The disappearance of the Reich did nothing, however, to stop the Reich fantasies. On the contrary: freed from ties to a real object, the visions of a new Reich could run wild. Both after the war and in the world economic crisis the vision of uniting with an Austria 'freed' from its non-German parts gained wide currency (Winkler 2000: Vol. 1, 524 ff.), and Moeller van den Bruck (see Ch. 5) was by no means alone in envisaging a grand new Reich. Fritz Büchner, for example, the editor of a volume entitled *What is the Reich?* (1932), wrote about the Reich as the 'great and tragic destiny of the Germans', because they allegedly, he claimed in obscure language, 'desire to find a unity in space and spirit beyond themselves and in themselves' (1932: 7).

While it is a strong claim to say that the Reich-myth alone was 'the most important bridge between Hitler and large parts of the highly educated Germany' (Winkler 2000: Vol. 1, 554), the term 'Third Reich' was certainly a catchy slogan. It had many strong positive connotations all connected with spiritual unity[18] and national might, but was in its vaguely utopian quality indeterminate enough to disguise the contradictory expectations connected with the call for reestablishing Germany as a major power. It stood for a new Germany united under a strong leadership, but also implied the demand for Germany to become the major European power. It seemed to connect Nazi Germany with the nation's glorious past, but also pointed at a new beginning. It did not sound overtly aggressive, but nevertheless implied a claim to German supremacy and expansion: the right and duty to integrate all Germans into the Reich, but also to establish an Empire dominating over weaker states. With time, Nazi Germany glorified itself even further by dropping the 'Third' simply to talk about the (allegedly unique) Reich and claiming a wider scope by introducing the term Germanic (not German) Reich to express the belief that it would unify the whole 'Germanic race' in a newly structured Europe. There are many states, a Nazi degree proudly proclaimed as early as 1939, 'but only one *Reich*' (quoted in Kettenacker 1983: 273).

The Nazis not only promised to reestablish the German nation as a great power, but equally to reestablish the wounded personal, primarily male, pride after military defeat. In the age of conscription, the ideal of manliness was closely related to military virtues. A man should be courageous and strong, prepared and able to defend his fatherland and loved ones. The dominance of military weapons over soldierly virtues in the First World War had already been a blow to a traditional concept of heroism in which individual qualities were supposed to be decisive,[19] and Germany's military defeat combined with its international weakness after 1918 were hard blows to the male ego. Paramilitary politics was partly motivated through revolution and civil war scenarios, but its continuation throughout the Weimar Republic under all political banners – even in Republican associations like the *Reichsbanner* (Rohe 1966; Ziemann 1998) – as well as the ubiquitous military symbolism, reveals quite clearly the desire to appear as a warrior for an important cause. An apocalyptic 'friend–foe-thinking' (Carl Schmitt) did not only cause paramilitary politics, but was also used in order to create one essential enemy, to hate him and fight him by all means. In confusing times, violent conflicts could produce ideological clarity, a decision. Not unlike Goebbels or Ernst Jünger, Ernst von Salomon stated about his time in a Free Corps: 'We did not know what we wanted ... You ask, what gives us our faith? Nothing but our actions' (1933: 72, 294). The military role provided protective armour against disorienting times (Sombart 1991; Theweleit 1987, 1989). A soldier was not to worry about ideological details, but could follow clear rules of behaviour, such as to develop physical strength and hardness in a glorification of the muscular male body (Wolbert 1982), show courage and determination, obedience and ruthless dedication to the chosen cause. Such seemingly amoral 'cool conduct' or 'matter-of-factness' (which was obviously not ideologically neutral, but simply took ideological premises to be unproblematic and thus rarely voiced fundamental principles) was widespread among both the Conservative Revolution and a young Nazi elite who made their career in the SS and other prestigious organizations in the Third Reich (Herbert 1991, 1996; Lethen 2002; Wildt 2002). Lower down the social ladder, paramilitary organizations like the SA fulfilled a similar function before 1933: the street fighters were often not primarily motivated by ideological reasons. In many cases, service in the SA provided shelter and a structure to life (especially for the many unemployed), social contacts through camaraderie and a legitimation for the use of violence (Reichardt 2002).

The Nazis always defined themselves through their connection with militarism and war. The movement, they emphasized, had its origin in the First World War. Hitler and others always stressed their military past, and the political struggle was presented as a continuation of military conflict. Hitler claimed that only the stab-in-the-back had convinced him to become a politician, and the party programme pointed out the Nazi leadership's readiness 'to sacrifice their very lives' for the cause (reprinted in Noakes and Pridham 1983 ff.: Vol. 1, 16).[20] Hitler praised the SA in *Mein Kampf* for its courageous battles against political enemies, and the Beer Hall Putsch was remembered as an act of death-defying commitment. The highest praise for workers, both in agriculture and industry, was the likening of their function to that of the soldier (see more generally Koonz 2003: Ch. 4). Defying death in serving the nation was the Nazis' highest value; and greatness was connected with the pathos – or *Kitsch* (Friedländer 1993) – of war and sacrifice, a world of Wagnerian fate and tragedy. One example from Albert Speer remembering the evening of 21 August 1939 shortly before the military conflict began may serve to illustrate the point:

> At night we stood on the terrace of the *Berghof* [Hitler's residence in the Bavarian Alps] and gazed at a strange spectacle of Nature [*Naturschauspiel*]. An exceptionally strong polar light illuminated the legendary mountain *Untersberg* for a whole hour with red light, while the sky above showed all the different colours of the rainbow. The last act of the *Twilight of the Gods* could not have been staged more effectively. The faces and hands of all of us were coloured by an unnatural red. The spectacle evoked a strange,

> thoughtful mood. Abruptly, Hitler said to one of his military adjutants: 'This time, things will not take their course without violence'. (1976: 177)

The public display of heroism and military grandeur not only served to advertise the Nazi movement, but also was a narcissistic display to the public. The SA was to present itself, as its Captain Pfeffer stated in November 1926, in a military fashion to show strength and determination. 'Calm bearing and matter-of-factness underscore the impression of power, the force of the marching columns and the cause for which they are marching. The inner force of the cause makes Germans jump to conclusions about its righteousness ... If whole groups of people in planned fashion risk body, soul, and livelihood for a cause, it simply *must* be great and true' (quoted in Merkl 1980: 166). The widespread belief that the Nazi movement was younger, more dynamic and more committed to fighting for a German reawakening was partly due to their marches, their martial uniforms and even their street fights. Violence could be viewed as a threat to the public order, but also as a sign of heroic commitment.

Michael Geyer has argued that Nazi Germany was characterized by a 'catastrophic nationalism', unable to accept the messiness of reality. Nationalists sought purity of belief and action – even at the risk of death or through death. Unable to face up to the mistakes they had made, the leadership could not admit defeat. Germans were prepared to fight to the bitter end and kill ever more enemy soldiers and civilians, despite the fact that more *Wehrmacht* soldiers were killed in action in the last year of war than in the previous five. 'German society, soldiers, and civilians, fought on long after the war was in effect lost and long after it had become apparent to everyone that the war could not but end in disastrous defeat' (Geyer 2002: 127).

An ideology of heroism, often inspired by aesthetic images, which provided a script one could follow to the catastrophic end certainly characterized many leading Nazis. Göring expected the battle of Stalingrad to be remembered as 'the greatest of the heroic battles which will ever have happened in our history'. He compared it with the Battle of the Nibelungs. 'The Nibelungs, too, stood in a hall of fire and flames and quenched their thirst with their own blood – but fought and fought to the last. This kind of battle is fought again today at Stalingrad, and every German, a thousand years hence, must speak the word with holy dread' (quoted in Krüger 1991: 180). Even at the very end of war, Hitler wanted just one more victory: 'It's the only chance to restore personal reputation ... If we leave the world stage in disgrace, we'll have lived for nothing' (quoted in Kershaw 2000: 795), and Goebbels released the film *Kolberg* in January 1945 to inspire further resistance.

Nazi Germany obviously worked hard to spread the readiness to give one's life for communal goals as defined by the Führer. Goebbels said at the occasion of Horst Wessel's death: 'The deceased, who is with us, lifts his tired hand and points into the distant future: move ahead beyond the graves! At the end there will be Germany' (quoted in Behrenbeck 1996: 136 f.). Hitler praised more heroic religions than Christianity, but hoped that ultimately a future generation would no longer need any illusions about an individual life after death to sacrifice itself for the *Volk* (2000: 83). The omnipresent cult around heroic death discussed above clearly left its mark: many hard-core Nazis did everything to force the whole German nation into fighting to the bitter end, and many chose death because they could not imagine a post-Nazi life.

If the Nazi message had been limited to such an extreme call for the ultimate sacrifice, however, they would have failed to gain a mass following. Their popular success depended on also accepting, in Orwell's words, 'the voice of the belly' tending towards safety and comfort. Apart from the bitter end, Germans were able to buy into the communal vision of heroism with surprisingly little self-sacrifice. The Nazis stylized life as a battle, but they were fully aware of the need to maintain a decent standard of living for the mass of the population. Germans could identify with the rituals of heroism and feel nationalist pride about the growing power of Germany as passive onlookers. They lived, propaganda told them, in a heroic age, where Germany was bound to triumph. Joining the Nazi movement was only a small risk before 1933 (even if you chose to be active in the SA), and for the first six years of the regime 'heroism' in Nazi organizations largely consisted of participating in glamorous rituals of self-glorification, in ruthless violence against defenceless minorities and some material profits. It is thus not surprising that a majority of the population wanted to continue these 'good years', as they were often described in hindsight, and not run the risk of another ruinous world war.

The Nazi leadership did not react to 'the voice of the belly' by a fanatical preaching of heroism and sacrifice, but also tried to show that this new war was diametrically opposed to a drawn-out war of attrition. Hitler called the weekly war reports 'a hero-epos as it never existed before' (2000: 71), but the emphasis was on showing a high-tech *Blitzkrieg*; in effect, the promise of minimal suffering for the Germans combined with maximum success. The war footage after 1939 did not show the hardship and suffering of German soldiers, but the easy triumph of German war planes over enemy towns (see, for example, the film *Baptism of Fire*). Even in war, great nationalist goals were to be achieved with minimal cost to the German citizens.

Nazism explicitly rejected any idea of compassion in favour of *völkisch* egotism. 'There is only one kind of law in this world', Hitler stated in 1928, 'and that lies in one's own strength'. The Minister of the Interior Wilhelm Frick echoed these sentiments by stating: 'Everything which is useful for the nation is lawful; everything which harms it is unlawful' (quoted in Noakes and Pridham 1983 ff.: Vol. 2, 474). In consequence, war was seen as a means to enrich the German nation, through plundering and through trying to establish a permanent, profitable dominance over other nations or races. Ideology and material gains were not seen as opposites, but as naturally intertwined. Within Nazi ideology, Germans could feel idealistic *and* follow their interests. While selfless service to the Reich and race was obviously the highest ideal, corruption, profiteering and promises for a better standard of living were rife (Aly 2005; Bajohr 2004). The Führer expressed the wish 'that victory should bring every German a better life' (quoted in Frei 2001: 70), and Robert Ley stated on 15 September 1940: 'The German people are going to be rewarded for their wartime sacrifices with an old age free of cares. In eighteen years Germany will not be recognisable. A proletarian nation will have become a master nation. In ten years' time the German worker will look better than an English lord' (quoted in Noakes and Pridham 1983 ff.: 289).

The vision of all Germans united in one communal faith always remained an elusive dream, but the Nazis got further towards realizing it than any other previous political movement. They tried hard to satisfy all those whom they considered worthy Germans and who should be integrated into the *Volksgemeinschaft*, but their fatal attraction was largely based on suggestive visions of the future which promised the reconciliation of the irreconcilable. With a policy of continuous rapid change and dramatic developments, they were surprisingly successful – at least for a long time of their rule and above all in the crucial moments of gaining and consolidating power – to divert attention away from the many contradictions and towards a widespread faith that the small practical achievements were mere indications for a bright and beautiful future.

Notes

1. For a convincing critique, however, of the claim that Hitler believed he was following God's command in the murder of the European Jews, see Rißmann 2001: 276–278.
2. The concept plays, however, only a marginal role in the remainder of the text. Burleigh 2006 contains more about the topic, but the book was published after the completion of this book's manuscript.
3. For critiques of this concept, see Introduction, footnote 14.
4. This might well be different for the activists, especially in the SA. The Abel collection, with 581 autobiographical reports about why activists joined the Nazi movement, shows that many SA members had a lower social position than their parents. One-third grew up in poverty, and two-thirds had experienced unemployment or bankruptcy (Merkl 1980: 154). Desperate economic conditions made people join the Nazi movement early and become particularly active and violent, but this does not hold true for the mass of the supporters.
5. Rosenberg 1927: 7–11. Apart from Chamberlain, Rosenberg also praised Lagarde, but the latter's intellectual influence was limited.
6. For his critique of Rosenberg, Himmler and Darré from this perspective, see Hitler 1999: 300 f. and Goebbels's diaries, 21 Aug 1938. He voiced his pseudo-scientific critique of religion, for example, in Hitler 1999: 100–102, 105 and in Domarus 1973: Vol. 2, 893).
7. He also fantasized how a group from occupied Kirgisin 'will be led through the capital to fill their imagination with the power and grandness' of the monumental buildings he intended to build (1999: 93).

8. All major Hitler biographies deal with the topic. See also Paul 1990: 17–44; Welch 1995: 10–12. Hitler's views were shaped primarily by war propaganda, especially that of the Allies, Socialist propaganda, commercial advertising and the ideas of Georges Sorel.
9. This distinguished him, for example, from the ideological crackpot Ludendorff, whose spectacular military career would have otherwise offered him a very good chance to become a charismatic leader.
10. Domarus 1973: Vol. 1, 449; Hitler 1999: 116, 610. Hitler summarized his ideas on art in a speech of 18 July 1937, printed in translation in Welch 1995: 170–174.
11. As other members of the Right, Goebbels took Socialism to mean, above all, service to the community (1929: 25), but he was quite concerned about social justice.
12. Quoted in Reichel 1993: 159, 180. Thus the Third Reich produced more seemingly apolitical than political films, and the amount of political broadcasting was strictly limited to assure enough entertainment (ibid.: 159–168, 181).
13. The whole letter is reprinted in Brenner 1963: 178–180.
14. The two temples were actually smaller than many of the buildings around them, in particular the Führer building, thus somewhat resembling guards in front of the larger building.
15. For Spoerer, see http://hsozkult.geschichte.hu-berlin.de.rezensionen/2005-2-143; for Tooze, http://www.taz.de/pt/2005/03/12/a="89.nf/textdruck.
16. See, for example, a Gregor Strasser speech reprinted in Noakes and Pridham 1983 ff.: Vol. 1, 41 f. Maschmann also describes a sense of class-transcending togetherness in a Nazi camp (1963: 41).
17. For example, the American journalist William Shirer noted: 'In 1914, I believe the excitement in Berlin on the first day of the world war was tremendous. Today, no excitement, no hurrahs, no cheering, no throwing of flowers, no war fever, no war hysteria. There is not even any hate for the French and the British' (1942: 162 f.).
18. The Reichs-idea was still associated, for example, with a people united in a Christian faith.
19. Even the writing of a soldierly nationalist like Ernst Jünger expresses the feeling of being just a puppet in the hand of overwhelming powers.
20. In his speech at the beginning of war, Hitler stressed again his willingness to sacrifice his life as a justification for asking others to do the same (Noakes and Pridham 1983 ff.: Vol. 3, 755).

CONCLUSION

The desire for a single communal faith was a core element of German right-wing ideology for more than a century. The entire tradition aimed at overcoming the plurality of modern society. The goal was a warm and harmonious community instead of pragmatic instrumental relations within an anonymous society; unanimity instead of diverse milieus and antagonistic classes; one culture permeating the whole of society instead of a separation between public and private; one faith instead of a multitude of religions and secularization; an up-to-date public faith giving orientation to the community instead of purely private religions; and shared national goals instead of clashes between antagonistic political ideologies. Beyond these core features, the manifestations of this tradition varied, but these differences can largely be explained through three historical trends: from individual artists and thinkers in the realm of high culture to a highly effective populist mass mobilization; from the belief in a spontaneous emergence of a single communal faith to an authoritarian and often manipulative top-down approach; and a growing radicalization, in particular the gradual emergence of polarized friend–foe-thinking in domestic politics (above all against Jews and Marxists), and expansionist dreams as a means both to unite the nation behind one vision and to establish a grand Reich. With repeated failures to achieve the elusive goal of uniting the nation in a single faith, the Right moved towards enforcing its will on to the nation and to identifying 'essential enemies' as scapegoats to explain their own lack of success.

While Romanticism was open enough to prove a strong influence on both the political Right and Left (witness, for example, the early Marx), a strong nationalism grew during the Napoleonic wars. It was still largely universal in the sense of demanding the right for all peoples to form into nations, and its fury against France is at least partly understandable as a reaction against a military invasion, but one can already note outbursts of raw hatred against everything French and calls for a 'pure' community with no space for 'others' like the Jews. Throughout the nineteenth century, the call for a nation united in a single faith continued, but for some decades it was largely expressed by individuals who only gained wider influence towards the end of the century. The political goal of state-building preoccupied the nationalist imagination, it seems, before 1871 (while a cultural unity was largely taken for granted), and it then took some time for the enthusiasm about unification to make space for a more sober or even pessimistic assessment of the degree of unity within the new nation. Towards the turn of the century, however, dissatisfaction increased dramatically among nationalists, because they came to realize that the deeply divided and politically antagonistic Empire was a far cry from all radically nationalist and *völkisch* ideals. In consequence, the desire for a second, spiritual unification gained unprecedented force in individuals and movements ranging from the veterans' and reservists' associations promoting social militarism as a unifying ideology, the many life-reform movements calling for an authentically German culture, and the Pan-Germans advocating an authoritarian regime which would lead the German people into a struggle for world power.

While 'August 1914' could appear at first as the long-awaited moment when an atomized society turned into a united force, eventually a horrendous war and defeat only further increased the divisions in society. The abhorrence about the reality of ideological gulfs, chaos and disorientation, domestic crises and international weakness after 1918 made the far Right shift towards an openly aggressive, authoritarian and populist style. As the extremists no longer saw anything worth preserving, they had no inhibition about destroying the present structure in order to create space for the emergence of something new and hopefully better. In contrast to an alleged nineteenth century 'Romanticism', now dismissed as idealistic and naive, they stylized themselves as a new generation marked by realism and decisiveness, heroism and cool conduct. Trying to escape a confusing reality, many fled into ideological rigour and extremist actions. Among both Conservative Revolutionaries and Nazis, the desire for a nation united in a single communal faith could finally take on wholly totalitarian forms.[1] While earlier, more open hopes for a communal faith envisaged a shared cultural horizon or 'mythology', which would provide the framework within which an infinite variety of individual humans and cultural products could emerge, a totalitarian vision advocated national homogeneity through ruthless *Gleichschaltung* (coordination) of all 'worthy' Germans and the violent exclusion of all 'otherness'. All Germans were to be moulded according to ethnic and racial stereotypes to play their clearly prescribed role within the whole.

This vision could not become reality. Ernst Jünger's *Der Arbeiter* (*The Worker*) aptly described and advocated such a pure totalitarian and militaristic world, but it was the amorphous and polycratic Nazi movement which was politically successful. Mass support could be won only by adapting to the many fears and desires of different parts of society and by presenting vague and often contradictory visions which seemed to promise – only temporarily, but for the crucial times during the rise and rule of Nazism – a more harmonious, affluent and grand future for the vast majority of the population. While the Nazi state never wholly succeeded in its attempt to unite the nation in a single faith, it was neither simply a traditional (conservative or reactionary) authoritarian regime nor primarily based on force and fear, but a wholly new phenomenon: a populist right-wing or fascist rule providing at least symbolic forms of political participation and finding majority support through integrative visions of a powerful, rich and harmonious national future. Nazism was popular because it promised to realize a true community of the people, a great and affluent Germany united in one political will.

The desire for a single faith was a key component of Nazism. The movement was obsessed by the will to realize German cultural, social and political unity, and it found widespread support because it seemed more able than any other force to achieve such unity. However, Nazism was neither the inevitable outcome nor culmination of this powerful cultural tradition in German history. It was not only the Nazis who believed in the need for a nation united in a single faith, but also the conservative resistance opposing them (Hammersen 1993; Mommsen 2000; Roon 1967). The wide majority of its members advocated a structure for the new nation in accordance with German tradition (often taking inspiration from the wars of liberation and von Stein's Prussian reforms), a harmonious and organic, but authoritarian (though explicitly non-totalitarian) *Volksgemeinschaft* overcoming class antagonisms, a German 'third way' between an allegedly egocentric 'Western individualism' and an anti-individualistic 'Eastern collectivism' and even a 'true' national socialism which the Third Reich was said to have betrayed.

It has been suggested that one can see repercussions of the desire for communal convictions in the Federal Republic of Germany, for example, in a stronger desire for a 'consensus politics' than in other Western European democracies or in the difficulties in accepting the reality of a multicultural society and the call for the communal acceptance of one dominant culture, or *Leitkultur.* Comparable ideas, however, are also discussed in other Western countries, and they have never become core ideals of the political culture in the Federal Republic. West Germany achieved more stability, more social harmony and more acceptance than any previous German state, but largely as a politically and culturally open, affluent consumer society with many international influences, in particular from the English-speaking world. A majority has come to value the choice between a wide variety of political opinions, cultural influences, fashions and lifestyles more than the security and ideological purpose of a nation united in a single communal culture and faith. In contrast, the ideal of a social and political order based on shared convictions and the end of alienation through an identity between individual and community remained powerful on the political left, both in the authoritarian form of state socialism in the GDR and other Eastern European states as well as in the more anti-authoritarian form of an unorthodox Left and the 'alternative culture' connected with it.

The many different historical forms which the dream of a harmonious and ideologically united community could take cannot be discussed here. An awareness about the wide variety in which such a dream can find expression can serve, however, to caution us against any sweeping condemnations of this way of thinking. The joy of feeling in harmony with one's social surrounding is known to all but the most emotionally deprived humans from intimate relationships, close friendships or like-minded groups. In contrast, more diverse, formal and regulated social institutions in the public sphere can be experienced as purely instrumental and anonymous, threatening and inhumane. It is thus not surprising that the will to turn a cold society into a warm and caring community has emerged within very different circumstances and ideologies, but especially in modern societies, which might well have lost a sense of secure belonging with the dissolution of a shared cultural horizon such as Christianity in the Middle Ages.[2] Closer to our topic, in particular a democracy without a political consensus about normative fundamentals (like the Weimar Republic) is bound to struggle, because such a political structure demands that all parties must be able to accept their political opponent as good enough to form a government and rule without destroying the country.

It might be unrealistic to expect too much unity within a nation under the conditions of modernity, but the vision only becomes truly dangerous if political actors try to enforce such unity through violent homogenization and exclusion. This was the direction taken by the *völkisch*-nationalist desire for a people united in a single faith: with time, 'Germanness' was no longer seen as open and opaque, but as a clearly defined concept to be used as a chauvinistic justification for expansion and as a strict measure for a violent domestic policy of inclusion and exclusion.

The desire for a single communal faith governing both private life and the public sphere contradicts the modern reality of religions, whose authority is limited by the laws of the religiously neutral state. From a liberal perspective, the modern state has to accept that its citizens have a variety of religious convictions so long as they obey the public law. As religious claims are in principle absolute, they do not lend themselves to rational discussions leading to a political agreement, but can easily provoke irresolvable conflict and, *in extremis*, civil war (as in early Modern Europe). To avoid this, religious faith needs to be restricted to the private or informal sphere: ultimately, believers have to obey the constitutional laws and use secular, rational and thus supposedly universal arguments in formal political discourse which involves, after all, participants who do not share their religious faith (Habermas 2005: 119–136). Religion is thus tolerated by the liberal state, because it is ultimately a personal whim; in the public sphere it is subordinated to both the authority of the secular state and of secular reason. The rest of the population should show tolerance and might appreciate religion, for example, to promote moral behaviour, to increase human happiness or to suggest ways towards a 'good' life, but faith has to adapt and prove itself to be compatible or even useful within a secular world.

Such an integration of religions into a state which is the ultimate arbiter is by no means 'normal' or easy. In the Old Testament, for example, God is said to have tested Abraham's faith by ordering him to sacrifice his son Isaac. God eventually stops him, but only after Abraham had proved his faith by laying his son on an altar and drawing the knife to slaughter him (Genesis 22). Modern believers would obviously read such a story, which is diametrically opposed to modern law and modern common sense, allegorically, but the problem that the Christian God claims to be the ultimate authority (even if he seems to demand highly immoral actions) cannot simply be brushed aside. The attempt, especially in the Lutheran tradition, to show the harmony between the spiritual and the worldly authority was bound to be challenged in times of political upheaval. Another example, this time closely connected with our topic, is The Barmer Declaration of May 1934 (Barth 2004: 1–5), the founding document of the Confessing Church which opposed a wholesale Protestant embrace of Nazism and rejected the state's intentions by emphasizing God's ultimate authority. Jesus Christ as 'attested for us in Holy Scripture', the first thesis states, 'is the one Word of God which we have to hear … and obey in life and in death'. The fifth thesis accepts the need for a worldly state authority, but stresses 'the responsibility of rulers and of the ruled'. Even in the political sphere, the church 'trusts and obeys the power of the Word by which God upholds all things'.

The declaration was cautiously phrased: it was, after all, a collective statement in a threatening political environment. In later interpretations, its main author, the highly respected theologian Karl Barth, emphasized the core message by stating in the same year that the revelation demands 'the totality of humans … As soon as a second stands next to the one and only, he has ceased to be truly *God* … State power cannot be the highest, cannot be the ultimate power. It remains the power of a human, limited by God's commandments and by God's justice' (2004: 18, 20 and 21).

Karl Barth continued to insist that the declaration should not be taken as a situational defence against a totalitarian claim. If anything, his claim for the supremacy of God only radicalized with time. He called the Barmer Declaration a mere 'minimum' and stated that Christians should not act according to 'the problematic authority of the so-called *natural law*' (2004: 230, 105), but only try to serve God. Throughout the Protestant Church, the Barmer Declaration has been held in the highest esteem, and in many German *Länder* it has gained the status of a religiously binding confession of faith. This continued affirmation of God's ultimate authority in all worldly matters, however, has never provoked a serious conflict between Protestantism and the democratic state since the Second World War, because there has been a general acceptance (1) that there is not one sole true reading of the Bible and (2) that Jesus' 'kingdom is not of this world' (John 18: 36). In consequence, the Protestant churches tried to promote a politics in accordance with their understanding of Christianity, but did not call for a Christian state or the realization of a godly order. While in principle the belief that God constitutes the highest and only authority challenges all worldly authority, a conflict has been avoided, because an open reading of Christianity secures an affinity with liberal democracy. In this vein, Barth claimed 'that the Christian politics of distinguishing, judging, choosing, willing and getting involved have a tendency towards an organization of the state which might not be realised in the so-called democracies, but is [at least] more or less honestly meant and attempted' (2004: 128).

It thus seems that in a world of religious pluralism the relationship between the authority of God and the state (or other political entities) must remain, in principle, a difficult one. If God is seen as the ultimate sovereign by the truly faithful, his authority can never be ignored, not even in the political sphere. God and world can work together harmoniously, but only as long as the religious and the political rest on mutually compatible principles.

If religious believers feel seriously threatened by modernization, fundamentalism is a possible and frequent response (Berman 2003; Ruthven 2005). The term was first coined to refer to 'back to the literal meaning of the Bible' movements in America, but has also gained a more general sense: a dogmatization and radicalization of religion in response to the seemingly overwhelming challenge of modernity. Instead of accepting the emergence of a metaphysical pluralism, fundamentalism aims at shaping the whole world according to its own religious faith, which is regarded as the one and only truth. Religious principles are not perceived as general guidelines in need of interpretation according to concrete circumstances, but as precisely formulated laws intended to govern humans in all spheres of life. The separation of a godly religious and a godless secular sphere is the prime scandal and provocation of the modern world; a religiously founded, homogeneous order united in a single communal faith is the utopian countervision.

Is it fruitful to view the desire for a single communal faith in Germany as a kind of fundamentalism? Certainly not in the narrow sense of the term, as the search for a single faith did not go back to a sacred text or traditional laws. On the contrary, the weakening of a religious tradition opened the space to hope for a new religion more suitable to one's own current political and ideological ambitions. Some wanted to adapt Christianity to the modern age, some wanted a wholly new religion by drawing on Germanic traits, but neither was justified as a return to a religion of old. It has been rightly noted that fundamentalist religions are also distinct from orthodoxy, as they emerge as (often violent) movements to overcome modern pluralism and as they are always selective (and frequently surprisingly innovative) in their reading of their sacred texts (Ruthven 2004: 17 f.), but the German case is obviously more extreme: many of the would-be founders of a new faith were consciously innovative and avant-garde in their aesthetic means. While Christian fundamentalists vehemently reject any scholarly reading of the Bible as a historical text, the callers for a new faith in Germany cherished the space this created for a new up-to-date communal world-view. By and large, they not only accepted that there was no way back, but even sought to be progressive by trying to provide something new – namely, a modern society united in a single communal faith. While they are thus different in being *consciously* innovative, they share with fundamentalists the desire to overcome the pluralism and differentiation of modernity by establishing a single communal faith, which was supposed to be an all-encompassing world-view to guide individual and collective behaviour, and give political direction to the nation. As with fundamentalist movements, this desire could culminate in the attempt to enforce a cultural totalitarianism.

Presenting himself as a detached onlooker, Max Weber dismissed the question of whether modern society needed a religion: 'The whirling of fashion will presently remove this subject of conversation and journalism' (1963: 137). The topic was, however, not simply a passing fancy, but a long and powerful tradition, driven by the desire to overcome what Weber himself so aptly named disenchantment: specialization and mechanization, the compartmentalization of modern existence into many different roles and the dominance of instrumental reason in administration and material reproduction. What Weber analysed as inevitable motivated others to promote a conscious 're-enchantment' (Bolz 1989).

Historians who believe in enlightened reason as the proper basis of the modern ideally democratic world have frequently rejected and condemned such 're-enchantment' as dangerously 'irrational'. This is quite a sweeping epistemological claim, which, to my knowledge, has never been supported by a thorough argument. It assumes that humans and societies should operate in a rational manner, and normally do so. But is such a conviction realistic? Is it not obvious that humans are, to a great extent, non-rationally motivated? Cultural and personal background, fears and desires, aspirations and dreams always play a crucial role in politics and discussions about a 'good life'. Humans have never fatalistically accepted Max Weber's diagnosis of disenchantment, but have continued to dream and scheme for an emotionally rich and meaningful life, not only in utopian thought, but also, for example, in the visual world of art and advertising. Modernity is not just characterized by abstract systems, in which we operate instrumentally according to rules and monetary incentives, but also by religions and ideologies, emotions and normative debates.[3] The term 'irrational' has largely served to dismiss something seemingly alien; but it is difficult to sustain such a judgement if we accept that emotions and reason are inseparably intertwined within human existence. It is true that the call for a new faith stood in tension with an enlightened concept of reason and a Western-style democracy, but beyond this the historical reality does not fit into a polar distinction of rational–irrational. Political goals are never wholly rational, and in trying to realize its political goals the German Right was not, it seems, any more irrational than its political opponents.

The other much overused label has been 'anti-modern' (Rohkrämer 1999, 1999b). Of course, the German Right was largely 'anti-modern' if we identify modernity with liberalism and democracy – these were, after all, their political opponents. But why use the more general label, if what is really meant is 'anti-liberal' and 'anti-democratic'? Such an identification of modernity with a democratic political orientation seems problematic because it is a normative definition in tension with the historical reality. Over the last two centuries, societies with highly developed economic and administrative systems have combined with a wide variety of political systems. Empirically there has been no necessary connection between industrialization and democracy; so it makes little sense to see the latter as a necessary ingredient of modernization. Political freedom is desirable, but frequently *not reality* in modern states. Of course, we can make a word mean what we want it to mean (as Humpty Dumpty has pointed out in *Alice in Wonderland*), but limiting the modern to the liberal and democratic tradition encourages one to downplay the modern features of the German Right, and thus its historical complexity. While the right-wing dream of a single communal faith largely rejected a liberal state, it tended to accept that history is irreversible. It drew on features of the past and fantasised about an essential 'Germanness', but explicitly called for the creation of something new. Many would-be founders of a new faith not only grudgingly admitted that the traditional religions had ceased to fulfil their communal function, but frequently enjoyed working towards a new and up-to-date faith in accordance with their own political ideals. They no longer saw their ideas as simply 'God-given' and obvious, but argued, persuaded and advertised to convert the public. Furthermore, most of the Right also came to accept that crucial material changes connected with modernization, above all the emergence of an industrial and technical world, were irreversible and even necessary to create social harmony and strengthen the German nation.

In the nineteenth century, the innovative and politically powerful forces among the German Right came to accept that one could not turn back the historical development as a whole. They remained conservative in working for a hierarchical and non-pluralistic community united in a single communal faith, but they wanted to achieve this in a historically unprecedented form. They thus envisaged a new future: a right-wing modernity – that is, an alternative modernity according to their own ideals and thus different and allegedly superior to that of the West.

There is no need for sweeping labels to recognize the problematic nature of the desire for a single communal faith. Aesthetics and culture as a whole came to be seen not as an open space in which to experiment with different perspectives or raise critical questions, but only as a means to establish one single communal faith. A plurality of opinions came to be regarded as dangerous; communality increasingly came to be confused with a uniform, at times even totalitarian, homogeneity.

Völkisch thinkers called for a faith in harmony with alleged ethnic traits, but in reality such faith did not emerge anonymously from the mystery of past times, but was consciously constructed, often even with clear political purposes in mind. Attempts at introducing a new communal faith thus tended to be top-down approaches from a self-declared cultural elite, which are in effect often indistinguishable from straightforward attempts to manipulate the population into accepting a new world-view. In the eyes of the actors and their followers, however, the ideas were not subjective opinions, but were elevated to the status of national myth or faith, that is, an up-to-date expression and concretization of eternal *völkisch* traits. The claim to such a semi-religious status could disguise the individual origins of these works and give them a seemingly objective or even sacred aura, thus removing them from the sphere of open and critical debate.

The dream of a new communal faith basically sought to combine the best of the traditional and the modern world. Its creators turned their back on traditional religion, which set limits to individual freedom by demanding obedience to sacred texts and church doctrine. They wanted the freedom of individual artistic creation, even the godly power to create a new communal faith, but at the same time the security which only a semi-religious world-view could offer. Individual freedom and the claim to shape the world according to one's own ideals (only for a cultural elite, of course, not for the mass of the population) was to be connected with the security of a comprehensive communal world-view.

The dream of a nation united in a single faith could serve as ideological justification of current conditions by emphasizing the primacy of national solidarity beyond the particular affiliations of citizens, churches or classes. It also served as a manipulative tool in the hand of right-wing party and state leaders to integrate the masses into a non-egalitarian and authoritarian hierarchy as well as mobilizing them for allegedly grand and heroic political goals. However, the vision of a nation united in a single faith was not only a convenient instrument to appease the masses and win them over for right-wing politics; it also contained strong utopian elements. The calls for a nation united in a single faith could play such a crucial historical role only because of the widespread existence of a desire for a secure world-view and for a harmonious and fair *Volksgemeinschaft* united in shared beliefs and shared political goals. It was a vision of the future, where all Germans would lead a fulfilled life: material security, social harmony and a clear orientation in life, heroism and national grandeur. This hope was wide and unspecific enough to mobilize, at least at a time of deep crisis, a mass movement for a change from a pluralistic Republic to a state promising unity under the slogan: 'One Reich, one *Volk*, one Führer'.

Winning over the masses was crucial for realizing a single communal faith, but this wooing of the people was always mixed with an elitist sense of superiority among right-wing activists. Traditional conservatism viewed the *Volk* with patriarchal contempt while *völkisch* nationalists glorified true Germanness, but both believed that only an elite could give appropriate expression to the best national traits. The belief that the genius of artists, thinkers and politicians could lead the *Volk* to realize its highest potential allowed nationalists to ignore all inconvenient expressions of the popular will as the babble of an amorphous and inauthentic mass. Manipulating the people could thus appear, if successful, as legitimate leadership towards realizing the *Volk*'s highest potential, while critical voices could be dismissed and rejected as allegedly 'un-German'. Authoritarianism and a policy of forced integration/exclusion did not only occur as a last desperate measure born from frustration, but was an integral part of the right-wing vision of a single communal faith.

If German nationalism ever fully accepted the rights of other nations, it soon came to put its own nation first. *Völkisch* nationalists, in particular, rejected any kind of universalism including the idea of human rights. Disregard for other nations' rights combined with visions of heroic grandeur led to a close connection between the desire for a single communal faith and war. Uniting the nation was seen as a necessary prerequisite for successful warfare in the age of peoples' war, and a military conflict as a way to unite the nation against an outside enemy. Social Darwinism and then the First World War and defeat marked stages of radicalization, until power alone seemed to be the sole basis of life.

The gradual radicalization of the drive towards a nation united in a single communal faith was not inevitable, but neither was it pure chance. If people try to realize the vision by any possible means, the dream is bound to turn into a nightmare.

Notes

1. The term 'totalitarian' is used to characterize a regime with a total claim to rule, with one exclusive ideology, and with the claim of a total identity between rulers and ruled, between individual and collective.
2. The need for individuals to act according to a wide variety of role expectations can also threaten a coherent sense of self and promote a feeling of alienation.
3. My thoughts about modernity alluded to here are most strongly shaped by Habermas 1984, 1987 and 2005 and the later Heidegger. Also particularly useful in this connection are Klinger 1995 and Latour 1993.

SELECT BIBLIOGRAPHY

Ach, Manfred and Clemens Pentrop, eds. 1991. *Hitlers 'Religion': Pseudoreligiöse Elemente im nationalsozialistischen Sprachgebrauch,* 2nd edn. Munich

Ackermann, Josef 1970. *Heinrich Himmler als Ideologe.* Göttingen

Ahlzweig, Klaus 1994. *Muttersprache – Vaterland. Die deutsche Nation und ihre Sprache.* Opladen

Akaltin, Ferdi 1997. *Die Befreiungskriege im Geschichtsbild der Deutschen im 19. Jahrhundert.* Frankfurt/M.

Albrecht, Clemens 1993. 'Kultur und Zivilisation. Eine typisch deutsche Dichotomie', in *Kultur und Technik,* ed. Wolfgang König and Marlene Landsch. Frankfurt/M., 11–29

Allen, William Sheridan 1984. *The Nazi Seizure of Power: The Experience of a Single German Town, 1922–1945,* 2nd edn. New York

Altenbockum, Jasper von 1994. *Wilhelm Heinrich Riehl 1823–1897: Sozialwissenschaft zwischen Kulturgeschichte und Ethnographie.* Cologne

Altgeld, Wolfgang 1991. 'Die Ideologie des Nationalsozialismus und ihre Vorläufer' in *Faschismus und Nationalsozialismus,* ed. Karl Dietrich Bracher and Leo Valiani. Berlin

—— 1992. *Katholizismus, Protestantismus, Judentum: Über religiös begründete Gegensätze und nationalreligiöse Ideen in der Geschichte des deutschen Nationalismus.* Frankfurt/M.

Aly, Götz 2005. *Hitlers Volksstaat. Raub, Rassenkrieg und nationaler Sozialismus.* Frankfurt/M.

Anderson, Benedict 1991. *Imagined Communities. Reflections on the Origin and Spread of Nationalism,* revised edn. London

Applegate, Celia 1990. *A Nation of Provincials: The German Idea of Heimat.* Berkeley

—— 1992. 'The Question of Heimat in the Weimar Republic', *New Formations* No 17, 64–74

Arendt, Hannah 1963. *Eichmann in Jerusalem: a Report on the Banality of Evil.* London

—— 1966. *The Origins of Totalitarianism,* 3rd edn. London

Arnim, Achim v. and Clemens Brentano 2006. *Des Knaben Wunderhorn: alte deutsche Lieder.* Frankfurt/M.

Arndt, Ernst Moritz 1803. *Germanien und Europa.* Altona

—— 1820. *Ein Wort über die Pflegung und Erhaltung der Forsten und der Bauern im Sinne einer höheren, dh. menschlicheren Gesetzgebung.* Schleswig/Leipzig

—— 1845. *Schriften für und an seine lieben Deutschen.* Leipzig
—— 1894. *Gedichte von Ernst Moritz Arndt. Vollständige Sammlung.* Vol. 2. Leipzig
Aschheim, Steven E. 1994. *The Nietzsche Legacy in Germany, 1890–1990,* paperback edn. Berkeley
Auerbach, Hellmuth 1993. 'Nationalsozialismus vor Hitler' in *Der Nationalsozialismus. Studien zur Ideologie und Herrschaft,* ed. Wolfgang Benz et al. Frankfurt/M., 13–28
Aufmuth, Ulrich 1979. *Die deutsche Wandervogelbewegung unter soziologischem Aspekt.* Göttingen
Bab, Julius 1914. *1914. Der Deutsche Krieg im deutschen Gedicht.* Berlin
Backes, Klaus 1988. *Hitler und die bildenden Künste. Kulturverständnis und Kunstpolitik im Dritten Reich.* Cologne
Baird, Jay W. 1990. *To Die for Germany: Heroes in the Nazi Pantheon.* Bloomington
Bajohr, Frank 2004. *Parvenüs und Profiteure: Korruption in der NS-Zeit.* Frankfurt/M.
Bald, Detlev 1982. *Der deutsche Offizier. Sozial- und Bildungsgeschichte des deutschen Offizierskorps im 20. Jahrhundert.* Munich
Bambach, Charles 2003. *Heidegger's Roots: Nietzsche, National Socialism, and the Greeks.* Ithaka
Bankier, David 1992. *The Germans and the Final Solution: Public Opinion under Nazism.* Oxford
—— ed. 2000. *Probing the Depth of German Anti-Semitism: German Society and the Persecution of the German Jews, 1933–1941.* New York
Baranowski, Shelley 2004. *Strength through Joy: Consumerism and Mass Tourism in the Third Reich.* New York
Barck, Karlheinz and Richard Faber, eds. 1999. *Ästhetik des Politischen – Politik des Ästhetischen.* Würzburg
Barkin, Kenneth D. 1970. *The Controversy over German Industrialization 1890–1902.* Chicago
Barlösius, Eva 1997. *Naturgemäße Lebensführung. Zur Geschichte der Lebensreform um die Jahrhundertwende.* Frankfurt/M.
Bärsch, Claus-Ekkehard 1998. *Die politische Religion des Nationalsozialismus. Die religiöse Dimension der NS-Ideologie in den Schriften von Dietrich Eckart, Joseph Goebbels, Alfred Rosenberg und Adolf Hitler.* Munich
Barth, Christian 2003. *Goebbels und die Juden.* Paderborn
Barth, Karl 1975. *Die protestantische Theologie im 19. Jahrhundert.* 2 Vols. Hamburg
—— 2004. *Texte zur Barmer Erklärung,* ed. Martin Rohkrämer. 2nd edn. Zürich
Bartov, Omer 1994. *Hitler's Army: Soldiers, Nazis and War in the Third Reich.* New York
—— 2001. *The Eastern Front, 1941–45: German Troops and the Barbarisation of Warfare,* 2nd edn. Houndsmills
—— 2002. *Mirrors of Destruction: War, Genocide and Modern Identity.* Oxford
Bartov, Omar and Phyllis Mack, eds. 2001. *In God's Name. Genocide and Religion in the Twentieth Century,* paperback edn. New York
Bauman, Zygmunt 1992. *Modernity and the Holocaust,* 2nd edn. Cornell
Baumgarten, Eduart 1964. *Max Weber: Werk und Person.* Tübingen
Bäumler, Alfred, 1929. *Bachofen und Nietzsche.* Zürich
—— 1931. *Nietzsche der Philosoph und Politiker.* Leipzig
—— 1934. *Männerbund und Wissenschaft.* Berlin

—— 1934. *Das Reich als Tat. Rede gehalten bei der Reichsgründungsfeier der Friedrich-Wilhelms-Universität Berlin am 18. Januar 1934.* Berlin
—— 1942. *Bildung und Gemeinschaft.* Berlin
—— 1943. *Alfred Rosenberg und der Mythus des 20. Jahrhunderts.* Munich
Bavyj, Ricardo 2003. *Die Ambivalenz der Moderne im Nationalsozialismus: eine Bilanz der Forschung.* Munich
Baycroft, Timothy and Mark Hewitson, eds. 2006. *What is a Nation? Europe 1789–1914.* Oxford
Becker, Frank 2001. *Bilder von Krieg und Nation. Die Einigungskriege in der bürgerlichen Öffentlichkeit 1864–1913.* Munich
Becker, Josef and Ruth Becker, eds. 1993. *Hitlers Machtergreifung 1933,* 3rd edn. Munich
Becker, Peter E. 1990. *Sozialdarwinismus, Rassismus, Antisemitismus und Völkischer Gedanke. Wege ins Dritte Reich.* Part 2. Stuttgart
Behnken, Klaus and Frank Wagner 1987. *Inszenierungen der Macht. Ästhetische Faszination im Faschismus.* Berlin
Behrenbeck, Sabine 1996. *Der Kult um die toten Helden. Nationalsozialistische Mythen, Riten und Symbole 1923 bis 1945.* Vierow bei Greifswald
Beiser, Frederick C. 1992. *Enlightenment, Revolution, and Romanticism: The Genesis of Modern German Political Thought, 1790–1800.* Cambridge, Mass.
Bendersky, Joseph W. 1983. *Carl Schmitt. Theorist for the Reich.* Princeton
Benjamin, Walter 1963. *Das Kunstwerk im Zeitalter seiner technischen Reproduzierbarkeit.* Frankfurt/M.
—— 1966. 'Angelus Novus', in his *Ausgewählte Schriften 2.* Frankfurt/M.
Benz, Wolfgang 2004. *Was ist Antisemitismus?* Munich
Berdahl, Robert 1988. *The Politics of the Prussian Nobility. The Development of a Conservative Ideology, 1770–1848.* Princeton
Berding, Helmut 1969. *Rationalismus und Mythos. Geschichtsauffassung und politische Theorie bei Georges Sorel.* Munich
—— 1988. *Moderner Antisemitismus in Deutschland.* Frankfurt/M.
—— 1998. 'Völkische Erinnerungskultur und nationale Mythenbildung zwischen dem Kaiserreich und dem "Dritten Reich"' in *Dimensionen der Historik. Geschichtstheorie, Wissenschaftsgeschichte und Geschichtskultur heute. Jörn Rüsen zum 60. Geburtstag,* ed. Hans Walter Blanke et al. Cologne, 83–91
Berggötz, Sven O. 2001. 'Nachwort' in Ernst Jünger, *Politische Publizistik,* 834–869
Berghahn, Volker 1966. *Der Stahlhelm. Bund der Frontsoldaten 1918–1935.* Düsseldorf
Bergen, Doris L. 1996. *Twisted Cross: The German Christian Movement in the Third Reich.* Chapel Hill
Berger, Stefan 1996. *The Search for Normality. National Identity and Historical Consciousness in Germany since 1800.* Oxford
—— 2004. *Germany.* London
Bergmann, Klaus 1970. *Agrarromantik und Großstadtfeindschaft.* Meisenheim am Glan
Berman, Paul 2003. *Terror and Liberalism.* New York
Bermbach, Udo 1994. *Der Wahn des Gesamtkunstwerks. Richard Wagners politisch-ästhetische Utopie.* Frankfurt/M.
—— 2003. *"Blühendes Leid". Politik und Gesellschaft in Richard Wagners Musikdramen.* Stuttgart
Bernhardi, Friedrich von 1912. *Deutschland und der nächste Krieg.* Stuttgart/ Berlin

Besier, Gerhard, ed. 1984. *Die protestantischen Kirchen Europas im Ersten Weltkrieg. Ein Quellen- und Arbeitsbuch.* Göttingen

Beßlich, Barbara 2000. *Wege in den "Kulturkrieg". Zivilisationskritik in Deutschland 1890–1914.* Darmstadt

—— 2002. *Faszination des Verfalls: Thomas Mann und Oswald Spengler.* Berlin

Bessel, Richard 1978. 'Militarismus im innenpolitischen Leben der Weimarer Republik: Von den Freikorps zur SA' in *Militär und Militarismus in der Weimarer Republik.* ed. Klaus-Jürgen Müller and Eckardt Opitz. Düsseldorf, 193–222

—— 1984. *Political Violence and the Rise of Nazism: The Stormtroopers in Eastern Germany.* London

—— 1991. 'Die Krise der Weimarer Republik als Erblast des verlorenen Krieges' in *Zivilisation und Barbarei. Die widersprüchlichen Potentiale der Moderne. Detlev Peukert zum Gedenken,* ed. Frank Bajohr et al. Hamburg, 90–114

—— 1993. *Germany after the First World War.* Oxford

—— 1995. 'The "Front Generation" and the Politics of Weimar Germany' in *Generations in Conflict. Youth Revolt and Generation Formation in Germany 1770–1968,* ed. Mark Roseman. Cambridge, 121–136

Blackbourn, David 1987. *Populists and Patricians.* London

—— 1993. *Marpingen: Apparitions of the Virgin Mary in Bismarckian Germany.* Oxford

—— 2003. *History of Germany 1780–1918. The Long Nineteenth Century,* 2nd edn. London

—— 2006. *The Conquest of Nature. Water, Landscape and the Making of Modern Germany.* London

Blackbourn, David and Geoff Eley 1984. *The Peculiarities of German History.* Oxford

Blackburn, Gilmer W. 1985. *Education in the Third Reich: A Study of Race and History in Nazi Textbooks.* Albany, NY

Blanning, Timothy C. W. 1983. *The French Revolution in Germany.* Cambridge

Blasius, Dirk 2001. *Carl Schmitt: Preussischer Staatsrat in Hitlers Reich.* Götteningen

—— 2005. *Weimars Ende. Bürgerkrieg und Politik 1930–1933.* Göttingen

Blitz, Hans-Martin 2000. *Aus Liebe zum Vaterland: die deutsche Nation im 18. Jahrhundert.* Hamburg

Bloch, Ernst 1962. *Erbschaft dieser Zeit.* Frankfurt/M.

—— 1976. *Das Prinzip Hoffnung,* 3rd edn. Frankfurt/M.

Boa, Elizabeth and Rachel Palfrey-Man 2000. *Heimat – A German Dream: Regional Loyalties and National Identity in German Culture, 1890–1990.* Oxford

Böhme, Hartmut 1988. *Natur und Subjekt.* Frankfurt/M.

Böhme, Hartmut and Gernot Böhme 1992. *Das Andere der Vernunft. Zur Entwicklung von Rationalitätsstrukturen am Beispiel Kants,* 2nd edn. Frankfurt/M.

—— 1996. *Feuer, Wasser, Erde Luft. Eine Kulturgeschichte der Elemente.* Munich

Böhme, Klaus, ed. 1975. *Aufrufe und Reden. Deutscher Professoren im Ersten Weltkrieg.* Stuttgart

Bollenbeck, Georg 1996. *Bildung und Kultur: Glanz und Elend eines deutschen Deutungsmusters.* Frankfurt/M.

—— 1999. *Tradition, Avantgarde, Reaktion. Deutsche Kontroversen und die kulturelle Moderne 1880–1945.* Frankfurt/M.

—— 2005. 'Kulturkritik als Reflexionsmodus der Moderne' *LiLi* 35, No 137, 41–53

Bollmus, Reinhard 1970. *Das Amt Rosenberg und seine Gegner. Studien zum Machtkampf im nationalsozialistischen Herrschaftssystem.* Stuttgart

Bolz, Norbert 1989. *Auszug aus der entzauberten Welt. Philosophischer Extremismus zwischen den Weltkriegen.* Munich

Borchmeyer, Dieter 1991. *Richard Wagner: Theory and Theatre.* Oxford

—— ed. 2000. *Richard Wagner und die Juden.* Stuttgart

—— 2002. *Richard Wagner. Ahasvers Wandlungen.* Frankfurt/M.

Borrmann, Norbert 1989. *Paul Schultze-Naumburg, 1869–1949. Maler, Publizist, Architekt. Vom Kulturreformer der Jahrhundertwende zum Kulturpolitiker im Dritten Reich.* Essen

Bosbach, Franz and Hermann Hiery, eds. 1999. *Imperium / Empire / Reich: ein Konzept politischer Herrschaft im deutsch-britischen Vergleich = An Anglo-German Comparison of a Concept of Rule.* Munich

Bösch, Frank 2002. *Das konservative Milieu: Vereinskultur und lokale Sammlungspolitik in ost- und westdeutschen Regionen.* Göttingen

Botermann, Frits 2000. *Oswald Spengler und sein Untergang des Abendlandes.* Cologne

Bracher, Karl Dietrich 1973. *The German Dictatorship: the Origins, Structure and Consequences of National Socialism.* London

—— 1978. *Die Auflösung der Weimarer Republik,* 5th edn. Villingen

—— 1984. *The Age of Ideologies: A History of Political Thought in the Twentieth Century.* London

—— ed. 1986. *Nationalsozialistische Diktatur 1933–1945. Eine Bilanz.* Bonn

Braun, Hans-Joachim 1992. 'Konstruktion, Destruktion und der Ausbau technischer Systeme zwischen 1914 und 1945' in *Propyläen Technikgeschichte,* Vol. 5: *Energiewirtschaft, Automatisierung, Information,* ed. Wolfgang König. Berlin, 9–279

Braungart, Wolfgang, ed. 1998. *Ästhetische und religiöse Erfahrungen der Jahrhundertwenden,* Part 2: *Um 1900.* Paderborn

Brenner, Hildegard 1963. *Die Kunstpolitik des Nationalsozialismus.* Reinbek

Brenner, Wolfgang 2005. *Walther Rathenau. Deutscher und Jude.* Munich

Breuer, Stefan 1993. *Anatomie der konservativen Revolution.* Darmstadt

—— 1995. *Ästhetischer Fundamentalismus. Stefan George und der deutsche Antimodernismus.* Darmstadt

—— 1999. *Grundpositionen der deutschen Rechten 1871–1945.* Tübingen

—— 2001. *Ordnungen der Ungleichheit – die deutsche Rechte im Widerstreit ihrer Ideen 1871–1945.* Darmstadt

—— 2005. *Nationalismus und Faschismus: Deutschland, Frankreich und Italien im Vergleich.* Darmstadt

Breuilly, John 1993. *Nationalism and the State,* 2nd edn. Manchester

—— 2001. *The Formation of the First German Nation-State 1800–1871.* London

—— 2002. *Austria, Prussia and Germany 1806–1871.* London

Brocke, Bernhard von 1985. 'Wissenschaft und Militarismus. Der Aufruf der 93 an die Kulturwelt! Und der Zusammenbruch der internationalen Gelehrtenrepublik im Ersten Weltkrieg' in *Wilamowitz nach 50 Jahren,* ed. W. Calder III et al. Darmstadt, 649–719

Brockhaus, Gudrun 1997. *Schauder und Idylle. Faschismus als Erlebnisangebot.* Munich

Brokoff, Jürgen 2001. *Die Apokalypse in der Weimarer Republik.* Munich

Broszat, Martin, ed. 1977–83. *Bayern in der NS-Zeit,* 6 Vol., Munich

—— 1988. 'Soziale Motivation und Führer-Bindung des Nationalsozialismus' in his *Nach Hitler. Der schwierige Umgang mit unserer Geschichte.* Munich

—— 1989. *Hitler and the Collapse of Weimar Germany*, 2nd edn. Leamington Spa
Broszat, Martin and Klaus Schwabe, eds. 1989. *Die deutschen Eliten und der Weg in den Zweiten Weltkrieg*. Munich
Browning, Christopher R. 1998. *Ordinary Men: Reserve Police Battalion 101 and the Final Solution in Poland*, 2nd edn. New York
Brubaker, Rogers 1992. *Citizenship and Nationhood in France and Germany*. Cambridge, Mass.
Bruch, Rüdiger vom, et al., eds. 1989 and 1997. *Kultur und Kulturwissenschaften um 1900*. 2 Vol. Stuttgart
Bruendel, Steffen 2003. *Volksgemeinschaft oder Volksstaat. Die "Ideen von 1914" und die Neuordnung Deutschlands im Ersten Weltkrieg*. Berlin
Brunner, Otto et al., ed. 1972–1997. *Geschichtliche Grundbegriffe. Historisches Lexikon zur politisch-sozialen Sprache in Deutschland*. Stuttgart
Brunschwig, Henri 1974. *Enlightenment and Romanticism in Eighteenth-century Prussia*. Chicago
Büchner, Fritz, ed. 1932. *Was ist das Reich? Eine Aussprache unter Deutschen*. Munich
Bucholz, Kai. et al., eds. 2001. *Die Lebensreform. Entwürfe zur Neugestaltung von Leben und Kunst um 1900*, 2 Vols. Darmstadt
Burleigh, Michael 1988. *Germany Turns Eastwards. A Study of Ostforschung in the Third Reich*. Cambridge
—— 2000. *The Third Reich. A New History*. London
—— 2005. *Earthly Powers. Religion & Politics in Europe from the French Revolution to the Great War*. London
—— 2006. *Sacred Causes. Religion and Politics from the European Dictators to Al Qaeda*. London
Burleigh, Michael and Wolfgang Wippermann 1991. *The Racial State. Germany 1933–1945*. Cambridge
Burrin, Philippe 2004. *Warum die Deutschen? Antisemitismus, Nationalsozialismus, Genozid*. Berlin
Buruma, Ian and Avishai Margalit 2004. *Occidentalism. The West in the Eyes of its Enemies*. New York
Buschmann, Nikolaus 2003. *Einkreisung und Waffenbruderschaft. Die öffentlichte Deutung von Krieg und Nation in Deutschland 1850–1871*. Göttingen
Bussche, Raimund von dem 1998. *Konservatismus in der Weimarer Republik. Die Politisierung des Unpolitischen*. Heidelberg
Busse, Carl, ed. 1916. *Deutsche Kriegslieder 1914/1916*. Bielefeld
Bussemer, Thymian 2000. *Propaganda und Populärkultur. Konstruierte Erlebniswelten im Nationalsozialismus*. Wiesbaden
Caldwell, Peter C. and William E. Scheuerman 2000. *From Liberal Democracy to Fascism. Legal and Political Thought in the Weimar Republic*. New York
Carsten, Francis L. 1964. *Reichswehr und Politik*. Cologne
—— 1988. *Geschichte der preußischen Junker*. Frankfurt/M.
Cecil, Robert 1972. *The Mythus of the Master Race. Alfred Rosenberg and Nazi Ideology*. London
Chamberlain, Houston Stewart 1904. *Die Grundlagen des 19. Jahrhunderts*, 2 Vols. 5th edn. Munich
—— 1905. *Arische Weltanschauung*. Berlin
—— 1914. *Kriegsaufsätze*. Munich

—— 1915. *Neue Kriegsaufsätze.* Munich
—— 1919. *Lebenswege meines Denkens.* Munich
—— 1921. *Mensch und Gott. Betrachtungen über Religion und Christentum.* Munich
—— 1925. *Rasse und Persönlichkeit. Aufsätze.* Munich
—— 1928. *Briefe 1882–1924 und der Briefwechsel mit Kaiser Wilhelm II,* 2 Vol. Munich
—— 1934. *Ausgewählte Werke.* Breslau
Châtellier, Hildegard 1996. 'Wagnerismus in der Kaiserzeit', in Puschner 1996, 575–612
Chickering, Roger 1984. *'We Men Who Feel Most German'. A Cultural Study of the Pan-German League 1886–1914.* London
—— 1993. *Karl Lamprecht: A German Academic Life (1865–1915).* Atlantic Highlands, NJ
—— 1998. *Imperial Germany and the Great War, 1914–1918.* Cambridge
Clark, Chris 1996. 'The Wars of Liberation in Prussian Memory: Reflections on the Memorialization of War in Early Nineteenth-Century Germany' *Journal of Modern History,* Vol. 68, No. 3, 550–576
Class, Heinrich (published under the pseudonym Daniel Frymann) 1914. *Wenn ich der Kaiser wär' – Politische Wahrheiten und Notwendigkeiten,* 5th enlarged edn. Leipzig
—— 1932. *Wider den Strom. Vom Werden und Wachsen der nationalen Opposition im alten Reich.* Leipzig
Clausewitz, Carl von 1976. *On War,* ed. Michael Howard and Peter Paret. Princeton
Clemente, Steven E. 1992. *"Mit Gott! Für König und Kaiser!" A Critical Analysis of the Making of the Prussian Army Officer, 1860–1914.* New York
Cocks, Geoffrey and Konrad H. Jarausch, eds. 1990. *The German Professions, 1800–1950.* Oxford
Coetzee, Marylin Shevin 1990. *The German Army League: Popular Nationalism in Wilhelmine Germany.* New York
Confino, Alon 1997. *The Nation as a Local Metaphor: Württemberg, Imperial Germany, and National Memory.* Chapel Hill
Confino, Alon and Peter Fritzsche, eds. 2002. *The Works of Memory: New Directions in the Study of German Society and Culture.* Urbana
Conway, Daniel W. 1997. *Nietzsche and the Political.* London
—— 1997a. *Nietzsche's Dangerous Game.* Cambridge
Corni, Gustavo 1990. *Hitler and the Peasants. Agrarian Policy of the Third Reich.* New York
Corni, Gustavo and Horst Gies 1994. *"Blut und Boden". Rassenideologie und Agrarpolitik im Staat Hitlers.* Idstein
Dann, Otto, ed. 1984. *Vereinswesen und bürgerliche Gesellschaft in Deutschland* (= Historische Zeitung, Beiheft Neue Folge 9). Munich.
—— 1996. *Nation und Nationalismus in Deutschland 1770–1990.* 3rd edn. Munich
—— 2001. 'Schiller' in *Deutsche Erinnerungsorte,* ed. Etienne Francois and Hagen S. Schulze, Vol. 2. Munich, 171–186
——, ed. 2003. *Patriotismus und Nationsbildung am Ende des Heiligen Römischen Reiches.* Cologne
Darré, R. Walther 1929. *Das Bauerntum als Lebensquell der nordischen Rasse.* Munich
—— 1930. *Neuadel aus Blut und Boden.* Munich
—— 1940. *Um Blut und Boden. Reden und Aufsätze.* Munich
Deist, Wilhelm 1992. 'Verdeckter Militärstreik im Kriegsjahr 1918' in *Der Krieg des kleinen Mannes,* ed. Wolfram Wette. Munich, 146–167

Deutsche Reden in schwerer Zeit 1914/15. Ed Zentralstelle für Volkswohlfahrt und dem Verein für volkstümliche Kurse von Berliner Hochschullehrern, 3 Vols. Berlin

Diehl, James M. 1977. *Paramilitary Politics in Weimar Germany.* Bloomington

—— 2003. 'No More Peace: The Militarization of Politics' in *The Shadows of Total War. Europe, East Asia, and the United States, 1919–1939,* ed. Roger Chickering and Stig Förster. Cambridge, 97–112

Dinnebier, Antonia 1996. *Die Innenwelt der Außenwelt. Die schöne "Landschaft" als gesellschaftstheoretisches Problem.* Berlin

Dittmer, Lothar 1992. *Beamtenkonservativismus und Modernisierung. Untersuchungen zur Vorgeschichte der konservativen Partei in Preußen 1810–1848/49.* Stuttgart

Domarus, Max 1973. *Hitler. Reden und Proklamationen 1932–1945,* 4 Vols. Wiesbaden

Dominick III, Raymond H. 1992. *The Environmental Movement in Germany: Prophets and Pioneers, 1871–1971.* Bloomington

Dörner, Andreas 1996. *Politischer Mythos und symbolische Politik. Der Hermannmythos: zur Entstehung des Nationalbewußtseins der Deutschen.* Reinbek

Dowe, Dieter, et al., eds. 1998. *Europa 1848: Revolution und Reform.* Bonn

Drehsen, Volker and Walter Sparn, ed. 1996. *Krisenwahrnehmung und Krisenbewältigung um 1900.* Berlin

Dreyfus, H. and H. Hall, eds. 1992. *Heidegger: A Critical Reader.* Oxford

Düding, Dieter 1985. *Organisierter gesellschaftlicher Nationalismus in Deutschland (1808–1847): Bedeutung und Funktion der Turner- und Sängervereine für die deutsche Nationalbewegung.* Munich

Düding, Dieter, et. al., eds. 1988. *Öffentliche Festkultur: politische Feste in Deutschland von der Aufklärung bis zum Ersten Weltkrieg.* Reinbek

—— 1991. 'Die deutsche Nationalbewegung als Vereinsbewegung: Anmerkungen zu ihrer Struktur und Phänomenologie zwischen Befreiungskriegszeitalter und Reichsgründung' in *Geschichte in Wissenschaft und Unterricht,* 42, 601–24

Dülmen, Richard van 2002. *Poesie des Lebens. Eine Kulturgeschichte der deutschen Romantik 1795–1820,* Vol. 1: *Lebenswelten.* Cologne

Dupeux, Louis 1985. *"Nationalbolschewismus" in Deutschland 1919–1933. Kommunistische Strategie und konservative Dynamik.* Munich

Durkheim, Emile 1915. *The Elementary Forms of the Religious Life.* London

Echternkamp, Jörg 1998. *Der Aufstieg des deutschen Nationalismus 1770–1840.* Frankfurt/M.

Echternkamp, Jörg, et al., eds. 2002. *Die Politik der Nation.* Munich

Eckart, Dietrich 1924. *Der Bolschewismus von Moses bis Lenin: Zweigespräche zwischen Adolf Hitler und mir.* Munich

Eghigian, Greg 2002. 'Injury, Fate, Resentment, and Sacrifice in German Political Culture, 1914–1939' in *Sacrifice and National Belonging in Twentieth Century Germany,* ed. Greg Eghigian and Matthew Paul Berg. University of Texas, 90–117

Eickhoff, Volker and Ilse Korotin, eds. 1997. *Sehnsucht nach Schicksal und Tiefe. Der Geist der konservativen Revolution.* Vienna

Eidenbenz, Mathias 1993. *"Blut und Boden". Zu Funktion und Genese der Metaphern des Agrarismus und Biologismus in der nationalsozialistischen Bauernpropaganda R.W. Darrés.* Bern

Eksteins, M. 1990. *The Rites of Spring.* New York

Eley, Geoff 1980. *Reshaping the German Right. Radical Nationalism and Political Change after Bismarck.* New Haven

—— 1986. *From Unification to Nazism. Reinterpreting the German Past.* Boston
—— 1990. 'Conservatives and Radical Nationalists in Germany: the Production of Fascist Potentials', in *Fascists and Conservatives,* ed. Martin Blinkhorn. London, 50–70
—— 1996. 'Introduction', in *Society, Culture and the State in Germany, 1870–1930,* ed. Geoff Eley. Ann Arbor, 1–42
—— 1996a. 'Is All the World a Text? From Social History to the History of Society Two Decades Later' in *The Historic Turn in the Human Sciences,* ed. Terrence J. McDonald. Ann Arbor, 217–21
Elsaesser, Thomas 2000. *Metropolis.* London
Emmerich, Wolfgang 1971. *Zur Kritik der Volkstumsideologie.* Frankfurt/M.
Engels, Friedrich 1895. *Ludwig Feuerbach und der Ausgang der klassischen deutschen Philosophie.* 2nd edn. Stuttgart
Epstein, Klaus 1966. *The Genesis of German Conservatism.* Princeton
Evans, Richard J. 2003. *The Coming of the Third Reich.* London
—— 2005. *The Third Reich in Power.* London
Faber, Richard, ed. 1991. *Konservatismus in Geschichte und Gegenwart.* Würzburg
—— ed. 1997. *Politische Religion, religiöse Politik.* Würzburg
—— 2005. *„Wir sind Eines". Über politisch-religiöse Ganzheitsvorstellungen europäischer Faschismen.* Würzburg
Falter, Jürgen 1991. *Hitlers Wähler.* Munich
Falter, Jürgen and Reinhard Zintl 1988. 'The Economic Crisis of the 1930s and the Nazi Vote' *Journal of Interdisciplinary History* 19, 55–85
Farias, Victor 1989. *Heidegger and Nazism.* Philadelphia
Farquharson, John E. 1976. *The Plough and the Swastika. The NSDAP and Agriculture in Germany 1928–45.* London
Farrenkopf, John 2001. *Prophet of Decline: Spengler on World History and Politics.* Baton Rouge
Faulenbach, Bernd 1980. *Ideologie des deutschen Weges. Die deutsche Geschichte in der Historiographie zwischen Kaiserreich und Nationalsozialismus.* Munich
Felken, Detlef 1988. *Oswald Spengler. Konservativer Denker zwischen Kaiserreich und Diktatur.* Munich
Fest, Joachim 1972. *The Face of the Third Reich.* London
—— 1977. *Hitler.* London
Feuerbach, Ludwig 1983. *Das Wesen der Religion.* Heidelberg
—— 1988. *Das Wesen des Christentums.* Stuttgart
Fichte, Johann G. 1944. *Reden an die deutsche Nation* (Die philosphische Bibliothek, Vol. 204). Leipzig
——1846/1971. *Sämtliche Werke,* ed. J. H. Fichte. Berlin 1846/1971
Field, Geoffrey G. 1981. *Evangelist of Race. The Germanic Vision of Houston Stewart Chamberlain.* New York
Figal, Günter and Enno Rudolph 2000. *Kritik der Moderne von innen. Kulturkritik und Konservative Revolution. Internationale Zeitschrift für Philosophie,* No. 2
Fischer, Bernd 1995. *Das Eigene und das Eigentliche – Klopstock, Herder, Fichte, Kleist: Episoden aus der Konstruktionsgeschichte nationaler Intentionalitäten.* Berlin
Fischer, Conan 1995. *The Rise of the Nazis.* Manchester
Fischer, Fritz 1977. 'Der deutsche Protestantismus und die Politik im 19. Jahrhundert' in his *Der Erste Weltkrieg und das deutsche Geschichtsbild. Beiträge zur Bewältigung eines historischen Tabus.* Düsseldorf, 47 ff.

Fischer, Hugo 1934. 'Der deutsche Infanterist von 1917' in *Widerstand,* ed. Ernst Niekisch, January 1934, 6 ff.
Flasch, Kurt 2000. *Die geistige Mobilmachung. Die deutschen Intellektuellen und der Erste Weltkrieg.* Berlin
Flemming, Jens 1978. *Landwirtschaftliche Interessen und Demokratie. Ländliche Gesellschaft, Agrarverbände und Staat 1890–1925.* Bonn
Flex, Walter 1918. *Der Wanderer zwischen beiden Welten: Ein Kriegserlebnis.* Munich
Förster, Stig 1985. *Der doppelte Militarismus: Die deutsche Heeresrüstungspolitik zwischen Status-quo-Sicherung und Aggression, 1890–1913.* Stuttgart
—— 1999. 'Dreams and Nightmares: German Military Leadership and the Images of Future Warfare, 1871–1914' in *Anticipating Total War? The German and American Experiences, 1871–1914,* ed. Manfred F. Boemeke et al. Cambridge, 343–376
—— 2000. 'Im Reich des Absurden. Die Ursachen des Ersten Weltkriegs' in *Wie Kriege entstehen. Zum historischen Hintergund von Staatenkonflikten,* ed. Bernd Wegner. Paderborn, 211–252
Forum für Philosophie, ed. 1989. *Die Ideen von 1789 in der deutschen Rezeption.* Frankfurt/M.
Francois-Poncet, Andre 1949. *The Fateful Years: Memoirs of a French Ambassador in Berlin, 1931–1938,* trans. Jacques LeClerq. New York
Frank, Manfred 1982. *Vorlesungen über die Neue Mythologie,* Vol. 1: *Der kommende Gott.* Frankfurt/M.
—— 1988. *Vorlesungen über die neue Mythologie,* Vol. 2: *Gott im Exil.* Frankfurt/M.
Frankel, Richard E. 2005. *Bismarck's Shadow: the Cult of Leadership and the Transformation of the German Right.* Oxford
Frei, Norbert 1993. *National Socialist Rule in Germany: The Führer State 1933–1945.* Oxford
—— 2001. 'People's Community and War: Hitler's Popular Support" in *The Third Reich: Between Vision and Reality. New Perspectives on German History 1918–1945,* ed. Hans Mommsen. Oxford, 59–78
Freud, Sigmund 1915. 'Zeitgemässes über Krieg und Tod' in his *Studienausgabe,* Vol. 9, Frankfurt/M.: 1982, 33 ff.
—— 1930. 'Das Unbehagen in der Kultur' in his *Studienausgabe,* Vol. 9, Frankfurt/M. 1982, 191 ff.
—— 1933. 'Warum Krieg?' in his Freud, *Studienausgabe,* Vol. 9, Frankfurt/M. 1982, 271 ff.
Frevert, Ute 1988. *Women in German History. From Bourgeois Emancipation to Sexual Liberation.* Oxford
—— 1991. 'Bourgeois Honour: Middle Class Duellists in Germany' in *The German Bourgeoisie.* Ed. David Blackbourn and Richard Evans. London, 255–292
—— 1995. *Ehrenmänner: das Duell in der bürgerlichen Gesellschaft,* 2nd edn. Munich
—— 2001. *Die kasernierte Nation. Militärdienst und Zivilgesellschaft in Deutschland.* Munich
Fried, Ferdinand [synonym for Ferdinand Friedrich Zimmermann] 1931. *Das Ende des Kapitalismus.* Jena
Fried, Jochen 1985. *Die Symbolik des Realen: Über alte und neue Mythologie in der Frühromantik.* Munich
Friedländer, Saul 1993. *Reflections of Nazism: an Essay on Kitsch and Death,* 2nd edn. Bloomington

—— 1997. *Nazi Germany and the Jews.* New York
Friedländer, Saul and Jörn Rüsen, eds. 2000. *Richard Wagner im Dritten Reich.* Munich
Friedrichsmeyer, S. et al., eds. 1998. *The Imperialist Imagination: German Colonialism and its Legacy.* Ann Arbor
Fritsche, Johannes 1999. *Historical Destiny and National Socialism in Heidegger's "Being and Time".* Berkeley
Fritzsche, Peter 1990. *Rehearsals for Fascism. Populism and Political Mobilization in Weimar Germany.* Oxford
—— 1998. *Germans into Nazis.* Cambridge, Mass.
—— 2004. *Stranded in the Present. Modern Time and the Melancholy of History.* Cambridge, Mass.
Fromm, Erich 1980. *Arbeiter und Angestellte am Vorabend des Dritten Reiches.* Munich
Fuchs, Stephan 2004. *"Vom Segen des Krieges." Katholische Gebildete im Ersten Weltkrieg. Eine Studie zur Kriegsdeutung im akademischen Katholizismus.* Stuttgart
Fuller, Steven N. 1997. *The Nazis' Literary Grandfather. Adolf Bartels and Cultural Extremism, 1871–1945.* New York
Gall, Lothar 1985. *Bismarck, The White Revolutionary,* 2 Vols. London
Garber, Jörn 1976. *Kritik der Revolution. Theorien des deutschen Frühkonservatismus 1790–1810,* Vol. 1: *Dokumentation.* Kronberg/Ts.
Gay, Peter 1974. *Weimar Culture: the Outsider as Insider.* Harmondsworth
—— 1993. *The Cultivation of Hatred.* New York
Geary, Dick 2005. 'Working-Class Identities in the Third Reich' in *Nazism, War and Genocide. Essays in Honour of Jeremy Noakes,* ed. Neil Gregor. Exeter, 42–55.
Gellately, Robert 2001. *Backing Hitler. Consent and Coercion in Nazi Germany.* Oxford
Gellner, Ernest 1964. *Thought and Change.* London
Gerwarth, Robert 2005. *The Bismarck Myth. Weimar Germany and the Legacy of the Iron Chancellor.* Oxford
Geyer, Martin 1998. *Verkehrte Welt: Revolution, Inflation und Moderne, München 1914–1924.* Göttingen
Geyer, Michael 1988. *Aufrüstung oder Sicherheit? Die Reichswehr in der Krise der Machtpolitik 1924–1936.* Wiesbaden
—— 2002. '"There Is a Land Where Everything Is Pure: Its Name Is Land of Death": Some Observations on Catastrophic Nationalism' in *Sacrifice and National Belonging in Twentieth-Century Germany,* ed. Greg Eghigian et al. University of Texas, 18–47
Geyer, Michael and Konrad Jarausch 2002. *Shattered Past: Reconstructing German Histories.* Princeton
Goebbels, Joseph 1931. *Michael. Ein deutsches Schicksal in Tagebuchblättern.* 10th edn. Munich
—— 1934. *Signale der Zeit. 25 ausgewählte Reden.* Munich
—— 1939. 'Rede zur Eröffnung der Automobilausstellung Berlin am 17.2.1939' in *Deutsche Technik,* März 1939, 105 f.
—— 1987. *Die Tagebücher [diaries] von Joseph Goebbels. Sämtliche Fragmente,* Part 1: *Aufzeichungen 1924–1941,* ed. Elke Fröhlich, 4 Vols. Munich
—— 1991. *Goebbels Reden 1932–1945,* ed. Helmut Heiber. Bindlach
Goedel, Denis 1984. *Moeller van den Bruck (1876–1925) un nationaliste contre la révolution.* Frankfurt/M.

Goldhagen, Daniel J. 1997. *Hitler's Willing Executioners. Ordinary Germans and the Holocaust.* New York
Gollwitzer, Heinz 1972 and 1982. *Die Geschichte des weltpolitischen Denkens,* 2 Vols. Göttingen
Golomb, Jacob and Robert S. Wistrich, eds. 2002. *Nietzsche, Godfather of Fascism? On the Uses and Abuses of a Philosophy.* Princeton
Goodrick-Clarke, Nicholas 1992. *The Occult Roots of Nazism. Secret Aryan Cults and their Influence on Nazi Ideology. The Ariosophists of Austria and Germany, 1890–1935,* 2nd edn. London
Götz von Olenhusen, Irmtraud 1987. *Jugendreich, Gottesreich, Deutsches Reich. Junge Generation, Religion und Politik 1928–1933.* Cologne
—— 1993. 'Vom Jungstahlhelm zur SA: Die junge Nachkriegsgeneration in den paramilitärischen Verbänden der Weimarer Republik' in *Politische Jugend in der Weimarer Republik,* ed, Wolfgang R. Krabbe. Bochum, 146–171
Graf, Friedrich Wilhelm 1996. 'Das Laboratorium der religiösen Moderne. Zur "Verlagsreligion" des Eugen Diederichs Verlags' in Hübinger 1996a, 243–298.
—— 2000. 'Die Nation – von Gott erfunden? Kritische Randnotizen zum Theologiebedarf der historischen Nationalismusforschung' in: Krumeich and Lehmann 2000, 285–317
Graf, Gerhard 1993. *Gottesbild und Politik. Eine Studie zur Frömmigkeit in Preußen während der Befreiungskriege 1813–1815.* Göttingen
Greenfeld, Liah 1992. *Nationalism: Five Roads to Modernity.* Cambridge, Mass.
Gregor, Neil 2005. 'Nazism – A Political Religion? Rethinking the Voluntarist Turn' in *Nazism, War and Genocide. Essays in Honour of Jeremy Noakes,* ed. Neil Gregor. Exeter, 1–21
Gregor-Dellin, Martin 2001. *Richard Wagner. Sein Leben. Sein Werk. Sein Jahrhundert,* 4th edn. Munich
Greiffenhagen, Martin 1986. *Das Dilemma des Konservativismus in Deutschland.* Frankfurt/M.
Greiling, Werner 2003. *Der Bismarckturm. Bürgerschaftliches Engagement und nationale Denkmalkultur.* Hain
Greverus, Ina-Marie 1991. *Auf der Suche nach Heimat.* Munich
Grießmer, Axel 2000. *Massenverbände und Massenparteien im Wilhelminischen Reich. Zum Wandel der Wahlkultur 1903–1912.* Düsseldorf
Griffin, Roger, ed. 2005. *Fascism, Totalitarianism and Political Religion.* London
Grimm, Jakob 1884. 'Über die wechselseitigen Beziehungen und die Verbindungen der Drei in der Versammlung vertretenen Wissenschaften' in Jakob Grimm and Wilhelm Grimm, *Werke,* Vol. 7, 553–559
Groh, Ruth 1998. *Arbeit an der Heillosikkeit der Welt: Zur politisch-theologischen Mythologie und Anthropologie Carl Schmitts.* Frankfurt/M.
Groh, Ruth and Dieter Groh 1991. *Weltbildung, Naturaneignung. Zur Kulturgeschichte der Natur.* Frankfurt/M.
—— 1996. *Die Innenwelt der Außenwelt.* Frankfurt/M.
Gröning, Gert and Joachim Wolschke-Bulmahn 1987. *Die Liebe zur Landschaft,* Part 3: *Der Drang nach Osten. Zur Entwicklung der Landespflege im Nationalsozialismus und während des Zweiten Weltkrieges in den "eingegliederten" Ostgebieten.* Munich
Gross, Raphael 2000. *Carl Schmitt und die Juden: eine deutsche Rechtslehre.* Frankfurt/M.

Großheim, Michael 1995. *Ökologie oder Technokratie? Der Konservatismus in der Moderne.* Berlin
Gründel, Günther 1933. *Die Sendung der jungen Generation. Versuch einer umfassenden revolutionären Sinndeutung der Krise.* Munich
Gumbel, Emil J. 1980. *Vier Jahre politischer Mord: und Denkschrift des Reichsjustizministers zu "Vier Jahre politischer Mord"*, with an introduction by Hans Thiel. Heidelberg
Habermas, Jürgen 1984 and 1987. *The Theory of Communicative Action*, 2 Vols. London
—— 1992. 'Work and Weltanschauung: The Heidegger Controversy from a German Perspective' in *Heidegger. A Critical Reader*, ed. H. Dreyfus and H. Hall.Oxford
—— 2003. 'Glauben und Wissen' in his *Zeitdiagnosen. Zwölf Essays.* Frankfurt/M., 249–262
—— 2004. 'Fundamentalismus und Terror' in his *Der gespaltene Westen.* Frankfurt/M., 11–31
—— 2005. *Zwischen Naturalismus und Religion. Philosophische Aufsätze.* Frankfurt/M.
Hagemann, Karen 2002. *"Mannlicher Muth und Teutsche Ehre". Nation, Militär und Geschlecht zur Zeit der antinapoleonischen Kriege Preußens.* Paderborn
Hagemann, Karen et al., eds. 2002. *Home / Front: The Military, War and Gender in Twentieth-Century Germany.* Oxford
Hagenlücke, Heinz 1997. *Deutsche Vaterlandspartei. Die nationale Rechte am Ende des Kaiserreichs.* Düsseldorf
Hahn, H. J. 2001. *The 1848 Revolutions in German-Speaking Europe.* London
Hamann, Brigitte 2003. *Winifred Wagner oder Hitlers Bayreuth*, 2nd edn. Munich
Hammer, Karl 1971. *Deutsche Kriegstheologie (1870–1918).* Munich
Hammersen, Nicolai 1993. *Politisches Denken im Deutschen Widerstand. Ein Beitrag zur Wirkungsgeschichte neokonservativer Ideologien 1914–1944.* Berlin
Hardensett, Heinrich 1932. *Der kapitalistische und der technische Mensch.* Munich
Hardtwig, Wolfgang 1990. *Geschichtskultur und Wissenschaft.* Munich
—— 1994. *Nationalismus und Bürgerkultur in Deutschland 1500–1914. Ausgewählte Aufsätze.* Göttingen
Harrison, Mark, ed. 1998. *The economics of World War II. Six Great Powers in International Comparison.* Cambridge
Härtle, Heinrich 1937. *Nietzsche und der Nationalsozialismus.* Munich
Hartwich, Wolf Daniel 2000. *"Deutsche Mythologie". Die Erfindung einer nationalen Kunstreligion.* Berlin
Haß, Ulrike 1993. *Militante Pastorale: Zur Literatur der antimodernen Bewegungen im frühen 20. Jahrhundert.* Munich
Hau, Michael 2003. *The Cult of Health and Beauty in Germany. A Social History, 1890–1930.* Chicago
Hayman, Ronald 1995. *Nietzsche: Critical Life*, 3rd edn. London
Heer, Friedrich 1989. *Der Glaube des Adolf Hitler. Anatomie einer politischen Religiösität.* Frankfurt/M.
Heidegger, Martin 1956. *Zur Seinsfrage.* Frankfurt/M.
—— 1961. *An Introduction to Metaphysics.* New York
—— 1962. *Being and Time.* London
—— 1971. 'The Origin of the Work of Art' in Heidegger, *Poetry, Language, Thought.* New York
—— 1971a. *Poetry, Language, Thought.* New York

—— 1977. *Nietzsche,* 4 Vols. San Francisco
—— 1978. 'The Question Concerning Technology' in *Martin Heidegger: Basic Writings,* ed. David F. Krell. London, 283–318
—— 1978a. 'Letter on "Humanism"' in *Martin Heidegger. Basic Writings.* Ed. David F. Krell. London, 189–242
—— 1979. *Prolegomena zur Geschichte des Zeitbegriffs.* Frankfurt/M.
—— 1989. *Hitherto Unpublished Heidegger Sources in Victor Farias, Heidegger and Nazism,* ed. Joseph Margolis and Tom Rockmore. Philadelphia
—— 1990. 'Bauen Wohnen Denken' in Heidegger, *Vorträge und Aufsätze.* 6th edn. Pfullingen, 139–156
—— 1991. 'The Self-Assertion of the German University' in Wolin 1991, 29–39
—— 1991a. '"Only a God Can Save Us". Der Spiegel's Interview with Martin Heidegger' in Wolin 1991, 91–116
—— 1999. *Gelassenheit,* 11th. edn. Stuttgart
—— 2000. *Gesamtausgabe,* Vol. 16: *Reden und andere Zeugnisse eines Lebensweges.* Frankfurt/M.
—— 2002. *Off the Beaten Track (Holzwege),* ed. and translated Julian Young and Kenneth Haynes. Cambridge
—— 2004. *Gesamtausgabe. Zu Ernst Jünger. IV. Abteilung: Hinweise und Aufzeichnungen,* Vol. 90. Frankfurt/M.
Hein, Annette 1996. *"Es ist viel 'Hitler' in Wagner". Rassismus und antisemitische Deutschtumsideologie in den "Bareuther Blättern" (1878–1938).* Tübingen
Hein, Peter Ulrich 1992. *Die Brücke ins Geisterreich. Künstlerische Avantgarde zwischen Kulturkritik und Faschismus.* Reinbek
Heller, Friedrich Paul and Anton Maegerle 1998. *Thule. Vom völkischen Okkultismus bis zur neuen Rechten,* 2nd edn. Stuttgart
Hentschel, Willibald 1904. *Mittgart: Ein Weg zur Erneuerung der germanischen Rasse.* Leipzig
Hepp, Corona 1987. *Avantgarde. Moderne Kunst, Kulturkritik und Reformbewegungen nach der Jahrhundertwende.* Munich
Herbert, Ulrich 1991. 'Generation der Sachlichkeit". Die völkische Studentenbewegung der frühen zwanziger Jahre in Deutschland' in *Zivilisation und Barbarei,* ed. Frank Bajohr et al. Hamburg, 115–144
—— 1995. *Arbeit, Volkstum, Weltanschauung. Über Fremde und Deutsche im 20. Jahrhundert.* Frankfurt/M.
—— 1996. *Best. Biographische Studie über Radikalismus, Weltanschauung und Vernunft, 1903–1989.* Bonn
—— 1996a. 'The Real Mystery in Germany. The German Working Class during the Nazi Dictatorship' in *Confronting the Nazis Past. New Debates on Modern German History,* ed. Michael Burleigh. London, 23–36
Herder, Johann Gottfried 1877. 'Vom neuern Gebrauch der Mythologie' in *Herders Sämmtliche Werke,* ed. Bernhard Suphan, Vol. 1. Berlin
—— 1877a: 'Germanien' in *Herders Sämmtliche Werke,* Vol. 29. 210–212
—— 1883. 'Iduna, oder der Apfel der Verjüngung' in *Herders Sämmtliche Werke,* ed. Bernhard Suphan, Vol. 18. Berlin, 483–502
—— 1995. *Ideen zur Philosophie der Geschichte der Menschheit.* Bodenheim
Herf, Jeffrey 1984. *Reactionary Modernism. Technology, Culture, and Politics in Weimar and the Third Reich.* Cambridge

Hermand, Jost 1981. *Orte. Irgendwo. Formen utopischen Denkens.* Königstein i. Taunus
—— 1992. *Old Dreams of a New Reich: Volkish Utopias and National Socialism.* Bloomington
—— ed. 1996. *Heimat, Nation, Fatherland: The German Sense of Belonging.* New York
Hermann, Arthur 1998. *Propheten des Niedergangs. Der Endzeitmythos im westlichen Denken.* Hamburg
Hermann, Ingo 2003. *Hardenberg: Der Reformkanzler.* Berlin
Heß, Rudolf 1987. *Briefe 1908–1933,* ed. Wolf R. Heß, with an introduction and comments by Dirk Bavendamm. Munich
Hielscher, Friedrich 1931. *Das Reich.* Berlin
Hildebrand, Klaus, ed. 2003. *Zwischen Politik und Religion. Studien zur Entstehung, Existenz und Wirkung des Totalitarismus.* Munich
Hitler, Adolf 1973. *Mein Kampf,* trans. Ralph Manheim, with an introduction by D. C. Watt, paperback edn. London
—— 1961. *Hitlers zweites Buch. Ein Dokument aus dem Jahr 1928,* ed. Gerhard Weinberger. Stuttgart
—— 1980. *Sämtliche Aufzeichnungen 1905–1924,* ed. Eberhard Jäckel. Stuttgart
—— 1981. *Hitlers politisches Testament. Die Bormann-Diktate von Februar und April 1945,* ed. Hugh R. Trevor-Roper and André Francois-Poncet. Hamburg
—— 1992 ff. *Reden, Schriften, Anordnungen. Februar 1925–März 1933,* ed. Institut für Zeitgeschichte, Vol. 1 ff. Munich
—— 1999. *Hitlers Tischgespräche im Führerhauptquartier,* ed. Henry Picker, 3rd edn. Berlin
—— 2000. *Monologe im Führerhauptquartier 1941–1944,* recorded by Heinrich Heim, ed. and commented by Werner Jochmann. Munich
Hobsbawm, Eric and Terence Ranger, eds. 1983. *The Invention of Tradition.* Cambridge
Hockert, Hans Günter 2003. 'War der Nationalsozialismus eine politische Religion? Über Chancen und Grenzen eines Erklärungsmodells' in *Zwischen Politik und Religion,* ed. Klaus Hildebrand. Munich, 45–72
Hoeges, Dirk 1994. *Kontroverse am Abgrund: Ernst Robert Curtius und Karl Mannheim.* Frankfurt/M.
Hoeres, Peter 2004. *Krieg der Philosophen: Die deutsche und die britische Philosophie im Ersten Weltkrieg.* Paderborn
Hof, Walter 1974. *Der Weg zum heroischen Realismus. Pessimismus und Nihilismus in der deutschen Literatur von Hamerling bis Benn.* Bebenhausen
Hofmannsthal, Hugo von 1927. *Das Schrifttum als geistiger Raum der Nation.* Munich
Holz, Klaus 2001. *Nationaler Antisemitismus. Wissenssoziologie einer Weltanschauung.* Hamburg
Hoover, Arlie J. 1986. *The Gospel of Nationalism. German Patriotic Preaching from Napoleon to Versailles.* Stuttgart
Hope, Nicholas 1995. *German and Scandinavian Protestantism, 1700–1918.* Oxford
Horne, John and Alan Kramer 2001. *German Atrocities: a History of Denial.* New Haven
Horstmann, Axel 1979. 'Der Mythosbegriff vom frühen Christentum bis zur Gegenwart' *Archiv für Begriffsgeschichte* 23, 7–54 and 197–245
Höss, Rudolf 1995. *Commandant of Auschwitz. The Autobiography of Rudolf Hoess,* trans. by Constantine FitzGibbon, introduced by Primo Levi. London
Höver, Ulrich 1992. *Joseph Goebbels – ein nationaler Sozialist.* Bonn

Hübinger, Gangolf 1994. *Kulturprotestantismus und Politik.* Tübingen
— 1996. 'Der Verlag Eugen Diederichs in Jena. Wissenschaftskritik, Lebensreform und völkische Bewegung' *Geschichte und Gesellschaft* 22, 31–45
— ed. 1996a. *Versammlungsort moderner Geister. Der Eugen Diederichs Verlag – Aufbruch ins Jahrhundert der Extreme.* Munich
— 1996b. 'Eugen Diederichs Bemühungen um die Grundlegung einer neuen Geisteskultur' in Mommsen 1996, 259–274
— 1998. 'Geschichtsmythen in "völkischer Bewegung" und "konservativer Revolution". Nationalistische Wirkungen historischer Sinnbildung' in *Dimensionen der Historik. Geschichtstheorie, Wissenschaftsgeschichte und Geschichtskultur heute. Jörn Rüsen zum 60. Geburtstag*, ed. Horst Walter Blanke et al. Köln, 93–104
Hübinger, Gangolf and Wolfgang J. Mommsen, eds. 1993. *Intellektuelle im Deutschen Kaiserreich.* Frankfurt/M.
Hughes, Michael 1988. *Nationalism and Society. Germany 1800–1945.* London
Humboldt, Wilhelm von 1903–1936. *Gesammelte Schriften*, ed. Bruno Gebhardt. Berlin
Humboldt, Wilhelm von and Caroline von Humboldt 1968. *Wilhelm und Caroline von Humboldt in ihren Briefen*, ed. Anna von Sydow. Osnabrück
Hürten, Heinz 1992. *Deutsche Katholiken 1918–1945.* Paderborn
Hutton, Christopher 1999. *Linguistics and the Third Reich: Mother-Tongue Fascism, Race, and the Science of Language.* London
Hyderhoff, J. and P. Wentzke, eds. *Deutscher Liberalismus im Zeitalter Bismarcks – Eine politische Briefsammlung.* Bonn
Izenberg, Gerald N. 1992. *Impossible Individuality: Romanticism, Revolution, and the Origins of Modern Selfhood, 1787–1802.* Princeton
Jäckel, Eberhard 1981. *Hitler's World View: a Blueprint for Power.* Cambridge, Mass.
Jahn, Friedrich Ludwig 1884. *Werke*, ed. C. Euler. Hof
James, Harold 1991. *A German Identity: 1770 to the Present Day.* London
Jamme, Christoph 1991. *"Gott hat ein Gewand an": Grenzen und Perspektiven philosophischer Mythos-Theorien der Gegenwart.* Frankfurt
— 1991a. *Einführung in die Philosophie des Mythos.* Vol. 2: *Neuzeit und Gegenwart.* Darmstadt
Jarausch, Konrad H. 1982. *Students, Society and Politics in Imperial Germany.* Princeton
— 1984. *Deutsche Studenten 1800–1970.* Frankfurt/M.
Jasper, Gotthard 1986. *Die gescheiterte Zähmung. Wege zur Machtergreifung Hitlers 1930–1934.* Frankfurt/M.
Jaspers, Karl 1977. *Philosophische Autobiographie. Erweiterte Neuausgabe.* Munich
— 1979. *Die geistige Situation der Zeit.* Berlin
Jay, Martin 1988. 'Should Intellectual History Take a Linguistic Turn? Reflections on the Habermas-Gadamer Debate', in his *Fin-de-Siecle Socialism.* Ch. 2. New York
Jefferies, Matthew 2003. *Imperial Culture in Germany, 1871–1918.* Basingstoke
— 2006. '"For a Genuine and Noble Nakedness"? German Naturism in the Third Reich' *German History*, Vol. 24, No 1, 62–84
Jeismann, Michael 1992. *Vaterland der Feinde. Studien zum nationalen Feindbegriff und Selbstverständnis.* Stuttgart
Joas, Hans 2000. *Kriege und Werte. Studien zur Gewaltgeschichte des 20. Jahrhunderts.* Weilerswist
John, Hartmut 1981. *Das Reserveoffizierskorps im Deutschen Kaiserreich.* Frankfurt/M.

Jones, Nigel H. 1987. *Hitler's Heralds. The Story of the Freikorps 1918–1923.* London
Jung, Edgar 1930. *Die Herrschaft der Minderwertigen, ihr Zerfall und Ihre Ablösung durch ein Neues Reich.* 2nd edn. Berlin
Jünger, Ernst 1922. *Der Kampf als inneres Erlebnis.* Berlin
—— 1925. *Das Wäldchen 1925. Eine Chronik aus den Grabenkämpfen 1918.* Berlin
—— 1929. *Das Abenteuerliche Herz. Aufzeichnungen bei Tag und Nacht.* Berlin
—— 1930. 'Die totale Mobilmachung' in *Krieg und Krieger*, ed. Ernst Jünger. Berlin, 9–30
—— 1932. *Der Arbeiter. Herrschaft und Gestalt.* Hamburg
—— 1978. 'Sturm' in his *Sämtliche Werke*, Vol. 15. Stuttgart
—— 2001. *Politische Publizistik 1919–1933.* Stuttgart
Jünger, Friedrich Georg 1930. 'Krieg und Krieger' in *Krieg und Krieger*, ed. Ernst Jünger. Berlin, 51–67
Karow, Yvonne 1997. *Deutsches Opfer. Kultische Selbstauslöschung auf den Reichsparteitagen der NSDAP.* Berlin
Kater, Michael H. 1971. 'Die Artamanen. Völkische Jugend in der Weimarer Republik' *Historische Zeitschrift* 213, 577–638
—— 2003. *Das "Ahnenerbe" der SS 1935–1945. Ein Beitrag zur Kulturpolitik des Dritten Reiches*, 3rd edn. Munich
Katz, Jacob 1986. *The Darker Side of Genius: Richard Wagner's Anti-Semitism.* Hanover
—— 1988. *Aus dem Ghetto in die bürgerliche Gesellschaft. Jüdische Emanzipation 1770 bis 1870.* Frankfurt/M.
Kedourie, Elie 1993. *Nationalism*, 4th edn. Oxford
Kehr, Eckart 1976. *Das Primat der Innenpolitik. Gesammelte Aufsätze zur preußisch-deutschen Sozialgeschichte im 19. und 20. Jahrhundert*, ed. Hans-Ulrich Wehler, 2nd edn. Frankfurt/M.
Kennan, George F. 1979. *The Decline of Bismarck's European Order.* Princeton
Kennedy, Ellen 2004. *Constitutional Failure: Carl Schmitt in Weimar.* Durham
Kershaw, Ian 1981. 'The Persecution of the Jews and German Popular Opinion in the Third Reich' *Yearbook of the Leo Baeck Institute*, 26, 261–89
—— 1987. *Popular Opinion and Political Dissent in the Third Reich. Bavaria, 1933–1945.* Munich
—— 1989. *The "Hitler Myth". Image and Reality in the Third Reich.* 2nd edn. Oxford
—— ed. 1990. *Weimar: Why did German Democracy Fail?* London
—— 1998. *Hitler*, Vol. 1: *1889–1936: Hubris.* London
—— 2000. *Hitler.* Vol. 2: *1936–1945: Nemesis.* London
—— 2000a. *The Nazi Dictatorship. Problems and Perspectives of Interpretation.* 4th edn. London
Ketelsen, Uwe-K. 1976. *Völkisch-nationale und nationalsozialistische Literatur in Deutschland 1890–1945.* Stuttgart
Kettenacker, Lothar 1983. 'Der Mythos vom Reich' in *Mythos und Moderne*, ed. Karl Heinz Bohrer. Frankfurt/M., 261–289
King, John 2003. *"Wann hat dieser Scheißkrieg ein Ende?" Writing and Rewriting the First World War.* Schnellroda
Kipper, Rainer 2002. *Der Germanenmythos im Deutschen Kaiserreich. Formen und Funktionen historischer Selbstthematisierung.* Göttingen
Klages, Ludwig 1974. 'Mensch und Erde' in his *Sämtliche Werke*, Vol. 3. Bonn, 614–636

Kleist, Heinrich von 1923 ff.. *Gesammelte Werke*, ed. Heinrich Deiters. Berlin

—— 1965. 'Über das Marionettentheater' in his *Sämliche Werke und Briefe*, ed. Helmut Sembdner. Vol. 2, 4th edn. Munich, 338–345

Klemperer, Klemens. von 1968. *Germany's New Conservatism. Its History and Dilemma in the Twentieth Century*, 2. edn. Princeton

Klemperer, Victor 2000. *The Language of the Third Reich: LTI, Lingua Tertii Imperii: a Philologist's Note Book*, trans. Martin Brady. London

Klepsch, Thomas 1990. *Nationalsozialistische Ideologie. Eine Beschreibung ihrer Struktur vor 1933*. Münster

Klinger, Cornelia 1995. *Flucht, Trost, Revolte. Die Moderne und ihre ästhetischen Gegenwelten*. Munich

Klugen, Alexander von 1938. *Die Absage an die Romantik in der Zeit nach dem Weltkriege. Zur Geschichte des deutschen Menschen*. Berlin

Kocka, Jürgen 1984. *Facing Total War: German Society, 1914–1918*. Leamington Spa

Köhler, Joachim 2000. *Wagner's Hitler: the Prophet and his Disciple*. Cambridge

—— 2004. *Richard Wagner: the Last of the Titans*. New Haven

Kohn, Hans 1965. *The Mind of Germany: The Education of a Nation*. New York

—— 1967. *The Idea of Nationalism*. 2nd edn. New York

Kondylis, Panajotis 1979. *Die Entstehung der Dialektik: eine Analyse der geistigen Entwicklung von Hölderlin, Schelling und Hegel bis 1802*. Stuttgart

—— 1981. *Die Aufklärung im Rahmen des neuzeitlichen Rationalismus*. Stuttgart

—— 1986. *Konservativismus. Geschichtlicher Gehalt und Untergang*. Stuttgart

Konersmann, Rolf, ed. 2001. *Kulturkritik. Reflexionen in der veränderten Welt*. Leipzig

Koonz, Claudia 2003. *The Nazi Conscience*. Cambridge

Korinman, Michel 1999. *Deutschland über alles: le pangermanisme*. Paris

Koselleck, Reinhart 1981. *Preußen zwischen Reform und Revolution. Allgemeines Landrecht, Verwaltung und soziale Bewegung von 1791–1848*, 3rd edn. Stuttgart

—— 1985. *Futures Past: On the Semantics of Historical Time*. Cambridge

Koselleck, Reinhard, et al., eds. 1994. *Der politische Totenkult. Kriegerdenkmäler in der Moderne*. Munich

Koshar, Rudy 1998. *Germany's Transient Pasts: Preservation and National Memory in the Twentieth Century*. Chapel Hill

—— 2000. *From Monuments to Traces: Artifacts of German Memory, 1870–1990*. Berkeley

Kraus, Hans-Christof 1993. 'Altkonservatismus und moderne politische Rechte. Zum Problem der Kontinuität rechter politischer Strömungen in Deutschland' in *Weltbürgerkrieg der Ideologien. Antworten an Ernst Nolte. Festschrift zum 70. Geburtstag*, ed. Thomas Nipperdey et al. Berlin, 99–121

—— 1995. *Ernst Ludwig von Gerlach. Politisches Denken und Handeln eines preußischen Altkonservativen*, 2 Vols. Göttingen

—— ed. 1995a. *Konservative Politiker in Deutschland. Eine Auswahl biographischer Portraits aus zwei Jahrhunderten*. Berlin

—— 1997. 'Politisches Denken der deutschen Spätromantik' *Literaturwissenschaftliches Jahrbuch* 38, 111–146

—— 2000. *Bismarck und die preußischen Konservativen*. Friedrichsruh

—— ed. 2003. *Konservative Zeitschriften zwischen Kaiserreich und Diktatur*. Berlin

Krebs, Diethart and Jürgen Reulecke, eds. 1998. *Handbuch der deutschen Reformbewegungen 1880–1933*. Wuppertal

Krieger, Leonard 1957. *The German Idea of Freedom: History of a Political Tradition*, 2nd edn. Chicago

Krüger, Peter 1991. 'Etzels Halle und Stalingrad: Die Rede Görings vom 30.1.1943' in *Die Niebelungen: Ein deutscher Wahn, ein deutscher Alptraum*, ed. Joachim Heinzle et. al. Frankfurt/M., 151–190

Krumeich, Gerd and Hartmut Lehmann, eds. 2000. *"Gott mit uns". Nation, Religion und Gewalt im 19. und frühen 20. Jahrhundert.* Göttingen

Kunz, Georg 2000. *Verortete Geschichte: Regionales Geschichtsbewußtsein in den deutschen Historischen Vereinen des 19. Jahrhunderts.* Göttingen

Kupisch, Karl, ed. 1965. *Quellen zur Geschichte des deutschen Protestantismus 1871–1945.* Munich

Krockow, Christian Graf von 1990. *Die Entscheidung: eine Untersuchung über Ernst Jünger, Carl Schmitt, Martin Heidegger.* 2nd edn. Frankfurt/M.

—— 2001. *Hitler und seine Deutschen.* Munich

Kroll, Frank-Lothar 1998. *Utopie als Ideologie. Geschichtsdenken und politisches Handeln im Dritten Reich.* Paderborn

Lagarde, Paul de 1920. *Deutsche Schriften. Gesammtausgabe letzter Hand.* 5th edn. Göttingen

Langbehn, August Julius 1922. *Rembrandt als Erzieher. Von einem Deutschen.* 56th edn. Leipzig

Langewiesche, Dieter 1989. 'Bildungsbürgertum und Liberalismus im 19. Jahrhundert' in *Bildungsbürgertum im 19. Jahrhundert*, Part 4: *Politischer Einfluß und gesellschaftliche Formation*, ed. Jürgen Kocka. Stuttgart, 95–121

—— 1992. 'Reich, Nation und Staat in der jüngeren Deutschen Geschichte' in *Historische Zeitung* 254, 341–381

—— 2000. *Liberalism in Germany.* London

——, ed. 2001a. *Die Revolution von 1848 in der Europäischen Geschichte.* Munich

Langewiesche, Dieter and Georg Schmidt, eds. 2000. *Föderative Nation. Deutschlandkonzepte von der Reformation bis zum Ersten Weltkrieg.* Munich

Large, David Clay 1997. *Where Ghosts Walked: Munich's Road to the Third Reich.* New York

Latour, Bruno 1993. *We Have Never Been Modern.* Hempstead

Leed, E.J. 1979. *No Man's Land. Combat and Identity in World War I.* Cambridge

Lees, Andrew 1985. *Cities Perceived. Urban Society in European and American Thought, 1820–1940.* Manchester

—— 2002. *Cities, Sin, and Social Reform in Imperial Germany.* Ann Arbor

Lehmann, Hartmut, ed. 1997. *Säkularisierung, Dechristianisierung, Rechristianisierung im neuzeitlichen Europa: Bilanz und Perspektiven der Forschung.* Göttingen

Leiser, Erwin 1989. *"Deutschland erwache!" Propaganda im Film des Dritten Reiches.* Reinbek

Lekan, Thomas M. 2004. *Imagining the Nation in Nature. Landscape Preservation and German Identity, 1885–1945.* Cambridge, Mass.

Lenger, Friedrich 1994. *Werner Sombart 1863–1941. Eine Biographie.* Munich

—— 1996. 'Werner Sombart als Propagandist eines deutschen Krieges' in Mommsen 1996, 65–76

Lenk, Kurt 1989. *Deutscher Konservatismus.* Frankfurt/M.

—— 1994. *Rechts, wo die Mitte ist. Studien zur Ideologie: Rechtsextremismus, Nationalsozialismus, Konservatismus.* Baden-Baden

Lenman, Robin 1997. *Artists and Society in Germany, 1850–1914.* Manchester
Lepsius, M. Rainer 1973. 'Parteisystem und Sozialstruktur: zum Problem der Demokratisierung der deutschen Gesellschaft' in *Deutsche Parteien vor 1918,* ed. Gerhard Ritter, Cologne
—— 1986. 'Charismatic Leadership. Max Weber's Model and Its Applicability to the Rule of Hitler' in *Changing Conceptions of Leadership,* ed. Carl F. Graumann and Serge Moscovici, New York
—— 1990. 'Nation und Nationalismus in Deutschland' in his *Interessen, Ideen, Institutionen.* Opladen, 232–246
—— 1992. 'Das Bildungsbürgertum als ständische Vergesellschaftung' in *Bildungsbürgertum im 19. Jahrhundert,* Part III: *Lebensführung und ständische Vergesellschaftung,* ed. M. Rainer Lepsius, Stuttgart, 8–18
—— 1993. *Demokratie in Deutschland: soziologisch-historische Konstellationsanalysen: ausgewählte Aufsätze.* Göttingen
Leske, Monika 1990. *Philosophen im "Dritten Reich": Studie zu Hochschul- und Philosophiebetrieb im faschistischen Deutschland.* Berlin
Lethen, Helmut 2002. *Cool Conduct: the Culture of Distance in Weimar Germany.* Berkeley
Ley, Michael and Julius H. Schoeps, eds. 1997. *Der Nationalsozialismus als politische Religion.* Bodenheim b. Mainz
Liepmann, Moritz 1930. *Krieg und Kriminalität in Deutschland.* Stuttgart
Link, Jürgen and Wulf Wülffing 1991. *Nationale Mythen und Symbole in der zweiten Hälfte des 19. Jahrhunderts.* Stuttgart
Linse, Ulrich 1983. *Barfüßige Philosophen. Erlöser der zwanziger Jahre.* Berlin
Lipp, Anne 2003. *Meinungslenkung im Krieg. Kriegserfahrungen deutscher Soldaten und ihre Deutung 1914–1918.* Göttingen
Liulevicius, Vejas Gabriel 2000. *War Land on the Eastern Front. Culture, National Identity and German Occupation in World War I.* Cambridge
Lohalm, Uwe 1970. *Völkischer Radikalismus. Die Geschichte des Deutschvölkischen Schutz- und Trutz-Bundes 1919–1923.* Hamburg
Longerich, Peter 1989. *Die braunen Bataillone. Geschichte der SA.* Munich
Losurdo, Domenico 1995. *Die Gemeinschaft, der Tod, das Abendland. Heidegger und die Kriegsideologie.* Stuttgart
Löwith, Karl 1983. *Weltgeschichte und Heilsgeschehen. Zur Kritik der Geschichtsphilosophie.* Stuttgart
—— 1986. *Von Hegel zu Nietzsche.* 9th edn. Hamburg
—— 1986a. *My Life in Germany Before and After 1933.* Urbana
Lübbe, Hermann 1963. *Politische Philosophie in Deutschland. Studien zu ihrer Geschichte.* Basel
Lüdtke, Alf 1994. 'The "Honor of Labor": Industrial Workers and the Power of Symbols under National Socialism' in *Nazism and German Society,* ed. David Crew, 67–109
—— ed. 1996. *Amerikanisierung. Traum und Alptraum im Deutschland des 20. Jahrhunderts.* Stuttgart
Lukács, Georg 1962. *Die Zerstörung der Vernunft.* Neuwied
Maengel, Manfred 2005. *Das Wissen des Kriegers oder der magische Operateur. Krieg und Technik im Frühwerk von Ernst Jünger.* Berlin
Mai, Günther 1997. *Das Kyffhäuser-Denkmal 1896–1996.* Cologne

Mai, Uwe 2002. *"Rasse und Raum". Agrarpolitik, Sozial- und Raumplanung im NS-Staat.* Paderborn
Maier, Hans, ed. 1996, 1997 and 2003. *Totalitarismus und Politische Religion, Konzepte des Diktaturvergleichs,* 3 Vols. Paderborn
—— 2002. 'Deutungen totalitärer Herrschaft 1919–1989' in *Vierteljahreshefte für Zeitgeschichte* 50, No. 3, 349–366
Makela, Maria 1990. *The Munich Secession: Art and Artists in Turn-of-the-Century Munich.* Princeton
Malinowski, Stephan 2004. *Vom König zum Führer: deutscher Adel und Nationalsozialismus.* Frankfurt/M.
Manemann, Jürgen 2002. *Carl Schmitt und die politische Theologie: politischer Anti-Monotheismus.* Münster
Mann, Thomas 1915. *Friedrich und die große Koalition.* Berlin
—— 1942. 'A Brother' in his *Order of the Day.* New York, 153–161
—— 1988. *Betrachtungen eines Unpolitischen.* Frankfurt/M.
—— 1993. 'Gedanken im Krieg' in Thomas Mann, *Essays,* Vol. 1, ed. Hermann Kurzki et al. Frankfurt/M., 188–205
Mannheim, Karl 1984. *Konservatismus. Ein Beitrag zur Soziologie des Wissens,* ed. David Ketteler et al. Frankfurt/M.
—— 1995. *Utopie und Ideologie.* 8th edn. Frankfurt/M.
Maschmann, Melita 1963. *Fazit. Kein Rechtfertigungsversuch.* 5th edn. Stuttgart
Mathieu, Thomas 1997. *Kunstauffassungen und Kulturpolitik im Nationalsozialismus. Studien zu Adolf Hitler – Joseph Goebbels – Alfred Rosenberg – Baldur von Schirach – Heinrich Himmler – Albert Speer – Wilhelm Frick.* Saarbrücken
McGowan, Lee 2002. *The Radical Right in Germany: 1870 to the Present.* Harlow
McLeod, Hugh 2000. *Secularisation in Western Europe, 1848–1914.* New York
Meier, Heinrich 1994. *Die Lehre Carl Schmitts. Vier Kapitel zur Unterscheidung Politischer Theologie und Politischer Philosophie.* Stuttgart
Meinecke, Friedrich 1906. *Das Zeitalter der deutschen Erhebung.* Bielefeld
—— 1914. *Die deutsche Erhebung von 1914, Vorträge und Aufsätze.* Stuttgart
—— 1958. 'Nationalismus und Nationale Idee' in his *Werke,* Vol. 2: *Politische Schriften und Reden.* Darmstadt, 82–95
—— 1958a. 'Politik und Kultur' in his *Werke,* Vol. 2: *Politische Schriften und Reden.* Darmstadt, 76–82
—— 1962. *Weltbürgertum und Nationalstaat,* ed. Hans Herzfeld. Munich
—— 1963. *The German Catastrophe: Reflections and Recollections.* Boston
—— 1976. *Die Idee der Staatsräson in der neueren Geschichte.* 4th edn. Munich
Meisner, Heinrich 1994. *Gedichte von Ernst Moritz Arndt. Vollständige Sammlung,* Vol. 2. Leipzig
Mergel, Thomas 2004. *Parlamentarische Kultur in der Weimarer Republik. Politische Kommunikation, symbolische Öffentlichkeit im Reichstag.* 2nd edn. Düsseldorf
Merkenich, Stephanie 1998. *Grüne Front gegen Weimar. Reichs-Landbund und agrarischer Lobbyismus 1918–1933.* Düsseldorf
Merkl, Peter 1980. *The Making of a Storm Trooper.* Princeton
Merlio, Gilbert and Gérard Raulet, eds. 2005. *Linke und rechte Kulturkritik. Interdiskursivität als Krisenbewußtsein.* Frankfurt/M.
Meuter, Günter 1994. *Der Katechon: Zu Carl Schmitts fundamentalistischer Kritik der Zeit.* Berlin

Meuter, Günter and Henrique Ricardo Otten, eds. 1999. *Der Aufstand gegen den Bürger. Antibürgerliches Denken im 20. Jahrhundert.* Würzburg
Michalka, Wolfgang, ed. 1994. *Der Erste Weltkrieg. Wirkung, Wahrnehmung, Analyse.* Munich
Missalla, Heinrich 1968. *"Gott mit uns": Die deutsche katholische Kriegspredigt 1914–1918.* Munich
Moeller van den Bruck, Arthur 1904–10. *Die Deutschen. Unsere Menschengeschichte,* 8 Vols. Minden in Westfalen
—— 1919. *Das Recht der jungen Völker.* Munich
—— 1932. *Das Dritte Reich.* Hamburg
Mohler, Armin 1974. 'Der faschistische Stil' in his *Von rechts gesehen.* Stuttgart, 179–221
—— 1989. *Die Konservative Revolution in Deutschland 1918–1932,* 2 Vols. Darmstadt
Modernism, Antimodernism, Postmodernism 2004. London
Mogge, Winfried and Jürgen Reulecke, eds. 1988. *Hoher Meißner 1913. Der erste Freideutsche Jugendtag in Dokumenten, Deutungen und Bildern.* Cologne
Mommsen, Hans 1985. 'Generationenkonflikt und Jugendrevolte in der Weimarer Republik' in Thomas Koebner et al., ed. *"Mit uns zieht die neue Zeit". Der Mythos Jugend.* Frankfurt/M.
—— 1989. *Die verspielte Freiheit. Der Weg der Republik von Weimar in den Untergang 1918–1933.* Berlin
—— 1991. *Der Nationalsozialismus und die deutsche Gesellschaft. Ausgewählte Aufsätze.* Reinbek
—— 1993. 'Preußentum und Nationalsozialismus', in *Der Nationalsozialismus. Studien zur Ideologie und Herrschaft,* ed. Wolfgang Benz et al. Frankfurt/M., 29–41
—— 2000. *Alternative zu Hitler. Studien zur Geschichte des deutschen Widerstandes.* Munich
—— ed. 2001. *The Third Reich. Between Vision and Reality. New Perspectives on German History 1918–1945.* Oxford
—— 2002. *Auschwitz, 17. Juli 1942. Der Weg zur europäischen "Endlösung der Judenfrage".* Munich
Mommsen, Wolfgang 1981. 'The Topos of Inevitable War in Germany in the Decade before 1914' in *Germany in the Age of Total War,* ed. Volker Berghahn and Martin Kitchen. London, 23–44)
—— 1984. *Max Weber and German Politics, 1890–1920.* Chicago
—— 1992. 'Der Geist von 1914: Das Programm eines politischen "Sonderwegs" der Deutschen' in his *Der autoritäre Nationalstaat. Verfassung, Gesellschaft und Kultur im deutschen Kaiserreich.* Frankfurt/M., 407–421
—— 1994. *Bürgerliche Kultur und künstlerische Avantgarde, 1870–1918. Kultur und Politik im Deutschen Kaiserreich.* Frankfurt/M.
—— ed. 1996. *Kultur und Krieg: Die Rolle der Intellektuellen, Künstler und Schriftsteller im Ersten Weltkrieg.* Munich
Mork, Andrea 1990. *Richard Wagner als politischer Schriftsteller: Weltanschauung und Wirkungsgeschichte.* Frankfurt/M.
Mosse, George L. 1975. *The Nationalization of the Masses.* New York
—— 1981. *The Crisis of German Ideology. Intellectual Origins of the Third Reich,* 2nd edn. New York
—— 1990. *Fallen Soldiers: Reshaping the Memory of the World Wars.* Oxford

Mühlberger, Detlef 2003. *The Social Bases of Nazism 1919–1933.* Cambridge
Müller, Adam 1819. *Von der Notwendigkeit einer theologischen Grundlage der gesamten Staatswissenschaft und der Staatswirtschaft im besonderen.* Leipzig
—— 1922. *Die Elemente der Staatskunst* with an introduction by Jakob Baxa. Jena
Müller, Jakob 1971. *Die Jugendbewegung als deutsche Hauptrichtung neukonservativer Reform.* Zürich
Müller, Klaus-Jürgen and Eckardt Opitz, eds. *Militär und Militarismus in der Weimarer Republik.* Düsseldorf
Müller, Sven Oliver 2002. *Die Nation als Waffe und Vorstellung. Nationalismus in Deutschland und Großbritannien im Ersten Weltkrieg.* Göttingen
Münchow-Pohl, Bernd von 1987. *Zwischen Reform und Krieg. Untersuchungen zur Bewußtseinslage in Preußen 1809–1812.* Göttingen
Münkler, Herfried 1996. 'Das Reich als politische Macht und politischer Mythos' in his *Reich – Nation – Europa. Modelle politischer Ordnung.* Weinheim, 11–59.
Murphy, David Thomas 1997. *The Heroic Earth: Geopolitical Thought in Weimar Germany, 1918–1933.* Kent, Ohio
Nanko, Ulrich 1993. *Die deutsche Glaubensbewegung. Eine historische und soziologische Untersuchung.* Marburg
Nathans, Eli 2004. *The Politics of Citizenship in Germany: Ethnicity, Utility and Nationalism.* Oxford
Naumann, Friedrich 1900. *Demokratie und Kaisertum.* 2nd edn. Berlin
Neitzel, Sönke 2000. *Weltmacht oder Untergang. Die Weltreichslehre im Zeitalter des Imperialismus.* Paderborn
Neuloh, Otto and Wilhelm Zilius 1982. *Die Wandervögel.* Göttingen
Neurohr, Jean F. 1957. *Der Mythos vom Dritten Reich. Zur Geistesgeschichte des Nationalsozialismus.* Stuttgart
Nevin, Thomas 1997. *Ernst Jünger and Germany. Into the Abyss, 1914–1945.* Constable
Niekisch, Ernst 1958. *Gewagtes Leben.* Cologne
Niethammer, Lutz, ed. 1983. *"Die Jahre weiß man nicht, wo man die heute hinsetzen soll": Faschismuserfahrung im Ruhrgebiet: Lebensgeschichte und Sozialkultur im Ruhrgebiet 1930 bis 1960.* Berlin
Nietzsche, Friedrich 1954. 'The Antichrist', trans. W. Kaufmann, in *The Portable Nietzsche*, ed. W. Kaufmann, New York
—— 1954a. 'Nietzsche contra Wagner', trans. W. Kaufmann, in *The Portable Nietzsche*, ed. W. Kaufmann, New York
—— 1954b. 'Twilight of the Idols', trans. W. Kaufmann, in *The Portable Nietzsche*, ed. W. Kaufmann, New York
—— 1966. *The Birth of Tragedy*, trans. W. Kaufmann. New York
—— 1966a. *Beyond Good and Evil*, trans. W. Kaufmann. New York
—— 1966b. 'Der Fall Wagner', *The Birth of Tragedy*, trans. W. Kaufmann. New York
—— 1968. *The Will to Power*, trans. W. Kaufmann and R. Hollingdale. New York
—— 1968a. *On the Genealogy of Morals*, trans. W. Kaufmann and R. Hollingdale. New York
—— 1968b. 'Ecce Homo', trans. W. Kaufmann, in *On the Genealogy of Morals.* New York
—— 1969. *Thus Spoke Zarathustra. A Book for Everyone and No One*, trans. and with an introduction by R.J. Hollingdale. London
—— 1974. *The Gay Science*, trans. W. Kaufmann. New York

—— 1983. *Richard Wagner at Bayreuth*, trans. R. Hollingdale. Cambridge
—— 1983a. *Untimely Meditations;* trans. R. Hollingdale. Cambridge
—— 1986. *Human, All-too-human*, trans. R. Hollingdale. Cambridge
Nipperdey, Thomas 1983. *Deutsche Geschichte 1800–1866. Bürgerwelt und starker Staat.* Munich
—— 1986. 'Der Kölner Dom als Nationaldenkmal' in his *Nachdenken über die deutsche Geschichte.* Munich
—— 1990 and 1992. *Deutsche Geschichte 1866–1918*, 2 Vols. Munich
Nitschke, August et al. 1990. *Jahrhundertwende. Der Aufbruch in die Moderne, 1880–1930*, 2 Vols. Reinbek
Noakes, Jeremy 1990. 'German Conservatives and the Third Reich: an ambigous relationship' in *Fascists and Conservatives*, ed. Martin Blinkhorn. London, 71–97
Noakes, Jeremy and Geoffrey Pridham, eds. 1983–1998. *Nazism 1919–1945. A Documentary Reader*, 4 Vols. Exeter
Nolte, Ernst 1965. *Three Faces of Fascism, Action Francaise, Italian Fascism, National Socialism.* London
—— 1992. *Martin Heidegger: Politik und Geschichte im Leben und Denken.* Berlin
—— 2000. *Nietzsche und der Nietzscheanismus.* Munich
Norris, Pippa and Ronald Inglehart 2004. *Sacred and Secular. Religion and Politics Worldwide.* Cambridge, Mass.
Norton, Robert E. 2002. *Secret Germany. Stefan George and his Circle.* Cornell
Novalis 1844. *Christendom in Europe.* Northampton
—— 1960 ff. *Schriften*, ed. Paul Kluckhorn and Richard Samuel. Stuttgart
Nowak, Kurt 1995. *Geschichte des Christentums in Deutschland: Religion, Politik und Gesellschaft vom Ende der Aufklärung bis zur Mitte des 20. Jahrhunderts.* Munich
Oberkrome, Willi 1993. *Volksgeschichte. Methodische Innovaton und völkische Ideologisierung in der deutschen Geschichtswissenschaft.* Göttingen
—— 2004. *"Deutsche Heimat". Nationale Konzeption und regionale Praxis von Naturschutz, Landschaftsgestaltung und Kulturpolitik in Westfalen-Lippe und Thüringen (1900–1960).* Paderborn
Ogan, Bernd and Wolfgang W. Weiß, eds. 1992. *Faszination und Gewalt. Zur politischen Ästhetik der Gewalt.* Nuremberg
Orwell, George 1968. *The Collected Essays*, ed. Sonia Orwell and Ian Angus, Vol. 2. London
Ott, Hugo 1994. *Martin Heidegger: A Political Life.* London
Ott, Konrad, Thomas Potthast, Martin Gorke and Patricia Nevers 1999. 'Über die Anfänge des Naturschutzgedankens in Deutschland und den USA im 19. Jahrhundert' in *Naturnutzung und Naturschutz in der europäischen Rechts- und Verwaltungsgeschichte*, ed. Erk. V. Heyen. Baden-Baden, 1–55
Overy, Richard 1996. *Why the Allies Won.* London
Panayi, Panikos, ed. 2001. *Weimar and Nazi Germany. Continuities and Discontinuities.* Harlow
Parin, Paul 1978. *Der Widerspruch im Subjekt. Ethnopsychoanalytische Studien.* Frankfurt/M.
Pauen, Michael 1997. *Pessimismus. Geschichtsphilosophie, Metaphysik und Moderne von Nietzsche bis Spengler.* Berlin
Paul, Gerhard 1990. *Aufstand der Bilder. Die NS-Propaganda vor 1933.* Bonn
Paul, Ina Ulrike 1996. 'Paul Anton de Lagarde', in Puschner 1996, 45–93

Pechel, Rudolf 1947. *Deutscher Widerstand.* Erlenbach-Zürich
Peters, Michael 1996. *Der Alldeutsche Verband am Vorabend des Ersten Weltkriegs (1908–1914). Ein Beitrag zur Geschichte des völkischen Nationalismus im spätwilhelminischen Deutschland.* 2nd edn. Frankfurt/M.
Petropoulus, Jonathan 1996. *Art as Politics in the Third Reich.* Chapel Hill
Petzet, Heinrich W. 1993. *Encounters and Dialogues with Martin Heidegger, 1929–1976.* Chicago
Petzinna, Berthold 2000. *Erziehung zum deutschen Lebensstil. Ursprung und Entwicklung des jungkonservativen Ring-Kreises 1918–1933.* Berlin
—— 1978. *Wegbereiter des deutschen Faschismus. Die Jungkonservativen in der Weimarer Republik.* Cologne
Petzold, Joachim 1980. *Generalprobe für Hitler.* Berlin
Peukert, Detlev 1985. 'Die Erwerbslosigkeit junger Arbeiter in der Weltwirtschaftskrise in Deutschland 1929–1933' *Vierteljahresschrift für Sozial- und Wirtschaftsgeschichte* 72, 305–328
—— 1987. *Inside Nazi Germany: Conformity, Opposition and Racism in Life.* London
—— 1991. *The Weimar Republic: the Crisis of Classical Modernity.* London
Philippi, Klaus-Peter 1979. *Volk des Zorns.* Munich
Planert, Ute, ed. 2000. *Nation, Politik und Geschlecht. Frauenbewegungen und Nationalismus.* Frankfurt/M.
Plenge, Johann 1915. *Der Krieg und die Volkswirtschaft,* 2nd edn. Münster
—— 1916. *1789 und 1914. Die symbolischen Jahre in der Geschichte des politischen Denkens.* Berlin
Plessner, Helmut 1959. *Die verspätete Nation. Über die politische Verführbarkeit bürgerlichen Geistes.* Stuttgart
Plewnia, Margarete 1970. *Auf dem Weg zu Hitler. Der "völkische" Publizist Dietrich Eckart.* Bremen
Pöggeler, Otto 1991. 'Heidegger's Political Self-Understanding' in Wolin 1991, 198–244
Pois, Robert 1986. *National Socialism and the Religion of Nature.* London
Poliakov, Léon 1993. *Der arische Mythos. Zu den Quellen von Rassismus und Nationalismus.* Hamburg
Prümm, Karl 1974. *Die Literatur des Soldatischen Nationalismus der 20er Jahre (1918–1933). Gruppenideologie und Epochenproblematik.* 2 Vols. Kronberg/TS.
Puhle, Hans-Jürgen 1967. *Agrarische Interessenpolitik und preußischer Konservatismus im wilhelminischen Deutschland (1893–1914).* Hannover
—— 1986. 'Konservativismus', in: *Pipers Handbuch der Politischen Ideen,* ed. I Fetscher and H. Münkler, Vol 4. Munich, 255–278
Pulzer, Peter G.J. 1988. *Antisemitism in Germany and Austria,* 2nd edn. Cambridge
—— 1992. *Jews and the German State: The Political History of a Minority, 1848–1933.* Oxford
—— 1999. *German Antisemitism Revisited.* Rome
Puschner, Uwe, et al., eds. 1996. *Handbuch zur "völkischen Bewegung".* Munich
—— 2001. *Die völkische Bewegung im wilhelminischen Kaiserreich. Sprache – Rasse – Religion.* Darmstadt
—— 2002. '"One People, One Reich, One God". The Völkische Weltanschauung and Movement' in *GHI London Bulletin,* 24 (1), May 2002, 5–28
Quinn, Malcolm 1994. *The Swastika. Constructing the Symbol.* London

Rabinbach, Anson 1997. *In the Shadow of Catastrophe. German Intellectuals between Apocalypse and Enlightenment.* Berkeley
Radkau, Joachim 1998. *Das Zeitalter der Nervosität. Deutschland zwischen Bismarck und Hitler.* Munich
Radkau, Joachim and Frank Uekötter, eds. 2003. *Naturschutz und Nationalsozialismus.* Frankfurt/M.
Rathenau, Walther 1977. *Hauptwerke und Gespräche* (= Walther Rathenau Gesamtausgabe, Vol. 2), ed. Ernst Schulin. Munich
Rauschning, Hermann 1938. *Die Revolution des Nihilismus.* Zürich
Reichardt, Sven 2002. *Faschistische Kampfbünde. Gewalt und Gemeinschaft im italienischen Squadrismus und in der deutschen SA.* Cologne
Reichel, Peter 1993. *Der schöne Schein des Dritten Reiches. Faszination und Gewalt des Faschismus,* 2nd edn. Frankfurt/M.
Reif, Heinz, ed. 1999. *Adel im 19. und 20. Jahrhundert.* Munich
—— ed. 2000 and 2001 *Adel und Bürgertum in Deutschland.* 2 Vols. Berlin
Repp, Kevin 2000. *Reformers, Critics, and the Paths of German Modernity.* Cambridge, Mass.
Retallack, James 1988. *Notables of the Right: The Conservative Party and Political Mobilization in Germany, 1876–1918.* London
Reulecke, Jürgen 2001. *"Ich möchte einer so werden wie die..." Männerbünde im 20. Jahrhundert.* Frankfurt/M.
Reuth, Ralf Georg 1995. *Goebbels. Eine Biographie.* Munich
Rhodes, James 1980. *The Hitler Movement. A Modern Millennarian Revolution.* Stanford
Ribhegge, Wilhelm 1992. *Konservative Politik in Deutschland. Von der französischen Revolution bis zur Gegenwart,* 2nd edn., Darmstadt
Richards, Donald R. 1968. *The German Bestseller in the 20th Century. A Complete Bibliography and Analysis.* Bern
Riehl, Wilhelm Heinrich 1854. *Land und Leute.* Stuttgart
—— 1873. 'Das landschaftliche Auge' (1850), in his *Culturstudien aus drei Jahrhunderten.* Stuttgart, 57–79
—— 1976. *Die bürgerliche Gesellschaft,* ed. and introduced by Peter Steinbach. Frankfurt/M.
Ringer, Fritz K. 1969. *The Decline of the German Mandarins.* Cambridge, Mass.
Rißmann, Michael. 2001. *Hitlers Gott. Vorsehungsglaube und Sendungsbewußtsein des deutschen Diktators.* Zürich
Ritter, Gerhard 1965. *Staatskunst und Kriegshandwerk. Das Problem des "Militarismus" in Deutschland,* Vol. 1. Munich
Ritter, Joachim 1963. *Landschaft. Zur Funktion des Ästhetischen in der modernen Gesellschaft.* Münster
Roehl, John C.G. 1998. *Young Wilhelm: the Kaiser's Early Life 1859–1888.* Cambridge
Rohe, Karl 1966. *Das Reichsbanner Schwarz-Rot-Gold. Ein Beitrag zur Geschichte und Struktur der politischen Kampfverbände zur Zeit der Weimarer Republik.* Düsseldorf
Rohkrämer, Thomas 1990. *Der Militarismus der "kleinen Leute". Die Kriegervereine im Deutschen Kaiserreich 1871–1914.* Munich
—— 1995, 'Das Militär als Männerbund? Der Kult soldatischer Männlichkeit im Deutschen Kaiserreich' *Westfälische Forschungen* 45, 169–187

—— 1997. 'Daily Life at the Front and the Concept of Total War' in *On the Road to Total War: The American Civil War and the German Wars of Unification, 1861–1871*, ed. Stig Förster and Jörg Nagler. Cambridge, 497–518
—— 1999. *Eine andere Moderne? Zivilisationskritik, Natur und Technik in Deutschland 1880–1933*. Paderborn
—— 1999a. 'Cultural Criticism in Germany 1880–1933, a Typology' *History of European Ideas* 25, 321–339
—— 1999b. 'Antimodernism, Reactionary Modernism and National Socialism. Technocratic Tendencies in Germany 1890–1945' *Contemporary European History*, 8 (1), 29–50
—— 1999c. 'Heroes and Would-Be Heroes – Veterans' and Reservists' Associations in Imperial Germany' in *Anticipating Total War? The German and American Experiences, 1871–1914*, ed. Manfred F. Boemeke et al., Cambridge, 189–215
—— 2001. 'Kult der Gewalt und Sehnsucht nach Ordnung – der soldatische Nationalismus in der Weimarer Republik' *Sociologus* 51, H. 1/2, 28–48
—— 2002. 'Contemporary Environmentalism and its Links with the German Past' in *The Culture of German Environmentalism. Anxities, Visions, Realities*, ed. Axel Goodbody. New York and Oxford, 47–62
—— 2003. 'Die Vision einer deutschen Technik. Ingenieure und das "Dritte Reich"' in *Utopie und politische Herrschaft im Europa der Zwischenkriegszeit*, ed. Wolfgang Hardtwig with Philip Cassier. Munich, 287–307
—— 2003a. 'Strangelove, or How Ernst Jünger Learned to Love Total War' in *The Shadows of Total War. Europe, East Asia, and the United States, 1919–1939*, ed. Roger Chickering and Stig Förster. Cambridge, 179–196
—— 2004. 'Nihilismus und Wille zur Macht. Zum Verhältnis von Sinnkrise und Schaffensfreude beim frühen Ernst Jünger' in *Anarch im Widerspruch. Neue Beiträge zu Werk und Leben der Gebrüder Jünger*, ed. Tobias Wimbauer, Schnellroda, 213–233
—— 2005. 'Heidegger, National Socialism and Environmentalism' in *How Green were the Nazis?* ed. Franz-Josef Brüggemeier et al. Athens, Ohio
—— forthcoming, 'Bewahrung, Neugestaltung, Restauration? Konservative Raum- und Heimatvorstellungen in Deutschland 1900–1933' in *Ordnungen in der Krise. Zur politischen Kulturgeschichte Deutschlands 1900–1933*, ed. Wolfgang Hardtwig
Rohrbacher, Stefan and Michael Schmidt 1991. *Judenbilder. Kulturgeschichte antijüdischer Mythen und antisemitischer Vorurteile*. Hamburg
Rollins, William H. 1997. *A Greener Vision of Home. Cultural Politics and Environmental Reform in the German Heimatschutz Movement, 1904–1918*. Ann Arbor
Roon, Ger van 1967. *Neuordnung im Widerstand. Der Kreisauer Kreis innerhalb der deutschen Widerstandsbewegung*. Munich
Rose, Paul L. 1992. *Wagner, Race and Revolution*. New Haven
Roseman, Mark, ed. 1995. *Generations in Conflict: Youth Revolt and Generation Formation in Germany, 1770–1968*. Cambridge
—— 1996. 'National Socialism and Modernisation' in *Fascist Italy and Nazi Germany*, ed. Richard Bessel, Cambridge, 197–229
Rosenberg, Alfred 1927. *Houston Stewart Chamberlain als Verkünder und Begründer einer deutschen Zukunft*. Munich
—— 1930. *Der Mythus des 20. Jahrhunderts*. Munich

—— 1930a. *Wesen, Grundsätze und Ziele der Nationalsozialistischen Deutschen Arbeiterpartei. Das Programm der Bewegung.* Munich

Rosenberg, Hans 1976. *Grosse Depression und Bismarckzeit. Wirtschaftsablauf, Gesellschaft und Politik in Mitteleuropa.* Frankfurt/M.

Ross, Chad 2005. *Naked Germany: Health, Race, and the Nation.* New York

Roth, Karl Heinz and Angelika Ebbinghaus, eds. 2005. *Rote Kapellen – Kreisauer Kreis – Schwarze Kapellen. Neue Sichtweisen auf den Widerstand gegen die NS-Diktatur 1938–1945.* Hamburg

Rürup, Reinhard 1984. 'Der "Geist von 1914" in Deutschland. Kriegsbegeisterung und Ideologisierung des Krieges im Ersten Weltkrieg' in *Ansichten vom Krieg,* eds. Bernd Hüppauf. Hanstein, 1–30

Rusinek, Bernd A. 1992. '"Das überall frech eindringende moderne Leben ...": Hohe Offiziere des Kaiserreiches als antidemokratische Denker' *Jahrbuch für Extremismus und Demokratie,* Vol. 4, 29–52

Ruthven, Malise 2005. *Fundamentalism. The Search for Meaning.* Oxford

Salmi, Hannu 1999. *Imagined Germany: Richard Wagner's National Utopia.* New York

Salomon, Ernst von 1933. *Die Geächteten.* Berlin

Schama, Simon 1995. *Landscape and Memory.* London

Schanze, Helmut, ed. 1994. *Romantik-Handbuch.* Stuttgart

Scheck, Raffael 1998. *Alfred von Tirpitz and German Right-wing Politics, 1914–1930.* New York

Scheler, Max 1915. *Der Genius des Krieges und der Deutsche Krieg.* Leipzig

Schelling, Friedrich 1856–1861. *Sämtliche Werke,* ed. Karl Friedrich Schelling. Stuttgart

—— 1975. *Materialien zu Schellings philosophischen Anfängen,* ed. Manfred Frank and G. Kurz. Frankfurt/M.

—— 1978. *System of Transcendental Idealism,* trans. Peater Heath. Charlottesville

Schildt, Axel 1981. *Militärdiktatur mit Massenbasis? Die Querfrontkonzeption der Reichswehrführung um General Kurt von Schleicher am Ende der Weimarer Republik.* Frankfurt/M.

—— 1987. 'Ein konservativer Prophet moderner nationaler Integration. Biographische Skizze des streitbaren Soziologen Johann Plenge (1874–1963)' *Vierteljahreshefte für Zeitgeschichte* 35, 523–570

—— 1995. 'Radikale Antworten von rechts auf die Kulturkrise der Jahrhundertwende. Zur Herausbildung und Entwicklung der Ideologie einer 'Neuen Rechten' in der Wilhelminischen Gesellschaft des Kaiserreichs' in *Jahrbuch für Antisemitismusforschung,* 4, 63–87

—— 1998. *Konservatismus in Deutschland. Von den Anfängen im 18. Jahrhundert bis zur Gegenwart.* Munich

Schiller, Friedrich 1995. *Essays.* New York

Schilling, René 2002. *"Kriegshelden". Deutungsmuster heroischer Männlichkeit in Deutschland 1813–1945.* Paderborn

Schleier, Hans 2000. *Historisches Denken in der Krise der Kultur. Fachhistorie, Kulturgeschichte und Anfänge der Kulturwissenschaften in Deutschland.* Göttingen

Schlegel, August 1983 ff. *Briefe von und an August W. Schlegel,* ed. Joseph Körner. Zurich

Schlegel, Friedrich 1979 ff. *Kritische Friedrich-Schlegel-Ausgabe,* ed. Ernst Behler. Paderborn

Schmädecke, J. and P. Steinbach, eds. 1985. *Der Widerstand gegen den Nationalsozialismus. Die deutsche Gesellschaft und der Widerstand gegen Hitler.* Munich

Schmidt, Jochen 1985. *Die Geschichte des Genie-Gedankens in der deutschen Literatur, Philosophie und Politik 1750–1945*, 2 Vols. Darmstadt

Schmitt, Carl 1982. *Politische Romantik.* 4th edn. Berlin

—— 1985. *Political Theology: Four Chapters on the Concept of Sovereignty.* Cambridge, Mass.

—— 1987. *Der Begriff des Politischen. Text von 1932 mit einem Vorwort und drei Corollarien.* Berlin

—— 1988. *The Crisis of Parliamentary Democracy.* Cambridge, Mass.

—— 1991. *Theodor Däublers "Nordlicht" – Drei Studien über die Elemente, den Geist und die Aktualität des Werks.* Munich

—— 1991a. *Glossarium. Aufzeichnungen der Jahre 1947–1951*, ed. E. von Medem. Berlin

—— 1994. *Positionen und Begriffe: im Kampf mit Weimar – Genf – Versailles 1923–1939.* Berlin

—— 1996. *The Concept of the Political.* Chicago

—— 1996a. *The Leviathan in the State Theory of Thomas Hobbes: Meaning and Failure of a Political Symbol.* Westport, Conn.

—— 1996b. *Roman Catholicism and Political Form.* Westport, Conn.

—— 1996c. *Politische Theologie II. Die Legende von der Erledigung jeder politischen Theologie*, 4th edn. Berlin

—— 1996d. *Politische Theologie. Vier Kapitel zur Lehre der Souveränität.* Berlin

—— 2003. *Tagebücher: Oktober 1912 bis Februar 1915*, ed. Ernst Hüsmert. Berlin

Schmitthenner, Heinrich 1891. *Erlebnisse eines freiwilligen badischen Grenadiers im Feldzuge 1870/71.* Karlsruhe

Schmitz, Peter 1985. *Die Artamanen. Landarbeit und Siedlung bündischer Jugend in Deutschland 1924–1935.* Bad Neustadt

Schmoll, Friedemann 2004. *Erinnerung an die Natur. Die Geschichte des Naturschutzes im deutschen Kaiserreich.* Frankfurt/M.

Schnädelbach, Herbert 1983. *Philosophie in Deutschland 1831–1933.* Frankfurt/M.

Schneider, Tobias 2001. 'Ideologische Grabenkämpfe. Der Philosoph Ludwig Klages und der Nationalsozialismus' in *Vierteljahreshefte für Zeitgeschichte* 49, 275–294

Schnurbein, Stefanie von and Justus H. Ulbricht, ed. 2001. *Völkische Religion und Krisen der Moderne. Entwürfe "arteigener" Glaubenssysteme seit der Jahrhundertwende.* Würzburg

Scholder, Klaus 1977 and 1985. *Die Kirchen und das Dritte Reich*, 2 Vols. Frankfurt/M.

Schotte, Walther 1932. *Der neue Staat.* Berlin

Schreiner, Klaus 1991. 'Politischer Messianismus, Führergedanke und Führererwartung in der Weimarer Republik' in *Was ist Gesellschaftsgeschichte? Positionen, Themen, Analysen*, ed. Manfred Hettling, Munich, 237–247

—— 1998, 'Politischer Messianismus in der Weimarer Republik' *Saeculum* 49 (1), 107–160

—— 2003. 'Messianismus. Bedeutungs- und Funktionswandel eines heilsgeschichtlichen Denk- und Handlungsmusters' in *Zwischen Politik und Religion*, ed. Klaus Hildebrand. Munich. 1–44

Schrenck-Notzing, Caspar von, ed. 2000. *Stand und Probleme der Erforschung des Konservatismus.* Berlin

Schreyvogel, Friedrich 1933, 'Der Dichter als Vorhut der Nation' in *Des deutschen Dichters Sendung.* Ed. Heinz Kindermann, Leipzig

Schubert, Gustav von 1909. *Lebenserinnerungen.* Stuttgart

Schüddekopf, Otto-Ernst 1960. *Linke Leute von rechts. Nationalismus in Deutschland von 1918–1933.* Stuttgart

Schüler, Winfried 1971. *Der Bayreuther Kreis von seiner Entstehung bis zum Ausgang der Wilhelminischen Ära. Wagnerkult und Kulturreform im Geiste völkischer Weltanschauung.* Münster

Schulin, Ernst 1977. 'Zu Rathenaus Hauptwerken' in Rathenau 1977, 499–595.

—— 1994. 'Die Urkatastrophe des zwanzigsten Jahrhunderts' in Michalka 1994, 3–27

Schulz, Andreas 2005. *Lebenswelt und Kultur des Bürgertums im 19. und 20. Jahrhundert.* Munich

Schulze, Friedrich, ed. 1913. *Urkunden der deutschen Erhebung. Originalwiedergabe in Faksimiledrucken der wichtigsten Aufrufe, Erlasse, Flugschriften, Lieder und Zeitungsnummer als Ergänzung aller Erinnerungsschriften.* Leipzig

Schulze, Hagen 1969. *Freikorps und Republik 1918–1920.* Boppard

Schumann, Dirk 2000. 'Einheitssehnsucht und Gewaltakzeptanz. Politische Grundpositionen des deutschen Bürgertums nach 1918 (mit vergleichenden Überlegungen zu den britischen middle classes)' in *Der Erste Weltkrieg und die europäische Nachkriegsordnung. Sozialer Wandel und Formveränderung der Politik,* ed. Wolfgang Mommsen. Cologne, 83–105

—— 2001. *Politische Gewalt in der Weimarer Republik. Kampf um die Straße und Furcht vor dem Bürgerkrieg.* Essen

Schumann, Hans-Gerd, ed. 1984. *Konservativismus.* Königstein

Schwabe, Klaus 1969. *Wissenschaft und Kriegsmoral. Die deutschen Hochschullehrer und die politischen Grundfragen des Ersten Weltkriegs.* Göttingen

Schwentker, Wolfgang 1988. *Konservative Vereine und Revolution in Preußen 1848/49: Die Konstituierung des Konservatismus als Partei.* Düsseldorf

Schwierskott, Hans Joachim 1962. *Arthur Moeller van den Bruck und der revolutionäre Nationalismus in der Weimarer Republik.* Göttingen

Scott, James C. 1998. *Seeing Like a State. How Certain Schemes to Improve the Human Condition have Failed.* New Haven

See, Klaus von 1975. *Die Ideen von 1789 und die Ideen von 1914. Völkisches Denken in Deutschland zwischen Französischer Revolution und Erstem Weltkrieg.* Frankfurt/M.

—— 1997. *Barbar, Germane, Arier. Die Suche nach der Identität der Deutschen.* Heidelberg

Seiberth, Gabriel 2001. *Anwalt des Reiches: Carl Schmitt und der Prozess "Preussen contra Reich" vor dem Staatsgerichtshof.* Berlin

Semmens, Kristin 2005. *Seeing Hitler's Germany: Tourism in the Third Reich.* Houndsmills

Sheehan, James J. 1989. *German History, 1770–1866.* New York

Shirer, W. 1942. *Berlin Diary.* New York

Silfen, Paul H. 1973. *The Völkish Ideology and the Roots of Nazism. The Early Writings of Arthur Moeller van den Bruck.* New York

Simmel, Georg 1915. *Der Genius des Krieges und der deutsche Krieg.* Leipzig

Sluga, Hans 1993. *Heidegger's Crisis. Philosophy and Politics in Nazi Germany.* Cambridge, Mass.
Smelser, Ronald and Enrico Syring, eds. 2000. *Die SS-Elite unter dem Totenkopf. 30 Lebensläufe.* Paderborn
Smith, Anthony D. 1998. *Nationalism and Modernism. A Critical Survey of Recent Theories of Nations and Nationalism.* London
—— 2001. *Nationalism.* Cambridge
—— 2001a. *National Identity.* London
—— 2003. *Chosen Peoples. Sacred Sources of National Identity.* Oxford
Smith, Helmut W. 1995. *German Nationalism and Religious Conflict: Culture, Ideology, Politics, 1870–1914.* Princeton
Sombart, Nicolaus 1991. *Die deutschen Männer und ihre Feinde. Carl Schmitt. Ein deutsches Schicksal zwischen Männerbund und Matriachatsmythos.* Munich
Sombart, Werner 1915. *Händler und Helden. Patriotische Besinnungen.* Munich
—— 1977. *Der Bourgeois. Zur Geistesgeschichte des modernen Wirtschaftsmenschen.* Berlin
Sontag, Susan 1981. 'Faszinierender Faschismus' in her *Im Zeichen des Saturns. Essays.* Munich, 95–125
Sontheimer, Kurt 1983. *Antidemokratisches Denken in der Weimarer Republik. Die politischen Ideen des deutschen Nationalismus zwischen 1918 und 1933,* 2nd edn. Munich
Speer, Albert 1976. *Erinnerungen,* 2nd edn. Berlin
—— 2002. *Spandauer Tagebücher,* with an introduction by Joachim Fest, 2nd edn. Berlin
Spengler, Oswald 1919. *Preussentum und Sozialismus.* Munich
—— 1932. *Der Mensch und die Technik. Beitrag zu einer Philosophie des Lebens.* Munich
—— 1951. *Reden und Aufsätze,* 3rd edn. Munich
—— 1963. *Briefe 1913–1936,* ed. Manfred Schröter. Munich
—— 1971. *The Decline of the West,* 7th edn. London
—— 1980. *Jahre der Entscheidung,* 2nd edn. Munich
—— 2002. *Man and Technics: a Contribution to a Philosophy of Life.* Honolulu
Speth, Rudolf 2000. *Nation und Revolution: Politische Mythen im 19. Jahrhundert.* Opladen
Spotts, Frederic 1994. *Bayreuth: A History of the Wagner Festivals.* New Haven
—— 2002. *Hitler and the Power of Aesthetics.* London
Stachura, Peter D. 1981. *The German Youth Movement, 1900–1945.* London
Stackelberg, Roderick 1981. *Idealism Debased. From Völkish Ideology to National Socialism.* Kent, Ohio
Stapel, Wilhelm 1917. *Volksbürgerliche Erziehung.* Jena
Stegmann, Dirk 1970. *Die Erben Bismarcks: Parteien und Verbände in der Spätphase des wilhelminischen Deutschlands. Sammlungspolitik 1897–1918.* Cologne
—— 1983. 'Vom Neokonservatismus zum Protofaschismus: Konservative Partei, Vereine und Verbände 1893–1920' in *Deutscher Konservatismus,* ed. Dirk Stegmann et al. 199–227
Steigmann-Gall, Richard 2003. *The Holy Reich: Nazi Conceptions of Christianity, 1919–1945.* Cambridge
Steiner, John M. 1986. 'Über das Glaubensbekenntnis der SS' in Bracher 1986, 206–223

Stern, Fritz 1961. *The Politics of Cultural Despair. A Study in the Rise of the Germanic Ideology.* Berkeley

—— 1999. 'National Socialism as Temptation' in his *Dreams and Delusion: the Drama of German History,* 2nd edn. New Haven, Ch. 2

Stern, Joseph. P. 1978. *Nietzsche.* London

—— 1984. *Hitler: The Führer and the People.* London

Sternhell, Zeev, Mario Sznajder and Maia Asheri 1999. *Die Entstehung der faschistischen Ideologie. Von Sorel zu Mussolini.* Hamburg

Stoecker, Adolf 1890. 'Unsere Forderungen an das moderne Judentum' (19.9.1879) in his *Christlich-Soziale Reden und Aufsätze,* 2nd edn. Berlin, 359–369

Strachan, Hew 2001. *The First World War,* Vol. 1: *To Arms.* Oxford

Strauß, David Friedrich 2003. *Das Leben Jesu,* ed. and introduced by Werner Zager. Waltrop

Strich, Fritz 1910. *Die Mythologie in der deutschen Literatur von Klopstock bis Wagner.* 2 Vols. Halle

Stromberg, Roland N. 1982. *Redemption by War. The Intellectuals and 1914.* Lawrence

Struve, Walter Ch. 1973. *Elites against Democracy. Leadership Ideals in Bourgeois Politics in Germany, 1890–1933.* Princeton

Süllwold, Fritz 2001. *Deutsche Normalbürger 1933–1945. Erfahrungen, Einstellungen, Reaktionen.* Munich

Swatos, William H., et al., eds. 2000. *The Secularisation Debate.* Lanham

Tal, Uriel 1975. *Christians and Jews in Germany: Religion, Politics, and Ideology in the Second Reich, 1870–1914.* Ithaca

—— 2002. *Faith, Politics and Nazism: Selected Essays by Uriel Tal.* London 2002

Tanera, Karl 1896. *An der Loire und Sarthe.* Nördlingen

Thamer, Hans-Ulrich 1986. *Verführung und Gewalt: Deutschland 1933–1945.* Berlin

Theweleit, Klaus 1987 and 1989. *Male Fantasies,* 2 Vols. Minneapolis

Thomas, R. Hinton 1986. *Nietzsche in German Politics and Society, 1890–1918.* 2nd edn. Manchester

Thomas, William I. and D.S Thomas 1928: *The Child in America: Behavior Problems and Programs.* New York

Tieck, Ludwig 1797: *Volksmärchen.* Berlin

Todt, Fritz 1941. 'Vorwort' in Alwin Seifert, *Im Zeitalter des Lebendigen. Natur * Heimat * Technik.* Dresden, 6

Tönnies, Ferdinand 2001. *Community and Civil Society,* ed. Jose Harris. Cambridge

Treiber, Hubert 1991. 'Im Westen nichts Neues: Menschwerdung durch Askese bei Weber und Nietzsche' in *Religionswissenschaft und Kulturkritik, ed.* Hans G. Kippenberg and Brigitte Luchesi. Marburg, 283 ff.

Treitschke, Heinrich 1879. 'Unsere Aussichten' *Preußische Jahrbücher,* Bd. 44, 559–576

Trippe, Christian F. 1995. *Konservative Verfassungspolitik: 1918–1923. Die DNVP als Opposition in Reich und Ländern.* Düsseldorf

Troeltsch, Ernst 1925. 'Das neunzehnte Jahrhundert' in his *Gesammelte Schriften,* Vol. 4. Tübingen

Trox, Eckhard 1990. *Militärischer Konservativismus: Kriege, "Militärpartei" in Preußen zwischen 1815 und 1848/49.* Stuttgart

Turner, Henry A. 1997. *Hitler's Thirty Days to Power: January 1933,* 2nd edn. London

Turner, Henry J. 1975. 'Fascism and Modernisation' in *Reappraisals in Fascism,* ed. Henry J. Turner. New York, 117–39

Ulbricht, Justus H. 1995. 'Kulturrevolution von rechts. Das völkische Netzwerk 1900–1930' in *Nationalsozialismus in Thüringen,* ed. Detlev Heiden and Gunther Mai. Weimar, 29–48

Ulbricht, Justus H., et al., ed. 1999. *Romantik, Revolution und Reform. Der Eugen-Diederichs Verlag im Epochen-Kontext 1900–1949.* Göttingen

Ulrich, Bernd and Benjamin Ziemann, eds. 1997. *Krieg im Frieden. Die umkämpfte Erinnerung an den Ersten Weltkrieg.* Frankfurt/M.

—— ed. 2001. *Untertan in Uniform: Militär und Militarismus im Kaiserreich 1871–1914. Quellen und Dokumente.* Frankfurt/M.

Urbach, Karina and Bernd Buchner 2004. 'Prinz Max von Baden und Houston Stewart Chamberlain. Aus dem Briefwechsel 1909–1919' *Vierteljahreshefte für Zeitgeschichte* 1, 121–177

Utz, Joachim 1990. 'Der Erste Weltkrieg im Spiegel des deutschen und englischen Haßgedichts' in *Kultur und Konflikt,* ed. Jan Assmann and Dietrich Harth. Frankfurt/M., 373–413

Verhey, Jeffrey T. 1997. *The "Spirit of 1914" in Germany 1914–1945.* Cambridge

Vierhaus, Rudolf 1972 ff. 'Konservativ, Konservatismus' in Otto Brunner et al., ed. *Geschichtliche Grundbegriffe,* Vol. 3, 531–565

Voegelin, Eric 1952. *The New Science of Politics.* Chicago

—— 1996. *Die Politischen Religionen* (1938), ed. Peter J. Opitz, 2nd edn. Munich

Vogel, Jakob 1997. *Nationen im Gleichschritt: Der Kult der 'Nation in Waffen' in Deutschland und Frankreich, 1871–1914.* Göttingen

Voigt, Rüdiger, ed. 2001. *Mythos Staat: Carl Schmitts Staatsverständnis.* Baden-Baden

Volkov, Shulamit 1978. *The Rise of Popular Antimodernism in Germany: The Urban Master Artisans 1873–1896.* Princeton

—— 2000. *Antisemitismus als kultureller Code: zehn Essays,* 2nd edn. Munich.

—— 2000a. *Die Juden in Deutschland 1780–1918,* 2nd edn. Munich

Vondung, Klaus 1971. *Magie und Manipulation. Ideologischer Kult und politische Religion des Nationalsozialismus.* Göttingen

—— 1988. *Die Apokalypse in Deutschland.* Munich

Wachsmann, Nikolaus 1998. 'Marching under the Swastika? Ernst Jünger and National Socialism' *Journal of Contemporary History,* 33, 573–589

Wacker, Bernd, ed. 1994. *Die eigentliche katholische Verschärfung: Konfession, Theologie und Politik im Werk Carl Schmitts.* Munich

Wagner, Cosima 1976. *Die Tagebücher.* Munich

Wagner, Richard n.d. *Richard Wagners gesammelte Schriften,* ed. Julius Kapp. Leipzig

—— 1975. *Sämtliche Briefe,* ed Gertrud Strobel et al., Vol 3. Leipzig

Waite, Robert G. L. 1970. *Vanguard of Nazism. The Free Corps Movement in Postwar Germany 1918–1923.* 2nd edn. New York

Walkenhorst, Peter 1996. 'Nationalismus als "politische Religion"? Zur religiösen Dimension nationalistischer Ideologie im Kaiserreich' in *Religion im Kaiserreich. Milieus – Mentalitäten – Krisen,* ed. Olaf Blaschke and Frank-Michael Kuhlemann. Gütersloh, 503–529

Walter, Dirk 1999. *Antisemitische Kriminalität und Gewalt. Judenfeindschaft in der Weimarer Republik.* Bonn

Walter, Franz 1995. 'Milieus und Parteien in der deutschen Gesellschaft. Zwischen Persistenz und Erosion' *Geschichte in Wissenschaft und Unterricht,* 46, 479–493

Wapnewski, Peter 2001. 'Das Niebelungenlied' in *Deutsche Erinnerungsorte*, ed. Etienne Francois and Hagen Schulze, Vol. 1. Munich, 159–165

Weber, Ernst 1991. *Lyrik der Befreiungskriege (1812–1815). Gesellschaftspolitische Meinungs- und Willensbildung durch Literatur.* Stuttgart

Weber, Marianne 1950. *Max Weber. Ein Lebensbild.* Heidelberg

Weber, Max 1963. *The Sociology of Religion.* Boston

— 1988. *Gesammelte Aufsätze zur Religionssoziologie*, Vol. 1, 9th ed. Tübingen

— 1993. *Max-Weber-Gesamtausgabe I/4: Landarbeiterfrage, Nationalstaat und Volkswirtschaftspolitik. Schriften und Reden 1892–1899*, ed. Wolfgang Mommsen and Rita Aldenhoff. Tübingen

Wegner, Bernd 1997. *Hitlers politische Soldaten: Die Waffen-SS 1933–1945. Leitbild, Struktur und Funktion einer nationalsozialistischen Elite.* 5th edn. Paderborn

Wehler, Hans-Ulrich 1985. *The German Empire 1871–1918.* Leamington Spa

— 1987. *Deutsche Gesellschaftsgeschichte*, Vol. 1: *Vom Feudalismus des Alten Reiches bis zur Defensiven Modernisierung der Reformära 1700–1815.* Munich

— 1987a. *Deutsche Gesellschaftsgeschichte*, Vol. 2: *Von der Reformära bis zur industriellen und politischen "Deutschen Doppelrevolution" 1815–1845/49.* Munich

— 1995. *Deutsche Gesellschaftsgeschichte*, Vol. 3: *Von der "Deutschen Doppelrevolution" bis zum Beginn des Ersten Weltkrieges 1849–1914.* Munich

—2003. *Deutsche Gesellschaftsgeschichte*, Vol. 4: *Vom Beginn des Ersten Weltkriegs bis zur Gründung der beiden deutschen Staaten 1914–1949.* Munich

— 2004. *Nationalismus. Geschichte, Formen, Folgen.* 2nd edn. Munich

Weinberg, Leonard et. al., ed. 2004. *Religious Fundamentalism and Political Extremism. London*

Weisbrod, Bernd 1992. 'Gewalt in der Politik: Zur politischen Kultur in Deutschland zwischen den beiden Weltkriegen' *Geschichte in Wissenschaft und Unterricht*, Vol. 43, 391–404

— 1998. 'Kriegerische Gewalt und männlicher Fundamentalismus. Ernst Jüngers Beitrag zur Konservativen Revolution' *Geschichte in Wissenschaft und Unterricht*, Vol. 49, 544–560

— 2000. 'Die Politik der Repräsentation. Das Erbe des Ersten Weltkrieges und der Formwandel der Politik in Europa' in *Der Erste Weltkrieg und die europäische Nachkriegsordnung. Sozialer Wandel und Formveränderung der Politik*, ed. Wolfgang Mommsen. Cologne, 13–41

— 2001. 'Violence and Sacrifice: Imagining the Nation in Weimar Germany' in Hans Mommsen 2001, 5–22

Weiss, John 1997. *Ideology of Death. Why the Holocaust Happened in Germany*, 2nd edn. Chicago

Weißmann, Karlheinz 1998. *Der nationale Sozialismus. Ideologie und Bewegung 1890–1933.* Munich

Welch, David, ed. 1983. *Nazi Propaganda: The Power and the Limitations.* London

— 1995. *The Third Reich: Politics and Propaganda.* London

—2000. *Germany, Propaganda and Total War, 1914–1918.* New Brunswick

Werner, Meike G 1996. 'Die Erneuerung des Lebens durch ästhetische Praxis. Lebensreform, Jugend und Festkultur im Eugen Diederichs Verlag', in Hübinger 1996a, 222–242

Werth, Christoph H. 1996. *Sozialismus und Nation. Die deutsche Ideologiediskussion zwischen 1918 und 1945.* Wiesbaden

Wette, Wolfram 1979. 'Ideologien, Propaganda und Innenpolitik als Voraussetzung der Kriegspolitik des Dritten Reiches', in *Das Deutsche Reich und der Zweite Weltkrieg*, ed. Militärgeschichtliches Forschungsamt, Vol. 1. Stuttgart, 25–173

—— ed. 1999. *Militarismus in Deutschland 1871–1945: Zeitgenössische Analysen und Kritik.* Münster

Whisker, James B. 1982. *The Social, Political and Religious Thought of Alfred Rosenberg.* Washington

Wildt, Michael 2002. *Generation des Unbedingten: Das Führungskorps des Reichssicherheitshauptamtes.* Hamburg

Willeke, Stefan 1995. *Die Technokratiebewegung in Nordamerika und Deutschland zwischen den Weltkriegen.* Frankfurt/M.

Williams, John A. 1996. '"The Chords of the German Soul are Tuned to Nature": The Movement to Preserve the Natural *Heimat* from the Kaiserreich to the Third Reich' *Central European History* 29 (3), 339–384

Williamson, George S. 2004. *The Longing for Myth in Germany. Religion and Aesthetic Culture from Romanticism to Nietzsche.* Chicago

Winiger, Josef 2004. *Ludwig Feuerbach. Denker der Menschlichkeit.* Berlin

Winkler, Heinrich August 1985. *Der Schein der Normalität. Arbeiter und Arbeiterbewegung in der Weimarer Republik 1924 bis 1930.* Berlin

—— ed. 1992. *Die deutsche Staatskrise 1930–1933. Handlungsspielräume und Alternativen.* Munich

—— 1993. *Weimar 1918–1933. Die Geschichte der ersten deutschen Demokratie.* Munich

—— 2000. *Der lange Weg nach Westen Deutsche Geschichte*, Vol. 1: *Vom Ende des Alten Reiches bis zum Untergang der Weimarer Republik;* Vol. 2: *Vom "Dritten Reich" bis zur Wiedervereinigung.* Munich

—— 2002. *The Long Shadow of the Reich. Weighing up German History* (German Historical Institute London. 2001 Annual Lecture). London

Wistrich, Robert 1996. *Weekend in Munich: Art, Propaganda and Terror in the Third Reich.* London

Wolbert, Klaus 1982. *Die Nackten und die Toten des Dritten Reiches: Folgen einer politischen Geschichte des Körpers in der Plastik des deutschen Faschismus.* Giessen

Wolin, Richard 1990. *The Politics of Being: The Political Thought of Martin Heidegger.* New York

—— ed. 1991. *The Heidegger Controversy.* New York

Woods, Roger 1982. *Ernst Jünger and the Nature of Political Commitment.* Stuttgart

—— 1996. *The Conservative Revolution in the Weimar Republic.* London

Wright, Harold R. C. 1996. 'Sombart and War' in *Werner Sombart (1863–1961). Social Scientist,* ed. Jürgen G. Backhaus, Vol. 1. Marburg, 211–215

Young, Julian 1993. *Nietzsche's Philosophy of Art,* paperback edn. Cambridge

—— 1997. *Heidegger, Philosophy, Nazism.* Cambridge

—— 2000. *Heidegger's Philosophy of Art.* Cambridge

—— 2002. *Heidegger's Later Philosophy.* Cambridge

—— 2006. *Nietzsche's Philosophy of Religion.* Cambridge

Zelinsky, Hartmut 1983. *Richard Wagner – ein deutsches Thema. Eine Dokumentation zur Wirkungsgeschichte Richard Wagners 1876–1976,* 2nd edn. Medusa

—— 1990. *Sieg oder Untergang: Sieg und Untergang. Kaiser Wilhelm II., die Werk-Idee Richard Wagners und der "Weltkampf".* Munich

—— 2000. 'Verfall, Vernichtung, Weltentrückung. Richard Wagners antisemitische Werks-Idee als Kunstreligion und Zivilisationskritik und ihre Verbreitung bis 1933' in Friedländer and Rüsen 2000, 309–341

Zeller, Thomas 2002. *Straße, Bahn, Panorama. Verkehrswege und Landschaftsveränderung in Deutschland von 1930 bis 1990.* Frankfurt/M.

Ziemann, Benjamin 1998. 'Republikanische Kriegserinnerung in einer polarisierten Öffentlichkeit. Das Reichsbanner Schwarz-Rot-Gold als Veteranenverband der sozialistischen Arbeiterschaft' *Historische Zeitschrift* 267, 357–398

—— 2000. 'Das "Fronterlebnis" des Ersten Weltkrieges – eine sozialhistorische Zäsur? Deutungen und Wirkungen in Deutschland und Frankreich' in *Der Erste Weltkrieg und die europäische Nachkriegsordnung. Sozialer Wandel und Formveränderung der Politik,* ed. Wolfgang Mommsen. Cologne, 43–82

Zimmermann, Harm-Peter 1989. *Der feste Wall gegen die rote Flut. Kriegervereine in Schleswig-Holstein 1864–1914.* Neumünster

Zimmermann, Jörg 1982. 'Zur Geschichte des ästhetischen Naturbegriffs' in *Das Naturbild des Menschen,* ed. Jörg Zimmermann. Munich, 118–154.

Zimmerman, Michael E. 1990. *Heidegger's Confrontation with Modernity.* Bloomington

Zippes, Jack 2002. *The Brothers Grimm: From Enchanted Forest to the Modern World.* 2nd edn. New York

Zmarzlik, Hans-Günther 1963. 'Der Sozialdarwinismus in Deutschland als geschichtliches Problem' in *Vierteljahreshefte für Zeitgeschichte* 11, 246–273

Zunkel, Friedrich 1974. *Industrie und Staatssozialismus. Der Kampf um die Wirtschaftsordnung in Deutschland 1914–1918.* Düsseldorf

Zweig, Stefan 1955. *Die Welt von Gestern. Erinnerungen eines Europäers.* Frankfurt/M.

INDEX